LOVE AND JUSTICE AS

For Elisa

In insecurity to lie,
Is joy's insuring quality

Emily Dickinson

LOVE AND JUSTICE AS COMPETENCES

THREE ESSAYS ON THE SOCIOLOGY OF ACTION

LUC BOLTANSKI

Translated by Catherine Porter

polity

First published in French as *L'Amour et la Justice comme compétences* © Editions Métailié, Paris, 1990

This English edition © Polity Press, 2012

Polity Press
65 Bridge Street
Cambridge CB2 1UR, UK

Polity Press
350 Main Street
Malden, MA 02148, USA

ISBN-13: 978-0-7456-4909-2
ISBN-13: 978-0-7456-4910-8 (pb)

A catalogue record for this book is available from the British Library.

Typeset in 10.5 on 12 pt Sabon
by Servis Filmsetting Ltd, Stockport, Cheshire
Printed and bound in Great Britain by the MPG Books Group

The publisher has used its best endeavours to ensure that the URLs for external websites referred to in this book are correct and active at the time of going to press. However, the publisher has no responsibility for the websites and can make no guarantee that a site will remain live or that the content is or will remain appropriate.

Every effort has been made to trace all copyright holders, but if any have been inadvertently overlooked the publisher will be pleased to include any necessary credits in any subsequent reprint or edition.

For further information on Polity, visit our website: www.politybooks.com

CONTENTS

Acknowledgements   *vii*
Foreword   *ix*

Part I: What People Can Do

1   A Sociology of Disputes   3

2   The Political Basis for General Forms   11

3   Ordinary Denunciations and Critical Sociology   18

4   The Sociology of Critical Society   28

5   A Model of Competence for Judgement   36

6   Principles of Equivalence and Justifiable Proofs   46

7   Tests and Temporality   59

8   Four Modes of Action   68

9   Below the Threshold of the Report   79

Part II: Agape: An Introduction to the States of Peace

10   Disputes and Peace   89
    10.1   The limits of justice   89
    10.2   Anthropology and tradition   94
    10.3   The theological tradition   100

11   Three Forms of Love   104
    11.1   An initial inventory   104

11.2	Love as reciprocity: philia	105
11.3	Eros and the construction of general equivalence	106
11.4	Agape and the withdrawal of equivalence	110
11.5	The insouciance of agape	114
11.6	Duration and permanence	116
11.7	The example of *Little Flowers*	120
11.8	Parable and metaphor	125
12	Agape and the Social Sciences	129
12.1	Agape: practical model, ideal or utopia?	129
12.2	Marx and the theory of justice	131
12.3	The paradoxes of gifts and counter-gifts	138
13	Towards a Sociology of Agape	145
13.1	The model of pure agape	145
13.2	Access to the states of agape	150
13.3	From love to justice	153
13.4	From justice to love	156
13.5	Agape and emotion	159

Part III: Public Denunciation

14	The Affair as a Social Form	169
15	The Actantial System of Denunciation	178
16	The Requirement of Desingularization	191
17	The Difficult Denunciation of Kith and Kin	199
18	Manoeuvring to Increase One's own Stature	207
19	What Not to Do by Oneself	220
20	Generalization and Singularity	229
21	Dignity Offended	239
22	Confidence Betrayed	253
Appendix 1	Building the Factorial Analysis	259
Appendix 2	A Sampling of Typical Letters	262
Notes		272
References		314
Index		327

ACKNOWLEDGEMENTS

The publisher wishes to thank the following for permission to quote copyrighted material:

KIERKEGAARD, SOREN; *WORKS OF LOVE*. © 1995 Postscript, Inc. Published by Princeton University Press, 1998 paperback edition. Reprinted by permission of Princeton University Press.

From WAITING FOR GOD by Simone Weil, translated by Emma Craufurd, copyright 1951, renewed © 1979 by G. P. Putnam's Sons. Used by permission of G. P. Putnam's Sons, a division of Penguin Group (USA) Inc.

We also wish to thank Editions du CERF and Chicago University Press for permission on additional materials.

FOREWORD

The three essays on love and justice brought together in this volume present the main lines of research that I have been pursuing for several years. Part III, 'Public Denunciation', appeared initially in a different form in Pierre Bourdieu's journal *Actes de la recherche en sciences sociales* (Boltanski et al. 1984). Part II, 'Agape: An Introduction to the States of Peace', was written in 1989. In the text that appears as Part I, 'What People Can Do', I sought to link 'Public Denunciation' and 'Agape' by retracing the path I had followed and also by suggesting some possible extensions. To do this, I had to refer to *Les Économies de la grandeur*, a work written in collaboration with Laurent Thévenot, published initially in 1987 and later revised for publication in a new version.* Chapters 5 and 6 focus on this work, whose principal elements had to be summarized in order to ensure the coherence of the texts gathered here. This is partly because themes that appear in an intuitive form in 'Public Denunciation' were clarified and further developed in *Économies*, and partly because 'Agape', as it attempts to shed light on behaviours that stem not from justice but from love, relies to some extent on the model of competence in justice that was the focus of *Économies*. The reader's thinking will thus have to gravitate among the various studies that form the whole.

These studies were carried out under the auspices of the Groupe de sociologie politique et morale (GSPM [Group for Political and Moral Sociology]) of the École pratique des hautes études en science

---

* Translator's note: This work, *De la justification*, was published in 1991; it appeared in English translation as *On Justification* in 2006. At the author's request, in-text references to *Les Économies de la grandeur* have been replaced in the present volume by references to *On Justification*.

sociale (EHESS [Practical School for Advanced Studies in Social Science]) and the Centre national de la recherche scientifique (CNRS [National Centre for Scientific Research]). They benefited from the intense intellectual activity that characterizes the GSPM, and from the collective research and discussions that took place in our seminar. Regarding Part III, I owe special thanks to Marie-Ange Schiltz, who handled the material involving statistics and computer science with remarkable skill, and to Yann Darré, who collaborated with me on the difficult task of codifying the raw data. Part II, 'Agape', resulted in large measure from conversations with Élisabeth Claverie. I am exceptionally indebted to this demanding scholar, who shared her erudition in a realm with which I was unfamiliar. The 'Agape' section also owes a great deal to discussions I had at various points in its development with Jean-Élie Boltanski – I am grateful for his knowledge, for his rigorous reasoning and for his untiring patience, which helped me believe in the existence of my object at times when I had doubts. I have also benefited greatly from contacts with Bruno Latour and from his work, especially his most recent books. I thank him for his generosity. Finally, a key stimulus of my work was a remark Michael Pollak made to me concerning the almost total absence of reflection on love in sociology; I hope this study will not disappoint his expectations too greatly.

The text has been read and discussed by several other colleagues. I have tried to take into account their invariably pertinent remarks. Since I have not always succeeded in solving the difficult problems they brought to my attention, the debate remains open on many points. I owe special thanks, for discussions during the writing process or for their attentive and often critical readings, to Nicolas Dodier, Charles Fredrikson, François Héran, Francis Kramarz, Paul Ladrière, Sebastien Mac Evoy, Pierre-Michel Menger, Patrick Pharo and Heinz Wismann. During the year I spent preparing and drafting the text on agape, the presence within the GSPM of Dénes Némedi (from Eotvös Lorand University in Budapest), who works on the theory of action, and of Allan Silver (from Columbia University), who is currently doing very interesting research on friendship, was extremely stimulating for me. As for Part I, 'What People Can Do', its occasionally polemical tone reflects first of all the difficulty of the debate that I had to engage with my own work. This part was discussed in GSPM seminars: I am particularly indebted to Philippe Corcuff, whose pertinent observations have been very useful to me, and to Francis Chateauraynaud, Nathalie Heinich and Claudette Lafaye. I owe much to a stimulating debate with Jean-Louis Derouet.

I must also thank Colette Plâtre and Danielle Burre, who have been of great help in establishing the manuscript. Finally, I have to express special gratitude to Alain Desrosières, who constantly encouraged this work, and to Laurent Thévenot, without whom completing the project that has preoccupied me for five years would have been simply impossible. The fact remains that, in keeping with the time-honoured formula, the final version of this work is the sole responsibility of its author.

15 February 1990

Part I

What People Can Do

— 1 —

A SOCIOLOGY OF DISPUTES

My attention was drawn to disputes during fieldwork I carried out from 1976 to 1981 in connection with research I was doing on the category of cadres, people at the management level in business (Boltanski 1987a). Among the hundreds of cadres I interviewed during that period, often repeatedly and at length, a good number of interlocutors – people I met on a variety of occasions, in interviews arranged by mutual acquaintances, in labour unions, or during training internships – had run into 'bumps in the road', to borrow the modest euphemism they often used, in their careers: events that had marked them deeply, sometimes irreversibly. These 'bumps', which in most cases resulted in loss of employment, were not dismissals carried out according to due process, but long processes of abandonment and exclusion that led them to resign of their own accord. In many instances the interviewees were left with a definitive loss of confidence in their own ability to pursue a work life of the sort they had been leading before. My interlocutors described these processes in a way that emphasized their absurd, unpredictable, incomprehensible aspects, the way the world is described in picaresque novels, where anything can happen: one day a prince bestows favour, the next day brings banishment or prison. Reproaches – unwarranted, as these people saw it – suddenly rained down on them. Individuals who had just been congratulating them on their success and dedication to their work, and who had been encouraging them to take on more responsibilities, to 'forge ahead', to commit themselves more deeply, suddenly and for no obvious reason stopped inviting them to meetings, placed 'incompetent' young directors over them, took away their secretaries, their telephones, their offices, and left them for months on end without a 'mission', without work. They were left in

3

the humiliating situation of having to beg for each day's assignment and having to perform tasks (for example, sweeping) that were in no way commensurate with their official title, salary or job description. Sooner or later, in their efforts to prove their good will or to point out the injustice that was being done them, they began to make repeated blunders and to produce a mishmash of verbal 'outbursts': demands for 'one-on-one' explanations, appeals to the unions and threats of 'legal' recourse, often to no avail. In the process, their colleagues and friends turned away, no longer recognized them, avoided them as if they feared that mere contact might drag them into the same process of degradation and exclusion. These fears were not unfounded, for the protagonists themselves constantly asked for support, sought to get others to testify on their behalf or to recall their past successes; in short, they kept trying to mobilize others in what they had come to call their 'affair', a situation whose outcome was often a quasi-pathological state described by those who suffered from it as 'nervous depression', while their adversaries, and also sometimes their former friends, referred to it sotto voce and in private as 'paranoia'.[1]

My first task was to describe these 'affairs', while seeking insofar as possible to capture their distinguishing characteristics and, above all, the extraordinary uncertainty that surrounded them. In each affair I examined, the versions provided by the various actors diverged. The victim's account was not the same as that of the union representative, or his best friend, or the human resources director, or his wife. Everyone had an opinion; each supplied an interpretation that purported to be truer, better informed, and more intelligent than that of the other partners. It seemed impossible to approach these affairs without being immediately swallowed up by them, without in turn getting ensnared in them, without aligning myself with one or another of the prevailing interpretations or supplying a plausible interpretation of my own. In other words, it seemed necessary to take sides, to choose a camp. Now, sociologists are well equipped for such situations. We have a host of interpretive tools in our arsenal, and, to put it bluntly, we have a method that positions us to say, in the final analysis, what the story is. Had I pursued that course, I would have been enlisted in turn by the victim, the union, the social worker, and so on. But I refused to follow that path. What interested me was the affair in itself: its unfolding, its form, the formal constants that seemed to emerge through a comparison of affairs that were quite dissimilar on the surface.

My goal was to constitute the 'affair' form as such and to make 'affair' a sociological concept. To this end, I had to collect a sufficiently

4

large corpus of affairs from a wide variety of contexts. An object of this sort is not accessible through the ordinary methods of sociology, questionnaires and interviews. To use these methods would have been to seek needles in haystacks. After making contact with the protagonists of affairs that had gone on long enough, or were important enough, to have had echoes in the press, and after noticing that the people involved in such affairs wrote constantly, often to newspapers, in attempts to mobilize as many others as possible in support of their cause, I undertook to find out whether there might be traces of such letters in the editorial departments of various newspapers, thinking that these might point me towards interesting objects of inquiry. My efforts were rewarded when I contacted the editors of the 'society' page of the newspaper Le Monde, which was headed at the time by Bruno Frappat. Frappat had the commendable habit – for motives I still haven't fully grasped, but in which a researcher's curiosity and a humanist's compassion were probably combined – of answering all the letters received in his department or passed along by other departments in the paper. He had saved this considerable influx of mail, and he generously granted me access. I found myself in the midst of several dozen boxes of letters accompanied by files that were sometimes voluminous. The files amassed items of all sorts – testimony, tracts, legal documents, bills for services, transcripts of trials, photocopies of letters, and so on – that the correspondents sent along with their letters, displaying them as proof of their good faith and the rightness of their cause. Here I had an experience familiar to historians who specialize in going through legal archives. Each of the files, once opened, brought to the surface a complex affair, impenetrable at first glance, sometimes very dated, sometimes tragic, with a multitude of protagonists, a procession of persons, objects, proofs, feelings: instances of devotion, inextinguishable hatred, abominable injustices, and so on. I spent several months just reading, taking notes, trying to establish classification systems that I kept having to revise, and speaking with journalists. In these conversations, the problem of normality immediately came to the fore. 'Some of these stories are genuine', they would say. 'But in many cases we're dealing with paranoia. In others, you can't really tell.' I questioned them about the signs that let them spot a correspondent's mental illness right away. Their semiology was roughly the same as the one I was beginning to practise spontaneously. For me, too, certain letters seemed normal and others seemed to be the product of illness or insanity. The question of paranoia, which I had already come across when I was doing research in business settings, came to occupy centre stage in my investigations. I opted to conceive of it not as would a psychiatrist, by seeking a substantive definition that could be used to support a diagnosis or the opinion of a legal expert, but as would a sociologist, by seeking to describe the sort of competence that allows anyone to make the same diagnosis. At the same time, I tried to understand the situations in which heretofore ordinary persons had been led to act in a way that would inevitably bring down on them a judgement of mental illness. What interested me was not illness as such, but the various manifestations of the ordinary sense of normality that we are all capable of putting into play in everyday life. My work along these lines had been preceded by Edwin M. Lemert's seminal article (1967; first published in 1962), and also by some research published in the *Law and Society Review*, especially an article by William L. Felstiner, Richard L. Abel and Austin Sarat (1980–81).[2] The question of normality and the sense of normality had a direct link with the question of justice and the sense of justice towards which I had been led by my investigation of affairs. In affairs, justice is always at issue, even for those that do not end up in a court of law (and most do not). In affairs, the persons who protest do so because their sense of justice has been offended. But even before the question of whether or not they are in the right is examined, another question, the precondition for taking the grievance into account, has to be answered: whether the author of the complaint is normal or not. It seemed to me that, even before facing the numerous and often very real obstacles that stood in the way of protest (obstacles belonging to the order of violence or to the related order of threats and fear), the author of a protest had to respect a no less important constraint imposed by the rules of normality if the complaint were to be deemed worthy of examination. Now, there is no a priori guarantee that these rules can always be respected on every occasion. Thus, even in the absence of violence or of explicit or implicit pressure, certain protests could not be lodged without risk in the space of public debates. The question I took as my object then became the following: what condition must a public denunciation of injustice satisfy in order to be treated as acceptable (without regard to its outcome)? To sketch out a response to this question, I had to use the same set of instruments to deal with complaints deemed normal and with those deemed abnormal, instead of being content, as had most often been the case in earlier studies, with a preliminary distribution, already established by the social arrangements responsible for a given protest and protestors – labour unions, the medical, psychiatric and legal establishments, law enforcement and social work agencies, and so on. Similarly, I had to give up the disciplinary compartmentalization that referred certain objects to sociology and others to social psychology, to psychology itself, or even to psychiatry. I needed to grasp the affairs all together, before they were parcelled out, in order to try to establish the properties of affairs in general and identify the distinctive features of normal affairs as opposed to abnormal ones. In short, I needed to try to constitute a *grammar* – understood as a set of constraints, imposed across the board – of claims that injustice had been done and of the accusations that are inherent in such protests.[3] For a person who is protesting an injustice that he or she has suffered and who is seeking reparations has to designate the author of the injustice. The protestor must thus launch a process of *accusation* that can in turn be characterized by the person accused as falling within the order of injustice. In affairs, one does not know, a priori, who is the persecutor and who is being persecuted.

But the intent to take affairs as my object and to deal with affairs as a social form, proper to a particular society and with a history that could be traced,[4] led to an even more radical break. The undertaking was possible only on condition that I give up the distribution that underlies the division between disciplines in the human sciences and on which the social sciences themselves, in a way, are based: the division between what is associated with the singular and what is associated with the general – or, rather, to use the term most familiar in sociology – with the collective. Thus I could no longer take into account the distinction between 'micro' and 'macro' social levels as sites for the phenomena I was investigating. In fact, among the affairs I had chosen to examine, some were tiny, involving a small number of actors for a limited period of time and mobilizing few resources (for example, a 'clash' between two technicians in a workshop one morning). Others were huge, spreading out over a very long period of time and mobilizing a significant number of actors along with a multitude of disparate resources. But, at the start of an affair, no one can say how far it will go. Who would have believed that the dishonourable discharge of a Jewish army captain, an alleged spy in Germany's pay, would in a few short years mobilize virtually the entire French nation and all the resources at its members' disposal – journalism, science, literature, politics – to support a cause and to bring proofs, creating cleavages between people united by the most solid of ties: members of the same family, the same party, the same literary circle or group of friends. Studying affairs thus presupposes that the researcher will refrain from assigning a priori qualifications to the object studied and will refrain in particular from specifying its dimensions.[5] Yet the assignment of a process to a particular place among the disciplines basically depends on its dimensions. If a secretary protests an injustice, and persists in her protest without managing to mobilize a significant number of persons or to get backing from representatives of institutions (union leaders, journalists, and the like), the problem will be treated as purely personal. She will remain an isolated case. Her personality will be open to question, and she will be sent to see a social worker, the house doctor or a psychiatrist. In contrast, if her protest is heard, if she has supporters, if authorized agencies and especially labour unions equate her affair with others characterized as 'similar', if her case, now defined as 'exemplary', is used to serve a cause that can be called 'general', her affair may spread; it may mobilize a significant number of persons, achieve the status of a collective problem and attract the attention of a sociologist. Far from accepting the a priori split between what is individual, and thus in the province of psychology, and what is collective, which would belong to sociology, the sociologist has to treat the way the affair is qualified – singular or collective – as a product of the actors' own activity. Instead of adopting collective bodies that are already constituted and ready for use, as it were, the sociologist can grasp the operations through which collectives are constructed by examining the formation of collective causes – that is, the dynamics of political action.

The very processes that the sociologist chooses to analyse are thus the ones that determine, finally, whether the object is individual or collective. These processes will elude him, for structural reasons, if he takes for granted the divisions that the actors contrive to establish. For, in the course of an affair, its very nature – individual or collective, singular or general – is the principal issue in the dispute in which the various protagonists are engaged. Depending on the way the affair is configured, certain actors work to 'deflate' it, trying to show that it is a 'complete fabrication' and seeking to 'put it back into perspective', while others, on the contrary, go to great lengths to reveal its 'true nature', to show 'what lies behind it' and thus to demonstrate that it concerns, 'in fact', many more people than might have been first supposed, that 'everybody' is involved. This is what it takes to forge a collective cause. For all causes, from the smallest to the largest, from those that appear strangest at first glance to those that are most obviously legitimate according to our sense of justice, have had to be created, constructed, established and proved at one point or another,[6] and, no matter how solidly established they may appear, they can also always be undone by the same procedures. In my own case, I was also seeking, indirectly, to develop a method I could use to

8

analyse the way persons build causes, good causes, collective causes. This was an extension, in a way, of my attempt to bring to light the immense collective effort that it took, between the 1930s and the 1960s, to construe cadres as a social category, a cause that deserved to exist and to be supported (Boltanski 1987a).

I shall not describe here the method I followed or the detailed results of the analysis; these can be found below, in Part III, which presents a revised version of the work I did in 1984. I decided not to modify this presentation substantially, in part because of the effort involved – I would probably have had to start all over – but also so that the research work, whose traces are necessarily eradicated in the finished product (or what tentatively passes for finished), would remain visible. I shall simply point out the aspects that strike me today as particularly deficient in this already dated work, and show briefly how the reflection on the summary model with which I ended up led me towards more sophisticated models, and thus brought up new questions.

For now, just a word about method: in my 1984 project, I opted for a procedure that involved coding and statistical analysis – the factorial analysis of correspondence, to be precise. It worked out fairly well. Feeling my way, I coded more or less everything I came across, everything that stood out in some way and seemed to have some relevance – including not only the characteristics of the affair, the context in which it appeared, its duration, and so on, but also stylistic or graphic properties such as the use of a typewriter or letterhead, the presence of abundant underlining or of insults. This work was bolstered, however, by two operations without which the analysis would not have been legible. On the one hand, I set up a jury, calling on ordinary persons who relied on their ordinary sense of normality and justice to assign a normality rating to each file after a rapid first reading. On the other hand, I defined an actantial system of denunciation that involved four functional roles or actants: a victim, a denouncer, a persecutor and a judge. Each of these actants was coded according to its *size* along a *singular–general* axis. The introduction of these two notions depended directly on the codification process. Initially, the desire to *reduce* the extreme diversity of the material by using a common nomenclature to code affairs that were entirely dissimilar in appearance was what prompted me to seek the dimensions that would allow me to qualify my objects in their most general form. But by the same token I was also led to displace the meanings of some of the most firmly established notions in sociology; this loosened their hold on my framework and allowed me to take a diversity of possible worths into account. Substituting the singular/general opposition for the individual/general opposition that was more familiar in sociological writing thus authorized a diversification of the operations that were conceivable along this axis, the shift from individual to collective being only one example. Similarly, I could speak about size (a notion that Bruno Latour uses in analyses of scientific controversies) without having to specify, at least in a first phase, what it entailed, so I could do without concepts such as 'status', 'power' or 'capital'. With this very general coding system, I could handle all the cases I encountered. Thus, for example, a fellow who was mugged in the street was coded as a small victim, while a militant espousing a collective cause – or, better yet, an association – would be coded as a victim of greater size. Only judges were not coded: I always viewed judges as stand-ins for 'public opinion', an entity that writers seeking to be published in a newspaper like *Le Monde* aspire to reach, and thus an actant of great size. I also coded the relations between actants according to their degree of proximity; this could go from identity, when the victim and the denouncer were one and the same person, to maximal alterity, when the two parties had no relationship whatsoever prior to the situation of injustice that had brought them together (as when someone wrote because he had seen a young North African being ill-treated by a police officer at a subway exit). Coding and the analysis of correspondence allowed me, rapidly and as it were synthetically, to come up with hypotheses about the grammar of protest and about the kinds of constraints recognized by the sense of normality and the sense of justice. The fact remains that this method consisted by definition in breaking down the material and constituting a priori equivalences (this is the very meaning of the coding operation, and the factorial analysis of correspondence can be reduced to a sort of coding of codings). The method did not allow me to follow, step by step, the relations established by the persons involved between the various reports that constituted the dossiers and their own interpretive work in each case. The method was detrimental in particular in that it no longer authorized me to take into account the place the various documents occupied in the history of a given affair. Yet in affairs, and particularly in affairs spread over a long period of time, the temporal dimension is absolutely essential, all the more so in that, over time, several different affairs may be grafted onto one another and become intertwined.

— 2 —

THE POLITICAL BASIS FOR
GENERAL FORMS

In retrospect, the chief critique I can offer of my earlier work has to do with the fact that the model I used was based largely on the positions occupied by the various actants on a single particular–general axis. My interpretation, in brief, was the following. A denunciation of injustice appears abnormal when the various actants occupy different positions on the singular–general axis. Since the judge was always an actant of large size in the cases I analysed, the affairs whose presentation remained in the order of the singular – that is, those that were not taken up by an agency whose collective character could be credibly defended and thus were not *desingularized* – appear abnormal (for example, the case in which the plaintiff wrote to accuse his neighbour of an injustice, and was himself accused in turn of having stolen his neighbour's ladder). Furthermore, I thought that the plaintiffs who were judged abnormal possessed the same sense of normality as normal people, and that it was precisely to try to satisfy the constraints of normality in particularly delicate situations that they produced a whole set of elements interpreted by others as signs of abnormality. Indeed, the aspects of these documents that appear abnormal are precisely the manoeuvres that the plaintiffs undertook in an effort to demonstrate their *greater worth* and thereby put themselves on the same (higher) level – an eminently collective level, since public opinion was at issue – as the judge to whom they were submitting their affair (for example, by alleging support from a defence committee of which they were president and sole member, or by giving themselves inflated titles, piling on official stamps, underlining numerous passages, and so on).

The following stages of the work, which led to the model of justice Laurent Thévenot and I presented in *OJ*, were devoted chiefly, first, to a reflection on the opposition between the particular and the general, and on what should be understood in our context as 'general'; second, to the substitution of the concept of *worth* for that of size; and, finally, to the shift from a universe that included a single particular–general axis to one that included several such axes, several ways of establishing generality and thus a plurality of possible worths. This last innovation led to a profound modification of the model: recourse to the concept of worth allowed me to encompass the dimension I had sought to grasp by speaking of 'size' in a more general form – 'size' being a notion linked to the possibility of recognition by others. (In the context of *OJ*, this notion was attached to a particular way of establishing worth, which we called *fame*.) In addition, reflection on what I placed at the top of the particular–general axis led me to establish a link between the form of generality that brings a constraint to bear on the denunciation of injustice and the form that supports the constitution of a political order. The establishment of this link was greatly facilitated by my reading of Louis Dumont (1977, 1980) and François Furet, both on the French Revolution (1981) and on Tocqueville's comparatist vision (1984); these works allowed me to recognize, in what sociologists simply called 'collectives', a particular political form that had been the object of a long and detailed description in political philosophy.

What had to be questioned, in order to understand the constraints that bore on public denunciations of injustice in France, was thus, first of all, the way one of the actants was constituted: one that, despite being the main character in the drama constituted by an affair, had been left in the dark in my 1984 work (continued in this volume) – namely, the judge. But, for a better grasp of what I had been calling 'public opinion' up to that point, I had to look closely at how the body politic, citizenship, was defined in France; I had to grasp the relation between each citizen taken separately and the totality of the body politic to which he or she belongs. What the public will deem credible or incredible, the types of argument or proof that can be presented, what will appear acceptable or unacceptable, normal or abnormal, licit or scandalous, all these depend in fact on the way the relation of the parts to the whole is defined in a particular political regime (Dumont 1977, 20). I sought first of all to grasp more fully what constituted the form of (civic) worth that results from operations of representation. These analyses were useful, since they would eventually allow me to consider the various forms of worth as various ways of *embodying* others – that is, of duplicating others in one's own person (standing in for them, identifying with them, and

12

so on; the representation associated with voting is only one particular modality of embodiment). My work then turned more specifically to the analysis of *scandals*, denunciations of which appeared quite frequently in the documents composing my corpus. It turns out that a denunciation of a scandal in our society always follows the same form. The act consists in unveiling the particular beneath the general, the singular person behind the representative or the judge, the particular interest hidden under a proclamation of adherence to the general interest, the secret personal ties that underlie relationships presented as official. The judge has been seen having dinner in a restaurant with the defendant; the real estate promoter who is building a new development is 'in fact' the cousin of the mayor who got him the necessary authorizations. They're in cahoots.

A scandal is thus always a conspiracy – that is, a secret alliance in favour of a particular interest where there ought to be only the agreement of all for a common good. Another example: a jury, in principle representing the general will, 'in fact' reached agreement at their hotel the night before the trial; moreover all the jurors came from the same village (Claverie 1984). Now, the schema of conspiracy, highly visible in the denunciations I was able to study, has a dignified pedigree: in *The Social Contract*, it figures as intrigue (Rousseau 1994b). Intrigue, for Rousseau, is a secret alliance in the interest of private persons that breaks the compact in favour of the common good. Nothing was more useful for my work than reading Rousseau's political writings and some of the many commentaries to which they have given rise, especially those of Robert Derathé (1970). The global architecture of *The Social Contract* makes it clear how the body politic was conceptualized and constituted in France, and it may also bring to light some of the fundamental constraints weighing on the construction of a political order that claims to be valid in the most general sense – that is, to be legitimate. The heart of Rousseau's construct lies, as we know, in the opposition between 'the will of all' and 'the general will'. The general will is not derived by summing up the will of each individual taken separately, as a particular person with private interests. Its emergence depends rather on the capacity of citizens to neglect their private interests in order to focus on the goal of a common good. The body politic is thus made up of two sets between which complex relationships are established: on the one hand the set of particular persons, locked into their own clusters of private and thus disparate interests, and on the other hand the entire set of citizens united by the goal of a single common good. These two sets consist of the same persons, but in different states of being, so that it is fair to say, with

Derathé, that in the architecture of *The Social Contract* each person is contracting with himself or herself. Now, if there is to be a viable passageway from one set to the other, if human persons are to escape the tyranny of particular interests, leave disparity, indifference and war behind and constitute themselves as a body politic, they have to be able to identify themselves by referring to a principle of order. It is through this work of identification that they become capable of realizing the possibilities embedded in their nature and can thereby accede to the fullness of their humanity. In this sense, Rousseau's construct can be rightly qualified as metaphysical, as can by the same token Durkheim's concept of society, moreover, in the sense that society includes two levels, one of which is not occupied by the incorporated bodies known as persons. At this second level, we find the conventions that define the humanity of persons and qualify their value – in other words, the ways in which persons may possess worth. (On the relation between the general will in Rousseau and collective consciousness in Durkheim, see *OJ*, 285–92.) Laurent Thévenot and I have called this bi-level construct a *polity*.

To create a polity, then, it is not enough to start with a set of persons. One must also define a *common good* that is superior to persons and that can institute equivalence among them. It is with the support of this equivalence that the just or unjust character of the relations maintained by persons among themselves can be established, because the possibility of establishing an order of worth among persons that is not arbitrary and that can therefore be qualified as just depends on the principle of equivalence adopted, the principle that qualifies the form of worth accessible to people in a given polity. I know of no way to define justice except with reference to equality. As Michel Villey explains clearly in his commentary on justice in Aristotle (Villey 1983), justice is ensured in a political order when the distribution of what has value among persons is carried out according to a principle of equality. But respect for this principle does not presuppose the arithmetical division of everything among everyone. For it has to take into account the value, or rather the relative *worth*, of those among whom the distribution is made. Now, in order to take this worth into account, judges have to rely on a principle of equivalence that they have not chosen, a principle that supports the construction of the entire political order from a vantage point anterior to that of judgement. The model of competence for judgement presented in *OJ*, which I shall summarize below, undertakes to elaborate this political metaphysics. Thus, for example, in the polity that Laurent Thévenot and I have qualified tautologically as 'civic', to distinguish it from other polities based on different principles of equivalence (this is the polity laid out by Rousseau), the worthy are those who embody the collective, represent the others and serve to express the general will. A judge is an embodied generality. Judges must act in such a way that their own bodies are forgotten, because those bodies, personal to them, can support only personal interests. This is probably why the pamphlets that frequently accompany protests of injustice in which a scandal is denounced so often employ scatological or pornographic allusions (Angenot 1983). A judge has interests owing to the fact that she has a body, interests whose satisfactions belong to her personally and cannot, by definition, be shared with others; when this judge fails to fulfil her responsibilities, these particular interests can be brought into the foreground in order to unveil, with the utmost conviction, her unworthiness – that is, her singularity – under the appearances of worth conferred on her by the claim that she is serving the common good.

But – and here is where we break with the model that supported earlier research on the logic of public accusation – what appears as unworthiness, with reference to the common good of a polity quali-fied in a specific way and thereby capable of supplying a principle of equivalence that makes it possible to posit an order among persons and to state their worth, can in turn be identified as a worth in another polity, one constructed according to a different principle of equivalence of which the first polity is unaware. Once again, it was in analysing the structure of scandal that I first observed the plurality of polities. For this I relied on the possibility, towards which I had been drawn in particular by Louis Dumont's work, to treat in symmetrical fashion the forms of construction of the political bond ('hierarchical' and 'individualist' in Dumont) that are most often opposed to one another in reductive reports. In the form of worth recognized in the civic polity, relations among persons are not singular relations. To be legitimate, they must always be mediated by reference to a collective that is working for the common good, an arrangement stemming, for example, from the state or from a philanthropic association. That is why only denunciations of injustice that had been subjected to the work of desingularization could be brought into the public space of debate without being disqualified on grounds of abnormality, as empirical studies had convincingly demonstrated. The actors in these affairs never figured in the act of denunciation on a personal basis, with their own names and their own singular properties; they appeared rather insofar as they embodied collective beings, quasi-personages, as Paul Ricoeur says in his analysis of 'emplotment'

15

(1984). What was at issue was no longer Mr X, who was well acquainted with Mr Y, an old family friend who had given him a job in his company, but rather – as union tracts make especially clear – 'the bosses', 'the employees', 'the state' as employer, and so on.[1]

Nevertheless, on the one hand, in-depth analysis of the multiple reports that came into play in an affair – and not simply of the reports that could be brought forward in public (before an arbitration board, for example) – brought to light other situations in which the accusation could take a singularized form and remain acceptable without being deemed abnormal. On the other hand, when we extended our research on the polity model beyond the civic polity, we observed other ways of constituting a political totality and founding it on a common good; in other words, we found other forms of generality. Thus one cannot understand, for example, the construction of the civic polity, in its Rousseauist version, if one does not know that it is oriented entirely towards denouncing the relations of personal dependency that prevailed under the Old Regime in France. It was precisely liberation from personal dependency that characterized, for Rousseau, what he called 'freedom.'[2] But we cannot stop with the disqualification of the Old Regime on which the Revolution based the construction of the republican order, or with the way the Revolution constructed the citizen as a man without qualities, detached from all forms of belonging that rested on the establishment of personal bonds – for example, membership in a local community or, in work contexts, membership on the basis of profession or trade.[3] For, as can be seen, for example, from an analysis of Bossuet's political writings (*OJ*, 92–6), the relations of personal dependency between people can also be construed as a principle of equivalence apt to support a legitimate order and thereby capable of serving as a basis for constructing a polity. This principle of equivalence, even if it no longer serves to establish the legitimacy of the state, has not disappeared from our world, and, in numerous situations often characterized as 'private', one can show that the judgements actors make about what is just or unjust, appropriate or inappropriate, are comprehensible only in relation to the principle of equivalence that underlies the domestic polity and the definition of the common good on which that polity relies.

By the same token, I could place myself at a certain distance from the denunciations of scandalous conduct as they appeared in the documents of the corpus. The definition of a different polity, in which the unworthy traits unveiled in misbehaving actors might be identified in other situations as worths, made it possible to reintroduce a symmetry that the entire denunciation aimed to exclude. By defining the denunciation of scandalous relations among public persons as an unveiling of the domestic relations they had been maintaining in secret, I could then go on to construct the contrary figure as well – that is, denunciation of the indecent conduct of those who, in situations involving family, friends or worldly connections, situations subject to the principle of worth that prevails in the domestic polity, persisted in behaving with the coldness, impersonality, distance and loftiness that characterize legitimate relations in the civic polity (*OJ*, 243–4). These two polities are not the only ones on which persons can rely today in order to form lasting bonds or to denounce the unjust character of relations between people. We shall look at several others in the model of justice to which *OJ* is devoted. But before recalling the architecture of this model in summary fashion (doing so will make it easier to follow the text presented in Part II of this volume, which is based on results already obtained), I shall have to return briefly to the rules of the method we adopted for that undertaking and what they taught us about the work of sociologists.

— 3 —

ORDINARY DENUNCIATIONS AND
CRITICAL SOCIOLOGY

It was not by chance that I decided to focus my work on disputes between people, the sense of justice manifested by the parties to disputes and the denunciations of injustice that people hurl at one another, not only in the most ordinary situations of daily life but also in situations marked by oddness or extravagance. Denunciation interested me for another reason as well, a more personal one in that it had to do with my own professional activity and the interests with which I was engaging in that context. For the persons whom sociologists label 'ordinary', when they are chosen as objects of study, are not the only ones who denounce injustices and bring their protests into the public sphere. In sociological literature, and perhaps especially in work done in France since the 1960s, one can find a multitude of denunciations which, although they are not presented as such, are nevertheless similar in every way to the accusations of injustice that appear in the documents I chose to analyse. The desire to maintain a radical distance between the denunciatory activity of persons and the scientific activity of sociologists presented a difficulty related to the fieldwork itself. It was not unusual to see persons involved in affairs of injustice attempting to prove their claims and shore up their positions by taking up explicitly, and almost word for word, a given analysis or concept borrowed from contemporary sociologists. The plaintiffs were acquainted with the work of these specialists because they had read it themselves, or had read about it in newspaper articles or mass-market books, or had heard about it on the radio, or even because they had learned some social science in school. This observation raised two questions. On the one hand, it led me to try to understand better the posture that sociologists whom I shall qualify schematically and summarily as 'classical' adopt in their work, a posture that can

18

come very close to that of the actors themselves. On the other hand, it also incited me to try to define an undertaking capable of giving me the means to analyse denunciations as such and to take as my object the critical work carried out by the actors themselves. For this, I had to abandon the critical intention of classical sociology.

How would a classical sociologist have approached my research area, that of 'affairs', if by chance, and without having established the concept, she had been attracted to such a topic? She would have gone to the sites or sent an investigator. She would probably have conducted interviews and distributed questionnaires in order to gather data on the characteristics of the public being studied – that is, data on those properties of the agents that appeared most stable, those that are impossible or difficult to modify: in short, the most irreversible properties, such as age, sex, profession, level of education or parents' profession. At the end of the investigation, and on the basis of the data assembled, the classical sociologist would have written a *report* – more precisely, to use the prevailing term, a 'research report'. The way a report of this type is conceived calls for two observations. On the one hand, a research report purports to convey truth. The social science researcher claims a capacity to shed a different light on reality, to offer insights superior to those available to the actors themselves. On the other hand, the validity of the researcher's insights does not depend on acquiescence by the actors. Quite to the contrary, classical sociologists, even if they recognize that they have supplied an interpretation that does not exhaust reality, believe they are bringing to light a dimension of reality that is not apparent as such to the actors. They will thus be inclined to see the actors' reluctance to acknowledge the truth of the report as evidence confirming the solidity of their analysis; in this respect, they resemble psychoanalysts whose system of interpretation anticipates and integrates the resistances of the analysand.[1] From this standpoint, it is precisely because they are parties to the affair that concerns them intimately that actors cannot grasp the truth of their actions. Bound to the social world by interests, they tend either to dissimulate the truth when it is contrary to their interests or (in the more sophisticated models at work in modern sociology) to conceal from themselves the truth of their acts and their positions. As a result, they tend to harbour a relation of bad faith with regard to social reality that results in self-deluding behaviour: the right hand stubbornly resists knowing what the left hand is doing. In this model, the gap between what the actors espouse as their ideal and the hidden reality brought to light by the sociologist is precisely what allows actors to perform actions compatible with the social

19

order, actions that they could not carry out if the reality of interest and the necessity of constraint were not concealed under a veil of disinterestedness or free will. The maintenance of order thus rests on an illusion. The task of the classical sociologist is to reveal the illusion as such, and this task presupposes the capacity to perceive and portray the interests that the illusion serves to hide.

This capacity depends on the possession of a specific competence, a method backed up by a science; in addition, simultaneously, it depends on a position of externality that allows one to disengage oneself from the interests in conflict in order to consider them from the outside and to describe them. This external site, instrumentalized by a method, is none other than the *laboratory*. It is because sociologists have access to laboratories that they can intervene in conflicts without getting caught up in them.[2] Outside of the laboratory, they are actors like the others. As the sociology of science has shown (I am thinking particularly here of Bruno Latour's work; see especially Latour 1987), the power acquired in the laboratory rests on a sacrifice. It is because they give up trying to grasp reality as a whole and focus only on isolated fragments transported into the closed space of instruments that scientists can domesticate their objects and make them 'speak', and a renunciation of this type can be shown to lie behind the very constitution of the experimental sciences.[3] Classical sociologists also agree to a sacrifice, and not a minor one: they must sacrifice *illusion*. It is because they give up the illusions of actors, and their own illusions when they are merely actors, that they can claim to have a grip on reality and to unveil its truth.

The opposition between reality and illusion, the idea that actors are dominated by their illusions and the concept of a social order resting on the maintenance of an illusion are central notions in the architecture of nineteenth-century sociology, where they occupied as important a place as they did in Freudian psychology. The assimilation of scientific activity to an operation of unveiling illusions can be attested, in various forms, in the work of Marx, Durkheim, Weber or Pareto, for whom social illusions are designated by a variety of terms – ideologies, pre-notions, representations, beliefs, residues, and so on.[4] Now, it can be shown, it seems to me, that the attention paid to the illusions of persons in society grew out of a reflection on religion. Classical sociology encountered at least two fundamental problems associated with the societies and the era in which it was constituted. First, the difficulty of maintaining social order in a historical situation marked by major inequalities and extreme poverty, in a society still imbued with the memory of revolutionary uprisings (in France, those of 1792, 1830 and 1848).[5] Here, the problem was justice – more precisely, the problem of creating appropriate conditions for ensuring social justice and thus a relative consensus that would make it possible to escape permanent civil war, in the framework of a nation-state. The second problem was religion. This issue arose not so much as a radical critique aiming to wipe out the religious illusion through relativization or irony, nor even as an effort to reconstruct religion that would make it acceptable by grounding it in reason (as Enlightenment thinkers sought to do); rather, it took the form of an attempt to preserve what was seen as truly useful in religion for human beings in society. To do this, religion had to be dismantled, its underlying principle revealed, so it could be replaced by a construct less detached from reality, less illusory and less absurd for the modern mind. Indeed, in the writings of the early sociologists, diverse as they are in other respects, the critique of religion cannot be dissociated from a theory of modernity shared by all, at least in its structure: a philosophy of history that accepts as self-evident the existence of a radical break between ancient and modern times, along with the constraint of an at once desirable and necessary evolution. The intent to provide an acceptable substitute for the old religious beliefs, particularly evident in Durkheim, was linked to the question of justice, and thereby to the problem of maintaining social order through the recognition of a moral imperative. As Durkheim asserts unequivocally, especially in his pedagogical writings, which are designed to ground the possibility of a secular morality transmitted by public schools in the science of sociology (Durkheim 1973, especially the introductory lesson, pp. 1–14), or in his disputes with the utilitarians (Durkheim 1975, vol. 2) and with the socialists (Durkheim 1958), the abandonment of morality leads to an anomic or anarchic society, and ultimately to a war of all against all (see below, Part II, chapter 11.3). Now, up to this point morality had been based on the religious illusion. The task of sociology was thus not only to remove that illusion but also to salvage morality by supplying it with a new foundation that could bring it closer to social reality.

But sociological unveiling of the religious illusion can also rely on more radical versions – that is, less on Marxism, which is hampered by the homology between the philosophy of history on which it rests and Christian eschatology (Kolakowski 1978), than on constructs inspired by the method Nietzsche used to objectivize the entire universe of values and subject it to an ironic critique; his schemas had a profound and lasting influence on sociology owing especially to Max Weber's writings (see *OJ*, 340–6). Nietzsche's critique consists, in sum, in using one particular value to contest the validity of another that is opposed to it – using the disinterestedness of the artist, for example, to reveal the crudeness of bourgeois calculations, or, conversely, using the omnipotence of interests to contest any hypocritical pretention to disinterestedness, and so on through the list of values, disparaging each by comparing it to another. The unveiling of the religious illusion served implicitly, and most often without the knowledge of those engaged in the endeavour, as a paradigm for approaching areas farther and farther removed from social activity, first and foremost those stemming from the theory of knowledge or the theory of art, which could easily be reinterpreted by applying Durkheim's theory of religion to them (Durkheim 1995). The process continues step by step until the entire social world has been embraced, treated as a system of symbolic relations that need not be further analysed once it has been revealed as a representation or a belief. Thus for this polemical sociology everything is belief, but everything 'is only' belief, which is also a way of saying that belief is nothing and, consequently, of suggesting – at least implicitly and in the register of nostalgia – that there could or should exist something that would not be mere semblance. For, if it is not to lapse into a scarcely tenable nihilism,[6] the unveiling of belief cannot completely renounce its reliance on a fixed point, on a reality truer than illusion on the basis of which belief can be denounced as such.[7] This fixed point is, in the first place, the laboratory and the science on which it rests. It is also, in the second place, the objects attached to persons and treated as symbolic forms destined to support their identity. The laboratory serves first of all to recognize and transport these objects. For – and this is what distinguishes them from persons – objects are reputed to be incapable of lying. Their objectivity – that is, their stability in being – prevents them from changing positions at will and thus rules out duplicity. Unlike persons, they are unacquainted with bad faith; from this perspective, it is through attachment to the objects that translate and symbolize them that persons can give themselves away and give up their truths.

Sociologists thus rely on laboratories to validate their work in the face of actors' illusions. For the research reports they produce are not intended solely for a public of colleagues. If this were the case, it is not clear what would underlie the reports' polemical aspects. Sociologists must also return, often by indirect routes (for example, via a state agency that has ordered a report or via the media – press, radio, television, and so on), to the public space in which actors settle their disputes. It is, moreover, in this respect that classical sociologists can call themselves 'critical' and lay claim both to the authority of science and to social utility. The idea of a critique forever cut off from those it critiques, forever hidden, is contradictory. But, reinscribed in the public space, the critical sociologist's report will have to compete, as we have seen, with many other reports produced by the actors themselves – letters, tracts, depositions, instructions, minutes, reports, 'informal' statements ('let me tell you what really happened . . .'), and so on – such as can be gathered when one is assembling documentation on an affair. The research report thus has every chance of becoming in turn an element of the dossier, a contribution to the debate,[8] a resource that can be mobilized to support arguments and advance the affair in which the actors are engaged; some of the actors will seek support in its objectivity, since it comes from an external laboratory, to prove the validity of their cause, while others will reject it as one interpretation among others and seek to show where it is biased, owing either to insufficient information or to its author's 'ideological' or 'political' presuppositions. For critical sociologists are not exempt from the type of critiques with which they confront the actors and which their colleagues, moreover, never stop turning against them. The laboratory is never powerful enough, the method never rigorous enough, to eliminate completely the risk that the adversary in turn may unveil the report-writer's illusions and the way these illusions are supported 'in fact' by hidden interests. This possibility in turn leads a sociologist who is honest and sensitive to criticism to undertake a preliminary self-analysis in an effort to identify any tacit presuppositions he might be harbouring, and thus to plunge into an infinite regression aimed at stripping his work of all impurity. Regressions of this sort may well have been present, moreover, in the movement recalled above that led the discipline to evolve from a sociology of religious illusion to a sociology of literary or artistic knowledge and from there to a sociology of science, of the human sciences, or of sociology itself.

When we compare a researcher's reports to those of actors, leaving aside insofar as possible the rhetorical or stylistic arrangements that often underlie the asymmetry between the two types of texts, we can only be struck by their similarities, in form and content alike. Like research reports, actors' reports include a claim of validity based on manoeuvres designed to establish proof. They offer interpretations, deploy arguments and single out facts by selecting the elements that can either be retained as necessary or rejected as contingent in the context of the affair; they invalidate objections, justify actions, engage in critiques, and so on. We note, moreover, that explanations supplied by actors do not differ radically, at bottom, from those contributed by sociologists (Cicourel 1973, 51); the differences are less marked than in the so-called natural sciences, where, for example, to account for the movements of the internal organs of the body, researchers resort to explanations that could not be derived from introspection or ordinary experience. But, in the social order, the reality with which the actors are familiar and the reality that a researcher unveils are not mutually opaque.[9] A large number of social theories produced by specialists can thus be treated as models of the competence of actors, in the sense that they re-elaborate, in a systematic form that purports to be explicit and coherent, constructs that underlie the arguments actors use when they have to account for the situations in which they find themselves – that is, when they have to explain the motives of their own or others' actions. What is more, re-engagement of research reports in debates in the public sphere provides the actors with resources whose directly sociological origin can be attested.[10] This movement of reappropriation can be grasped even while fieldwork is under way. For example, a study undertaken by Claudette Lafaye on activities of critique and justification in the municipal services of a medium-sized city in northern France made it possible to identify a large number of arguments based directly on critical resources contributed by the social sciences or, more generally, by the human sciences. Seeking to understand the causes of the injustices of which they think they have been the object, people construct interpretations that draw on notions derived from psychoanalysis ('he suffers from polymorphous perversity') or sociology ('she's a jealous lower-class type' or an 'upper-class type who's trying to stand out'), or they use concepts such as 'interest', 'power' or 'power relations' in a way that was not accessible before they were given form by the modern social sciences (Lafaye 1989). The social sciences, especially in their most recent developments, have in fact helped to popularize a representation of the world according to which one can interpret the behaviours of anyone at all, when one has understood that these behaviours are always oriented towards the search for satisfaction of personal interests, the most widespread being the interest in gaining power ('here everything is about power') and, consequently, that relations among persons can always be reduced to 'power relations' between those who have power and those who do not. This universal key makes it possible not only to deprecate all claims made by others that they are acting for the common good by revealing the underlying interests, but also, in extreme cases, to claim for oneself, in the name of realism, the right to perform actions that abandon the aim of justice in favour of

24

the quest for power and that, without the support contributed by reference to the natural laws of society as revealed by the social sciences, would be immediately denounced as cynical and unjust.[11]

Thus we can see how difficult it is to push to the extreme limit the hypothesis of a social unconscious, of a radical discontinuity between what people grasp consciously and the realities of the social world in which they live. Even though the hypothesis of the unconscious was never really constructed theoretically, except in psychology, it was probably the unifying principle of the human sciences in the 1960s. It has certainly constituted one of the central elements of the paradigm that has dominated sociology and the social sciences more generally in France over the last thirty years. Moreover, in different senses, it constitutes the cornerstone of linguistics, ethnology, sociology and, in a way, history as developed by the *Annales* school.[12] As we know, the *Annales* historians, with their dual reference to Marx and to Durkheim, shifted their focus away from the history of events (*l'histoire événementielle*) and even away from political history towards the long term (*longue durée*), which presupposes the construction of statistical series in order to reveal the meaningful orientations that underlie particular events treated as incidental (*la petite histoire*), or else towards the 'history of mentalities', which, as its name indicates, orients historical research towards the discovery of largely unconscious mental structures that characterize the members of a given society at a given period. And yet, if persons inhabited a world accepted as self-evident, if they were in the grip of – dominated by – forces working on them without their knowledge, one could comprehend neither the eminently problematic character of the social environment that is revealed by the constant anxiety about justice nor the very possibility of raising questions and offering critiques.

My intention here is not to make a case against critiques. The critical sociologist is perfectly entitled to engage in political and social struggles, and often has the duty to do so. Nothing would be farther from my positions than the attitude that consists in denouncing denunciation out of respect for scientific purity or, worse, in the name of a sacralization of values that would authorize rejecting sociological critiques inasmuch as they encourage ethical relativism. Adopting for myself, on this point, the arguments Bruno Latour developed in *Irreductions* (1988b, 151–236), I am suspicious of 'purity', whether scientific or ethical – that 'vitriol of the soul', as Latour calls it, citing Michel Tournier (Latour 1984, 171). Far from holding the critical sociologists' commitments against them, I would reproach them rather for not maintaining those commitments to the end. In fact, the critical sociology of the last thirty years has focused, particularly in France, on the problem of social inequalities – that is, inequalities among the citizens of a nation-state. (The term society has often been used, as we see with wonderful clarity in Durkheim, as a synonym for 'country', 'nation' or 'state'; in most cases these different labels can be substituted for one another in a given utterance without changing the meaning.) Relying heavily on statistics, in numerous studies often commissioned by state agencies associated with centralized planning, critical sociology has brought to light inequalities in the distribution of public goods – for example, in education and medical care, or in the distribution of consumer goods, particularly durable goods and equipment (Desrosières 2008). In this respect, sociology can be treated as a sociology of justice. It places, as I do, the question of justice at the centre of its interrogations and, by approaching justice in its relations with the state, treats justice as a problem of political sociology. But it has the defect of revealing inequalities, described as so many injustices, without clarifying the position of justice on the basis of which they can be defined as such.

In fact, what has been said about the denunciations of injustice produced by ordinary persons is just as valid for sociologists. Bringing to light an injustice – that is, a division of material or immaterial goods that does not respect the legitimate order of worth among persons – could entail making explicit the principle of justice to which the critique is linked and clarifying the definition – supported by the denunciation from below – of what constitutes the value of things and people. Clarifying its own implicit scale of values would allow critical sociology to progress as a science. Yet critical descriptions have often dispensed with this work of clarification in the name of a division between judgements of reality and judgements of value, often relying on the authority of Max Weber, whose views probably constitute one of the least questioned dogmas in the practical epistemology of sociology. To defend simultaneously a position of retreat with respect to values – which recognizes their relativity – and the legitimacy of a critique, sociology claims, when it becomes conscious of the tension between these two requirements, to be doing nothing but opposing the 'realities' revealed by science to the discourse that society holds about itself and its declared *ideals*, without taking sides on the question of justice. But this position is hard to sustain, because the simple description of inequalities exercises an effect of selection and specification, and because it contains in itself a vague and implicit definition of what equality should be.

Nevertheless, we should not underestimate the importance of this distinction in the judgement that sociology passes on itself. It serves most often to sort out what belongs to the realm of science and what escapes science, to separate science from tradition and from philosophy and, more precisely, social science from social philosophy. Speaking of scholars who say how society should be arranged in order to be just, who attempt to depict a just and harmonious polity, a modern sociologist with scientific aims will say that those scholars are doing social philosophy and so they cannot claim scientific validity for their work. Thus in Durkheim's work, for example, one may be tempted to distinguish between texts that belong to social philosophy and those that belong to social science, between the numerous texts that speak of happiness and conditions for a happy social life and the ones that speak the language of law and method. The first will be treated as objects of sociology or, more specifically, of the sociology of knowledge. Attempts will be made to interpret them with reference to their author's beliefs, interests or origins, or else with reference to the 'historical context' of the period – in short, to reduce them to contingency. The second will be taken as solid, positive and necessary results, still valid and contributing to ongoing research. However – and this would be easy to demonstrate in Durkheim's case – this division is impossible: the methodological rules that are the most rigorous and seemingly the most detached from the preoccupations of practical reason are meaningful only in relation to Durkheim's construction of social justice and, more fundamentally still, to his anthropology. Critical sociology has to harden the split between facts and values in order to keep on sheltering from any critical enterprise, including its own, an islet of positivity on which to base the ambition of a radical unveiling. But it is through that very ambition that it rejoins the political philosophy from which it means to distinguish itself. For the critical operations on which critical sociology claims a monopoly and the justifying operations that, in its view, disqualify political philosophy constitute two ways of achieving the same competence to make judgements. But this competence is not the privilege of the philosopher or the sociologist. It is constantly put to work by actors themselves. It is precisely this incessant work of constructing causes, in the sense in which one invokes 'good causes' in order to justify action, and of calling into question, in the sense of critique, that critical sociology, speaking from the bastion within which it has closed itself off, can no longer take as an object.

— 4 —

THE SOCIOLOGY OF CRITICAL SOCIETY

From its own perspective, critical sociology cannot take the critical operations carried out by actors as objects of its analysis. Yet such objects are essential if we are to understand our own societies, which can be defined as *critical societies* in the sense that the actors in them all possess critical capacities; all have access to critical resources, although to varying degrees, and they call on these resources more or less continuously in the ordinary course of social life.[1] They do so even though their critiques have very uneven chances of modifying the state of the world that surrounds them; the effectiveness of a critique depends on the degree to which the actors have mastered their social environment. We belong to a society in which operations of critique and justification have become necessary if one is to respond to critiques or to forestall them, and thus these operations are continually brought into play. I am not referring here solely to major public causes, to denunciations shaped by institutions of political representation and publicized by the press or other media; I am referring as well to the countless accusations of wrongdoing that are conveyed from person to person in public places, workshops and offices, corridors and dining halls. It suffices to pay attention in order to hear the incessant murmur attesting to the indignation, pain and anxiety triggered by the feeling of injustice, a murmur that manifests the capacity of persons to put their sense of fairness to work. The social world is riddled with such challenges in its most ordinary situations; on a daily basis, denunciations point out injustices and call for reparations.

To study such denunciations as sociologists, we have to modify our position with respect to our object. To begin with, we have to give up the idea that we can have the last word by producing – and imposing on the actors – more powerful reports than the ones they themselves

28

are able to produce; in other words, we have to abandon the way classical sociology has conceptualized the asymmetry between researchers and actors. However, in order to construct an adequate research position, it is not enough to ask researchers to give up their hubris and stop claiming to rely on the legitimacy of science; it is not enough to demand that they involve themselves in participatory investigations and recognize that they are always implicated in their objects, that they occupy positions within the arrangements they are studying. All these steps are entirely consistent with the position of critical sociology, where researchers simply take the concern for ethical involvement and turn it into a methodological imperative. To move from critical sociology to the sociology of critiques, it is not ever more interiority that we need, but ever more exteriority. In the final analysis, exteriority is what defines critiques. To critique is to disengage oneself from an action so as to occupy an external position allowing the action to be considered from a different viewpoint, rather like persons who remain at the back of the room, looking on without joining in the fun, at a party where everyone else is drinking and dancing freely. Thus in the *OJ* model, where anthropology takes critical capacity as the criterion that allows us to distinguish persons from other beings, we base the possibility of critiques on the hypothesis that the existence of several polities allows persons to disengage themselves from any given situation. It is in fact by relying on a principle of justice stemming from a different polity that persons can detach themselves from the model of justice on which the situation in which they find themselves depends.

To study the critical activities of actors and to take critical society as my object, I must thus acquire a higher-level exteriority than the one for which critical sociology settles. This does not mean that I can no longer rely on my laboratory or maintain any asymmetry between researchers and actors. Asymmetry is by no means abolished, although it may take a different form. My activity will consist essentially in attempting to reconstitute as fully as possible the critical space within which an affair takes shape and plays out. In this respect, my approach can be related to a broader movement that has affected the social sciences as a whole, a movement often associated with the 'linguistic turn'. In the field of sociology, and, more specifically, in the theory of action, one can characterize it, as Nicolas Dodier does, by the shift from a 'sociology of agents' to a 'sociology of translation' (Dodier 1989). Instead of defining agents by means of stable attributes, endowing them with interests and tendencies that are inscribed in the body and capable of generating objective unconscious intentions, and then assigning itself the task of explaining the actions of these agents when they encounter external obstacles, the sociology of translation shows how actors develop discourses about these actions, how they shape their actions into a plot (Ricoeur [1984] calls this 'emplotment'). I shall adopt this paradigm provisionally; later, I shall have to step back in order to avoid being caught in a sociology that knows nothing of the social world beyond what belongs to the order of discourse. More specifically, within my own analytic framework I shall have to take into account things and their importance in social activities, while at the same time I shall have to open up my research to modes of relations between persons that are particularly difficult for actors to translate in their reports. The paradigm I need to deploy will thus require me, in my fieldwork, to accumulate the greatest possible number of reports produced by actors themselves. The work of a sociologist of critique is comparable in this respect to that of a judge investigating a case who keeps on postponing the moment of decision, the moment when, relying on the proofs accumulated or on an 'inner conviction' – that is, on the ability to make synthetic judgements (Dodier 1989) – the judge supplies her definitive report on the affair so as wrap it up by condensing it in a narrative 'requiring no supplementary information for a listener to understand the meaning of the actions being reported' (Chateauraynaud 1991, 21). Like judges, as sociologists of critique we stage the trial by gathering and recording the actors' reports, and our research reports are above all transcriptions of these recordings – reports on reports. We limit ourselves, in effect, to following the actors as closely as possible in their work of interpretation, making our way through the reports they have constituted. We take their arguments seriously, along with the proofs they offer; we do not attempt to diminish or disqualify them by contrasting them with a more powerful interpretation. We are attentive to the way in which the actors themselves construct reports that are coherent and that aim for objectivity and generality while making a selection between the elements that may be deemed necessary, in the context of the affair, and those that may be viewed as contingent. The work of simplification on the actors' part is intended, like our own, to constitute a coherent reality, by 'testing the solidity and coherence of the material situations' (Chateauraynaud 1991, 24) and giving that reality form (Thévenot 1984) in an account that is satisfying, in the sense that it finds an equilibrium between brief utterances lacking in consistency and narratives so dense in relational networks that they are uninterpretable. Sociologists of critique thereby give up the possibility of basing their own interpretations on

a stable form, one that could be constructed by exploiting the material resources at their disposal, a form of what classical sociologists
commonly call 'social structure'; instead, they allow themselves to be
guided by the stable forms that appear in the actors' accounts.

But, as we have seen, as sociologists of critique we do not abandon
our reliance on laboratories, and we do not suppress the asymmetry
between our own positions and those of the actors. There are basically two reasons for this. On the one hand, as professionals, we are
external to the affair, we have more resources at our disposal than
any of the actors taken separately, and we also have more time,
since we are not under pressure to rush to judgement, not obliged to
reach a conclusion quickly. Thus we can put together a set of reports
that none of the actors in isolation is in a position to assemble, even
though each of them may have knowledge of certain reports (made by
telephone, for example) to which a researcher will never have access.
Above all, we can compare the actors' reports with one another in a
single space, something the actors themselves are not in a position to
do. The trial staged by sociologists is in this respect an imaginary trial
that has no chance of taking place in reality in just the same way. In
fact, as we can see from the analysis of the way the actors prepare
for the trial, and from the immense work of selection and shaping
required when union leaders are preparing to present a legal case,
for example (Corcuff 1989), the reports that a sociologist of critique
has the means to bring together – a note from headquarters, remarks
exchanged by protagonists in private or during a meal, and so on –
have very little chance of appearing on stage as such and at the same
time in the space of the debate. Since as sociologists we do not close
off the list of reports a priori, we have to face the thorny problem of
where to end the investigation. Knowing that we will never collect
all the reports and will never have access, for example, to telephone
conversations between protagonists that took place during our
absence and without our knowledge, at what point do we decide that
we know enough to give a satisfactory representation of the critical
operations carried out by the actors, and by the same token bring the
investigation to a close?

Furthermore, the utterances that figure in the actors' reports are
often hasty and laconic. As a sociologist of critique, I cannot deal
with these utterances without clarifying them. While I do give up
the possibility of challenging the actors' interpretations with a more
powerful one, I cannot do without an analysis designed to explain
and clarify the actors' statements – that is, to test the degree to which
these statements are contingent by attempting to see to what extent

they hold up in association with stable elements. Am I dealing with remarks exchanged 'in passing', casual remarks 'of no account', as people say when they are striving to *relativize* their utterances, or are these remarks that 'count' – in other words, do they support a claim to consistency and aspire to generality? To be consistent with my own analytic framework, I cannot test these utterances by relating them to stable elements that would consist in properties inscribed once and for all in persons, as one has the right to do in sociologies of agency in which utterances and actions are apprehended only as markers and traces referring to underlying properties that are themselves defined with reference to a cartography of 'social structure'. To clarify the actors' statements, I thus have to test them in relation to stability of a different order: more precisely, I have to relate them to conventions that underlie their intelligibility and their acceptability to an indefinite number of other actors. Clarification consists, in this case, in deploying the 'et cetera' (to borrow a concept from ethnomethodology), the additional content that each of the interlocutors could draw from the utterance by reflecting independently even while remaining in the same semantic space; or it consists in 'exhausting the series of "because"', as Ricoeur puts it (1991, 189)[2] – in other words, in going back up the argumentative chain to utterances of higher generality in the sense that they are acceptable to unspecified actors and their validity no longer depends on the contingent dimensions of the situation. By resorting to clarification, researchers bring together a greater number of relations than those included in the utterance. To do this, we need models that validate general utterances and that explicitly represent the conventions on which the utterances rely, models to which we can compare the utterances gathered through empirical procedures.[3] This is the sense in which we can speak, in the present context, of analytic sociology. The work of analysis, comparable in some respects to that of analytic philosophy, aims here to bring out elements that actors may have been content to leave implicit; this allows us, as researchers, to formulate hypotheses about the categories these actors are calling on to orient their actions and 'to describe the very complex logical mechanisms presented to us by the concepts of everyday life' (Strawson 1962, 107). My undertaking can be related in this way to a 'descriptive metaphysics', to use Strawson's term (1959, 9), but with a difference: it does not aim to clarify universals but seeks rather, as cognitive anthropology does for exotic societies, to make explicit the metaphysical implications of the actions and arguments of ordinary persons in our society.

To carry out this task, the sociologist of critique has to associate each of the actors' utterances with models developed in the laboratory. To build these models, researchers adopt the position, fictitious or real,[4] that would be theirs if they had to program a robot capable of carrying out acceptable actions during a dispute inscribed in the arrangement of a given situation; this implies both defining the objects the robot would have to be able to recognize and writing the rules it would have to learn so it could generate judgements adjusted to the constraints of the situation. I shall argue that we are in a position to *understand* the actions of persons when, by putting this model to work, we have grasped the constraints that they have had to take into account, in the situation in which they found themselves, in order to make their critiques or their judgements acceptable to others. But the models themselves result from an effort at elaboration based on the arguments that have been put forward by actors and that bear on the situations in which the arguments were developed.

The work of model creation seeks to reconstitute the competence that actors must be able to enact in order to produce arguments that are acceptable – 'convincing' – to others in specific situations: in other words, arguments that can support a claim to intelligibility and that are endowed, too, with a high degree of objectivity and thus of universality. The possibility that an argument can lay claim to universal validity is in fact what upholds its objectivity and thereby makes it acceptable to others, or, as some would say, incontestable. The existence of such competence must be presupposed if we are to account for the empirically debatable capacity that actors utilize when they have to make judgements, develop justifications, or exit from a dispute by concluding with robust agreements – that is, in this context, legitimate ones. It is cognitive competence in the sense that we have to hypothesize that it has an equivalent in the mental equipment of persons. As in the case of generative grammar, from which the concept of competence is borrowed (Chomsky 1975), we can leave the task of exploring the modes of storing this competence to the psychologists; still, light shed on the way this competence is internalized is nevertheless apt to prove useful for analysis of the cognitive work done by the actors (Boltanski and Thévenot 1983). But speaking of competence does not imply adhering to a mentalist representation of the workings of social life. In fact, if competence is worthy of the name, if its use is to be effective and thus distinguishable from a phantasmagorical or utopian activity, it has to be adjusted to the order of the worlds to which it is applied. The construction of a model of competence thus has to be based on an analysis of the way situations in which persons are led to carry out operations of critique or justification are set up;

it must also take the situational arrangements and their components into account. *On Justification*, whose major arguments will be outlined below, is devoted to the construction of a model of competence of this type – namely, a model of justice. The book seeks to clarify the principles of justice on which people rely when they engage in critiques or produce justifications, and when they make explicit the operations by means of which they establish the well-foundedness of their assertions by using proofs to relate them to reality.

The use of models of competence is necessary to clarify the utterances of actors, because in the concrete situations of ordinary life people are rarely led to pursue to the end the work of going back to the principle of justice that supports their arguments (Dodier 1989). The work of justification is rooted in the need to respond to a critique (Habermas 1984). Apart from situations involving critiques, justification is useless. Now, on the one hand, persons are not continually engaged in situations involving critiques – even if such situations arise much more frequently than classical sociology would have it. Classical sociology tends to focus either on situations in which power relations prohibit critiques by ensuring the absolute domination of certain actors over others, or else on situations of tacit adjustment, in which the order of the world seems to be taken for granted. On the other hand, persons can exit from critiques and turn again towards agreement without fully carrying out the work of going back to principles, as we see in two sample cases analysed in *OJ* – compromise and relativization – and also in cases analysed in the second part of that work involving a shift into states in which equivalence is no longer sought and which thereby diverge from the demand for justice. It follows that the accounts produced by actors and collected by sociologists of critique during their fieldwork present utterances in which the principles of justice to which the argumentation refers, and which guarantee the validity of that argumentation, will not all be explicit to the same degree. Only in relatively rare situations, marked by a heightened tension and by a very elaborate work of shaping, mobilizing all the available resources, will these principles of justice figure with full transparency in the actors' utterances.

But while a sociologist of critique may retain the support of a laboratory, and while, as I have suggested, the various ways of constructing a laboratory can be characterized by different types of sacrifices, what sacrifice has the researcher agreed to make in the present case? Clearly, it can no longer be the sacrifice of illusions about which critical sociologists boast. For, by operating the necessary conversions in order to take critiques as such as my object, I

34

have penetrated into a world without illusions. The illusion I had to give up presupposed a space with two levels, that of the actor's beliefs and that of the underlying reality to which the sociologist alone could have access. Now that space is no longer mine, and I can no longer rely on the form of asymmetry on which it was based. I take the actors' arguments as they come, without subjecting them to my own critique; I simply confront them with models that are themselves the product of an effort to describe the common competence explicitly and systematically. By the same token, my colleagues in the sociology of critique and I are no longer subject, as persons, to the doubling that affected the critical sociologist, who was forced to abandon his illusions when he entered his laboratory but could pick them up again when he went back out, for example when he left the sociology of art behind to go to an art exhibit – for, as an ordinary person, he was no better able than anyone else to get along without the values and prin-ciples of judgement described in his work as common illusions. In our paradigm, the sacrifice is of a different order. Renouncing any claim to an analytic capacity that would be radically different from the actor's, on the basis of which we could explain the actor's behaviour in his place and better than he could do it himself, we are making the sacrifice of our *understanding*, in the sense in which Eric Weil (1968) uses this term to describe at once an attitude towards the world and a philosophical category. When we give up the possibility of present-ing our own version and of having the last word, we reject engaging in an activity that the actor does not have to renounce. Thus, as in the case of illusion, it is by not allowing ourselves to take liberties that the actor can exercise that we re-establish an asymmetry that grounds and justifies our research activity. In the concluding section of Part I of this book I shall examine the extent to which taking into account modes of relations that the actors themselves have difficulty translating can give us more room to manoeuvre with respect to actors' reports, and thus to transgress the ethical and methodological requirements associated with the linguistic turn. But first I must offer some remarks about the model of competence for justice presented in *OJ*. These observations are a necessary prelude to Part II, which at once relies on this model and seeks to shed light on a mode of activity for which the model cannot account.

— 5 —

A MODEL OF COMPETENCE
FOR JUDGEMENT

The framework Laurent Thévenot and I developed together and presented in *On Justification* aims principally at supplying an instrument for analysing the operations that actors perform when they develop critiques and have to justify them, but also when they justify themselves in the face of critiques advanced by others, or when they collaborate in the search for a justified agreement. Thus our privileged objects are situations subjected to an imperative of justification; these are not at all uncommon in everyday life, as the empirical research that accompanied the construction of the *OJ* framework attests. In this respect the book breaks with constructs that ultimately seek to associate all social relationships with power relations (as was often the case with works of Marxist inspiration) or else to link social relationships with the strategies actors use to optimize their interests (as in the various forms of sociology derived from utilitarianism) and thus cannot be attentive to the requirements of justice expressed by the persons involved; these are treated as ideological masks when they are not simply ignored. Alternating between fieldwork and model construction, we sought in *OJ* to contribute to empirical research on the way persons use their sense of justice to engage in critiques, justify their actions or veer towards agreement. By the same token, we did not seek to offer a theory of society that would compete with the numerous theories that have already been proposed to account for these social phenomena. The *OJ* framework does not propose principles of explanation that would allow us to reduce the disparity among social phenomena by relating them to underlying causes. Our framework is not based on the establishment of stable statistical connections between social phenomena of the morphological, demographic or economic order, and it does not rely on reference to social

36

structures or systems. If it fits into a theory of action rather than a theory of social phenomena (Némedi 1989), it nevertheless does not seek to account for the behaviour of agents by relating these agents to determining factors that would make them act. Thus it does not aim to reveal causes definitively programmed into agents that would guide their behaviours in any and all situations in which they might find themselves. Leaving explanation aside, it does not aspire to exhaustive understanding, either, and it would be useless to seek in it a grid making it possible to describe social reality in all its aspects. The analytic framework presented in *OJ* is built around the question of *justice*. It seeks to supply a model of the type of operations in which actors engage when they turn towards justice, and of the arrangements on which they can rely, in the concrete situations in which their actions take place, in order to ground their claims to justice. These claims are clearly not limited to cases – observable especially in drawn-out affairs that have taken on a certain amplitude – in which the actors submit their affairs to the legal system for arbitration.

Now, people are not continuously oriented towards justice, and the requirement of justice is not present – far from it – in all situations in which people interact. The *OJ* framework in fact seeks to do justice to justice, as it were, by taking seriously the ideal of justice[1] and the claims to justice advanced by persons on many occasions of everyday life, instead of denouncing them as so many illusions dissimulating judgements of a different nature (that is, essentially belonging to the realm of interest or power), and it thereby recognizes, without subjecting it to systematic suspicion, the possibility that persons may base their critiques on these requirements of justice or may veer towards justifiable agreements. Nevertheless, it does not seek to reduce the social phenomenon entirely to the question of justice. Actors are not always oriented towards justice and not all situations are subjected to the same degree to an imperative of justification. The requirement of justification is in fact inseparably tied to the possibility of critique. It is a necessary basis for supporting critiques or responding to them. Yet, on the one hand, critiques are not equally possible in all situations; on the other hand, the persons critiqued are not always obliged to explain themselves and to respond to arguments with other arguments. Instead, they can impose their positions by relying on an implicit or explicit threat of violence, or – much the same thing – on the justification of urgency; this is easy to see in military situations, where the urgency of combat rules out any discussion of orders. But these extreme situations cannot be extended everywhere; justice thus has to be dealt with as one of the registers capable of ordering the relations that ground social activity. Further on I shall offer a look at the way I think we can approach other modes of action, but at that point we shall have to go beyond the *OJ* framework, which focuses on the analysis of situations subjected to an imperative of justification.

To analyse these situations and the type of actions that take place in them, I shall not start from a definition of justice based on an a priori construction whose validity would be independent of the claims manifested by persons. To this extent, our model does not have a transcendental project, even if taking claims to justice into account always presupposes a reference to a logical level that transcends the diversity of concrete situations;[2] the model is not even normative in the sense that it would seek to establish an imperative of justice claiming universal validity, whether or not it is in harmony with the conventions on which actors' claims rely. As I have already had occasion to emphasize, the *OJ* model rests on an analysis of the justifications brought by actors and on the arrangements underlying these justifications, insofar as these can be gathered through investigative work, even if the transition from field observations to model construction presupposes recourse to other sources and the use of formal operations that are not in direct continuity with the empirical work. The model is thus presented as a *model of competence* – that is, as a shaping of the competence that the actors deploy when they act with reference to justice, and as a schema for the arrangements that, in reality, underlie and support this competence by ensuring that it has the possibility of being effective.

The competence I am attempting to analyse involves more than language use. It has to allow persons both to form arguments that are acceptable in terms of justice and to construct assemblages of objects, arrangements that hold together and that can thus be qualified as fair. The need to deploy this model in a formal construction is a direct consequence of the decision to take actors' demands for justice seriously. In fact, to make sure that these demands will hold up, and to avoid reducing them too quickly to hypocritical manoeuvres bound up with the defence of private interests or with unfounded illusions, actors must be able to show how they are going to satisfy conditions of validity that meet a requirement of universality and how they are going to make explicit the type of rationality on which their arguments rely. Now, this requirement that arguments be grounded on a form of rationality that is defensible at the highest level of generality cannot be directly tested simply by recording the utterances of actors, for, as we have seen, actors often skip the step of going back to first principles and instead settle for compromises.

The requirement cannot be tested, either, by simply observing the arrangements without relating the empirically observable reality to the formal model whose existence has to be presupposed in order to account for the robustness of the utterances and arrangements in question when they are put to the test of a critique. But this does not mean that the formal models have a rightful claim to universal validity without further examination. These models reflect the way the competence for justice that can be attested in our society today has taken shape; they cannot be extended to other societies or to other eras without a detailed analytical effort to test them against the arguments developed by persons belonging to these societies, and against the situations in which these arguments could be mobilized, insofar as we have access to such information. Without careful examination we cannot determine their range of validity or the modifications that would have to be made in order to permit their extension to other societies or other historical periods. Indeed, the various polities that the model needs to subsume in order to account for the competence for justice possessed by members of our own society have a historical character, although the study of their genesis, barely sketched out in *OJ*, has not been the object of extensive research. When we took on the task, in *OJ*, of constructing a model that would make it possible to understand how persons in our society put their sense of justice to work today, we could at least initially forego the work of seeking the origin or doing the genealogy of the resources on which operations of justification or criticism could rely (that task would have taken us well beyond the framework of our book). The brief summary that follows will focus on the features that define the specificity of the model and on the main concepts that it utilizes.

First, some observations about the beings recognized by the model: the model recognizes, first and foremost, the existence of persons who act in situations. It begins by seeking to grasp the constraints that limit the possibilities of action available to persons when they position themselves in the regime of justice. But these constraints are not treated as internal determinations. In *OJ*, we are not seeking to identify properties that would be inscribed irreversibly within agents and in their bodily habits and that would determine their behaviour in all circumstances. In fact, such properties, which have to be taken into account in other constructs, do not come into play in the operations that people carry out in order to do justice; it is precisely when people mean to denounce the unjust character of a situation that they seek out the contextual constraints in order to make their impact visible. The constraints that *OJ* seeks to bring to light are thus constraints that affect the arrangements in the situation in which the persons are placed. We consider that the ability to grasp these constraints and take them into account lies within the competence of all normal members of a given society. Like grammar rules, these are not unconscious constraints in the sense that censorship arising out of interests or taboos would oppose their being made explicit by the actors, even though, in most practical situations, the actors do not need to make them explicit or to go back to the basic principles that give meaning to their actions. In our view, the operative constraints can always be made explicit under certain pressures – for example, the pressure to respond to a direct critique proffered by an adversary, or to answer questions posed by an investigator. But even when they are not formulated explicitly, these constraints remain present, particularly through the way the objects that make up the situation are arranged. In our framework, when a person considered to be demented, eccentric or not in possession of good sense is identified as abnormal, this is also a way of saying that the person is incapable of taking these constraints into account.

It follows that we do not base the possibility of agreement on the fact of belonging to a single group on which the possibility of a common culture would depend – culture being understood as a set of norms and schemas shared in an implicit way, in the mode of going-without-saying, whatever the group's origin in terms of ethnicity, region, class, and so forth. This refusal is in line with my earlier work, focused on *cadres*, which led me to abandon a view according to which group unity and cohesion resulted from substantial similarity among the members and from a shared objective interest. I began to be attentive to the immense historical work that is needed to unify disparate beings around a single system of representation, in order to constitute the reality of that heterogeneous set, to inscribe it – by an intense effort of objectivization – in arrangements, and to define a common interest for it. I also sought to show that, even in the case of a strongly objectivized group, this work would have to be continued, begun over and over again, and that all of its members would repeat the work on their own account when they had to rule on their own identity (Boltanski 1987a). But that is not all. In the case of justice, constructs that present themselves as basic units of groups and cultures can account only in terms of power relations for agreements reached among people belonging to different groups, with their divergent cultures and interests. While the existence of power relations clearly has to be acknowledged, it was important for me to show that, in certain situations, people can reach justifiable and universalizable agreements that are capable of holding up in the face of denunciations that characterize them as mere power relations disguised as relations of justice.

This perspective is necessary if one is to follow the arguments of persons when they engage in critiques or propose justifications, and it led me to break with the two principal types of explanations used in social theory. The first set of explanations refers to *force*, domination, power. From this perspective, order reigns in appearance only: it results from domination – power exercised by the strong over the weak. The appearance of coordination is thus the result of permanent and tacit *violence*. This thematics can be oriented along two somewhat different paths, according to the relation that it introduces between justice and power. It can contain an implicit denunciation in the name of justice. The goal of a just order will then be contrasted with the reality of present injustice: order in society ought to be just, but present reality is ruled by the arbitrariness of domination of the strong over the weak. The task of people in society is to achieve this goal of justice. The harmonious polity to come may be the object of a detailed description, as in a utopia, or it may remain in the indeterminacy of the future, but in all cases the eschatological thrust presupposes reliance on an anthropology that specifies the capacities of human beings and that thus opens the way to reflection on the conditions that must be fulfilled if their humanity is to be fully realized. This eschatological thrust is present, for example, in Marx's work. If Marx develops the description of a harmonious polity only minimally (much less, for example, than Durkheim does), as has often been remarked, his writings nevertheless contain an anthropology that insists on human creative capacities, and particularly on the creative value of work: freed from exploitation and subject to the law of desire, work can be in itself a source of gratification apt to ensure happiness. Associated with a philosophy of history (history as ultimate judge), this anthropology supports Marx's overall critique of the present world, and, by extension, it supports ordinary denunciations of everyday injustices (see below, chapter 12.2).

The thematics of power takes on a completely different orientation when it stops trying to base critiques on the goal of a harmonious polity in a possible future world and abandons the question of justice, treating it as illusory or – as Max Weber does to virtually the same effect – viewing it as a contingent matter of personal choice (having the courage to 'listen to one's own demons'). In the modern world, the propagation of this thematics, which finds its fullest formulation in Nietzsche, emerges in the social sciences, which have adopted it to a very large extent. It too offers the possibility of a critical attitude. Freed from the tyranny of values, one can take up one value at a time and turn it against another by unveiling the underlying *interests* in each case – that is, by reducing the common good in every instance to a private interest (a procedure Marx adopts, for example, in his critique of the Hegelian concept of right, although he does not position it as a general attitude towards the social world [Marx 1970]). The reference to each value in turn is thus subordinated to a critical project that seeks to surpass them all; identifying underlying forces everywhere, it perceives every judgement as a negation of lateral possibilities, the result of violence. One effect of this generalization is that it no longer allows any distinction between what we recognize as 'violence', in our ordinary experience of the social world, and what we identify as acquiescence, right, discipline freely accepted. The way in which a denunciation is carried out will thus take an entirely different direction depending on which of these two orientations it adopts.

The second set of explanations, which has several variants (some more Durkheimian in orientation, others more culturalist), refers to common values, to a common culture, to representations and often to an unconscious: persons display orchestrated behaviours because they have internalized the same models, the same values or the same schemas, which guide them from within, take on the contours of their will, shape behaviours in the mode of habit and give the characteristics of naturalness to constraint. In the Durkheimian form, analysed in more detail in *OJ* (pp. 285–92), the coordination of individual actions is the result of a double process of externalization and internalization: the group, which is not reducible to the simple sum of its parts, is the space of collective representations that are reinternalized by the persons involved.

I am not unaware of the role – uneven according to the situation, the society and the era – played by violence in political relations among people, nor am I unaware of the degree to which habits depend on internalization by the body. But I contest the claim that all situations can be accounted for by violence or habit. The *OJ* model seeks to establish that, in certain situations – namely, those in which persons are, or may be, confronted with critiques (and these are numerous) – in order to reach agreement one must be in a position to justify oneself through reference to a principle valid for all. Such agreements are necessary to bring a dispute to an end or to avoid one altogether. These situations, in which persons are confronted with an *imperative of justification*, are the ones on which the *OJ* model focuses. A shift into violence is always a possibility, one that I shall attempt to examine a little more closely later in this study. But at that point I shall then have to adopt a perspective from which it is possible to constitute the relevance of modes of action that do not stem from justice, and, consequently, I shall have to exit from the framework of OJ. For, on the basis of the OJ model of competence for justice, one can only set aside as irrelevant situations that dispense with justifications and that are either attributed to violence, on which the model has nothing to say, or else rejected as contingent.

The type of agreement sought in OJ is thus active agreement. Persons work towards producing agreement. Our emphasis on the work persons have to do in the here and now to construct the social world, to endow it with meaning and to guarantee it a minimum of sturdiness, brings our enterprise closer to that of phenomenological sociologies, which are equally attentive to the performative activities of the actors. But, in order to simulate the constraints that weigh on actors when they involve themselves in justice, our model cannot limit its purview to persons in situations. It must also recognize two other types of entities, whose relevance is not always acknowledged by sociologies of a phenomenological bent. We have to take into account metaphysical beings, on the one hand, in particular what we call polities, and objects, on the other hand, especially things, as we shall see later on. Unlike ethnomethodology, for instance, which addresses all the possible states of the world that can present themselves in the here and now without making the methodological decision to use resources external to the situation, the OJ model seeks to account for justifiable states, those whose justification calls upon common resources that extend beyond the situation. And it is precisely the recourse to principles of construction extending beyond the situation that allows us to identify the situations and the selection of arguments and configurations that are relevant to it, an immense and almost impossible task if one takes on a universe, as ethnomethodology does, in which any being at all may be involved in any situation at all, and in which situations are grasped in the absolute indeterminacy of a here and now offered without resistance to free interpretations by the actors.

In the OJ model, the very possibility of a social order is based on a bi-level construction: on one level there are persons, while on the other there are forms and common goods that make it possible to establish equivalence among beings and thereby to define their relative worth. At the heart of this model of competence there is thus what might be called a *metaphysical capacity*. We credit human persons with a metaphysical capacity, and we consider that this capacity is essential for understanding the possibility of a social bond. In fact, in order to converge towards agreement, persons have to refer to something other than persons, something that transcends persons. This common reference is what we call a principle of equivalence. When agreement is difficult to establish, in order to achieve it persons have to clarify their positions with regard to justice; they have to conform to an imperative of justification, and, in order to justify, they have to remove themselves from the immediate situation and rise to a higher level of generality. Thus they are inclined to seek a position based on a principle that is valid across the board – that is, a principle that can claim universal validity.

We seek to show in OJ, and this is the first part of our construction, that, although the social sciences presuppose such a metaphysical capacity, they do not draw all of its consequences. We begin with the controversy between Durkheimian sociology and liberal economics, which is a form of the more general controversy between holism and individualism. The terms of the argument are well known: the tendencies linked to the tradition of liberal economics reproach Durkheimian sociology for its holism, which they associate with metaphysics. The 'groups' recognized by Durkheimian sociology do not exist. Collectives are artefacts. Only individual persons supplied with interests exist. Durkheim, for his part, establishes the existence of collective realities in his polemical exchange with liberal economics; this polemic is at once inextricably ethical and scientific. The rational individual of liberal economics is an egoist (Durkheim uses this term when he criticizes individualism), and this individual is an artefact, an abstract man belonging to no era and no country. We recognize, with the individualist tradition, that the Durkheimian schema is based on a metaphysics. But we try to show that the construction of a just political bond on the basis of market relations also presupposes a metaphysics: persons in a market are not in a state of individuality, in the ordinary sense of the term 'individual'. If they were plunged into individuality, they would have no reason to seek the same goods, to agree on the search for the same goods, or to find themselves in competition for those goods. We say, then, that persons in a market are *moral beings*, in the sense that they are capable of abstracting themselves from their particularity to reach agreement on external goods, the list and the definition of which are universal (Thévenot 1989). We do not regard this underlying metaphysics as a failing in the social sciences. It is precisely by having recourse to conceptualizations that can be viewed as metaphysical that the social sciences recognize the role played by the human capacity to conclude justifiable agreements in the construction of society.

Such an agreement, then, justified by reference to a principle that transcends the situation because it claims to be valid across the board, is what we call a *legitimate* agreement. Justification does indeed support a claim to universality (Habermas 1984). In fact, if a person who finds herself in disagreement sets aside the possibility of violence and thereby gives up the possibility of imposing her views by eliminating her adversaries, she must express her disagreement by basing it on arguments. But the arguments on which she relies cannot be valid solely for the person who expresses them, for this would tip the exchange into the register of insult, which is defined precisely by the will to evade justification ('Why are you telling me this?' 'Because I don't like your looks!') or by pure idiosyncrasy, as a form of personal, poetic or delirious expression. The arguments used cannot be valid just for certain people, either – for example, in order to stabilize a *deal* among the persons present – for they must be robust enough to be able to stand up to the questions of an indeterminate number of new partners, not yet specified, who, if they were introduced into the situation where the disagreement is posited, could be in a position to demand in turn that the previously advanced arguments be clarified in order to stabilize the social bond among the participants. To make convergence towards agreement possible, operations of justification must thus hypothesize some common knowledge on which the arguments or arrangements subject to critique or approval by the others can rely. Our work also aims, then, to help clarify what is understood, in sociology, as 'legitimacy'. This concept, which constitutes one of the common references of sociology, is subject to ambiguous use. Sociology views legitimacy sometimes as a necessary component of social action, sometimes as the after-the-fact legitimizing of a coordination achieved by other means – that is, essentially, by force: in the latter case the term 'legitimation' is often used (as for example when a legal text is said to be a 'legitimation' of a 'power relation').[3] In *OJ*, we treat legitimacy as stemming from the very competence of actors. We are in effect hypothesizing that the actors are capable of making the distinction between, on the one hand, arguments or configurations that are legitimate in the sense that, when confronted with critiques, they can be the object of justifications that are valid across the board and can be used to support universalizable agreements and, on the other hand, illegitimate arguments or configurations that can indeed be mobilized by actors in certain situations to support deals that benefit the parties involved but can neither justify nor support agreements aiming at the generality of the common good.

— 6 —

PRINCIPLES OF EQUIVALENCE AND JUSTIFIABLE PROOFS

When persons present critiques that they want others to find acceptable, even if the opposing arguments are not in harmony with their own, or when they construct justified and legitimate agreements capable of forestalling a dispute or bringing one to an end, the critique or agreement will bear on the just or unjust character of the situation. To qualify what must be understood as justice here, and to introduce the possibility of using a single notion to bring together disputes that appear to be quite different, I posit that disputes conducted with reference to justice always have as their object the order of *worths* in a situation. Let us take a trivial example, namely, the problem of distributing food among people seated for a meal. When the table is large and there are more than a few tablemates, people cannot readily serve themselves, as they can when the dishes are presented at a buffet and the participants are free to move about and choose the food they will put on their plates – although the latter situation does not preclude questions of order, as attested by the widespread reluctance to be the first in line at the buffet. During a meal served from the head of the table, the question of the temporal order in which the plates are filled cannot be avoided, and it has to be settled in public. One can of course try to remove all significance from the order of service, try to detach it from the order among persons and thereby relativize its import, by opting to adjust the temporal order to a spatial order; this happens when the host or hostess, choosing not to serve certain persons first, simply passes the dish around the table, 'family style'. But in all other cases, the temporal order of service is apt to be interpreted as an order of precedence, established according to the relative worth of the persons present, as when the oldest persons are served first and the children last (in this case the worth in question is domestic, according to the terminology I shall introduce later on). But the achievement of this order can obviously pose difficult problems, especially if several principles of order are present simultaneously (should one serve the grandmother first, or the boss whom the head of the household has invited to dinner?), and the order adopted can be challenged. If the scene is to play out harmoniously, without argument or scandal, the participants have to be in agreement about the relative worth of persons to be recognized in the order of service. And this agreement on the order of worths presupposes in turn a more fundamental agreement with respect to which the relative worth of the beings present can be established. Even if the principle of equivalence is not invoked explicitly, it must be sufficiently clear and present in everyone's mind if the episode is to unfold naturally. I designate these principles of equivalence with an expression borrowed from Rousseau, *common higher principles*. Reliance on these principles of equivalence is what allows us to reach agreement on the relative worth of persons.

One cannot put a requirement of justice to work, in fact, without referring to a scale of values. The requirement of justice can be equated with a requirement of equality. Yet since Aristotle we have known that, in a polity, equality does not necessarily signify an absolutely identical distribution among all members of the material or immaterial goods valued in that polity; rather, as Michel Villey aptly puts it, equality signifies a just 'proportion between the quantity of things distributed and the various qualities of persons' (Villey 1983, 51). To define a relation as equitable or inequitable – a judge's task (and the task taken on by sociologists when they bring inequalities to light) – thus supposes a pre-existing definition of what constitutes the value of things and persons, a scale of values that requires clarification in the case of disagreement. Such a definition necessarily has a normative character: it refers to the principle of worth that makes it possible to relate persons and things in a just and acceptable configuration. Why do I speak of worth and not of value, a term more commonly used in sociological literature? What I call *worth* is different from what sociology commonly calls value in several respects that can be identified briefly here. Values are not necessarily oriented towards justice (we also speak of aesthetic values, tastes, opinions, and so on), while the term *worth*, as I construe it, always presupposes a reference to an order whose just character can be revealed: a justifiable order. Secondly, and the two arguments are not unrelated, sociologists tend to identify 'values' with the preferences revealed by opinions that emerge from responses to interview questions or to batteries of items on questionnaires ('scales of values'). It is clear that, when this is the case, every option disclosed can be the manifestation of a 'value' and that, as a result, everything can be a 'value'; this is consistent with the postulate according to which values are arbitrary. Certain persons will be said to have bureaucratic values, or values that are authoritarian, racist, religious, rural, hedonistic, and so on. And people can indeed rely on such 'values' – for example, a shared racist attitude – to establish a bond in a given situation. But my construct aims precisely to distinguish these private 'deals' from agreements that can be generalized. These 'values', defined as 'arbitrary', allow the actors, or a subset of the actors, present in a situation to reach mutually beneficial agreements by mutual consent, but they cannot establish agreements that are valid across the board. Conversely, 'worths', in the sense in which I am using the term, are based on general principles of equivalence whose validity transcends the present situation, and they can thus be the basis for agreements that are acceptable to all, agreements oriented towards universality. This distinction is consistent with the project of taking the concept of legitimacy seriously and clarifying it. Agreement on worths is the condition for legitimate agreement. Finally, the values to which sociology usually refers are attached to groups and to persons insofar as they belong to – or define their 'identity' with reference to – these groups (this presupposes an architecture connecting 'persons' and 'groups' that would include mechanisms of externalization and internalization, mechanisms that may be Durkheimian or culturalist in orientation). In the *OJ* model, worths are attached neither to groups nor to persons insofar as the latter are attached to groups; instead, they are attached to the situations in which persons find themselves. When, among the multitude of possible states, the situation represents a state of the world that is justifiable, it incorporates a reference to a principle of equivalence that can claim universal validity, a principle in relation to which the worth of the beings present can be defined.

If the claim to universal validity constitutes one of the characteristics of what I call a worth, it does not follow, however, that I am attempting to reduce all behaviours to a single principle of equivalence. The confrontation between Durkheimian sociology and liberal economics, whose broad outlines I have recalled above, has already shown us two forms of possible agreement, corresponding to two higher common principles, one established with reference to a collectivity and the other with reference to a market. In *OJ*, we sought to identify additional worths that fall under a constraint of legitimacy – that is, we tried to establish the properties that a scale of values must manifest in order to be the support for a legitimate worth. Classical sociology in effect defines for itself a world that contains a plurality of values because it contains a plurality of groups. But it then becomes difficult to raise the question of agreement among different groups endowed with different values. Explanations based on the existence of a shared culture no longer suffice, and this most often leads to the invocation of effects produced when one group dominates another. Conversely, theories of justice, which take on the task of establishing the conditions that make a just society possible, are most often oriented towards the search for a universal principle that makes it possible to establish a convention recognized by all. But such constructs – which are valid first of all owing to the requirement of systematicity that must be accepted by any enterprise aiming to establish the possibility of a just polity based on a single normative principle, and which thus possess certain of the properties one can expect from models – turn out to be utopias when they are confronted with the diversity of situations familiar to people in complex societies. In the *OJ* model, we posit that the worth of persons can be established on the basis of a plurality of principles of equivalence. Because these different principles of equivalence are attached not to different groups but rather to different situations, it follows that a normal person must be capable of shifting, in the course of a single day, among situations arising from different principles of worth. Normal persons must thus agree to see their own worth vary (since nothing assures them that the worth to which they have access in a situation defined by one principle of equivalence will follow them into a different situation governed by a different principle of equivalence). Finally, because the various worths are incompatible (since each of them is posited, in the situation in which its validity is guaranteed, as universal), in any given situation persons have to have the ability to ignore the principles on which they have based their justifications in the situations they have traversed.

To define these worths, Laurent Thévenot and I went back and forth systematically between empirical data gathered from fieldwork on disputes – data that supplied us with a corpus of arguments and situational arrangements that guided our intuition towards the type of justifications that are often used in daily life[1] – and constructions that had undergone systematic elaboration in the tradition of political philosophy and thus had the character of models apt to be used profitably in our task of creating models of common competence. Connecting data gathered from fieldwork among ordinary persons with scholarly texts belonging to the cultural tradition is not a problem for anthropologists who study exotic societies, but it is unfamiliar in sociology, which is concerned with maintaining a distinction between everyday life and the universe of texts (or between popular culture and scientific culture); our decision to adopt this practice was anchored in a reflection on the place of tradition in our society and, more specifically, in our political universe. One can show indeed that the constructs of political philosophy today are inscribed within institutions and arrangements (for example, polling stations, workshops, media, concerts or family reunions) that continually let actors know what they have to do to behave normally. But one can also show that the same traditions inform research activity in sociology because they are inscribed in the tools researchers use – tools bequeathed to them by their discipline, which was itself established on the basis of an often polemical debate with political philosophy.[2] This double observation helped to found a conception of sociology, set forth above, which breaks with the intent to unveil something hidden or to explore an unconscious, and instead defines the sociologist's activity as an operation of clarification inscribed most often within the framework of a hermeneutics (this point is developed below in chapter 10.2 and 10.3).[3] Moreover, only such a framework allows us to assume fully, and to reinsert within the architecture of research, the actors' reappropriation of the results of the sociologist's activity (analysed above in chapter 3) instead of denying this reappropriation, denouncing it as a compromise, or seeing it as an obstacle to the achievement of a truly 'objective' science.

The analyses that enabled us to identify the various polities are based on classical works of political philosophy. For this purpose, we sought to use works that present themselves explicitly as political and that articulate the principles of justice governing the polity; we chose the earliest – or one of the earliest – texts in which the polity considered is presented in a systematic way. These are always well-known texts that have been widely disseminated and have most evidently inflected institutions or arrangements that are still operative today. We treated these texts not as philosophers or historians would have done, by seeking to resituate them either in the history of philosophy or in their properly historical context, but rather by viewing them as works by grammarians of the political bond: political philosophers propose a general formulation valid for all, one that validates customary games, procedures or rules that are constituted locally. The analysis of the six texts on which we relied allowed us to sketch six harmonious polities founded on six different principles of equivalence.[4]

In the determination of legitimate worths, it was very important for us to maintain symmetry between principles derived from arguments developed by ordinary persons and the kinds of arguments sociologists usually evoke to explain people's behaviour: in other words, it was important to align the actors' resources with those of researchers. If analysis had brought to light sociological principles of explanation that had no analogues in the principles of worth invoked by persons to support their claims to justice, the possibility of explaining actions by underlying causes beyond the actors' reach would have remained open. If that had been the case, we would not have been in a position to break with a sociology of unveiling that is always tempted to engage itself anew in analyses. Now, it can be shown that the various worths we have identified also support the manoeuvres of sociological unveiling, which can thus be treated symmetrically with the arguments of persons. Sociologists, like ordinary persons, rely on domestic worth when they unveil the real relationship among people that is concealed under the artefact of official relations – which is to say, most often, civic relations. Similarly, they rely on the worth of fame when they purport to discredit the claims to inspiration put forward by actors, for example in the case of the sociology of art or science, by making 'recognition by others' or 'credit' the only 'real' criterion of work acceptable to a truly scientific sociology. This list could be extended, through a series of successive intersections, but it would quickly become tedious. In this respect, our approach partakes of a radical relativism, since it renounces the possibility of appealing to a reality more robust than that of the various worlds in which justifications of persons are deployed. Reality, in this perspective, is precisely the critical space opened up by the possibility available to the actors of moving into different worlds, of involving themselves in these worlds or finding support in one of them in order to denounce the validity of another.

But, to build this space, we had to deploy the alternative worlds that compose it while satisfying two contradictory constraints. On the one hand, we had to reveal each world in its specificity and focus on those aspects that are irreducible to those of all the others; this implied adopting a vantage point external to these worlds, since from the standpoint of each one the others can certainly be internalized, although at the price of ignoring what constitutes their worth: they can be submitted to an order according to which one form of generality is endowed with the legitimacy of the polity's common good while all the others are reduced to particular goods with which only selfish enjoyment is associated. This external vantage point is accessible because persons are always free to exit, by means of a thought experiment, from the world in which they function when they are dealing with their relationships in justice, in order to find support in a position that eludes the regime of justice, a position from which the space of what is subject to judgement can be apprehended as a whole. On the other hand, and this is the second constraint, we also had to deploy these different worlds in such a way as to shed light on their symmetrical character – that is, we had to try to build them according to a common architecture and then to describe them by means of standardized tools and according to a common grid. This approach, congruent with the scientific aim of our enterprise, gave an industrial tonality to the shaping to which the description of the various natures was subjected, however foreign to the industrial world those natures might be. If it were otherwise, since each world has its own way of establishing proof and thus its own mode of knowing, for our depictions of the various worlds in *OJ* (chapter 6) we would have had to adopt a different mode of exposition in each case, presenting the inspired world in the form of enigmas, the domestic world in the form of examples, the civic world in the form of laws, and so on. But this is not how we chose to proceed. On the contrary, we strove to standardize the presentations so we could compare the different worlds. In so doing, we carried out a task of reduction by apprehending each of them from a viewpoint close to that of the industrial world. This reduction comes close to denunciation, since it consists in associating beings from one world with ways of establishing proof derived from a different world. But the successive presentation of the different worlds within a single chapter, using a common grid, helped to achieve the effect of relativism necessary for our demonstration. The decision in favour of relativism – which we limited, moreover, by bringing to light the constraints of legitimacy that weigh on the construction of worths – brought our enterprise into line with structuralist tendencies. But, unlike structuralist anthropology, which shatters the opposition between the rational and the irrational by substituting the concept of system for that of reason and by endeavouring to show that the human world is always systematic, even in its seemingly most incoherent myths, we did not give up the possibility of a reasonable universe or of practical reason; instead, we subjected this possibility to the constraint of a plurality of incompatible worlds. If people are to act reasonably, they must be in a position to develop critical capacities. Now, the possibility of using critiques depends on the possibility of having access to an externality on the basis of which which one can disengage oneself from the present situation so as to

52

bring judgements to bear on it. It is this possibility of disengagement, always open, that is offered by the existence of a plurality of worlds. But this possibility can be real only if one conceives of these worlds as so many incompatible universes in which fairness is supported by different principles.

We also sought to identify the constraints that bore upon the construction of these six polities, constraints constitutive of the model they had in common. To be legitimate, worths have to satisfy *constraints of construction*, and the works of political philosophy we used to identify the various worths had to be confronted with these constraints, although the latter turned out to be unevenly stabilized insofar as they were written in very different historical periods and in different contexts. Thus, if the principles of equivalence that we grasped in contemporary French society do have a historical character, if they can disappear and be replaced by others (for their number is of course not determined once and for all, so that one has the right, for example, to try to identify, in the contemporary period, worths that are in the process of being constituted – pre-worths, as it were), the fact remains that the need to satisfy constraints of construction is one of the elements that helps limit the number of legitimate worths on which the justification of persons can rely. By bringing to light the constraints that a scale of values must satisfy if it is to support a legitimate worth, we accounted for the relatively restricted number of principles of equivalence that, at a given moment in time, can lay claim to universal validity. To recognize that there exists a plurality of worths thus does not necessarily signify that these can be unlimited in number (like the values familiar to sociology). It is on the basis of this model that we were able to describe the competence that actors put to work when they manifest their ability to distinguish between arguments relying on legitimate worths and value judgements incapable of supporting a claim to legitimacy. This model, which cannot be developed here in detail, is articulated around the tension between two constraints. The first, which we call a constraint of *common humanity*, posits a fundamental identity among the persons apt to enter into agreement, the members of the polity, who belong in this respect and by the same token to humanity: the constructs of political philosophy that we use include, at least potentially, a common definition of humanity in which all human beings are equally human. Political philosophy thus tends to posit a fundamental equality among human beings. The second constraint applies an *order* to that humanity.

Let us note that, if the first constraint is partially identical in the various political philosophies on which we relied, the principle of equivalence that makes it possible to establish an order among beings varies, as we have seen, from one construct to another. This double constraint generates tension, because persons have in common the fact of being equal with regard to their membership in humanity, even though they are ordered according to a principle of worth. To resolve this tension, one must introduce into the model other hypotheses that I shall not spell out here; it will suffice to indicate their three principal thrusts. First, a *formula of economy* that links access to the higher states with a *cost*, and thus with a *sacrifice* required for this access. Second, an equivalence between the happiness associated with higher states and the *common good* of the entire polity: a sacrifice benefits everyone and spills over onto the least important members. Finally, a principle of uncertainty: the various states of worth are not attached once and for all to persons; this would be in contradiction with the principle of common humanity. Persons thus always exist *potentially* in all worths. It follows that the determination of the state of worth in which persons find themselves is subordinated to the completion of a *test*, which we call the test of worth.

The notion of test plays a central role in our construct; a major part of our study is devoted to it. In fact, for persons to be able to reach agreement in practice and not only in principle, this test must take place concretely in reality, and it must be accompanied by a form of proof: it is a reality test. To account for the completion of such a test, we had to introduce into the situation not only persons, as political philosophy does, but also things, material or immaterial objects. In our view, in fact, reality tests result from the capacity of persons to confront objects and decide on their *value*. This observation holds true in all orders: for example, when two computer scientists have to demonstrate their competence by assigning value to computers with reference to a principle of the industrial order, or when two potential heirs reveal their capacity to attribute value to real property with reference to a principle of the domestic order. Thus each principle of justice is associated with a universe of objects, qualities and relations that we call natures or models. In our book, we depict these different worlds by cataloguing the objects, persons and relations that figure in manuals intended for everyday life. We chose a manual for each of the principles of justice discussed earlier, and, in order to be consistent with the hypothesis according to which the principles of worth are not attached to localities but to situations, we chose these various manuals from a single space, that of a company: in a company, in the course of a single day, the same person can pass from situations of production that are industrial in nature to a situation in which personal relations play a role – for example, in the lunch room (relations stemming from domestic worth) – and then to a market situation or to a union situation that is civic in nature. The analysis of the objects and relations that figure in these manuals constitutes a first element of empirical validation of the model that has been broadly confirmed by fieldwork.

To grasp persons as they carry out operations of justification and to clarify the competence that they put to work when they engage in a dispute in the mode of justice, it is thus of no use to endow them with personalities in the psychological sense, whether one locates the origin of personality traits in the earliest familial or sexual experiences (as in psychoanalytic interpretations) or in the earliest social experiences. To orient themselves in the worlds in which their actions are justifiable, persons have to possess capacities of the cognitive type (the capacity to make associations and to recognize equivalences, for example), but they do not need 'personalities' understood as a set of response patterns that are established and fixed in the way habits are bound up in the body, patterns that would be apt to guide them from within and – often unconsciously – induce behaviours whose consistency would be ensured by repetition.[5] The decision to centre our investigations on the question of justice led us to emphasize the plasticity of persons, their aptitude to change situations and to reach agreement in different situations, rather than stressing their rigidity. In contrast, when the social sciences face the test of creating a biography, they typically produce a stylized, coherent portrait by bringing together behaviours adopted in different periods and situations by a single individual so as to bring out his or her systematic character.[6] Our way of constructing human persons may seem counter-intuitive, because it does not take into account the persistence of persons over time. But it is congruent with the trends that, after Dilthey, refuse to take persistence as a given inscribed once and for all in the nature of the body itself; their goal is to analyse the arrangements in which persons are led to associate their present actions with actions that they have carried out in past situations, and to analyse the procedures through which these persons establish coherence among acts that are associated in temporal terms. Without going into the detail of such analyses, one may suggest that these procedures have to be open to treatment as particular instances of procedures of justification. In fact, the question of persistence over time does not come up for persons in all situations or at every moment of their lives. It arises essentially in quite specific situations in which persons have to pass judgement on acts that have been committed in the past and on the relation between those past acts and more recent ones (as is shown, for example, in debates over the statute of limitations on criminal charges, in the unease often aroused by condemnations for acts committed long before they were formally judged, or in situations where anticipatory judgement has to be made about future acts and the probable fairness of that judgement is evaluated, for instance, in tests that accompany hiring procedures). Similarly, biography and, especially, autobiography, which aim to reconstruct a coherent life story, are oriented with reference to judgement, and more precisely still with reference to what can be called a last judgement. Thus, from this perspective, a reference to justice and an imperative of justification have to guide the analysis of biographical arrangements and procedures.

The model whose broad outlines I have just summarized can be used to analyse the critical operations in which actors engage. Critiques following the logic of the model presuppose that objects deriving from different worlds will be brought together. In situations of dispute, beings of several different natures are valorized simultaneously. Such clashes interest me especially when they provoke challenges to the validity of a test. A challenge arises when, in a test, the presence of beings foreign to the nature of the test is revealed. We can identify, at bottom, two characteristic cases. In the first, the principle of the test is not challenged; rather, the accusation bears on the fact that the test has not been carried out in conformity with justice, because the persons passing judgement have taken a different worth into account. Let us consider, for example, a test administered in a school, a test that is supposed to measure pupils' abilities and is thus predominantly industrial in nature. One can denounce the fact that a pupil has exhibited his family's wealth – by his clothes, his manners, and so on – and that the examiner has noted these elements foreign to the nature of the test (an 'expensive' jacket, a 'distinguished' accent) and has taken them into account in her assessment. The situation is not equitable because there has been a *transport of high worth* (in such cases the term 'privilege' is often used). If, on the contrary, the evaluators consider that the rigour of their judgement has to be attenuated because the pupil comes from a poor family or has not had good working conditions, we will say that they are taking into account a *transport of low worth* (the pupil has suffered from a 'handicap'). In the second representative case, which we call *denunciation*, the very validity of the principle governing the test is challenged by someone relying on a different principle. The dispute then bears on what matters in reality; what really matters, in the academic institution, is not producing efficient workers (industrial worth), it is forming responsible citizens (civic worth). In this case, resolving the dispute implies reverting to a single test, organized with reference to one of these principles or the other. We should note that the way a situation is structured may make it easier or harder to carry out a denunciation. The murky situations in which beings of several different natures are involved are particularly apt to invite denunciations. This is why test situations are usually structured in such a way as to be pure, by excluding beings of different natures, in order to make it difficult to challenge the outcome. And it is precisely because the situational arrangements encountered in everyday life, especially those that include the possibility of tests involving the worth of persons, have been structured in advance that the cognitive competence of persons to make just judgements is relatively realistic – that is, attuned to the world as it is. To support their claims to justice, persons may in fact rely on reality – that is, on the objects that matter, in the arrangement of the situation, in relation to a justifiable world; in the case of compromise, which we shall examine later on, they may rely on objects that associate the relevance of two incompatible worlds in a single form. But the fact remains that, though it may be more or less difficult or more or less realistic according to the situation, a denunciation is always possible: since the persons exist, precisely as persons, prior to any qualification, they always have the possibility of realizing themselves in the world that assures them relevance and justice here and now. I express this by saying that persons always have two possibilities: they can *close their eyes* while involving themselves in the nature of the situation, and act in such a way as to be present in what they are doing, or, conversely, they can *open their eyes* – that is, withdraw from the situation and denounce it by considering it from the vantage point of a different nature. It is this critical capacity, always open, that defines the free will of persons.

But I also envisage another way of concluding a dispute and reaching agreement: by setting up a *compromise*. In a compromise, persons agree to *settle* – that is, to maintain the simultaneous presence of beings of different natures without clarifying the principle of their agreement and while maintaining an intentional disposition oriented towards the common good. Compromises are easy to denounce. Persons act in effect as if there were a principle of higher rank capable of supporting a state of equivalence among objects arising from different natures. Thus, for example, a reference to workers' rights opens up a compromise between civic nature and industrial nature. Such compromises are consolidated by the way objects, institutions and other elements are set up, borrowing from the two natures involved; these disparate entities, identified as such, come to constitute indivisible objects. One cannot challenge the compromise without destroying them.

The model I have just outlined may be useful as a way of expanding and modifying the interpretations I had initially provided for the data presented in 'Denunciation' (Part III, below). In fact, by relying essentially on the size of the actants, size being defined with reference to a single particular–general axis, and thus to a single form of generality, I had concluded that denunciations judged abnormal could be distinguished from denunciations judged normal essentially by a significant disparity in the size of the various actants. A second interpretation is also possible. A denouncer who submits an affair to the verdict of public opinion thereby brings it into a civic world, even though such affairs are often domestic in nature and often include an important inspired component; by so doing, the denouncer establishes a murky arrangement in which objects arising from different worlds are brought together in an incongruous way. According to this second interpretation, the desperate manoeuvres that denouncers undertake in order to try to hold together a chaotic arrangement – manoeuvres that consist, for the most part, in attempts to inscribe their affairs more clearly within a civic arrangement (for instance, when someone invokes the existence of a 'support committee' of which he or she is the sole member) – are precisely what would constitute signs of abnormality in the reader's eyes. Conversely, in cases judged normal, because the affairs in question had been taken in hand by collectives constituted along civic lines and had thus already undergone a work of desingularization, these affairs would be sufficiently supplied with objects belonging to the civic world that they could be taken into the space of public debate without creating a feeling of embarrassment or prompting an accusation of insanity. It will become clear later on how departing from a model centred uniquely on justice and analysing the relations between love and justice make it possible to develop a third interpretation of the same data (see below, chapter 13.5).

— 7 —

TESTS AND TEMPORALITY

At the end of Part II of this book, the reader will find a sketch of a third way – one that I now find more relevant – to interpret affairs that never come to an end, but also to deal with the related question of bringing disputes in justice to a close. This third interpretation is supported by an analytic framework designed to embrace a broader horizon with respect to which justice can be treated as one way among others to support social bonds. But before describing this framework, and in order to clarify the logic of my undertaking as best I can, I would like to show how the decision to take other dimensions of action into account – dimensions that do not stem strictly speaking from justice – follows from questions that come up when the *OJ* model is put to empirical use. As I see it, when any model of justice is applied to actual situations in life, even one that refers, as the *OJ* model does, to a plurality of possible worlds, we have to know its limits, and thus we have to know how it opens onto modes of relation that do not stem from justice.

When we use the *OJ* model to analyse the way people face up to the pragmatic conditions of testing, we are forced to confront the difficulties people encounter in seeking to achieve justice, and by that very token we face the impossibility of endowing ourselves with a universe in which the relevant judgements could be entirely absorbed by the problematics of justice. A world located wholly in justice is no less utopian than the world located wholly in violence sometimes depicted by classical sociology. This train of thought, stimulated in large measure by questions that arose regularly during my fieldwork, led me to emphasize the gaps between the model and the world, and then to deepen the analysis of the relation between, on the one hand, a capacity oriented towards the realization of an ideal of justice, of

59

which *OJ* provided an analogue (and which I needed to confirm by actually encountering it among people in certain states of the world, in harmony with reality, if it were not to be written off as utopian), and, on the other hand, constraints of a different order that people encountered when they put this capacity to work. Moreover, this latter gap was implied by the model itself. In a universe in which justice met no resistance – that is, in a universe where all gaps with respect to justice were perfectly transparent and immediately repaired by the concerted action of persons – critiques would be no more useful than on the 'isle of the blessed' of which Augustine speaks, so that critical capacity, the potential establishment of which is the object of the model, would be without an object of its own because it would not find in reality any situations that would warrant its application.

The constraints that weigh on the realization of a requirement of justice have to do with the administration of a test. In the *OJ* model, tests occupy a central position. The notion of testing is in fact what allows us to articulate the ideal of justice of which persons in our society have an intuitive sense, an ideal that is deployed in the axiomatics of a given polity and put into practice in situations of dispute under the regime of justice. When we shift from the ideal of justice found in pre-model form in political philosophy to situations of dispute in justice, the list of beings in presence is considerably modified. In effect, the ideal of justice recognizes only *persons* and a metaphysical being capable of connecting them. The question that arises is essentially the question of equality among persons according to a principle that makes it possible to establish equivalence among them. But, to move towards the realization of this ideal, we have to make room for other beings of which reality is composed – that is, things and non-material objects (such as codes, regulations, and so on) that are supported by things. The execution of justice can be reduced in this way to the achievement of a justifiable ranking of persons and things. Now the whole weight of this ranking and the demonstration of its well-foundedness is borne by tests. But tests are not foreign to the axiomatics of the polity that presupposes them. In fact, the axiomatics that founds the ideal of justice rests to a large extent, on the one hand, on a principle of uncertainty that is necessary to reconcile common humanity and order of worth and, on the other hand, on the possibility of proceeding to a test when the fairness of the world is the object of critiques, or to repeat a test when its integrity is in question.

Achieving justice through testing poses no special problems as long as the testing arrangement is set up without regard to the existence of persons in time. This restriction is consistent, moreover, with the ideal of the polity: always bound to its origin in Greek political philosophy, the polity offers an answer to the question, which arises outside of history, of the equilibrium among citizens facing a division of goods. The polity model offers a satisfying solution to this question provided that it is endowed with a disequilibrium that is punctually absorbed by a test with no aftermath. But it runs into daunting difficulties when the introduction of a temporal vector makes it necessary to raise the question of memory. For, if time is taken into account, every test must be envisaged in its relation to the tests that have preceded it and those that will follow. Now, the various tests are linked in a sequence through the intermediary of memory, mental or textual, that persons provide for themselves. Memory in effect transports the recollection of the results obtained from past tests into the present, where the current test is taking place. But immersing the testing arrangements in time does not simply make it necessary to endow the persons involved in them with memory. If the model is to remain realistic, it also requires that persons be given the possibility of anticipating the future and, consequently, of conferring on the results of the current test a certain validity over a certain period of time. But recollections of previous tests and anticipations that rely on the results of current tests become problematic when they are confronted with the requirements of uncertainly and renewal, without which justice remains an ideal devoid of practical applications.

Let us look more closely to see where the requirements of uncertainty and renewal may lead. According to the axiomatics of polities, the existence of worths attached once and for all to persons would contradict their common humanity; thus the worth of persons, when it is contested in a dispute in justice, must be concealed 'under a veil of ignorance', to borrow an expression from John Rawls (2005). Uncertainty thus appears as a condition for the integrity of the test. In order to be fully realized, this condition presupposes that persons are equally naked before the test. This does not mean that they are equal, since testing will in fact reveal an inequality between them that will justify their ranking according to an order of worth. However, they are equally stripped of any mark that would support the inscription of a pre-existing worth. For if access to the test is subordinated to the possession of a worth resulting from a pre-existing worth, the possibility that persons deemed less worthy could take the test again would no longer be ensured, and in that case a test that had been unfavourable to them before would no longer be renewable. The principle of uncertainty, in its most radical form, thus implies that

61

all memory of prior tests has to be eradicated. But it also follows that the results of the current test cannot be registered in a definitive way. For if the result of a test could be attached definitively to the persons involved, nothing could keep them from presenting themselves to a new test with the worth that had been attributed to them in a past test, and this would contradict the principle of uncertainty. Let us imagine a universe that conforms to this principle. Let there be a test consistent with the sense in which a literary prize, a sporting event, or admission to a university can be construed as a test. In this universe everyone may present himself or herself for testing, without exception. Everyone arrives at the test stripped of any mark that might provide information about his or her worth insofar as that worth resulted from previous tests. The test establishes a ranking among persons, but this order is not retained in any way. The test is always renewable, so that those who have shown themselves of lesser worth can always, at any time, present themselves anew before their judges. Such a world is difficult to conceive. Each test would be extremely difficult to set up, since the number of postulants would be by definition uncertain, but in all probability very high. Tests would be very numerous and probably continuous, since, given the way this universe is constructed, all requests for renewal would have to be satisfied. But it is especially difficult to understand what purpose the test would serve, since its results would have no lasting effects and, indeed, would be obliterated from memory as soon as they had been obtained. This last consequence leads us to suppose, moreover, that in time the test would no longer be requested, since it would serve no purpose, so that a world in which tests would be perfectly fair, because the principle of uncertainty would be perfectly respected, would end up excluding from its order the very notion of test. What gives meaning to a test, makes it desirable and thereby puts something at stake, is precisely the possibility inherent in it of establishing among people an order of worth valid for a certain time period or, to put it another way, the possibility of inserting it into a sequence of tests whose accumulated results can be the object of a calculation.

It is thus almost impossible to imagine tests being carried out in a situation where people are unable to retain the memory of the results of prior tests and transport them through time when they have to face new tests. If we reintroduce the possibility of memory into this purified construct, the existence of a mechanism for selection in advance of a test can be justified by a concern for maintaining the test's uncertainty. For we may suppose that someone who has been shown to be less worthy during prior tests has no chance of succeeding in the new one. Now, in order for the outcome of the test to remain uncertain, it must be impossible to predict any candidate's chance of success. But this way of maintaining the test's uncertainty under the constraint of commitment to memory is achieved, as we see, at a high price: the maximal homogenization of the candidates retained. For their pre-evaluated worths must be very similar, and the possibility that persons reputed to be less worthy according to prior tests can ask for a renewal of the tests that have been, in a more or less remote past, unfavourable to them is considerably reduced.

Another weighty argument militates in favour of pre-selection. A test that conforms to its concept is, as we have seen, a reality test. It thus engages not only persons but also objects that are present in reality. Now, real objects are objects that exist in the world of human beings, and whose use consequently affects an indeterminate number of persons. The person who assigns value to them is thereby responsible for his or her acts before the other persons who may be affected by these objects when they are in active use. Let us take, for example, an automobile and a driver put to the test by driving on a highway. The uncertainty principle would have it that any candidate could take the wheel and be tested. But it is obvious that the risks that such a situation would pose to other drivers make such a test highly implausible. The same arguments would apply to a large number of other situations – for example, giving someone a leadership position in a business, assessing a family estate, celebrating a liturgy, or organizing an important family event. Moreover, this is why many tests considered as such by the actors, and in particular school tests that involve uncertain beings – children and adolescents – are tests that could be called *factitious*, not in the sense that they are illusory, but in the sense that they are set up on a reduced scale. They are often 'paper-and-pencil' tests, as the psychologists call them – in other words, tests that do not involve real objects, objects that are activated in the ordinary world where people use them and that are therefore capable of affecting other persons: showing my inability to fix a leaky tap does not risk flooding my neighbour's apartment. The fact remains that, like the preceding argument, this one can be invoked in order to avoid responding affirmatively to requests for retesting, even when candidates base their demands on the possibility of a change in personality or capability that has come about over time. In a great number of cases, the requirement of *security* thus offers a solid argument in favour of pre-selection or in favour of refusing a demand for retesting that is aimed at abolishing the results, committed to memory, of a prior test.[1]

The requirement of pre-selection by relying on the results of past tests recorded in memory, on the one hand, and the degree of predictability attributed to a test, on the other, are not unrelated. The more the results of the test are deemed to contribute information that is valid over time about the candidate's abilities, or lack thereof, the more the requirement of pre-selection seems to be considered normal. Moreover, people ordinarily use the term *test*[2] only for this type of probatory activity, the results of which are subject to some form of recording. The tests that conform most closely to the ordinary concept of a test thus most often have a formal character that is necessary for several reasons: to ensure the pre-selection of candidates; to control the conditions for taking a test by eliminating circumstances or setting aside objects stemming from other worlds, so as to remove all ambiguity about the results and about the order of worths that follows from them (through grading, for example) and thereby to disarm critiques; and, finally, to solidify the connection between test results and the very person of the test-taker. This solidifying can take different forms, the most customary being the awarding of a title whose validity may extend beyond the bearer's life span (when it is transmissible to heirs); alternatively it may be coextensive with the bearer's life, as is the case with most academic titles, or it may be limited in time, as with sports titles (which are regularly open to competition) or with the scientific or literary prizes that are awarded on an annual basis.[3]

As these remarks suggest, a universe immersed in time, in which people retain the memory of earlier tests and rely on the results of current tests to make predictions about the future, resembles our own, but it can be exempted more easily than can a universe conceived without reference to time from the requirement of justice that conforms to the ideal of the polity. More precisely, a universe immersed in time introduces tension between, on the one hand, the adjustments that make a world stable by preventing constant disputes over order and, on the other hand, the requirements of persons whose power, as 'power-to-be in action', cannot be fully revealed by the acts they accomplish in their 'current states' (Grenet 1962, 32–6). In the ordinary metaphysics of members of our society, a person is in effect defined by the fact of being endowed with an 'aptitude' or 'capacity' that is structurally 'always prior to observation of the body' (Ricoeur 1977a, 24) and, on the other hand, not knowable in its totality or once and for all, not even by the person himself, who, in action, must be 'willing to risk the disclosure' without knowing 'whom he reveals when he discloses himself in deed' (Arendt 1958, 180). Outside the

64

realm of action, power is unknowable, and, between acts, one cannot say with full certainty what people are capable of doing. It follows that, in the absence of any manifestation through acts, the existence of a specific power may be viewed with suspicion, so that acts attesting to it have to be repeated at more or less regular intervals in order to support its factuality – that is, in order to make sure the possibility of its realization always remains present.[4] Many everyday disputes, of which Aristotle's famous example concerning the architect who does not build constitutes the paradigm,[5] bear precisely on the existence of powers recognized as a result of tests taken but not currently attested by acts, and whose recording in memory, for example in titles that open up access to positions or jobs, is denounced as unjust (Bourdieu and Boltanski 1975). Conversely, in many situations the no less acceptable contrary argument is invoked: it consists in denouncing as unjust a test that involves a contemporary action and that is restricted so as to preclude taking the worth of past acts into account.[6]

The relation between act and power, according to the ordinary metaphysics brought into play by members of our society when they have to judge tests, thus entails a tension that can be explained briefly as follows. An act in itself has no probative interest. It has value only to the extent that it is capable of revealing some power in the person who carries it out – that is, some disposition that is more durable than the act and that is thus capable of manifesting itself anew in future acts. The persistent character of the power revealed by the act is thus what confers on the act its character of being a test. The act counts as a test inasmuch as it brings power into daylight. But, conversely, in structural terms, a person's power must remain unknowable in its totality. It is precisely the imputation of an unknowable power, a power never exhausted by the acts that reveal it, that qualifies the person as a person in our everyday metaphysics.[7] This way of constructing persons, foreign to the immediacy of the polity model, probably has deep roots in Christian anthropology, which is dependent on an eschatology and which sets aside the question of contemporary judgement and of the just equilibrium between human beings who are unequal in the present instant in favour of a problematics immersed in time and conceived as a history of salvation that shifts the unveiling of powers and the practice of judgement to the horizon of *parousia*.[8] This is in fact the property of persons that is taken into account by the requirements of uncertainty and renewal when they demand, for example, that a freed prisoner be given a chance to wipe out his past so that he can rebuild his life and once again prove himself in the world without bearing the weight of his fault forever.

Now, if tests are to be capable of supporting predictions about people's future actions – and, as we have seen, without this capability they would be of no use – they must make it possible to work back from act to power. But, if they are to be considered fair and humane, they must also – and this may seem contradictory – take as a given that powers cannot be reduced to the acts that bring them to light. The example of school tests,[9] which can support predictions about what people are capable of doing because they are reputed to bring to light the hidden power of persons, power whose renewal is most often governed by an explicit convention, will allow us to understand better the disputes in which the possibility of wiping out a failure and proving oneself anew is at stake. School tests are ordered in sequences of which each stage can be the object of a predetermined number of renewals. At each stage, the candidates who have exhausted their possibilities of retesting are eliminated from the competition. This elimination is justified by the recognized capacity of tests to exhaust knowledge of the candidate's power. But, as critiques of school tests have shown (Derouet 1989), critiques that often bear on the question of the age at which the selection of the best candidates (that is, the elimination of the least good) should be made, their capacity to end disputes can be denounced as inhumane in that they claim to reduce the powers of persons to what is revealed of these powers by the acts accomplished on a specific occasion during a test. It is precisely to respond to such critiques that supplementary tests have been instituted: make-up tests, gateway tests or continuing education, for example. These tests are supposed to offer people once again a range of probative acts through which they can prove themselves; as a secondary effect, they increase the extent of the domain that is under the constraint of school testing.

Analysis of the problems posed by carrying out testing in a universe harmonized with time thus supplies arguments that help problematize the possibility of a world under the regime of justice. For either the model of competence for justice is put into practice, and nothing permits bringing the dispute in justice to a close (because it can always be relaunched by critiques and by the deployment of new tests), or else the configurations are relatively stabilized by arrangements that take memory into account in order to prolong the test results in time, in which case the conditions of justice are no longer met (because persons whose powers are treated as if they could be known once and for all find themselves endowed with the

66

irreversibility that, in the justice model, specifically qualifies things) (Chateauraynaud 1991).

These remarks, which may appear purely theoretical, were corroborated by the results of fieldwork that reported on a number of disputes whose closure did not seem to have been accompanied by a return to basic principles (Dodier 1989) or by the manufacture of a compromise, but seemed rather to have been accomplished, as it were, 'all by itself', as if under the effect of abandonment or forgetting (an example can be found in the case analysed in chapter 13.5). In the final analysis, a universe existing wholly in justice would recognize only objects qualified by their participation in a nature whose coherence is sustained by a principle of equivalence that can be activated during a dispute, for example a principle of justice capable of sustaining critiques or agreement. But adopting such a position would amount to endowing the model of competence for justice presented in *OJ* with the capacity of generating an ontology of the objects of the universe. Now, as we can see from the insoluble problems raised by the empirical question of registering things that figure in a situation that does not include disputes (but where a dispute might arise),[10] only the way in which objects are identified in a test makes it possible to qualify them with reference to a particular world, and this is the case even if the coherence of pre-existing rankings brings to bear a constraint on the way in which people identify the relevance of the objects on which they base their justifications. A model of competence for justice thus clearly includes an ontological opening, but this ontology concerns only the objects that enter into disputes, not things in themselves. Thus, to grasp anew the very diverse modalities according to which people qualify their actions, we cannot limit ourselves to situations of justification in which the actors contest the parity between *persons* and *things* whose ordering has become problematic. It is also necessary to grant actors the possibility, foreign to the regime of justice, (1) of letting themselves be guided by the equivalences that are tacitly enclosed in the silence of existing things, (2) of setting aside things and the equivalences they bear so as to focus on persons, or, finally, (3) of setting persons aside so as to encounter only things liberated from equivalence – that is, forces. I shall now try to sketch out these different modes of action, which are situated outside the realm of justice.

— 8 —

FOUR MODES OF ACTION

As I suggested earlier when I was analysing the competence that actors deploy when they conduct their disputes in a regime of justice (without losing sight of the possibility that they may shift into a regime of violence), the idea of a universe operating wholly according to justice is as utopian as the idea of a universe totally given over to violence is dystopian. I shall now seek to defend the idea that, if we are to understand what people are capable of doing, we cannot limit ourselves to disputes; we have to envisage as well the possibility of relations that do not include disputes and that are nevertheless not purely contingent. I propose to call these regimes of peace. The analytic framework I am about to outline has to allow us to conceptualize the way people place themselves under different modes and also the way they can shift from one mode to another, sometimes very rapidly. I shall attempt to draw up a 'theoretical construction [*theoretische Gedankengebilde*]', as Max Weber (1949, 88) might call it, of some of the properties of the various modes, to which we can then compare the behaviours, most often composite ones, that individual persons manifest in the ordinary situations of daily life. The question of equivalence remains at the heart of my undertaking. I posit that the regimes of dispute and of peace are distinguished according to whether relations under these regimes invoke principles of equivalence or not. For disputes in a regime of justice that is associated with principles of equivalence, there is thus a corresponding regime of peace, equally associated with equivalence, which I shall call fairness. The impossibility of converging towards a principle of equivalence is what differentiates a dispute in violence from a dispute in justice. A dispute in violence leads away from equivalence, even if, at the close of the dispute, some residual equivalence appears, a

68

form of equivalence unknown before the test, in the shape of a power relation. But violence is not the only mode that is unacquainted with equivalence. I envisage the possibility of a different regime, equally detached from equivalence, which is a regime of peace: the regime of love as agape, to which Part II of this work is devoted. In this schema, the dual opposition regime-of-dispute vs. regime-of-peace and regime-recognizing-equivalence vs. regime-not-recognizing-equivalence is mediated by the way in which each regime resolves the tension between *persons* and *things*. For the person–thing relation undoubtedly constitutes a central node in the ordinary metaphysics of members of our society. Regimes that recognize equivalence associate persons and things, while regimes that do not recognize equivalence either set things aside and recognize only persons (agape) or set persons aside and endow themselves with a universe of things overcome by forces (violence). In these different modes, as I shall attempt to show, people use language in different ways.

In disputes in justice, people present critiques and offer justifications. To do this, they must make a particular use of language that consists in moving to a higher level of generality, so as to bring out the principles of equivalence that support the prevailing order of worths in a given situation. In contrast to situations in which equivalences reappear on the surface of discourse, I shall try to define a first regime of peace in which equivalences are tacitly at work in the uses persons make of things. To say that equivalence is tacit does not mean that it cannot be identified in discourse. But, in this regime, discourse accompanies and accomplishes the work of equivalence without contesting equivalence or taking it explicitly as an object. Reports on the state of things have a local character and do not aim to reconstitute the situations fully, as is the case in justice, where the interplay of critique and justification leads the actors to use the possibilities of discourse to bring together and embrace a considerable number of objects and relations. In fairness, reports serve to stabilize local connections, as we see in the case of instructions, users' manuals, labelling, and so on. To be sure, the possibility of tacit equivalence is envisaged in *OJ*, where it is supported by the relation between justice and fairness. But I think it is necessary to make a clearer distinction between these two ways of achieving equivalence. Doing so will make it easier to perceive the complete change of regime that comes about when one shifts from peaceful situations, in which people comply with the equivalences that are tacitly inscribed in the things that surround them, to situations in which they identify these equivalences and take them as objects of their disputes. To a regime of *disputes in justice*, I shall thus oppose, first of all, a regime of *peace in fairness*.

To establish the possibility of a second regime of peace, I shall turn to what constitutes the foundation for the two previous regimes – that is, the matter of equivalence – and turn it upside down: I shall envisage the possibility of persons entering into relations without going through the intermediary of equivalence. This possibility, which may seem hard to conceive of at first, is nevertheless amply developed in one of the traditions we have inherited, that of Christian theology, especially the theology of agape, which lies perhaps at Christianity's very core. I shall turn to this tradition for support in Part II in an attempt to construct a regime of peace in agape characterized by the setting aside of equivalence. In this regime, as in the preceding ones, persons are endowed with speech. But they cannot use language to reflect back on the love that connects them in the here and now. Discourse does not allow them to move up to equivalence in an aim of totalization and calculation; thus the possibility of a relation aiming to qualify the present situation, to totalize the objects that compose it and make them calculable, implies shifting into a different regime. It is first and foremost in this respect that a regime of peace in love is distinguished from a regime of peace in justice.

To specify the different regimes in somewhat greater detail, I shall have to characterize the way in which the question of the relation between persons and things is treated in each one. In a regime of peace in fairness, equivalence may be present in a tacit fashion because things are themselves present among persons. Thus the connection among the actors is stabilized according to equivalence not only by the equipment that is internalized, even incorporated, but also by things operating in their own way – that is, silently. Things tell people what to do (in the way a train schedule tells us the time of departure); they keep people in place and propose constraints that play the role of tacit conventions capable of harmonizing people's relationships and their movements. But in this regime people develop the inner being that can harmonize with things because it has the nature of things: people confer on themselves and on others the character of irreversibility that qualifies objects according to their metaphysics (Chateauraynaud 1991), and they do not use language to call into question the equivalences inscribed in the stability of things and in the steadfastness of people when they present those aspects that are constant in themselves.[1]

Conversely, in a regime of dispute in justice, the possibilities of language are exploited to bring equivalences to the surface and to

70

consider them as such, to make them work, as it were, either challenging them through the goad of critique or reaffirming them through justification. The work of developing a narrative – 'emplotment' – is carried out by human beings, who alone are endowed with language. But, through them, things abandon their call to silence. They begin to make demands, and people become their spokespersons (Latour 1987). For, if it is true that disputes in justice bear fundamentally on equivalence, their principal focus is the inappropriate attribution of things. To critique is to contest the state of worths in place; it is in effect to demand that things change hands. The best computer ought to be assigned to the researcher able to use it to best advantage; the property with the most potential should go to the most capable heir; the Legion of Honour medal must be awarded to someone truly honourable; the department requires a new director if it is to function well. To say that people contest the attribution of computers, the Legion of Honour or academic titles is also to say that they are serving as spokespersons for these material or immaterial objects when the return to fairness demands a change in attribution. Thus in disputes like these people never speak only for themselves. They become spokespersons, first and foremost, for the things that surround them; through the mouths of these persons, things demand a change of ownership so that, once justice is satisfied, the tacit fairness of people and things can be restored. But in the same operation they also become spokespersons for other people, insofar as the valorization of things can affect these others in turn. For if the department or the state is badly led, if the property is badly managed, if the automobile is badly driven or public opinion is badly informed, people in greater or lesser numbers find themselves, too, confronting injustice. Things are in fact mixed up with the people whose solidarity they establish. They are most often common to those people, even when they are subject to private appropriation; consequently, as we have seen in connection with reality tests, an inappropriate attribution of things – that is, an attribution that does not allow their valorization – affects a greater or lesser number of persons. Speaking for things thus always leads to surpassing one's own singularity in order to move up to a higher level of generality that includes other people; it also means distinguishing oneself from things by valorizing a property of persons – namely, the ability to undo irreversibility by using critiques to call into question the state of things as they are.

Finally, in a regime of peace in agape, persons can be present together while excluding equivalence because they also exclude from their world the importance of things. If our vocabulary were

71

adequate, if we had a sufficient gamut of terms to designate people as they are qualified in different modes, it would behoove us to reserve the term 'person' for beings when they are in a regime of agape. The regime of peace in agape brings persons as such to full realization. It exempts them from the constraint of things, which do not necessarily disappear completely but which appear as subordinated. And in extreme representations of this regime – that is, in certain tendencies of Christian mysticism, exemplified by St Francis or Meister Eckhart, among others – the animals and even the things that figure in the world of description are affected, as if by contagion, with certain properties that we recognize as belonging to human persons, in whose way of being they participate inasmuch as they are *creatures*. In the peace of agape, things have no weight and the worths they once supported also fade away; disputes in justice, born in sites where persons and things are connected, are lost and forgotten; people know one another as persons without the support of equivalences, which vanish with the objects that had served to support them.

As for the regime of dispute in violence, its position with respect to justice and fairness is symmetrical but inverse to that of agape. In justice/fairness, people and things are ordered in terms of equivalencies; in fairness these equivalencies are tacit, because people keep quiet and conform to the constraints of things, while in justice they are proclaimed aloud, as people develop their human capacity for critique and become spokespersons for things that have been misattributed. But whereas agape exempts itself from equivalence – that is, from the existence of a stabilized relation between things and persons – in order to endow itself with persons considered as such, the regime of dispute in violence, although it too frees itself from the control of equivalence, ignores persons, and, as many have observed, by concentrating on things it opens up the possibility of treating human beings as things. But the things recognized in violence are no longer the things stabilized in fairness by the equivalence of persons and things. These are things without persons – that is, they are also things exempted from equivalence. No convention connects them to one another (Thévenot 1984, 1989), so that nothing is known about what they are capable of doing. Things in violence – and the category includes people, too, when they are in violence – are no longer human things, stabilized by their association with persons, but beings of nature, forces of nature. Hence they show themselves as foreign and unknown. One does not know what they are made of, what they want, who inhabits or controls them, or how far they may go. Their mode of being is that of force in the sense of unknown power realized only in the encounter with other forces – that is, in a test of strength, a power struggle (Latour 1987). In this regime, people themselves recognize one another only as opposing and unknown forces putting one another to the test, and, as we have seen, their struggle is in no way different in its underlying principle from the relation they might have with a thing. But in this regime, where things are no longer in the grip of equivalence and are no longer by that very token obliged to respect pre-established conditions or to satisfy the expectations placed upon them, people lose all hold over them. They can neither conform to things, so as to remain in their grasp (fairness), nor challenge them and become their spokespersons (justice). Things have broken the conventions that bound them to people and that bound them to one another (Chateauraynaud 1991), in such a way that they are only manifested in the form of forces that can be appropriately halted by force. In violence – that is, in the presence of force – each actor becomes a force in turn, identifying an unknown internal force that can be deployed without controls and that can be measured only when tested by other forces. In this respect, a struggle with a recalcitrant or threatening object – a tap or an overflowing oil well – is in no way different from a battle against other men in a state of force. The desertion of things, when they withdraw abruptly from the conventions that have bound them and go off in all directions, unstoppable, may well constitute one of the most frequent occasions for the shift from fairness to violence, moreover, because the objects of the world are then manifested as inaccessible to language, and one does not know what gestures to make that would appease them; it is precisely the capacity to remain calm that characterizes the competence of the professional, plumber or doctor.[2] In both cases, the situation is overcome by urgency. For a force does not wait, does not reflect, does not deliberate, does not withdraw to talk things over, but applies itself to whatever applies itself to it in turn and resists. To stop a force, one must apply oneself to it in the mode of force and resist it. This is the way force communicates, in the application of body to body; this is how it enters into a relationship, establishes a connection that no longer involves categories in the celestial sphere of ideas but rather bodies, as when we speak of 'hand-to-hand combat'.[3]

A central question that I shall have to try to clarify through more in-depth empirical research, in developing the programme sketched out here, is that of the shift from one regime to another. If each of the four regimes that I am positing in order to analyse action is utopian when it is generalized in such a way as to include the entire set of relations among people, which means, also, among people and things, it is indeed necessary to conceive of potential shifts in rapid succession from one to another: the acceptance of established objects; a gesture of violence towards a thing that resists, dissipated in the rediscovered equivalence of a critical argument; a dispute withdrawn from justice by a lightning bolt of love; a moment of love that is undone in the reciprocity of a calculation; and so on. My hypothesis is the following. People stay in the regime in which they are installed and that establishes itself in them as a state. They exit from this regime, in spite of themselves, as it were, only when the situation confronts them with another person installed in another regime. This shift is analysed in detail in Part II in the case of the shift from love to justice and from justice to love ('Agape', chapter 13.3–4). Without examining the other shifts with the same care (for example, from fairness to love or from fairness to justice) for the time being, I should like to suggest a way in which shifts into violence could be envisaged. If there does exist, as I believe, a strong link between violence and urgency, the shift to violence might be understood as a reduction in the time delays that are acceptable in interactions either with people or with things. As in the case of relations between love and justice, this approach has the advantage of leaving room for the possibility of a gradual shift, with tipping points beyond a certain threshold. If my interpretation is correct, violence can be reduced to a decrease in the delays considered acceptable before one responds to an action. For what is realized as force is precisely that which does not tolerate delay. Examples include a raging sea, an erupting volcano, a gas leak, a man rendered inaccessible to reasoning by passion or by alcohol: all these are things in expansion, things with which one cannot reason and with respect to which one must make oneself a thing in one's turn in order to resist and conquer them. To be sure, agape offers a different path: not the path of justice, which reasons, but the path of passivity in love, which exhausts force by remaining unaware of it and conquers force by non-resistance, non-violence – although at its own risk. Involvement in a test of strength, where each participant is available only as an unknown force, decreases delays in responding and increases the urgency of the situation in which the exchange of blows and counterblows can be stopped before the destruction of one of the two parties only by the intervention of a third, who is in a different state and who, not yet governed by urgency, can attempt to get involved in the situation to pacify it – that is, to disengage it from violence by reintroducing the possibility of a delay. In the case of violence, it is the possibility of a delay – that is, of a subsisting present that would not be immediately absorbed in the scuffle between past and future – that makes the situation reversible and opens up the possibility of a shift to a different regime, whether it is a matter of a discussion refereed in justice – that is, brought back to a convention of equivalence – or of a return to agape, for example, in which those who had been ready to kill one another forget the henceforth futile object of their dispute, falling into one another's arms and setting aside the thing that separated them, the service not rendered, the gift refused, as we see with marvellous clarity in love affairs in crisis.

The regime of justice remains the pivot of this construct. The silent equivalences deposited in things that make relations of peace in justice possible are thus clearly – as Bruno Latour's work shows, especially the concept of the 'black box', which he uses to account for technological arrangements that are taken for granted – the result of extinguished controversies, ancient conflicts absorbed by their inscription in established conventions whose implantation in objects considerably increases the cost of challenging them. To be sure, relations established in fairness can always be viewed differently. One can criticize the ordering as unfair or even denounce it as violence, no doubt especially in cases where demands that a test be repeated bump into a state of the world that, whether given as irreversible or changed according to iron-clad laws, then presents itself in itself in its entirety with the inhumane harshness of forces of nature. For the constraint of things, when it is no longer tolerated, can appear as imposed violence; this happens when one denounces the tacit violence of the established order, of regulation, law, technology, and so on. But the operation that unveils determination as violence and affirms reversibility of the irreversible calls for moving up towards justice, a move that results in withdrawal from the regime of fairness; if a denunciation succeeds, that regime collapses into crisis. The denunciation of reality as violence is often attached to the observation of some urgency, moreover. The world, such as it is, imposes its priorities and controls people by holding them to the fire of urgency, so that the first gesture of crisis destined to ensure the shift into a regime of justice that is vulnerable to critique is a gesture of stopping: going on strike, quitting one's job, rebelling against an order whose execution can perfectly well wait, and so on. If fairness remains contiguous to justice, the same remarks hold true for violence: as strange as violence may seem, it does not readily let justice out of its sight, either, so that pure, absolute violence constitutes for me an almost unthinkable and hardly operative limit; this is shown, for example, by Clausewitz's abandoned effort to understand war using the model of the rise to extremes conceived in the mode of a duel between two partners each determined to conquer the other no matter the cost.[4] For, given what we know about violence, it is difficult to conceive of it without attaching it, at least in its beginnings, to a feeling of indignation in the face of a being that, behaving in denial of all established conventions, shows itself to be unpredictable – that is, in the face of the experience of an injustice, in the specific sense that Hobbes gives this term;[5] this is the way 'holy anger' carries one beyond justice through passion for justice. As we see clearly in the extreme cases described in the literature on paranoia – for example, in the 'Aimée' case presented by Jacques Lacan (1980) – *indignation* is the interface between love and justice. Indignation, in paranoia, is presumably preceded by a loss experienced in a state of agape, a loss of something that cannot be recuperated in other regimes – especially not in the regime of justice (see chapter 13.5), since, as I shall show in the next chapter, the various regimes are separated by something incommensurable that translation cannot exhaust.[6] In paranoia, indignation betrays a demand for recognition, in two incompatible senses: it arises both in the regime of agape, where it is an unformulable demand for recognition of the person without limits, and in the regime of justice, where it takes the form of recognition of a debt that can be the object both of a claim and of a calculation of reciprocity.[7] A person in a situation of paranoia – that is, at the interface between love, justice and violence – cannot obtain satisfaction because she demands the chimera that is constituted, to borrow an expression Paul Ricoeur used in a different context, by 'a demand for settlement of an infinite unpaid debt'.[8] This unquenchable indignation surfaces as it finds support in a requirement of justice offended by a scandal on display in the world, and it engages in violence through the intermediary of the emotions aroused (and these are particularly strong at the interface between different regimes)[9] by the impossibility of formulating the denunciation in a way acceptable to others, the impossibility of getting the denunciation accepted and shared. Thus Lacan writes that 'one has to make room for Aimée's moral system, of which we find a coherent exposition in her writings; room for the indignation she feels at such an importance being granted in public life to "artists"' (Lacan 1980, 162). If it cannot be absorbed in a world of shared equivalences, indignation abandons the path of argumentative justification for justification through gestures – that is, through a symbolic act offered to the interpretation of others, an act that may open up the way to a 'shift into action' and, in this case, a shift into violence. The project that seeks fulfilment in paranoia, and that can actually be characterized as 'delirious', consists in the intention of maintaining oneself permanently on the dividing line between the various regimes at a point where, without tipping into one regime or another, one can have an overview of them all and maintain them in continuous presence.

The fact remains that, in the case of disputes in violence, unlike what we see in disputes in justice, the space in which injustice is calculated remains proper to each of the parties. Persons involved in disputes in violence never converge towards the search for a space of calculation that they would share, that would include the same objects and the same relations, and that would thereby permit prior agreement on what matters in their discord and, consequently, on what the dispute may be about. In the indignation that animates and underlies, at least subjectively, the violent outburst of a driver whose bumper has just been scratched, a host of factors can figure, pell-mell: the illness of his wife, who had had to be rushed to the hospital the night before, the bad grade his son had received at school, his boss's tyranny, his own sore foot, other things he is worrying about, and so on. For, added to this unexplained series of accumulated misfortunes, a scratched bumper is just too much, more than he can bear. But the same may hold true for his adversary, whose mother has just died, whose tax bill is unreasonably high, and so on. Between these two universes, in which each actor calculates the good and bad things in his or her life, no accommodation is possible. Why should the former take the latter's loss – of which he is unaware – and behave courteously? And why would the latter have taken into account the bad grades of a child who is not her own to grant the right of way, which, rightfully speaking, belonged to her?

The coherence of the worlds governed by conventions of equivalence recognized by all and subjected to the same principle of justice, a principle brought to light by the *OJ* model, comes into play here. By moving up towards equivalence and towards the principle of justice with which it is in solidarity, the partners in a dispute can agree at least to exclude certain objects from the list of those on which their discord bears; they can exclude the wife, the illness, the foot, the son, the boss and the mother, and centre their debate on the eminently civic principle of right of way. They can then bring up the relatively contingent character of the situation (the sign was hard to see), introduce objects of a different nature – industrial, for example (the pavement, badly maintained, was slippery) – and even seek out a policeman who can help them agree on a report – that is, a document attesting, in a form acceptable to all parties, to the record of their test. By immersing their relations in a coherent world of things under equivalences, they can, through the same operation, exit from their indeterminacy in agape, as ungraspable *persons* and, in violence, as impenetrable *forces*, and accept a *judgement*, because they are in turn *qualified* with reference to the objects whose relevance they identify, and this supports their claim to a worth that can be demonstrated in a test and legitimized by a principle of justice developed in a polity (a law-abiding driver, a professional driver, and so on).

Without the possibility of converging towards a common space of calculation offered by the existence of these domains of relevance harmonized with a principle of equivalence whose objects may be identified in order to establish proof in the course of a dispute (domains that in *OJ* we called natures or worlds), people would probably slip constantly, or at least much more often than is the case in a critical society in which the dispute can proceed freely in justice, from violence to love and from love to violence, from gratuitous blows and insults to the gift of self; they would be incapable of stabilizing their relations in the peaceful silence of things firmly in place, or of treating their disagreements by means of arguments that point out what is lacking in the ordering of things and people, bring proofs and propose tests that can give rise to agreement. And it is no doubt because they are ill-equipped to recognize the salience of these coherent worlds of things that can support equivalences and thus qualify relationships and persons, and because they are less disposed than others to allow themselves to be carried away by these worlds and things, that people labelled 'paranoid' seem to maintain themselves in the impossible place constituted by the dividing line between different regimes in which one can only shift ceaselessly from one to another. But this is probably valid as well for all situations, and especially those characterized as 'extreme' (Pollak 1986), in which these worlds become particularly precarious and come apart, so that people, no longer finding themselves in the presence of stable objects on which they can base their justifications and their critiques, tend to slip, more easily than is the case in ordinary life, from the disinterestedness of gratuitous love into the deployment in violence of impenetrable forces, without managing to find the ground of a justifiable agreement.

As for the states of agape, which will be examined in detail later on, we shall also see that they can be taken into account only in relation to justice. But this last consideration will bring us back to problems of method, because it also involves the question of how these states can be observed and reported by sociology.

BELOW THE THRESHOLD OF
THE REPORT

The states of agape become accessible to analysis only if we make a detour through justice. The exit from equivalence into agape can be inscribed in discourse in terms of deviations from justice, and more precisely by means of metaphoric narratives that open up a space of which justice is one of the boundaries; this is especially clear in the case of parables (chapter 11.8). This property is linked to the principal characteristics of the regime of love in agape – that is, the preference for the present, the pre-eminence of gifts over desire and the refusal to compare, totalize or calculate, the rejection even of calculations intended to ensure the reciprocity of exchanges. In love in agape, persons – because this regime is indeed filled by persons – are not deprived of the use of language, and, whatever the regime to which their actions may conform, human beings never abandon this prerogative; they even use it in violence, to proffer insults, curses or blasphemy. But not all forms of discourse are equally accessible from the various regimes. Thus it can be shown (chapter 11.6) that one particular form of discourse is incompatible with agape, so much so that its use would lead persons to shift into a different mode: this is the *report*, in the sense in which I use the term to speak of the way people make plots out of the affairs in which they find themselves involved. In this sense, a report is a kind of transcript intended to operate serial associations in order to bring to light, by means of a totalizing interpretation, the order of worths and relations that make all the relevant beings intelligible.[1] Let me offer an example, to make palpable this particularity of the regime of agape, which I shall develop in detail in Part II. The utterance 'I gave to you without counting' is completely acceptable. But it immediately refers to a situation in justice in which partners are taking a retrospective look

at their relationship and arguing over whether the one who gave
has received in exchange – that is, whether the reciprocity of their
exchanges has been assured. 'I gave to you without counting' undeni-
ably contains a nuance of reproach: 'I gave to you without counting'
and I have not been repaid; and it was very naïve of me to act that
way; and so on. Now let us take the utterance 'I give to you without
counting'. We immediately feel that there's something amiss here, and
we cannot clearly conceive of the type of situation to which it would
correspond. For if in the present situation the speaker is indeed in
the oblatory disposition of someone who gives without counting, he
cannot simultaneously report on his state, because that report would
immediately reintroduce into the situation the possibility of a calculation, or even a threat ('I could do otherwise, and not give to you
without counting', or 'I could give to you and keep count'), which
would discredit the reality of the disposition he is affirming.[2] Now the
report form, the form of discourse in which the demand for justice is
customarily expressed, occupies a privileged position for the social
sciences, because it is also the form in which our disciplines bring the
results of their investigations into the order of language.

Even when sociology gives up the possibility of producing its own
report, one that would be more powerful than those of the actors,
it produces an original construct, as we have seen, by accumulating and juxtaposing the reports of the various actors involved in a
given affair, and by following, step by step, the divergent ways in
which these actors interpret the affair and turn it into a narrative.
This procedure, which no longer requires sociologists to give up
'illusions', nevertheless requires another sacrifice, as has been noted
– that of their 'intelligence'. For, in order to take the critical operations conducted by the actors as their object, sociologists have to give
up the possibility of producing their own critiques. This leads them
to develop an epistemology and a methodology aimed at controlling
and limiting the interpretations they have the right to deploy in order
to deal with the actors' reports – that is, to establish the transcript
of the transcripts formulated by the actors during their affair. These
rules require sociologists to maintain themselves constantly *as close
as possible* to the actors' own formulations and interpretations. Thus
the rules all aim, in the final analysis, at subordinating researchers'
reports to those of the actors.

The procedure whose broad outlines I have just recalled is entirely
adequate to treat the registers of action that are attached, more or
less closely, to a regime of justice, and that thereby involve operations
of *establishing equivalence*. It is doubtless no accident that it was

first developed, to cite only a few examples, in the realm of identity construction (Garfinkel 1967), judicial procedure (Cicourel 1968), medical diagnosis (Freidson 1970), scientific controversies (Latour and Woolgar 1979), statistical codification (Desrosières and Thévenot 1979; Thévenot 1983), political legitimacy (Pharo 1985) and labour regulations (Dodier 1988). Constrained to follow the way in which actors construct their reports, this procedure is in fact directly applicable in the realms mentioned, owing to the fact that in these realms the actors engage in intense interpretive and process-focused activity. But the same remarks hold true, more generally, whenever actors pursue their actions while involving themselves in a regime of justice, whether during the course of a passing family argument, in work relations, or in some other situation. For, when persons involve themselves in this regime, the method that consists in following their reports is directly in harmony with the way the action finds its translation in the order of discourse – that is, the way it is constructed as a narrative. But if the hypotheses I developed in the previous chapter have any relevance, it is clear that this claim does not apply to other regimes, regimes that do not include to the same degree, according to their inherent modes of instrumentation, the possibility of access to the report form. It follows that the actors' establishment of reports on the actions they carried out while they were in these other regimes necessarily passes through operations of translation (Dodier 1989) that can profoundly modify relevant aspects of the reports. This is doubtless especially true when the report is delivered to the researcher in an interview situation, whose similarity to judicial situations cannot be overemphasized; in the interview situation the actor is expected to report on actions that he has carried out in different situations, including, in many cases, actions taken under regimes that do not stem from justice and thus do not involve the necessity of a report.

I do not know the exact nature of the translations imposed by the production of a report, because I have not explored these translations systematically. But, by transposing what is known about the work of autobiographical construction (Boltanski 1975), work already evoked above in connection with the subsistence of the person, I can suggest some of the aspects that this work must presumably display. To ask someone to deliver her biography indeed consists in asking her not only for a report on her life, but also, more precisely, to submit herself to a test in justice. For to put oneself in an autobiographical position is to commit oneself to passing judgement on one's life as a whole – that is, to adopt, through a sort of thought experiment, the position of a last judgement. The situation in which an autobiography is delivered thus appears as a situation of justification. A person who engages in it has to make a selection of relevant acts, evaluate them separately at first, with reference to atemporal moral requirements, but also judge them for their consequences, then apprehend them sequentially, organize them in series, relate them to one another and submit them to a test of coherence, as we see clearly in the case of episodic political biographies – 'traversals of the century', to borrow the title of Bertrand de Jouvenel's autobiography. In this work of biographical justification, factual information about the actions accomplished will often be accompanied by metadiscourse bearing on the intentions that have presided over their accomplishment and that the acts, or their unpredictable consequences, may have betrayed. As this example shows, the shift to reporting presupposes the adoption of a retrospective position that withdraws for a moment from the present action to embrace the past according to a constraint generated by the tension between the need to make a selection and the requirement to be sincere and transparent – that is, thorough – so as to transport into the present of the report all past events that are sufficiently pertinent to be subjected to a biological calculation – that is, not only the acts as an external observer might describe them but also the mental events that preceded or accompanied the accomplishment of the acts. For the perspective of last judgement inherent in the autobiographical enterprise encompasses not only the requirement of retrospective totalization but also the need to calculate the value of the actions, put their coherence to the test, stabilize imputations and specify intentions in such a way as to allow the formulation of a synthetic judgement on the person.

The features that have just been identified, while they take on an exemplary character in the case of autobiography, are probably not foreign to the report form in its most general sense. The order of reports, as it is practised in a regime of justice, presupposes the adoption of a retrospective position and encompasses, like biography, a requirement of selection, serialization, coherence, imputation, expression and clarification of intentions, so the situation being reported on will be calculable. Now, as I try to show in the case of the regime of love in agape, the other regimes are not subjected to the same degree to a requirement of calculability, even when this requirement is not incompatible with them. It follows that one of the principal effects of the translation inherent in the production of a report, inasmuch as it implies a projection of the action onto the level of justice, is no doubt to confer a character that can be totalized (Bourdieu 1990b,

82–3), calculated, finalized, intentionally oriented towards a horizon that thought can dominate, on actions that could have dispensed with these determinations when they were immersed in the completeness of the present moment. And these gaps cannot be interpreted in the logic of bad faith. For, in changing regimes, the actor can no longer accede to the recognition of actions whose characterization depends entirely on the mode on which they are accomplished. Under the effect of a constraint that is in some sense technical rather than ethical, linked to the position he adopts with respect to language, the actor is obliged to requalify his acts – that is, to replace them by acts of a different order, one that is pertinent in the world, real in a report, but not in other modes where people have at hand the instruments they need to deploy strategies consciously. To adopt a 'strategy', one must in fact have a space available for calculation, a temporal horizon, knowable means and identifiable goals; as Jon Elster has shown (Elster 1985, 51, 96) with regard to Pierre Bourdieu's *Distinction* (Bourdieu 1984), the idea of an unconscious strategy is hard to defend. Like memories of war, reports are worth what war stories are worth. They do not restore the uncertainty of one's presence to gunfire that so upset Fabrice del Dongo, when he asked himself if he had really participated in the battle at Waterloo.[3]

The logic of bad faith has to be dismissed here because in fact it supports the inverse hypothesis. In works that mean to take into account the lack of transparency of actors to themselves, it is precisely the accomplishment of a strategic action that is supposed to be denied and repressed by actors who would be inclined by their ethical code of honour to stress the moral character – either gratuitous or oriented towards a common good – of actions whose principle would actually reside in the will to satisfy particular interests. These works thus take as their object the unveiling of strategies based on selfish calculations, situations in which the actors would invoke gratuitousness or altruism. In this respect they are in harmony with the main tendency of sociology, which since the earliest empirical works of its founders has most often chosen as a test its capacity to reveal a calculable order under the appearance of gratuitousness or contingency; to be comprehensible, this approach requires viewing actors as endowed with means of calculation of which they themselves are unaware. It is in this sense that one can speak, in the case of the social sciences (but this would also be true for psychoanalysis) – especially in the form that these sciences adopted in the second half of the twentieth century, at the price of a reinterpretation of the anthropologies of the preceding century – of a heuristics of evil, in the same way one speaks (starting from roughly the same time period, moreover) of an 'aesthetics of evil' for which the requirement of truth presupposes ferreting out the shameful, secret, calculating and selfish motives underneath the false motives of gratuitousness or altruism that the actors hasten to produce as soon as they are given the floor. This precept does not have the generality with which it is credited. On the contrary, what strikes the researcher, when he knows how to be attentive to what his informants are telling him and to the way they express themselves in his presence, is precisely the extraordinary propensity of people, especially when they are confronted by a sociologist who is questioning them and whom they want to please, to attribute selfish motives to themselves, to reconstruct strategies, to bring to the surface a closed universe in which everything is calculable and in which everyone calculates, and to immerse in this universe what they still remember of already accomplished acts – acts whose modality they no longer recognize, thus acts that they are incapable of describing any better than could a neophyte model-constructing sociologist who is particularly eager to respect the constraints of exhaustiveness and transparency that satisfy the requirement of formalization at the least cost. When actors set out to recount their lives as plots and also to theorize them, more and more often by borrowing tools from the social sciences, they are thus in no better position than the sociologist, to whom they are delivering what they think is the fruit of their experience, to grasp the mode in which they have accomplished actions that they are transforming as they transport them into the ordered presentation of a report. Now, if the world were not only the way the sociologists describe it but also the way people very often describe it when they put themselves in the position of 'informers', it would be not only unlivable but also impossible to achieve with the means available to men and women.

If actors excel at reporting only those actions whose relevance is established in a regime of justice, a sociology of action can no longer settle for following the actors in all their reports in order to see the way they turn their actions into narratives. Unless it posits a radical opposition between a logical universe, whose objects would be of the order of what is said, and a mystical universe whose objects would be of the order of what is shown and would remain unavailable for clarification in discourse, the sociology of action has to seek to endow itself with the theoretical instruments and the methods necessary to delve 'beneath' the reports by rummaging in their gaps, their interstices. For if in fact 'everything is a report', including the field notes that sociologists record in their notebooks, this commonplace among

84

linguistic turns does not preclude directing the investigation towards the constraints that weigh upon the production of a report. To go in this direction does not necessarily lead back towards the sociology of the agent, to use Nicolas Dodier's terms (1989); instead, it may lead investigators to combine various methods in an effort to bring out whatever offered some resistance, in advance of the report, to the establishment of a narrative. This requires, first, that we be especially attentive to the traces of actions whose translation is especially problematic, traces that may have been left in the report, and for this reason we have to endow ourselves, according to the programme Dodier proposes, with interpretive prudence, or, to go back to his terms, with an 'economy of interpretation'; once again, this opens up to sociologists a margin of play with respect to the actors' reports, even as it limits the power of the means that sociologists can use – a necessity if sociology is to avoid falling back into the infinite regressions that characterized the forms of interpretation founded on the postulate of an unconscious of the analytic type.

Another strategy might consist in granting more space to observation, and especially to the relation between what is observed and what is reported by the actors. One of the constraints on observation would consist, in this case, in maintaining it on the horizon of the situation by setting aside both any prior information about the actors in earlier situations and any predictions about situations to come. This would allow sociologists, returning to their field notes later on, to compare those aspects of the situation that were abandoned or forgotten by the actors and those the actors identified when they integrated them into a narrative. Social action consigned to a report is like a statue sculpted out of a block of wood. The form appears, but there is a price: the chips cut away from the wood disappear. If it is true that knowledge progresses by dipping into what is left over, mere residue that was not relevant for an earlier approach, we have to use these chips, going against sociology's ordinary tendencies, to restore life to the aspects of the situation that could not be integrated without difficulty into a retrospective report and lend itself to strategic reduction, for example; this would presuppose translation into a different logic. This is the approach that I adopted spontaneously when I began to work on affairs: I focused my attention on *anecdotes*, precisely on the aspects of an affair whose singularity seemed to resist the intention of scientific totalization; for instance, when I sought to inform myself by listening to colleagues who specialize in the sociology of work speak about social conflicts, I paid closer attention to the little stories they told in the cafe, after the seminar, than to the constructs armed with powerful concepts that characterized our discipline at the time. Observation was supposed to allow us in particular to establish tools for describing chains of actions, if it is true that actors spend their lives shifting among different modes (justice, which is perhaps easiest to grasp, is only one of these), often in rapid succession. Such a project must thus be supported by a renewal of field studies. In our disciplines, which like others cannot do without theory, fieldwork remains at once the source of all our knowledge and the decisive test. If it is true that our task consists in clarifying and giving form to the competence of actors, so that sociology is to common sense what epistemology is to science, only fieldwork allows us to reveal, in chunks, pieces of ordinary competence that have remained underestimated, minimized or unknown up to now.[4] In the process, a source of human dignity is brought to light: people are capable of more than they generally believe.

Part II

Agape: An Introduction to the States of Peace

— 10 —

DISPUTES AND PEACE

10.1 The limits of justice

Justice is understood as an alternative to violence; this is part of its definition. Simone Weil expresses this law in its raw state in a discussion of Thucydides:

> The Athenians, who were at war with Sparta, wanted to force the inhabitants of the little island of Melos, allied to Sparta from all antiquity and so far remaining neutral, to join with them. It was in vain that the men of Melos, faced with the ultimatum of the Athenians, invoked justice, imploring pity for the antiquity of their town. As they were unwilling to yield, the Athenians razed the city, put all their men to death, and sold all their women and children as slaves.
>
> Thucydides has put the lines in question into the mouth of these Athenians. They begin by saying that they will not try to prove that their ultimatum is just.
>
> 'Let us rather treat of what is possible . . . You know it as well as we do; the human spirit is so constituted that what is just is only examined if there is equal necessity on both sides. But if one is strong and the other weak, that which is possible is imposed by the first and accepted by the second.'
>
> The men of Melos said that in case of a battle they would have the gods with them on account of the justice of their cause. The Athenians replied that they saw reason to suppose so.
>
> 'As touching the gods we have the belief, and as touching men the certainty, that always, by a necessity of nature, each one commands wherever he has the power. We did not establish this law, we are not the first to apply it; we found it already established, we abide by it as something likely to endure forever; and that is why we apply it. We know quite well that you also, like all the others, once you reached the

same degree of power, would act the same way.' (Weil [1966] 1973, 141)

Commenting later on the same text, Weil writes:

> Except the cases where one human being is brutally subjected to another, who deprives him for a time of the power of thinking in the first person, everyone disposes of others as he disposes of inert things, either in fact, if he has the power, or in thought. There is, however, still one more exception. This is when two human beings meet in such circumstances that neither is subject to the other and each has to an equal degree need of the consent of the other. Each one then, without ceasing to think in the first person, really understands that the other also thinks in the first person. Justice then occurs as a natural phenomenon. The legislator's aim must be to make these occasions as numerous as possible. (Weil 1957b, 173)

Such convergence does not in itself presuppose agreement or, as Weil puts it, 'harmony'. As a form of dispute, justice is a substitute for violence. In a dispute in justice, the persons involved no longer measure one another simply *against* one another, as in violent comparisons. To provide a basis for their assessments, they rely on a principle of general equivalence, which they treat as universal. This general equivalence introduces into their relations a reference to a second level that is not occupied by persons, since even a judge can rule only by referring to it. The judge's task, which is not indispensable to the pursuit of a dispute in justice, consists solely in helping all the parties in conflict to detach their attention from the person of the adversary and redirect it towards that second-degree equivalence, by reactivating the common knowledge they have of the principle. Thus a dispute can shift from violence to justice when each party recognizes the principle of general equivalence and recognizes that the other recognizes it, and when the other recognizes that he or she recognizes it as well, and so on (Lewis 1969).

In the cycle of violent reciprocity, whoever takes a blow reciprocates in kind, following the principle of *lex talionis*, 'an eye for an eye'; the response to a death on one side is the greatest possible number of deaths on the other. This cycle is transformed by the shift to justice. In justice, a test is no longer a test of force conducted over time, with the loser simply the first one to stop; tests can be immobilized in the present and settled through reference to the principle of general equivalence. Convergence on common knowledge allows the adversaries to establish their relative worth and to recognize the superiority of one of the parties without relying, as they would in violence, on the chronological order of the blows exchanged. Finally, and most importantly, externalizing the principle of equivalence in relation to the persons involved requires referring to an equivalence that is not a matter of persons but that generalizes one of the abstract properties of personhood – a property potentially given to all, or so we choose to believe, although it is present in each person to varying degrees and concealed behind the veil of ignorance that is stripped away in a test. This reference makes it possible to avoid all-or-nothing comparisons and thus to construct a test whose outcome need not be the destruction or exclusion of one of the adversaries.

This bifurcation is not insignificant. However, it does not suffice to exhaust the question of how to end disputes. For, if a dispute cannot be stopped, retreat into violence always remains possible, if not probable, whenever power relations shift. Justice handles disputes by relating them to a principle of general equivalence and by subjecting the parties to a test defined with reference to that equivalence. But, to the extent that several legitimate principles of equivalence exist, the test can always be repeated with reference to a different equivalence, equally endowed with universal validity, as Laurent Thévenot and I sought to demonstrate in *On Justification*. Such a move allows a dispute in justice to be reactivated and even expanded. Indeed, the persons involved in this process will constantly seek new objects, new arguments, new persons deemed trustworthy, to defend them, support their cause and provide evidence. This is why the regime of justice is always insufficient in itself. It can channel disputes at least for a while by subjecting them to its own order. But it is powerless to stop them. To end a dispute in justice, one always has to seek out something other than justice. This is what confers on justice its relatively arbitrary character, which is often denounced and is intuitively known to all. For the central question remains that of closure; anything that halts the process will do, as Henri Levy-Bruhl astutely remarked in his book on judicial proof (1964). Whatever brings a trial to an end is sufficient proof, and in this respect the divinely sanctioned judgement in medieval courts – where a judge had a legal obligation to rule and could use his authority to invoke his own 'inner conviction' – is equivalent to the most sophisticated scientific proof.[1]

The inability of justice to exhaust disputes and restore peace is one reason why constructs limited to justice may be seen as inadequate. In a world envisaged from the standpoint of justice, only three kinds of situations can exist: situations susceptible to justification and, in contrast, either situations of violence or situations of contingency. About the latter two, justice has nothing to say. But, while justice remains

91

a regime for addressing disputes, not everything that escapes it can be reduced to contingency. Peace cannot be reduced to contingency, or to a situation in which a justifiable (even if not actively justified) ordering of persons and things would forestall a dispute for a while. Yet peace is also a matter of concern for human beings: we have an intuition for it, and often some nostalgia.

In the brief sketch that follows, I shall try to identify instruments that will facilitate a cognitive approach to peace. In order to maintain the homogeneity of the model developed in *OJ*, I shall also try to relate this new approach to the problem of comparison and equivalence. Peace excludes disputes in violence – that is, any comparisons of persons that, pursued to the end, lead to the destruction of one of the parties. It also excludes states that may be calm and stable in appearance but that are nevertheless marked by the seal of violence. These are states in which the silence of some persons is simply the result of a threat brought to bear on them by others believed to be stronger; the apparent calm thus depends entirely on each participant's ability to make anticipatory judgements about violence and its outcome. These anticipations are effective because they oblige the persons involved to subordinate their thinking about the future to what they know or do not know about the future as conceived by the others.

But peace also excludes disputes in justice – disputes characterized, as we have seen, by the active engagement of principles of general equivalence that make it possible to impose an order of worths on persons by means of tests. The potential outcome of violence, the derivation that substitutes reference to general equivalences on a different level for two-way comparisons, and that absorbs the energy engaged in violence so as to redirect it towards a rule-governed test, is nevertheless not the same thing as peace, since the process it institutes allows participants to renew the dispute over and over again, endlessly. Peace is made manifest by the silence of equivalences. When persons are at peace, reference to equivalence is useless. Equivalences are not involved in the situation. If there is no dispute, why engage in measuring?

The state of peace itself can be conceived in various ways. One way to silence equivalences is to objectivize them. As all of Bruno Latour's work shows (especially Latour and Woolgar 1979), the world of objects is pacifying because it establishes equivalences in an irreversible form by installing them in agreements that are difficult to dismantle. We do not constantly call into question the measurements of the beings that surround us: time, the gap between railroad ties, the width of doors, and so on. When an object takes shape in reality, the dispute to which the conception of that object quite probably gave rise is brought to a close; thus we pay for today's peace today at the price of yesterday's disputes. These measured beings impose on us the necessity inscribed in them; in so doing, they order and orchestrate our behaviours. Thus, through the constraints they bring to bear on us, they play the role Durkheim attributed to supra-individual norms inscribed in the firmament of collective consciousness. And it is only when a dispute about persons arises and is handled in the regime of justice that objects are actively qualified with reference to the principle of justice that underlies the situation; they are then valorized in a reality test that can establish justifications and support a judgement (*OJ* 127–38).

But I shall no longer concern myself here with the peace of things, because this form of peace does not require that persons put complex cognitive capacities to work. When objects serve as mediators among persons, each person can adjust his or her behaviour so as to be guided by things in the environment (a train schedule, for example), without having to take direct charge of the difficult problem represented by the human ability to make demands or to enter into states that surpass the present situation. Things suffice to ensure peace as long as 'everyone disposes of others as he disposes of inert things' (Weil 1957b, 173). This state of indifference closely resembles the state of nature that Rousseau described in his *Discourse on the Origin of Inequality* (Rousseau 1994a) (although things ensure a coordination of behaviour that Rousseau's naked savage can achieve only by submitting to a contract), but it does not allow us to understand behaviours that develop in situations in which the arrangements of things are minimally constraining, and even less in the still more frequent situations that do not lend themselves at all to the tacit control exerted by things.

I shall thus envisage a fourth possibility and posit that there are states in which, by making an active effort and not simply taking their lead from the world of objects, persons can establish reasonable relations with others without recourse to equivalences. To try to establish a basis for this possibility, I propose to examine texts that speak of friendship or love. Love, like justice, is said to be an alternative to violence. However, its means are radically different. Justice starts with a comparison between two people who are confronting one another in an all-out test, and it absorbs their violence by substituting reference to a universal equivalence for a two-way comparison, whether or not the equivalence is objectivized in law. Love takes a shorter path. It turns away from comparison and does not reckon with equivalences.

93

This is why love has always been presented not only as an alternative to violence but also as an alternative to justice. But it is also why the sort of state engendered by love has always been cast into doubt – if not always in principle, at least as unlikely to be realized – and either rejected as idealistic or utopian or else (but this amounts to the same thing) relegated into an eschatological future. My goal in this study is to try to assess the extent to which the presumption that persons can engage in relations of love is realistic. In schematic terms, relations of love are relations in which reference to equivalence is set aside. My hypothesis is that people in our society, persons we encounter in our daily lives, are in fact acquainted with this state, that they actually engage in it in practice, as one of the possible states – others being violence, justice and tacit concession to the peace of things – among which they can shift, though not always simultaneously (persons installed in one state can interact with persons settled in another), according to processes that may give rise to rational formations.

Whereas our work in *OJ* focused largely on the way situations were arranged, my interest here lies in the states in which a person is situated when he or she enters into a relationship. This means that I shall position myself on the level of a psychology of relationships, as it were. I shall assume that the nature of the situational arrangement is especially constraining when persons shift into a state of justice since, in this state, they have to valorize the world of objects in order to satisfy a reality test (*OJ* 130–8). This is why, in a situation that is in a calm state, without disputes and consequently without any active engagement of equivalences, a theory of justice – that is, a theory constructed from the standpoint of justice – can legitimately recognize arrangements that are set up in advance according to the principle of equivalence that prevails in the situation, precisely in order to forestall disputes. But, apart from these states, the prevailing arrangements, without being entirely irrelevant, exercise a weaker constraint. One can fight in the street, in a workshop, even in a church; one can let oneself be guided by things in any environment except a desert – and, even in a desert, the stars remain; people can love one another, although with varying degrees of facility, in a large number of possible worlds.

10.2 Anthropology and tradition

According to Aristotle, there is something antecedent to justice: he calls it *philia* (friendship). We know that, for him, the term does not merely designate what it evokes for us – lasting relations among private persons – but that it has a much broader extension. Philia also applies, for Aristotle, to relations among persons in a city-state and to relations among city-states themselves.[2] It thus has an immediate political dimension. For Aristotle, philia precedes justice and makes justice useless; this certainly suggests that, for him, justice is still a form of dispute, even if he does not say so explicitly:

> Moreover, friendship appears to be the bond of the state; and lawgiv-ers seem to set more store by it than they do by justice, for to promote concord, which seems akin to friendship, is their chief aim, while faction, which is enmity, is what they are most anxious to banish. And if men are friends, there is no need of justice between them; whereas merely to be just is not enough – a feeling of friendship is also necessary. Indeed, the highest form of justice seems to have an element of friendly feeling in it. (Aristotle 1926b, VIII.i.4)

Aristotle's hypothesis has to be taken seriously, first of all because it converges with the ordinary intuition that constitutes the sole form of acceptable validation for anthropology (as it does for other disciplines as well – linguistics and analytic philosophy, for example). I shall try to take the hypothesis seriously in this sketch. But to do so I shall have to veer away from philia and from Aristotle's commentary in order to reimmerse the hypothesis in the larger whole to which it belongs – that is, in what one would want to call the dimension of love, if that term, eroded by overuse and with its meaning almost forgotten today, evoked for us something other than a confused literary mix of whims, passions, attachments and appetites endlessly repackaged in love songs and stories. I hope to bring some order to this muddle; for this reason, I shall not follow the most common practice in sociology and take ordinary intuition or literary displays as my starting point.[3] There is nothing to be seen from those vantage points, because everything is mixed together in confusion. I shall have to turn away from intuition and ordinary meaning for the time being and try to reconstruct the system of incompatible constraints among which compromises are made, the compromises that we are given to understand by common sense and that are the only things whose existence common sense recognizes, as if it were necessary to forget the tensions that these compromises had provisionally appeased and the hard labour that was required to achieve them. Everyone repeats this labour on his or her own account, in the face of the practical exigencies of everyday life, and without knowing the extent or the specific nature of the cognitive capacities that have had to be mobilized in the process.

To take some distance from the commonplaces of discourse about love, and to provide instruments that will make it possible to analyse the cognitive capacities that persons deploy when they return to peaceful relations whose reference to justice is nevertheless set aside, I shall start, as I did for the study of the sense of justice, with constructions borrowed from tradition. Thus I need to return to the reasons for which I find the recourse to tradition useful. My current endeavour is in fact a direct extension of my earlier efforts to explore the cognitive structures persons can use, in our society, to enter into relationships. I shall thus remain within the strict framework of anthropology, with one difference, with respect to most anthropologists: my terrain is not an exotic society, remote in space or time, but our own. Now an anthropology of cognitive capacities in our society is necessarily in close proximity to the work of other disciplines, notably psychology and philosophy, analytic philosophy in particular.

The fact of taking one's own society as the terrain, while it allows one to dispense with travel, with learning indigenous languages, and more generally with the difficult work of insertion undertaken by ethnologists, is nevertheless not without its challenges. This approach in fact entails a need to grapple directly with the body of questions that distance often allows anthropologists and historians to neglect in practice, for the simple reason that the persons who serve as their informants are radically separated from those who will be their readers. From this often repeated observation, it seems to me that not all the consequences have yet been drawn. There has frequently been a tendency to see only an easily denounced facility, because the persons whose knowledge is given shape by an ethnologist cannot control or critique the representation that has been produced. But this is not the essential point. The primary advantage available to historians and ethnologists by virtue of this asymmetry is that their object is hidden away – naturally hidden, as it were – since it is obscured by space and time. In my case, everything is here, ready at hand. If in the final analysis anthropology can always be reduced to an epistemology, since it is the science of the science of the actors and thus constitutes second-degree knowledge (see chapter 9), the problem is posed in one way when the resources of the observers and those of the actors are different, at least in part, as is the case in the anthropology of distant or past societies, and in quite another way when these resources are identical, as is the case in the anthropology of our own society.

The gap between the two situations is fundamental, because it induces a different relation to tradition. In anthropology, the tradition in question belongs to the actors. In seeking to shed light on the object of study, an Indian village, for example, an anthropologist sees no reason not to associate the actors' observed behaviour and discourse with traditional texts or ancient stories transmitted orally. Similarly, historians of ancient societies can draw on multiple sources to reconstruct the culture of people who have disappeared from the world in which the researchers are writing history, and, like Georges Dumézil, for example, they can speak in very general terms of an 'Indo-European mind'. This work on tradition never brings anthropologists – and still less ethnologists – back to the tradition from which they themselves have emerged and of which they can pretend to be unaware. When the human sciences were established at the end of the nineteenth century, they broke with the prevailing philosophical, legal and theological traditions. Those who practised the human sciences (like a good many who still practise them today), themselves trained in the humanities, could continue to look to tradition for concepts and fundamental notions for their activity, but they did so in the way one dips discreetly into a secret treasure, a storehouse of tools that are powerful although hardly adequate in terms of technological legitimacy, and these practitioners were not subject to the imperative of control that weighs so heavily on those whose activity is inscribed explicitly on the path laid out by traditional knowledge. This discreet practice, sheltered from critique, allowed them in particular to underestimate the degree to which their surface knowledge, the knowledge they presented to others and submitted to the direct control of the scientific community, was dependent on traditional schemas that they had incorporated and often reinterpreted.

Similarly, the will to forge their own specific object, different from that of the traditional disciplines, led the human sciences, and especially sociology, to overestimate the gap between the mental instruments with which observers themselves were endowed and those of the ordinary persons they took as their objects. The notions of 'the people', tradition and popular culture arose in Germany in the late eighteenth century and marked the beginning of research into folklore; it doubtless played an important role in creating this gap, which has persisted into our time in an often reaffirmed opposition between 'scientific' and 'popular' knowledge, despite the many field studies that have brought to light the existence of ongoing communication, today and in the past, between these two bodies whose distance from one another has been dogmatically affirmed.

When we give up these two sharp distinctions, between the human sciences and the traditional disciplines in which they are rooted, on the one hand, and between the cognitive competences of ordinary persons and the notions, divisions and concepts that have been worked and shaped by tradition, on the other, we are led to reconsider the work of anthropology and to distance ourselves from the canonical model of the ethnology of exotic societies. For those who accept these premises, the object of an anthropology of our own society is nothing other than a self-referential loop that closes around tradition. The anthropologist's work can then be defined by the entire set of operations of clarification that are inscribed within this loop.[4]

To gain access to their chosen object, the cognitive competencies of ordinary persons, anthropologists can proceed by going back and forth between the tradition and the intuitions gleaned from their informants. Thus, in *OJ*, we continually moved from field observation, and in particular from recording the arguments developed by actors in their disputes, to the traditional constructs of political philosophy. In fact, as we have already seen, persons do not have the capacity to clarify and present in a systematic form the entire set of procedures they use to develop arguments or to set up situations that hold together. They lack this capacity not because they are impelled by an 'unconscious', in the sense that they could not tolerate transparency, but because they have no need for it. When they are not obliged to do so, persons have no reason to clarify the principles that underlie their actions. Clarification seems to obey a law of least effort, as linguists would say. As we showed in *OJ* (31–7), persons commit themselves to the work of clarification only in situations of justification – that is, in situations in which they are confronted with a critique and from which they are unable to extricate themselves by force: they are obliged to take their contradictor into account, and they seek to converge towards some common knowledge capable of stabilizing an agreement. This effort will be developed to differing extents according to the situation, and especially depending on whether the actors can exit from the test through a compromise without going back to the principles of general equivalence that make it possible to validate an action as legitimate across the board. Yet compromises, which are at the heart of what any anthropologist brings back from an expedition into the field, do not in and of themselves reveal all the work of conciliation among incompatible persons that has to be accomplished to shape them and make them common property. The tensions they enclose and neutralize, at least temporarily, most often remain underdeveloped, and thus underestimated by the observer. For *OJ*, we turned to political philosophy to find the instrument we needed to develop the principles that are tacitly enclosed in the arrangement of ordinary situations or set in tension in compromises. Political philosophy offered us these principles in purified form, because its aim is normative. Taking as their object the utopia of a just world organized in all respects around a single principle, classic political philosophies – the work of specialists – are in fact confronted with constraints of construction and clarification that do not weigh to the same degree on persons acting in practice. These philosophies require rigour in order to convince us that, even if the world whose purification they are tracing is judged utopian at a given moment, this world is possible – that is, logically possible, cohesive and robust. A highly rigorous clarification is then necessary to show that in the nooks and crannies of the model there are no hidden flaws, no internal contradictions that would make its enactment impossible.

How to counter the obvious objection: that these old utopian constructions, aiming at an inaccessible ideal, have nothing to do with the people of today's world, who for the most part have never opened a book by Hobbes or Saint-Simon or Rousseau, and could care less? I maintain that the terms 'utopia' or 'ideal', as opposed to 'reality', are the pivots of the critique. They cannot be set aside without examination, for utopias do exist. It is possible to construct imaginary worlds that offer at least some degree of systematicity and coherence. To make my undertaking convincing, then, I must be in a position to establish the difference not only between impossible and achievable utopias but also between achievable and achieved utopias. For this, an objective indicator is available. A utopia is achieved, and thus deserves the name of polity, when the society in question encompasses a world of objects that make it possible to set up tests that rely on a particular principle of equivalence, the one whose logical possibility is deployed in this utopia. A complete demonstration would obviously presuppose a historical analysis of the way the world in question was set up, with its objects and its two-way relations woven between the logical constructs of philosophers and the empirical constructs of persons who have assembled coherent universes of objects. But even in the absence of such studies, the empirical analysis of tests allows us to identify the relationship between the models of political philosophy and the type of cognitive instruments that must be available to the persons involved if these persons are to confront one another while behaving in a reasonable manner. In fact, in each of these reality tests, tradition is in a sense set before the actors once again, reactualized in the process of its 'application', in Gadamer's sense (Gadamer 1982, 274–305), although this practical reappropriation does not presuppose recourse to a text.

But the task of the anthropologist studying our own society does not stop here. Anthropologists who study exotic societies would be perfectly prepared to accept what I have just said about the relation between tradition and the ordinary behaviour of persons; this seems strange to sociologists only because we are accustomed to taking for granted the existence of an unbridgeable divide between scientific thinking and the cognitive capacities of ordinary persons. When we study our own society, the confrontation between tradition and field observation has an additional effect: it prompts us to clarify the relation between the tools proper to our own discipline, on the one hand, and tradition, on the other. In fact, if we take the arguments of ordinary persons seriously, we are led to minimize the gap – which positivism has expanded to an extreme – between the arguments persons make and the schemas that our discipline provides to account for their behaviour. Now, this similarity is incomprehensible if we fail to see that the very schemas presented by the tradition are the ones brought together here, actualized by the actors in tests, and by the observer in the particular test constituted by the intention to achieve mastery by explaining the behaviour of others. Throughout these operations, which appear to have nothing in common with the work of philosophers when that work is defined as uniquely focused on texts, the tradition is continually both enacted and clarified. The anthropologist's clarification of the way tradition is enacted in the tests to which the actors are subjected contributes in itself to the enactment of tradition. In fact, when the work of sociology is undertaken as the anthropology of our own society, it is not performed in an ivory tower. The actors latch onto the variations on tradition offered them by the anthropologists – a tradition the two groups share – and re-engage the tradition in the world in which they function.

10.3 The theological tradition

Classic political philosophy would be of little use for the project I am outlining in this section. Focused on the establishment of justice in the framework of nation-states, it ignores the relationship, so powerfully present to consciousness in the ancient world, between friendship, or love, and justice. A different tradition has to be invoked here, one whose presence, in a work claiming to belong to the social sciences, may seem more incongruous and, frankly, less legitimate than that of political philosophy, which has been adapted to the climate of anthropology today owing in particular to the efforts of Louis Dumont (1977, 1980, 1986). In the work presented here, I have come to attribute particular importance to a notion of love that is most often designated by *agape*, 'a term of Christian jargon' (Collange 1980, 146) that has been taken seriously and studied by theologians and almost no one else. In Christian theology, agape designates first and foremost the relation of God to humankind, although it also applies to the relations of human beings among themselves inasmuch as the relation of agape is made possible by God's gift of love for humanity. Because I am not a theologian but a sociologist, I shall attempt to detach agape from its specifically supernatural dimension and focus on the way it can regulate relations among human beings; in particular, I shall use a model to deploy the intuitive understanding of agape that I believe all of us share.

But this effort to secularize agape stems purely from a methodological decision; it is not inscribed within a sociological theory of religion. My intention is not to reveal the social foundations of religious belief in divine love, in a spirit that would conform to Durkheim's theory of religion, nor do I mean to unveil the 'truth' of agape by rooting it in the relation of non-recognition that society could be said to maintain with itself. I do not mean that human beings claim that God loves them in order to establish the obligation of loving one another. My work is positioned, instead, within research on pacified relations (Latour 1988a) between the social sciences and religion. The social sciences were established in the nineteenth century by means of, and as part of, a critique of religions (Moscovici 1988). This was virtually their only object, along with pauperism. For the early social sciences, it was a question not of abolishing religion but of replacing it with an acceptable equivalent. And this project, while it did allow the construction of a science of society, failed completely in one respect: it made it almost impossible to develop an anthropology of religion. Worse still, it blocked the reappropriation of religious knowledge by anthropology. This is particularly true for the Christian tradition: as René Girard has rightly remarked, this tradition is conspicuous by its absence in the modern social sciences, which nevertheless do not hesitate to attach 'an immense importance to a number of ancient Greek tales about a certain Oedipus and a certain Dionysos' (Girard 1987, 261). My undertaking would be satisfying if the construction sketched in here, even as it conforms to the rules of my discipline, remained compatible – as one says of two software programs that they are compatible – with interpretations that aim to reinsert it into the theological corpus. I can perhaps suggest a passageway opened up by Rudolf Bultmann (1947): if the revelation of agape is to be recognized, however partially and incompletely, instead of being simply

101

shunted aside as absurd, agape must already be known in a different way: it must be known in practice. I can thus propose the hypothesis that this practical relation is what the revelation of agape unfolds and clarifies.[5] We shall see, moreover, how the notion of 'practice' (Bourdieu 1977, 1990b) or 'a practical form of knowledge' (Weber 1978, 545) reactualizes certain characteristics that have been thematized in the theology of agape.[6]

An issue remains, however, that makes my position more difficult to maintain than it was when Laurent Thévenot and I were attempting to clarify the meaning of justice for ordinary persons, in *OJ*, by turning to political philosophy. If it is true that justice is not merely a matter of argumentation and thus of language, since argumentation relies on the arrangements of objects that persons discover in the situations in which they find themselves (*OJ* 127–44) – and this claim distances my position from that of Habermas, for example (Habermas 1984) – the fact remains that disputes in justice cannot always remain silent. At some point, persons have to express themselves in the trials in which they are engaged. These trials lead them to clarify their positions – that is, to move up to the principles of equivalence that political philosophy has systematized. As I have tried to show in the first part of this book, justice thus maintains a privileged relation with the order of *reports*. A report is a retrospective construction that posits imputations and justifies them by relying on an architecture of proof. However, the situation is entirely different in the case of love. Indeed, we shall see that one of the properties of the relation of agape is precisely that it posits strong constraints on the uses that can be made of language. It is not that persons are forbidden to express themselves. But when they are *in* love, they cannot talk about love itself without risking its destruction.[7] In situations of love, it is hard to use language self-referentially. This state of affairs has several consequences, both for the shaping of the theory of love and for the relation between that theory and the practice of persons in a state of love. The theory of agape, which has as one of its central themes precisely the irreducibility of love to discourse, poses quite specific problems for those seeking to formulate it. I shall come back to this point. But it also follows that the theory of love cannot be reduced to an argumentative resource to which persons might turn in order to justify a particular mode of relation. The theory does not supply them, as an ideology would, with discursive resources that they could immediately re-engage in their practice, common knowledge that could help them conclude an agreement that would be at once verbal and effective. Relations in agape cannot be attributed to an 'effect of theory' (Bourdieu 1990a, 180–2). Does this mean that there is no relation between the traditions that speak of love and the degree to which this state is available to persons? Such a hypothesis would make it impossible to comprehend the very existence of discourse about love. But to account for the way in which the relation between theory and action is established here, we shall no doubt have to examine, as I try to do below (chapter 13.3 and 13.4), the way people shift intermittently between agape and other regimes such as justice or even violence. For in a world in which everyone is constantly immersed in love, the theory of love – like the theories of equity and non-violence, moreover – would have no place (chapter 13.1). The theory of love is addressed to those who are not in love – that is, to all persons, at one time or another. By developing the possibility of love as a regime of action and by inscribing it in arrangements that ensure its presence, it offers persons *mediations* on which they can rely in order to undertake the work of passage, in order to let themselves go – that is, to exempt themselves from the constraint of urgency and at the same time to take active control of the present moment while silencing the ability, one that is always active in the other regimes, to look back or to look ahead. These mediations are first and foremost references to persons, present or represented – for, as we shall see, it is to the extent that persons are not all in the same state at the same time that such passages are possible. But to speak of the work of passage does not mean that abandoning calculation – which is one of the characteristics of the state of agape, as I shall show later on – is still the result of a calculation. This work is focused first of all on the emotions and, more particularly, no doubt, on fear. The mediations that sustain a reference to persons in the state of agape incite others to make the passage, assuring them that they will come through it alive.

— 11 —

THREE FORMS OF LOVE

11.1 An initial inventory

To make love an object of anthropology, we cannot just use what the moderns say about it as the starting point, because the formulations they have to offer tend to be too complex and too rich; they take experiences and intuitions rooted in different states and blend them without distinction. I propose to begin simply by drawing up an initial inventory of the states of love. These can be combined in empirical manifestations of love, but, if we are to have the means to analyse the combinations, we need tools that can give us access to each state in its purest possible form. To forge such tools, I have to turn away from everyday experience for a moment and seek out what tradition tells us about the forms of the social bond that are built on the basis of love. For our own single word 'love', Greek has four lexical forms, of which three in particular have served to support various theories of love (on the Greek lexicon of love, see Spicq 1955, 1–70). I shall review these concepts briefly here, trying to pinpoint their contrastive features. I shall recall the properties of *philia* and *eros* – which will be familiar to the reader because they have thoroughly penetrated not only our culture but also modern social science – only in order to bring out more sharply the relevant features of *agape*. Finally, in examining the various concepts of love, I shall focus on the varying relations they maintain with justice and, in the case of agape in particular, with the order of jurisprudence and law.[1]

11.2 Love as reciprocity: philia

Of the pages Aristotle devotes to philia in the *Nicomachean Ethics*, I shall be concerned in particular with the strongly marked connection between friendship and reciprocity. Philia, a term that extends from 'friendship between two people' to the 'cardinal virtue of political morality' (Spicq 1955, 32), and that, as a 'principle of every community, can ... designate sociability' (Fraisse 1976, 191), is an interactionist notion based on the recognition of reciprocal merit. If a friendship is to be established, the partners first of all have to be meritorious; both have to be 'worthy of being loved'. This requirement implies that friends must be equally able to evaluate another person's merits, and thus that they share a common knowledge of what constitutes worth. Moreover, they have to interact in order to communicate the evaluation that they make of one another; as Aristotle indicates, they have to know each other's feelings.[2] The need for mutual recognition accounts for the importance Aristotle attributes to the conditions of space and time. The realization of philia is conditioned on simultaneous presence in the same space. Friendship tends to unravel when people are far apart.[3] Since the good will that one friend bears towards another must be 'known to its object' (Aristotle 1926b, VIII.ii.4), if it is not to remain unnoticed it must be manifested to both parties through an encounter in a common space. Moreover, good will based on the evaluation of merits must be reciprocal. Thus it presupposes not only a common measure allowing for the evaluation of merits but also a rule of equality in mutual dealings.[4]

The connection made here between friendship and the evaluation of merit, on the one hand, and between friendship and reciprocity, on the other, brings the theory of friendship into association with the theory of justice; indeed, the two are not completely separate. Aristotle's description of philia always presupposes a pre-existing principle of equivalence that allows friends first to evaluate their reciprocal merits, and then to control the reciprocity of their dealings and maintain the equality of exchanges between them. For, in friendship, reciprocity is not exercised blindly. It is an object of expectation on the part of each partner; each expects from the other a return equivalent to his or her own contribution. Aristotle's stress on reciprocity and on the expectation of reciprocity accounts for the hierarchical classification of friendships, based on pleasure, interest or virtue. The increasing perfection of friendship, when one moves from pleasure to virtue, is first of all based on the notion of stability over time. Yet the steadfastness of friendships, their capacity to resist the assaults of time, depends essentially on the degree to which reciprocity binding the friends can resist the changes that time may bring in one or the other. Friendship is most perfect between virtuous people, not only because 'either party receives from the other the same or similar benefits, as it is proper that friends should do' (Aristotle 1926b, VIII. iv.1), but also because, since its source is more stable (since the pleasure that one provides the other, which characterizes the friendships of young people, or the interest that one takes in interacting with the other, which characterizes the friendships of the elderly, depend on contingent properties like beauty or wealth), it is surer to last,[5] and the same principle applies to alliances between city-states (ibid., VIII. iv.4). Starting from these premises, Aristotle undertakes a calculus of friendship (ibid., VIII.vi.7–vii.6). Since friendship should be proportional to the merits of each person involved, the combinations of friendships are diversified according to the hierarchical positions of the partners. Indeed, since friendship is defined, like justice, by equality, persons who are unequal in other respects have to compensate for the gaps by manifestations of friendship in order to maintain reciprocity in their exchanges.[6] Beyond a certain distance, it is not possible to compensate for the gap; reciprocity can no longer be exercised, and this excludes friendship. This is why Aristotle deems friendship with God impossible: 'when one [friend] becomes very remote from the other, as God is remote from man, [the friendship] can no longer continue' (ibid., VIII.vii.5). The reciprocity that must rule relations of friendship is ultimately attached to a more general rule of reciprocity, since it also orders relations among enemies, and 'hate for the enemy is as virtuous as delight in the friend' (Spicq 1955, 30).[7]

11.3 Eros and the construction of general equivalence

It is customary to define the properties of agape by distinguishing it not only from philia but also and especially from eros, understood in Platonic terms. Thus to mark the place of eros in my own construction I shall take my lead directly from theological commentaries like those of Anders Nygren (1953), which highlight agape's paradoxical properties by contrasting them with those of eros. Among the features of eros that are relevant to my schema, I shall focus especially on the omnipotence of desire and the role desire plays, as I see it, in the construction of a relation between the particular and the general. It is widely recognized that the distinction between eros and agape cannot be reduced to an opposition between human physical love and transcendent love. If eros, a force that drives the world, is defined first and foremost in terms of desire, if it is above all the product of deprivation and the expression of a feeling of deprivation and incompleteness on the part of beings (and is thus unknown to the gods, whose completeness excludes the possibility of desire), this human desire, which as such is inclined primarily towards other humans, can veer off in two opposing directions. Eros is initially attracted by what is beautiful, and principally by the beauty of bodies, which awakens a feeling of deprivation. Far from being indifferent to the value of its object, eros depends first of all, just as philia does, on the quality, or merit, of the beings towards which it is attracted; it can thus descend towards its *terrestrial* state and seize the object of desire. Under this influence, a man 'gives himself up to pleasure and like a beast proceeds to lust and begetting' (Plato 1914, 251a). Alternatively, eros can go in the opposite direction: it can rise up towards its *celestial* state and renounce immediate possession. It can then force itself to bring deprivation to a peak by placing itself above the disparate multiplicity of sensations so as to contemplate perfection in the world of ideas – that is, perfection in its most general form. The soul, moved by eros, is, as Paul Ricoeur says, 'the very movement from the sensible toward the intelligible; it is *anabasis*, the rising toward being; its misery is shown in that it is at first perplexed and searches' (Ricoeur 1986, 7). Connected in Plato's *Phaedrus* to the myth of transmigration of souls, this concept of love, the inspiration for all constructs based on a radical dualism between the senses and ideas, remains profoundly 'egocentric', as Nygren notes, since it remains oriented, whether its direction is downward or upward, towards the feeling of deprivation that haunts human beings. The dualist structure of eros generates a specific construction of the relation between the particular and the general that contains an irreducible tension. Love, which according to this theory is always the desire to rise from a lower to a higher state, can be satisfied only by following the first movement, which directs it towards singular beings. To be fully realized, it has to detach itself from the immediate object and rise up towards the general ideas that actually subtend desire. Thus violence, which permeates the Platonic description of terrestrial eros, is averted.[8] But this comes at a high price: renouncing all individual attachments to particular beings. Love of beings is replaced by something that establishes equivalence among beings, love of the 'higher common principle', as Rousseau puts it to express the higher generality of law, without which the initial apprehension of the merits of another being, and thus the awakening of desire, would be impossible. It is in this respect, as has

107

often been noted, that the theory of eros connects with the political theory of justice, since the orientation towards the contemplation of the most general forms is also the disposition that the leaders of a polity must inspire (Plato, *The Republic*).

The concept of love evoked rapidly here is familiar to us not only through education in the humanities, of which it is one of the commonplaces, but also, more directly, because it has inspired most of the theories in our cultural tradition that have sought to account for the very possibility of a social order.[9] In my own context, in particular, it has inspired the social theories of Freud and Durkheim, both of whom posit the primacy of desire and its destructive effects when it is oriented, as it naturally tends to be, towards the possession of particular beings and thereby leads human beings into mortal competition.

With Freud, it is in the theory of sublimation that we see most clearly how the relation between the particular and the general underlying the Platonic model of eros is constructed. If we set aside the biological bias that grounds desire in sexuality – conceived as an instinct – for Freud (Sulloway 1979), at the root of Freud's social theory, in addition to the postulate of the omnipotence and destructive character of desire, we find a mechanism that accounts for the deviation of desire towards other objects. In the myth to which *Totem and Taboo* is devoted (Freud 2000; here I am following Roger Bastide's summary), we know how 'free sexuality' – which is 'anti-cultural' in Freud's view because it 'pushes males towards combat and children towards incest', and this 'makes families impossible' – encounters 'the constraint of the father, a constraint that is at first wholly selfish, without any social purpose, based on pure jealousy', but that nevertheless introduces a 'first order': from then on 'there will be a control on the sexual, and the social will never be anything but the result of the clash between the libido and the external control imposed on it. Just as a ball that encounters an obstacle transforms its kinetic energy into caloric or luminous energy, the libido, encountering the control, becomes social energy.' This mechanism transforms a 'dangerous' energy, which is thus 'inhibited, displaced, deviated towards other activities' (Bastide 1947, 114–15). But the mechanism, located at the origin of the history of societies and played out over and over in every person, also initiates a passage from the particular to the general. The drive is not only deflected from the violence in which the negative reciprocity of desire would engage it, and reoriented towards the positive reciprocity of relations of solidarity, but it is also detached from the singular towards which it had tended, and redirected towards humanity in general. The same mechanism that establishes the possibility of culture is thus found again in the principle of altruism, conceived as a passage from the particular to the general, from attachment to particular beings, whose possession may be, on this basis, an object of rivalry with others, towards love of humanity in general. Freud says this very explicitly, for example, in the text devoted to the Schreber case, in which he makes an effort to untangle the aetiology of paranoia: the derivation of desire represents the contribution of 'an erotic factor to friendship and comradeship, to *esprit de corps* and to the love of mankind in general'.[10]

In Durkheimian anthropology (no doubt inspired in part by Schopenhauer [Chamboredon 1984], which would account for the homologies with Freud's political philosophy [Nisbet 1966, 82–3]), human beings are also driven by unrestrained desires. Unlike the appetites of animals, those of humans are not naturally limited by instincts, and this makes them all the more formidable: 'there is nothing within an individual which constrains these appetites' (Durkheim 1958, 199). If these appetites become 'insatiable', they can drag people into no-holds-barred competitions that exercise a destructive effect on the social bond, even when they do not degenerate into violence (here Durkheim is targeting the social constructs of the utilitarians and especially those of Spencer); thus the appetites 'must be contained by some force exterior to' the individual (ibid.). This force is supplied by the collective representations – and, in the case in point, the moral representations – that emanate from society, from the social body, from the *group* as a supra-individual agent of practical reason (and not as the mere aggregate of its members). Only groups, sites in which morality is generated, possess the authority necessary to restrain individual appetites, whose unbridled expression would bring society back to a state of disaggregation and conflict close to the state of nature; only groups can impose on each person the 'sacrifice' that allows 'private utility' to be subordinated to 'common utility'.

In this schema, as in Freud's, the existence of a social order is ensured by the possibility that desire can circulate on an axis running from the singular to the general, from the individuality of personal appetites for singular objects to the generality of collective representations placed above the private satisfaction of those appetites and reassimilated by persons in the form of external, constraining laws.[11] In fact, the same energy that animates human desires, invested in the same persons but in a derivative and transmuted form, externalized as collective representations and reinternalized as moral values, is what ensures the control of appetites in each person. If the authority of the collective body is to be effective, each individual must experience it internally, even bodily. Solidarity, to be effective, thus presupposes a double movement. Externalization towards the collective consciousness must be accompanied by a movement of reinternalization in order for society to be able to offer resistance to the destructive anarchy of desire. Individual persons, even taken separately and in isolation, can be in accord with morality, because they have internalized the collective representations. It is this dual movement of externalization and internalization that ensures the orientation of individual activities towards 'solidarity'. Thus, with Durkheim as with Freud, it is when a brake is applied to the private desires of private persons that individuals can contribute to the common good, to the collective interest at its most general. Destructive 'egoism' is thus replaced by 'altruism', a name attributed in Durkheim's schema to love, in the sense of love in general for humanity: socialized love.[12]

11.4 Agape and the withdrawal of equivalence

Both philia and eros are in a relation of complicity with justice, since both require some pre-established notion of general equivalence that will allow the parties involved to evaluate the merits of the beloved object, whether by making a calculation of reciprocity or by rising above their disparate sensations to the principle underlying them. The features I have identified in these two forms of love will allow us to pinpoint, in contrast, the properties of agape that interest anthropology. Agape is a term whose reference is initially theological, since it designates in the first place the love of God for men, love that is a free gift, and consequently a relation directed from above to below rather than from below to above, as with love for God in celestial eros (Feuillet 1972, 192–3). However, the term is also used to designate 'love towards God' and, finally, love for other human persons; this latter form is defined as 'neighbourly' (Nygren 1953, 123, 127). It is in this last sense that agape is most directly relevant to my research. The fact remains that, from a theological standpoint, these three dimensions are inseparable. In fact, as Édouard Cothenet shows (1988), agape takes the place of the divine *Pneuma* – the principle of cohesion of the cosmic order for the Stoics – and realizes the world's 'aspiration' towards 'unity'. But for 'the depersonalizing unity of the Great Whole' it substitutes 'the unity of love willed by a personal God'. Agape is thereby 'the structure of the redeemed world'. For God's love makes its presence known in the teaching of love for one's neighbour, which is in turn a manifestation of love for God. In Christian – and especially Pauline – theology, the *mediation* between the different meanings of agape is assured by the Church, defined as a 'mystical body', as 'mother', and especially as 'bride'. As an institution, the Church is, as Hans Urs von Balthasar puts it, 'the condition of presence' (1980, 244–9). It is through the Church that God's agape is revealed to the 'community', whose 'bond of charity' then maintains cohesion, and it is in the Church that agape is embodied, likened, in a thematics borrowed from Hosea and Isaiah, to the faithfulness of bride to groom (Cothenet 1988, 240–5). But agape among men and women is not limited to the ecclesiastic community. It is called to manifest itself in the presence of any person at all, no matter how that person may be qualified in other respects. This is the sense in which the notion is available to anthropology.

An initial property of agape requires particular attention. Agape is built entirely on the notion of gift. Unlike eros, it does not rise up towards what is higher, and it does not contain the idea of desire. Agape is independent not only of the desire to possess that dominates terrestrial eros, but also of the desire to transcend that orients celestial eros.[13] The awakening of eros depends fundamentally on the value of its object, since according to Plato it is directed primarily towards 'beautiful bodies' (although it can detach itself from these and move up to the principle of all beauty). In contrast, agape does not depend on the value of its object: not owing to ascetic detachment, but because it is unable to recognize value. The question of the value of the object to which it is addressed does not even arise: value has no pertinence for agape. The gratuitousness of this form of love is qualified by its indifference to merit.

Agape is nevertheless not indifferent to persons, in their concrete, singular aspects. It is not caught up, as eros is, either in the dilemma of bad love, which is directed towards particular objects but with a goal of possession capable of arousing desire and provoking violence, or in the dilemma of good love, which attaches itself to essences, but at the price of detachment with respect to embodied objects. Just as it does not know desire, agape is unacquainted with ideas detached from the senses; it does not recognize pure ideas. Thus it has nothing in common with love of the idea of humanity, love of humanity in general as expressed in the altruism that characterized the secularized religions of the nineteenth century. To be sure, agape has no preferences and knows no favouritism. But if it does not recognize 'the respect of persons', this is not owing to concern for equity, for giving everyone what is due him or her, as in Aquinas's version, which is already a compromise with the juridical (Aquinas 1947, 2: 1462–5 [Part 2, section 2, question 63]). Agape can be active only when it is aroused by the presence of unique persons, but the persons to whom it is addressed are the ones it happens to encounter along its way, those whose gaze it returns. Thus the notion of agape does not contain – as Jean Brun notes in his introduction to Søren Kierkegaard's book on love (to which I shall return at greater length) – the idea of an 'imperative born from the universalization of a law . . . and does not address itself to man in general but to its neighbour'. This is also why the same work 'contains an implicit – and sometimes explicit – critique of humanisms like Feuerbach's for which . . . solidarity constitutes the foundation of a rational social ethics' (Brun 1980, xv, xvii).[14]

The way 'neighbours' are construed in the theory of agape also breaks with the classical notions of proximity associated either with natural, instinctive love comparable to that of animals for their offspring or with the familiarity characteristic of philia. With agape, neighbours are detached from 'any relation of family, friendship, or nationality' (Spicq 1958, 1: 186).[15] But, compared to philia, the notion of agape reveals still other no less remarkable properties. In fact, in contrast with philia, based on the notion of reciprocity (one of the fundamental concepts in modern social science, especially in anthropology),[16] agape as a gift expects nothing in return, either in the material form of objects or in the immaterial form of requited love. The gift of agape has nothing to do with counter-gifts. For a person in a state of agape, what is received cannot be related to what he or she has given at an earlier moment. In this sense, unlike philia, agape is not based on an interactionist schema. Actors in a state of agape do not model their behaviour on the way they think others will respond to their acts. They do not incorporate in their own acts the anticipated response of the person or persons to whom they are addressing themselves, and thus, in defiance of all modern theories of action, whether they stem from psychology, sociology or economics, they do not envisage the relation to others in the form of a sequence of strikes and counter-strikes.

This property of detachment is clearly associated, first and foremost, with the absence of general equivalence. The refusal of equivalence is the first feature that distances agape from philia as well as from eros. Not required to be proportional to the merit of its object, agape has no need to fall back on a standard of value. In this respect it is distinct from justice, which Aristotle defines by a 'kind of equality', the 'adequate measure' of which is a 'just proportion' between 'the quantity of things distributed and the various qualities of persons'; as we have seen, this presupposes a higher-level principle of equivalence on which to base judgement (Villey 1983, 50–1). But recourse to an equivalent, no matter how summarial, is also what undergirds the theory of reciprocity as a whole. For a counter-gift to have some common measure with a gift, even and especially if – as the anthropological conception of the relation between gift and counter-gift would have it – the exchange is deferred in time and accomplished by means of different objects, the persons involved have to be able to call on some instrumentation in order to make connections, however approximate, among the offerings that compose the sequence.

In the classical theory of agape, the refusal of equivalence is governed by the relation to law, and more particularly by the opposition between the *old law* and the *new law*. Here, the old law – the law revealed in the form of a code that includes a set of rules – symbolizes the externality of equivalence with respect to persons. By its very structure, a system of law implies the possibility of moving up towards a principle of equivalence that establishes justice, and this is how it can be applied to disputes among persons who disagree about their worth, who assess one another, and who, when they recognize the law, find in it a common measure. In the presence of the law, the work of a judge, learned in the law, consists essentially in bringing together in a just way the general law and the particular case presented; the judge interprets the code in order to derive from the law a response appropriate to the case. This interpretation, to be valid, has to be justifiable – that is, presented in the form of arguments linked together in a discourse whose coherence establishes proof. This indispensable recourse to language is what situates judges among the learned.

Unlike the old law, the new law has agape at its core, and most of its features express a denunciation of legalism. The opposition between the two systems has less to do with content than with form, with ways of holding in reserve, means of access, and procedures for putting into practice. This is the sense in which the new law can say that it has come not to abolish the old law but to accomplish it.[17] The two legal systems are opposed as exteriority is opposed to interiority. The old law, inscribed in a code, engraved on tablets locked up in a temple, is replaced by the new law, inscribed in the heart, internalized and thus disengaged from all formalism.[18] The validity of the acts in which the new law is carried out no longer depends on a judgement passed by a third party who is competent with respect to the code and who has the authority to establish the relation between the acts and the rule; it depends rather on the intentionality of the person who acts. As a

113

consequence, practices in keeping with the law no longer need to be visible. It is better to perform them in private than in public, and it is precisely this detachment with respect to the judgement of a third party that liberates these practices from formalism. For formalism is inscribed in an expressive economy. Formalism makes it easier to confront acts with rules, and thus easier for others to assess the validity of the acts. In the absence of judgement, formalism is useless. Now, the new law rests on the refusal of judgement. It deprives human beings of their ability to judge. This fundamental property is obviously associated with the new relation that Revelation institutes between man and God. But the supernatural foundation can be bracketed here. For if the new law cannot do without the eschatology of judgement, the fact remains that the expectation of parousia, or the second coming, does not modify the modalities of the relationships among human beings that it prescribes for the present. And what it prescribes in the first place is the impossibility of judging, and thus the uselessness of prescribing. St Paul marked his opposition to legalism in concise terms: 'there are no forbidden things' (1 Corinthians 10: 23). In the absence of judgement, equivalence, which is the foundation of justice, is useless. It is in this sense that the new law, the law of love, can be said to have come to 'abolish justice' (Nygren 1953, 70–1).

11.5 The insouciance of agape

Because it is not acquainted with equivalence, agape is also unacquainted with calculation. If it is ill-equipped to establish a relation of worth among the beings in presence, it is no better able to calculate for the long run, and its capacity to establish equivalence in diachrony is still worse than its ability to do so in synchrony. Beings under the law of agape do not accumulate 'more than for the present day' and they do not 'take thought for the morrow', in keeping with the Jewish parable of the manna, a free gift that is the 'bread of life' when everyone takes some according to daily need, and the germ of destruction when it is 'hoarded', for it will spoil (Di Sante 1991, 142–5.) In short, agape does not come equipped with temporal space for calculation, and this is why it is often said to be without limits. This inaptitude for calculation, which, combined with a weak ability to look ahead, inhibits the expectation of any return, also suppresses debt. Persons in the state of agape neither hold onto things nor expect things. They remember neither offences to which they have been subjected nor good works they have accomplished, and, along with the ability to give freely, the ability to pardon is quite rightly the property most often associated with the notion of agape. Hannah Arendt thus makes forgiveness an indispensable ability for the conduct of human affairs, because it alone offers, along with 'punishment', the possibility of 'freedom from vengeance', of putting an end to a process that 'by itself need never come to an end' (Arendt 1958, 240–1). In other words, forgiveness brings closure to disputes that could only be stopped by dissimulation if they were pursued in violence or even in justice, because they do not incorporate their own solutions. Without the intervention of a radically foreign resource, a dispute cannot come to an end, and this is why, as we have seen, justice is only barely able to turn a dispute away from violence, to channel it by engaging it in the path appropriate to it; justice cannot produce peace (ibid., 236–43). And the idea of forgiveness may be too strong to be applied to all the cases that concern us, because it seems to suggest that the debt has been retained before being cancelled. Indeed, forgiveness implies the intention to forget which, conferring a mental presence on what one would like to wipe out, possesses a self-destructive character, as Jon Elster has shown (Elster 1981, 436–8). Now, agape does not so much insist that trespasses must be forgiven as that they must be dismissed, in order to allow 'life to go on', in Arendt's apt phrase (Arendt 1958, 240). It is the letting-go, the release – in short, the capacity to forget – that characterizes agape's relation to past offences. Good and bad deeds alike are cancelled because there is nothing to retain them, no instrumentation to calculate them and install them in memory.[19] But this capacity itself is only the result of applying to a particular set of objects – misdeeds, 'trespasses' – the more general property that defines the relation that persons maintain with time when they are immersed in this sort of love. In opposition to the order of justice, but also unlike eros, agape has an original temporal orientation. Justice gives itself a space of calculation oriented towards the past, since our actions must have been carried out in order to be judged, with misdeeds and good deeds retained and accumulated before being weighed and calculated in a necessarily retrospective judgement; eros, fully given over to the incompleteness of its desire, that 'spirit of adventure which rises from the body to willing' (Ricoeur 1966, 265), turns towards the always deferred moment of accomplishment – that is, towards the future. Agape, in contrast, remains stubbornly grounded in the present (Latour 1988a). Opting for the present is what finally ensures coherence among the main properties that define agape. But the present is not, or not only, the here and now starting from which past and future may be conceptualized negatively.

115

The present of agape is temporalized on the basis of the past, as a memorial of the Revelation, and on the basis of the future as an eschatological announcement of the Kingdom. In this sense, present time is itself a manifestation of agape, a 'gift given', which 'is governed by the memorial and *epektasis*', or constant progress (Marion 1982, 175; more generally 169–76).

11.6 Duration and permanence

To grasp the temporal dimension of agape and see how it is connected with the other faculties of persons in this state, let us turn to Søren Kierkegaard, whose book *Works of Love* (1995) constitutes a highly systematic attempt to set forth the properties of agape and integrate them into a coherent model. Studying this work will also allow us to identify other properties of agape, properties of interest to anthropology that have not been particularly emphasized in theological writings.

Kierkegaard, seeking to construct an anthropology based on love, re-examines the principal properties of agape as it has traditionally been defined. He critiques the notion of reciprocity inherent in philia ('if a person really has love people will then also love him' [Kierkegaard 1995, 120]). This notion reduces love to barter, he says, 'just as in the commercial world' (ibid., 237): love becomes a transaction. But Kierkegaard also differentiates agape from eros, which has an elective preference for beauty and which leaves the world behind when it moves up to the abstract generality of ideas. The object of agape, according to Kierkegaard, is 'the person one sees': 'to love is to love precisely the person one sees. The emphasis is not on loving the perfections one sees in a person, but . . . on loving the person one sees, whether one sees perfections or imperfections in this person, yes, however distressingly this person has changed, inasmuch as he has not ceased to be the same person' (ibid., 173). The way agape bears on the being who is seen is opposed to the 'pure thought' of 'pure persons', and on this basis it constitutes a token of realism: 'When it is a duty in loving to love the people we see, *then in loving the actual individual person it is important that one does not substitute an imaginary idea of how we think or could wish that this person should be.* The one who does this does not love the person he sees but again something unseen, his own idea or something similar' (ibid., 164).

However, in *Works of Love* Kierkegaard places particular emphasis on the opposition between love and justice, insisting especially, on the one hand, on the opposition between the externality of law and the internality of love and, on the other, on the tension between the legalism of rules and the immanence of practice; finally, he stresses the mortal risks that comparison and calculation impose on love – that is, the impossibility of establishing equivalence in love. The latter theme comes up again and again in his work, with regard to jealousy first of all. Jealousy, which leads 'from the greatest happiness' to 'the greatest torment' (Kierkegaard 1995, 35), has 'comparison' at its root. It posits 'proportions' and enters into a 'calculation'. 'Jealousy loves as it is loved. Anxious and tortured by the thought of whether it is loved, it is just as jealous of its own love, whether it is not disproportionate in relation to the other's indifference, as it is jealous of the manifestation of the other's love . . . It is comparable to spontaneous combustion' (ibid.). In contrast, love in agape, 'simple love', is exempt from trials and immune to jealousy, because 'it does not love by way of comparison' (ibid., 36). Persons in the state of love must work incessantly to remove from their mental environment everything that could put them in the presence of equivalence. In order to 'be kept alive', love has to be maintained in the 'immeasurability' which is its 'element' (ibid., 180). In the 'incommensurable', according to Kierkegaard, 'reciprocity is infinite on both sides': 'In the one case, it is the beloved, who in every manifestation of the lover's love lovingly apprehends the immeasurability; in the other, it is the lover, who feels the immeasurability because he acknowledges the debt to be infinite' (ibid., 181). Thus a person who is in a state of love must see the immeasurability in every manifestation of the other. But this activity does not imply any calculation. For

> if this is so, it does indeed express that an actual bookkeeping arrangement is inconceivable, is the greatest abomination to love. An accounting can take place only where there is a finite relationship, because the relation of the finite to the finite can be calculated. But one who loves cannot calculate. When the left hand never finds out what the right hand is doing, it is impossible to make an accounting, and likewise when the debt is infinite. To calculate with an infinite quantity is impossible, because to calculate is to make finite. (Ibid., 178)

This is why love, beyond the fact that it excludes calculations of interest and 'bargaining, compromising, partisan agreement' (ibid., 100), can be said to be 'limitless' (ibid., 105): *there is no limit to love; if the duty is to be fulfilled, love must be limitless, it is unchanged, no matter how the object becomes changed'* (ibid., 167).

For Kierkegaard, renouncing equivalence is what keeps love

immune from despair. In fact, in his construct, the refusal of equivalence is associated with the inhibition of expectations. When love is agape, knowing 'whether [one] will continue to love or not' does not depend 'on whether the other will love'; only in this way can love be protected from despair (Kierkegaard 1995, 39). 'The inwardness of love must be . . . without the requirement of any reward': the absence of expectation is what separates agape from the ordinary reciprocity expected by someone who 'only wants to be loved' in return (ibid., 130–1). This is the sense in which Kierkegaard interprets the injunction to give to the poor rather than to the rich; we are to grant priority to those who, unable to give anything in return, do not threaten to shift the relationship into a cycle of gifts and counter-gifts.

To escape from equivalence and protect itself against comparison, love has to submit to a fundamental constraint, namely, never to look back at itself. In self-reference, love is undone: *'there must be eternal vigilance, early and late, so that love never begins to dwell on itself, or to compare itself with love in other people, or to compare itself with the deeds that it has accomplished'* (Kierkegaard 1995, 179). It is this constraint that confers on love its eminently practical character. Love is commitment to 'immediate action': the injunction that guides it is 'Go and do likewise' (ibid., 46); it 'imprisons' the individual in the task (ibid., 97), and this is how it distinguishes itself, among other things, from a 'promise', which 'is deceptively like a beginning yet without being that' (ibid., 98). It is also in this sense that love is 'the downfall of the Law' as such, which it annuls by substituting 'fulfilment' for 'requirement' (ibid., 99). The Law, *'despite all its many provisions . . . is still somewhat indefinite'* (ibid., 104). 'The concept of the Law', Kierkegaard adds,

> is to be inexhaustible, limitless, endless in its provisions; every provision begets of itself an even more precise provision, and in turn a still more precise provision by reference and in relation to the new provision, and so on infinitely. . . . The Law starves out, as it were; with its help one never reaches fulfilment, since its purpose is to take away, to require, to exact to the utmost, and in the continually remaining indefiniteness in the multiplicity of all its provisions is the inexorable exaction of the requirements. (Ibid., 105)

Without access to self-reference, love is unacquainted with 'curiosity', and it remains without answers in the face of questions. It does not respond to language with language, and this is why 'justification' is foreign to it. The interplay of questions and answers engenders only 'quarrels and evasions', to which love opposes the authority of the act, for the defining feature of authority is to 'press the task' (Kierkegaard 1995, 96–7). Only practice puts an end to explanation by uniting it with being: it is 'only when the explanation *is* what it explains, when the explainer *is* what is explained . . . only then is the relation the right one' (ibid., 101).

The constraint that limits self-reference is closely connected with the refusal of equivalence through the intermediary of time. The necessity of setting equivalence aside in order to remain in the state of love also applies to temporal equivalence. This is why love's refusal of equivalence, its inability to engage in self-reference, its realization in the practical mode and its preference for the present are structurally interrelated. Everything else derives from this basic structure. Thus the preference for the present is what maintains commitment in the practical mode and forbids self-reference. In fact, self-consideration presupposes the availability of duration. To consider oneself, one has to linger, take one's distance, look back or look ahead; in short, one has to situate oneself in a temporal space treated as a space for calculation. Kierkegaard addresses the relation between commitment, practice and duration in his analysis of 'busyness'. To be busy is to be not completely present to the task, thus to be not entirely present to the *present*. 'To be busy is to occupy oneself, divided and scattered (which follows from the object that occupies one), with all the multiplicity in which it is simply impossible for a person to be whole, whole in all of it or whole in any particular part of it, something only the insane can succeed in doing. To be busy is, divided and scattered, to occupy oneself with what makes a person divided and scattered.' Conversely, love is 'whole and collected, present in its every expression' (Kierkegaard 1995, 98).

The temporal analysis of agape culminates in the opposition to duration and permanence. Duration inscribes the action on the horizon of a time that is being completed. It is this finite horizon that calls for expectations and renders them problematic. In contrast, plunged into permanence, action is at every moment present to itself. In this way, Kierkegaard says, it is protected from tests. What 'undergoes its test' manifests its capacity to endure. But 'testing is always related to possibility; it is always possible that what is being tested would not stand the test' (Kierkegaard 1995, 33). Conversely, 'the enduring continuance of the enduring will not and *cannot* manifest itself in standing a test':

it is not self-evident that what exists at this moment will also exist at the next moment, but it is self-evident that the enduring exists. We say

119

that something stands the test and praise it when it has stood the test. But this is said of something imperfect, because the enduring continuance of the enduring will not and *cannot* manifest itself in standing a test – it is, after all, the enduring, and only the transient can give itself the appearance of enduring continuance by standing a test. (Ibid., 32)

Installed in enduring continuance – that is, always reinstalled in the present – love is protected from 'anxiety' because it can neither calculate – since the temporal horizon has no limits – nor consider whether it might change. The question of change would require both sensitivity to the responses of the object to which it is addressed and a relation of self-reference that would allow it to appreciate its own change – that is, to compare its present state in love to a previous state. Both of these operations are excluded from the model, as we have seen.

11.7 The example of *Little Flowers*

To look at love in a different light and pursue this provisional characterization of agape along different paths, let us now consider some passages excerpted from an anonymous collection of anecdotes in the Tuscan dialect dating from the second half of the fourteenth century, the outcome of a long process of selection, translation and compilation. The text we know as *Little Flowers of St Francis of Assisi* (Anonymous 1965), inspired by the *Actus beati Francisci et sociorum eius*, was produced in the situation of conflict that arose after St Francis's death between the community, concerned with discipline, and the Spirituals who drew on Francis's sparse writings, especially his 'Testament' (Lambert 1977, 183), to take the Franciscan precepts of charity and poverty to an extreme, critiquing the transformations that had affected the order (the valorization of knowledge, the acceptance of positions of authority in the Church, ownership of real property and material goods, and so on). As Ivan Gobry remarks in his introduction to the French translation, *Little Flowers* expresses the Spirituals' viewpoint, and thus constitutes 'a work with a thesis', written by 'members of a party, to defend a doctrine' (Gobry 1962, 13). The band of vagabonds whose adventures are related in *Little Flowers* had no money or property of any kind and no defined occupations; they lived on alms, among lepers, animals, the poor and the wealthy, uniquely guided by brotherly love; the sometimes extreme fantasy that permeates these narratives – and that accounts in part for their appeal – stems precisely from the principle that all demands other than those of love are to be treated as contingent. The partiality of this collection of stories, its edifying aim and its systematic privileging of love make it a precious source for identifying the features most durably attached to the description of agape. Of the fifty-three anecdotes in the collection, many of which are subdivided into several stories, we shall look at just a few examples that directly illustrate our topic.

Francis is always in the state of agape, as are his companions, most of the time, and also, though less consistently, a significant number of the many individuals with whom they interact during their wanderings. Unaware of their own desires, they are oriented towards the needs of those they meet, preoccupied with a concern to satisfy them and thus always ready to give. This permanent disposition is never presented in a general sense. In each anecdote it is manifested by singular beings (usually people, but sometimes also animals) that are encountered in particular conditions, meticulously set forth in the text, during the random course of the vagabond life of these 'ragged gypsies', as Gobry calls them. The great diversity of people who cross their path – paupers, nobles, peasants, thieves, kings – is not organized in a series; it is there precisely to bring out the requirements of the situations that bring them into presence. The companions' availability to give is indifferent to the value and merits of those they meet. It is offered to the generous gentleman who feeds Francis and washes his feet (chapter 37), but also, for example, to the malefactor, caught in the act, 'who had been condemned to have both eyes torn out' and whose punishment the young man from San Severino tried to lighten by going 'boldly to find the rector in the middle of a meeting' to ask 'that one of his own eyes be taken, and another from the criminal, so that the latter would not be deprived of both' (chapter 41). The sun, which is usually associated with the symbolics of equality, for it shines on everyone, here also expresses the gratuitousness that allows sun to shine and rain to fall 'on the just and on the unjust' alike, out of courtesy (chapter 37). In the state of agape, the brothers do not judge. Thus Francis avoids spending much time with brother Bernard, who has made him promise to take him in hand and to correct him, 'fearing lest, out of holy obedience, he might be obliged to reprove him' (chapter 3). In this state, calculation is also foreign to their nature. Before the avaricious Silvester (later one of the brothers), who believes Francis to be wealthy because he gives to the poor and thus demands more and more money for the stones he has sold him, Francis, not being in a regime of justice, was 'surprised at such a demand, but . . . not wishing to dispute with him, gave it to Silvester, saying that, if he wanted more, he would give it to him' (chapter 2). It is this refusal to calculate that leads to the choice of poverty. If praise of poverty, of *pauperes* and *illiterati* (Le Goff 1973), is indeed a constant in *Little Flowers*, poverty is nevertheless not loved for itself and is not desired only as a manifestation of asceticism. Brother Elias was wrong to desire 'that none of the brethren should eat flesh' (chapter 4). There is much discussion of food in these stories, and certain descriptions of the 'good things' to eat that come to the brothers, 'carts laden with bread and wine, with beans and cheese' (chapter 18), the 'supper composed of the choicest meats' set up next to a 'great fire' that a nobleman offers Francis (chapter 37), often make one's mouth water. The preference for shedding possessions is the result of suspicion, not towards work,[20] but towards industry, because the achievements of industry depend on a relation to time based on sacrifice of the present and investment in the future; industry requires foresight to give itself a horizon on the basis of which calculation is possible. The copious abundance of 'good things', an object of praise and gratitude, is all the more valuable in that it owes nothing to industry. In the company of brother Masseo, Francis begs for bread among people who, not being entirely in a state of love, give to each according to his merits as revealed by appearances. Francis receives only 'a few bits of dry bread', because he was 'a little man, with a mean exterior' and therefore 'did not attract much attention'; he was taken for a poor wretch by those who did not know him. Brother Masseo, on the contrary, 'being tall and good-looking, received many large pieces of bread, with several whole loaves'.

> When they had ended their task of begging, they met on a spot outside the city where there was a beautiful fountain and a large stone, on which each placed what he had collected. St Francis, seeing that the pieces of bread which Brother M[a]sseo had collected were much larger and better than those he had received, rejoiced greatly, and said: 'O Brother Masseo, we are not worthy of this great treasure'; and he repeated these words several times. At this Brother Masseo answered: 'Father, how canst thou talk of a treasure where there is so much poverty, and indeed a lack of all things? For we have neither cloth, nor knife, nor dish, nor table, nor house to eat in, nor servant or maid to wait upon us.' St Francis answered: 'This is indeed the reason why I account it a great treasure, because man has had [no] hand in it.' (Chapter 13)

The abundance of 'good things' is given to those who produce it by the conversion of the gaze that allows them to see the begged-for bread, the 'beautiful fountain' and the 'large stone' table (chapter 13). Agape, entirely in the present, receives everything from the lack of foresight. People who are in the state of agape, like birds that are fed though they 'neither sow nor reap' (chapter 16), owe their existence to gifts they do not expect. They live 'only by means of what nature or men voluntarily donate' to them (Weber 1978, 547). Francis commands his listeners 'to take no thought what you shall eat or what you shall drink'. St Dominic, 'who was present, wondered much at this order of St Francis, considering it as indiscreet, for he could not understand how such a great multitude could exist without taking thought for the body.' But 'presently', people arrived 'from all the neighbouring country', from Perugia, Spoleto, Foligno, Spello, Assisi, 'with horses, and asses, and carts laden with . . . good things [to eat] of which the poor . . . had need'; and 'those who could carry most and serve the best rejoiced greatly, and the knights, barons, and other noblemen, who were present, waited on the brethren with great devotion and humility' (chapter 18). To those who do not recognize their own desires, goods arrive only through gifts.

But why do others respond to gifts with gifts? The question takes different forms according to the initial state of the persons involved, so that the brothers' behaviour is somewhat different depending on whether they are together, equals in love, or whether they are dealing with other persons who are in different states, usually desire or violence. Among themselves, since all are in a state of agape, each reaches out of his own accord to meet the needs of the others. Brother Masseo is the doorman. He has 'the office of porter, of almoner and of cook'. But 'his companions . . . began to feel in their hearts great remorse, considering . . . how all the work of the convent fell to his share, and none to theirs.' With all in agape, their actions are coordinated by their coexistence in the same state: moved by the same will, 'then went they all to St Francis, begging him to divide among them those charges, since they could not in conscience allow Brother Masseo to bear all the burden of the convent' (chapter 12).

In the face of desire that demands – or, in a different way, in the face of violence, which is often treated as the consequence of a desire that is impossible to satisfy – the brothers act by offering no resistance and thus no toehold for demands. One of the most striking features of their behaviour is their complete passivity in the face of the often exorbitant desires of people outside their community with whom they come into contact. They satisfy demands and give to the extent of their means. A raging leper, caught up in his own unhappiness, tries the brothers' patience. St Francis replies:

'My son, I myself will serve thee, seeing thou art not satisfied with the others.' 'Willingly', answered the leper; 'but what canst thou do more than they have done?' 'Whatsoever thou wishest I will do for thee', answered St Francis. 'I will then', said he, 'that thou wash me all over; for I am so disgusting that I cannot bear myself.' Then St Francis heated some water, putting therein many odoriferous herbs; he then undressed him, and began to wash him with his own hands, whilst another brother threw the water upon him. (Chapter 25)

Passivity in giving exhausts desire, and recipients in turn shift into love. This is the case with the murderous thieves, to whom Francis gave 'a sack of bread and a little vessel of wine' that he had just received by begging (chapter 26), or the wolf of Gubbio, which had been terrorizing the region. Francis brings them peace by recognizing their desire. He acknowledges the hunger of the wolf, which, fed 'courteously' every day by the inhabitants, lived with them in peace; when the wolf 'died of old age . . . the people of Gubbio mourned his loss greatly' (chapter 21). Similarly, passivity is the response to violence. But the operator here is patience, which does not recognize violence as such. Brother Bernard

set out for Bologna; but when he arrived in that city, the little children in the streets, seeing him dressed so strangely and so poorly, laughed and scoffed at him, taking him for a madman. All these trials Brother Bernard accepted . . . with great patience and with great joy, and . . . having seated himself [in the marketplace], a great number of children and men gathered round him, and taking hold of his hood pushed him here and there, some throwing stones at him and others dust. To all this Brother Bernard submitted in silence, his countenance bearing an expression of holy joy,

uncomplaining and untroubled (chapter 5).[21] Constancy in the state of love in fact presupposes a non-response. The relation is not interactive, since one party is acting, the other not. Similarly, dialogues often do not communicate, as in the long exchange between Francis, who calls for reproof, and Leo, who does not know how to avoid praising (chapter 9). For – and this is a constant in *Little Flowers* – love does not hold any discourse about itself, as when 'St Louis, king of France, went in person in a pilgrim's garb to visit the holy brother Giles in Perugia':

They both knelt down and embraced each other with great reverence and many outward signs of love and charity, as if a long friendship had existed between them, though they had never met before in their lives. Neither of them spoke a word; and after remaining clasped in

124

each other's arms for some time, they separated in silence, St Louis to continue his journey, and Brother Giles to return to his cell.

And to his brothers' questions, Giles replied: 'If we had explained in words that which we felt in our hearts ... words would have been to us rather a hindrance than a consolation', so imperfect is human language (chapter 34).

11.8 Parable and metaphor

The imperfection of human language in the regime of agape (Latour 1988a) has to do with the constraints surrounding the self-referential activity that is necessary to narrative. In the regime of agape, as we have seen, we cannot construct a theory of love, since the effort to theorize implies the adoption of a general viewpoint that brings with it the space of comparison between people and, over time, shifts the situation out of love. The tension between engagement in love and thematization of love constitutes the central problem of the parabolic relation. For critics, parables – expressions by way of enigmas – pose a problem that has long been subject to controversy. Most parables (and all those we are considering here) are presented in effect as 'plots' (Ricoeur 1975) that include 'implausible' features (Fusco 1989, 51) or, to use another of Ricoeur's terms, 'extravagances' (1975). In the etymological sense, a parable establishes a parallel (Léon-Dufour 1975, 406); thus it has the distinctive feature of including two references. The narrative initially proposed for attention, which includes its own reference, then leads to 'a second-level reference' (Zumstein 1989). These disconcerting tales are thus modelled on a typical form. The first part of the narrative presents a story of daily life; the second part gives the story a paradoxical conclusion.

The tension inherent in this duality is the focal point for a new approach to parables, born of the 'post-Bultmanian problematics' (Fusco 1989, 31), which turns away from historical interpretation (Dodd 1961; Jeremias 1963)[22] and takes as its object of predilection the 'fissure' that puts reality 'in crisis' (Marguerat 1989, 71). Today, these interpretations rely especially on the theory of metaphor, particularly in the form that Paul Ricoeur (1977b) gave it and that Ricoeur (1975) himself applied to the parable texts. Critiquing the formal analyses inspired by structuralism, Ricoeur saw parables as products of the conjunction between a metaphoric form and a narrative process. In fact, the parables make reference to something other, something that does not figure explicitly in the narrative and that thus cannot be reached if the parable is treated as a self-contained whole in keeping with structuralist methods. How, then, we may well wonder, does the narrative on its own trigger the interpretative process that transforms it into a parable? The modern theory of metaphor (Ricoeur 1975) solves this problem in part by positing that metaphoric utterances are based on an internal tension that is resolved by means of a semantic innovation and that includes the power to 'redescribe' reality.[23] Thus a metaphor, which for the old rhetoric was merely the replacement of the usual term by a different one, is treated in its modern conception as a 'phenomenon of tension capable of releasing new meanings.[24] The unexpected juxtaposition of two different realities, of two lexemes belonging to ordinarily distinct semantic fields ... provokes an almost visual superimposition that makes us see things in a new light' (Fusco 1989, 33). Metaphors thus account for the 'productive' character of narratives that call for interpretation. Parables apply the metaphoric process to a narrative form. They can be described as 'extended metaphors' (ibid., 35). The metaphoric tension thus has to be identified in the plot itself.[25] Now, as we have seen, the striking feature of the plot is the contrast between the realism of the anecdote, stressed by the historical school, and what Ricoeur calls the 'extravagance' of the dénouement: 'The *extraordinary in the ordinary*: this is what strikes me in the dénouement of the parables' (Ricoeur 1975, 115). The 'metaphoric tension of the parable results from the shock produced between two conceptions of reality: an initial conception that stems from the ordinary and the everyday comes into tension with an extraordinary conception'; it is 'in this double distortion ... that the meaning of the parable is presented' (Zumstein 1989, 97–9). The tension that puts 'ordinary reality' in 'crisis' brings something new to language, something that could be expressed in no other way; it institutes a surplus in the order of language (ibid., 97). The tension created in a narrative by an extended metaphor thus makes it possible to constitute a meaning that could not have been directly attained in discursive language. The tension created by this contrast gives rise to reference to objects that are not included in the story itself, objects that Ricoeur defines (by analogy with Karl Jaspers's concept of 'limit situation') as 'limit-experiences'. They can be revealed only by means of the limit form of expression known as a parable.[26]

To be completely pertinent in the analytic framework outlined here, the application of the theory of metaphor to parabolic discourse has to qualify with more precision the referent that is least problematic, the one addressed to the world in its most ordinary aspects. We are told that the first part of a parable narrative, the part that appeals to 'common sense', is 'realistic' (Zumstein 1989, 89). It stems from the 'narrative framework of everyday life' (Marguerat 1989, 70), from 'the ordinary and the everyday' (Zumstein 1989, 98); as the work of the historical school has emphasized, it is rooted in dailiness and more precisely in first-century rural Palestinian society. But the interpreters do not put enough stress, in my view, on the nature of the everyday problems that are presented as crises. In a significant number of cases ('The Prodigal Son', 'The Vineyard Workers', and so on), these problems entail classic issues of justice – that is, of equitable distribution – where the relative worth of persons is taken into account. It is in relation to justice that the paradoxical character of the response is established. In fact, the solution provided does not take into account the principle of equivalence that is clearly deployed in the premises, one that could be associated with different forms of worth (for example, fidelity to the ancestral line in the case of the Prodigal Son, the usefulness of work in the case of the Vineyard Workers), so that the signification drawn from the metaphoric tension refers directly, at least in a large number of cases, to the opposition between the regime of justice and that which, abolishing the regime of justice, belongs to agape.[27]

Agape is hard to formulate in discursive language because it cannot be simultaneously described in words and engaged in practice in relationships. The parables, as we know, are not theoretical discourses in a position of metalanguage with respect to the situations in which they are uttered. The texts in which they appear offer a written record of acts, and it is accurate to say, with J. D. Crossan, that a parable can be expressed in gestures as well as in verbal narratives.[28] Parable narratives must also be related, as the historical interpretation would have it, to the concrete situation confronting the speaker (Jeremias 1963, 131–2), taking the interlocutors present into account; as Grégoire Rouiller has shown, these narratives often constitute a *mise en abyme* of the conflictual relation involved in the situation of utterance with which it maintains a specular relation (Rouiller 1981). Thus what the extended metaphor compares, often by means of a 'proportional analogy' (Sider 1985) whose principle of comparison is not made explicit, does not seem to be without relation to the situation itself, for there are also, as Vittorio Fusco notes, 'comparisons that would seem simply absurd, meaningless' otherwise (Fusco 1989, 50). The opacity of parabolic language has to be related to the pragmatic context of the situation. Now, in the interlocutory context in which a

127

given parable is inscribed, the narrator is positioned stably in a state of agape, and what distinguishes him from the other actors is that he is not willing to acknowledge the possibility of attaining other states. Practically involved in the situation from within the state of agape and that state alone, he cannot develop the theory of agape in a discursive utterance that would presuppose the possibility of exiting from that state in order to consider it from the outside. As Ricoeur stresses, the paradox that inhabits parables and that initiates their interpretation is necessary because, in this case, irony, scepticism and even distancing are ruled out ('There is paradox . . . because the distance of irony and skepticism is excluded, and because paradox disorients only to reorient' [1975, 126]). A parable, through its extravagances, thus makes it possible to 'redescribe . . . human experience' (ibid., 127) in a way that is inaccessible to a theoretical formulation, for the latter would presuppose a critical distance that is incompatible with practical engagement. The chance that this language may be received is not zero, for the experience targeted by the paradox, one that owes its limited character in the first place to the difficulties of expression that it encounters, is also, as Ricoeur emphasizes, a human experience, of which the interlocutors can thus become aware. The parabolic narrative can make its way in the speech situation defined here by the real or potential state of the interlocutors present, who are presumed to be endowed with the capacity to recognize the signification that the extravagant comparison brings to the surface, at the price of a change of state which, inherent in the process of constructing meaning, is at once the result and the condition of possibility of that process.[29]

— 12 —

AGAPE AND THE SOCIAL SCIENCES

12.1 Agape: practical model, ideal or utopia?

The status of the theory of agape is a central problem. Is it a construction that lets us describe actions carried out by real persons, a partially achievable ideal, a utopia or a fraud? This is not just a problem raised by social scientists. It has been a problem for theologians, too, in their efforts to formulate an ethics applicable to the everyday world (on this point, see Collange 1980). Confronted by a requirement on which it was easy to rely, either to denounce the hypocrisy of those who proclaimed it without putting it into practice[1] or, conversely, to demand its radical achievement (this demand lay behind a large number of uprisings that were regularly condemned as heretical),[2] or else to denounce fraud globally: where evangelical morality was viewed merely as a tool the powerful could use to ensure the servitude of the dominated, the reasonable attitude was to treat agape as a respectable but ultimately unattainable goal. The compromise solution often found in recent works consists in relegating agape to the limits of a horizon out of reach as a regulatory model for behaviour; justice is represented as its accessible and realistic equivalent (see, for example, Schnackenburg 1965).[3] A flaw in such conceptions is that they reincorporate into agape the legalism it is structured to resist, and thus they attenuate the opposition between agape and justice by gradually effacing agape's paradoxical properties along with the perspectives opened up by the investigation of these properties.

Already troubling for theology, the question of how realistic agape may be has been resolutely set aside by the social sciences and the disciplines from which they emerged. Modern political science has been established as an autonomous field on the basis of an anthropology

129

that leaves no room for the possibility of achieving peace except through the constraint of law or force, and that virtually ignores the notions arising from the New Testament corpus; Hannah Arendt makes this point in *The Human Condition* when she examines the question of forgiveness (1958).[4] The same can be said about economics, which, if we are to believe Schumpeter, has nothing to say about texts in which people are told they 'should sell what they have and give it to the poor, or that they should lend without expecting anything (perhaps not even repayment) from it'. What we have here, Schumpeter writes, are 'ideal imperatives that form part of a general scheme of life and express this general scheme and nothing else, least of all scientific propositions' (1954, 71). But what does Schumpeter mean when he refers to ideal imperatives? Is the scientific economy not also built according to an ideal of rational choice that optimizes the dictates of interests, an ideal treated as an imperative that persons cannot evade?

Sociological approaches based on the notion of interest have similarly avoided engaging with agape. When they are directly derived from individualism as it has developed in economics, they simply ignore the tradition in which the notion of agape is inscribed, because they do not acknowledge the possibility that persons might enter into relationships in this state; when they are inspired instead by the Nietzschean critique, itself built on an inversion of Christian apologetics (Nietzsche 1968), they denounce the illusion of gratuitousness and unveil the interests hidden under the appearance of disinterestedness.[5] Once again, the possibility of gifts remains most evident in Durkheimian sociology. In his unending controversy with utilitarianism, Durkheim produced a theory of *altruism* as a *sui generis* mode of relation to others that is irreducible to the logic of interest,[6] and he developed an opposition between the inclinations that draw people towards selfishness and the altruistic inclinations that are realized in the development of morality. But altruism, for Durkheim, is directed towards the group.[7] 'Self-love' is contrasted with 'love of society' (Durkheim 1975, 263). A product of collective constraint, altruism returns in the form of social solidarity. This orientation towards the generality of the rule, the preference for the general, distinguishes Durkheim's conception from the notions whose features I am attempting to spell out here.

In the next two sections, I shall try to shed new light on the problem that concerns us by examining summarily, with a purely descriptive aim, constructs that stem from or are accredited by the social sciences and that use more familiar language to raise questions we have already encountered in the tradition from which the notion of agape arises. I shall seek to specify the kind of relations in which persons can be engaged when they are in a state of agape, by distinguishing situations in which everyone is in this state from situations in which some persons are in it and others are not. In fact, the problem of the reality of agape takes different forms according to whether it is envisaged as the only permanent state for all persons, which is the case whenever the imperative of morality is stressed, or as one state among others, in which persons can be engaged to varying degrees according to the situation. This reflection will lead me to propose hypotheses about the way persons, in their encounters, can be led to leave their initial state and shift into another. Finally, I shall describe some empirical problems to which I think this model might usefully be applied.

12.2 Marx and the theory of justice

The question of the theory of justice in Marx's writings is problematic in that Marx often exercised his polemical verve against the claim of economics, that 'most moral of sciences', that it was laying the foundations of a just society; more generally, his critique targeted the normative aims of the social sciences of his time. This has led his detractors to charge him with ethical relativism, a sin to which our contemporaries are particularly alert. The fact remains that Marx's works offer insights about justice that he does not explicitly develop as such but that are necessary if his critique of capitalist exploitation is to be fully coherent. The problem is thus the following: either one has to acknowledge a lack of consistency in Marx's positions – he criticized the supposed ideological justice of his adversaries, but he based his own critique on a concept of justice that was condemned to remain implicit – or else one has to seek to reconstruct the position on the basis of which justice can be critiqued without that critique presupposing the abandonment of all normative positions. As Guy Haarscher has shown, normative utterances of two very different types undergird Marx's work. Statements of the first type, linked to the theory of historical materialism – which claims to supply the framework for an analysis of the 'objective tendencies of reality' and thereby to support the denunciation of the hypocritical moralism of 'utopian conceptions' – concern the distribution of economic goods in capitalist society. Statements of the second type, which appear in his early works, such as *Economic and Philosophic Manuscripts of 1844* (Marx 1964), and then reappear in the texts of the final period (a fact that invalidates the hypothesis of a break), especially in *The Gotha Program* (Marx 1922), are associated with the problematics of the 'ontology of generic being' (Haarscher 1984). This duality leads Jon Elster to say, in *Making Sense of Marx* (1985), that there are two distinct theories of justice in Marx (Elster's book is probably the most successful effort to extract Marx's work from the muck in which Marxism has buried it, Engels's version included). Unlike many commentators who deny that Marx even refers to absolute values, whether they approve or condemn him for this, Elster seeks to show that Marx's work contains a specific notion of distributive justice and a specific conception of 'the good life'; according to Elster, this double normative underpinning, even though it is not explicitly developed in the construction of a political philosophy of the just polity,[8] is precisely what supports the critique of industrial society in its capitalist form. One of the difficulties has to do with Marx's indifference to the opposition between judgements of reality and normative judgements. He brings out features that 'can be developed by men' in a construct designed to describe the way the world ought to be deployed in full reality (Elster 1985, 61; see also Dumont 1977, 169–74).

The two concepts of justice that appear in Marx correspond to two critiques of the capitalist society of his time and have to be achieved in two successive historical phases. The first principle of justice supports the critique of the exploitation of labour in capitalist society, a term that designates here, and denounces, the compromise between industrial and market arrangements (*OJ* 43–61). This principle, which can be expressed as 'to each according to his contribution', presupposes, if its robustness is to be assured, the construction of a theory of labour-value (Elster 1985, 51). Inspired, as Haarscher shows, by the principle 'each according to his labour', which Adam Smith placed in the original state of relations (Haarscher 1984), it can legitimately be qualified as industrial to the extent that it establishes an equivalence between labour and social utility.[9] The first critique (the theory of capital gain) seeks to show, by relying on arguments with scientific validity, that capitalism does not fulfil this principle, which leads to its ruin. This is the principle that socialism must fulfil. The second critique, which focuses on capitalist alienation as an externalization that can no longer be recognized in the objectivized products of its activity (Haarscher 1980, 17), and which remains implicit throughout Marx's work – this is especially apparent in the early texts – is different. It is based not on a thematics of man at work, but on an anthropology of man as creator and a metaphysics of self-creating humanity. In fact, Marx's critique of alienation has meaning only in opposition to

132

the normative definition of what Elster terms the good life for man. This good life, as deducible from the critique and from a few positive remarks in *The Gotha Program*, is a life of creative activity developing in multiple directions and in which economic production, in the strict sense, is only one form among others. It can be expressed positively as a life in which 'each [receives] according to his needs'. According to this anthropology, the need that takes precedence, to the point of absorbing all others, is the need to create.[10] In this 'ontology of activity', as Haarscher puts it, activity does not represent a means adapted to certain ends; rather, it is an end in itself (Harscher 1980, 91). It is this need for creative activity that is to find the conditions for its realization in communist society: 'self-realization through creative work is the essence of Marx's communism' (Elster 1985, 521). In a communist society, all persons have equal access to the possibility of full self-realization (ibid., 524). This is what makes Elster say that Marx has a hierarchical theory of justice, since the principle of contribution is the second best criterion when the principle of need is not historically ripe enough to be applied. The principle of just compensation for contributions in fact constitutes the chief instrument for denouncing capitalist injustice. But, in fully developed capitalist society, that principle is condemned in the name of a higher principle: that of the free realization of needs – that is, of free access to self-realization through creation (ibid., 229).

The possibility of satisfying this primordial need, once the vital needs have been met, leads to a decline in the artificial desires that are developed, in the industrial-market society, by mimetic competition for the appropriation of goods. The pessimistic concept of desire that is present in Freud's anthropology, and also in Durkheim's, is foreign to that of Marx. Here we find it only in the description of alienation at the heart of industrial-market society. The need to create – freed from the desire to possess and from competition to acquire – that develops in communist society realizes in this way the reconciliation between the particular and the general. In industrial-market society, society as a whole is dissociated from the individuals who constitute it. More precisely, progress in society as a whole is achieved to the detriment of individual persons, or most of them, and at the price of a growing gap between an elite, whose members are like gods, and the rest of the people, who are condemned not to realize the properly human properties with which they are endowed. It is first of all for its *holism* that Marx (on the same grounds as John Rawls [2005]) reproaches the utilitarian theory of justice in industrial-market society. Utilitarianism has as its aim the maximization of the

133

collective good, even if it calls for the sacrifice of individuals; it does not aim at the happiness of individual persons. Marx denounces all discourse that puts the group above individuals because he sees this as a way for certain individuals to achieve their own humanity to the detriment of others. In capitalism, the increase in creative power that accrues to some people, ensuring the development of society, is achieved at the cost of loss of dignity for the majority. On the basis of this refusal to postulate the existence of society as an abstraction vis-à-vis the individual, Jon Elster offers an interpretation of Marx that is compatible with methodological individualism (Elster 1985, 88), and Michel Henry relies on this same refusal when he salutes in Marx the appearance, 'as obvious as it is exceptional', of a 'metaphysics of the individual' in Western philosophy devoted to the 'teleology of the universal' (Henry 1976, 2: 442–5). Not only is communist society expected to allow each individual – and not just a small elite – self-realization through creation, but it also abolishes – as the state withers away – the dissociation between private individuals, with their heretofore antagonistic desires, and the community, which comes into being when the desires of each are satisfied in it, and satisfied to its advantage; for, when the need to create spontaneously is given free rein, the convergence of activities is assured. In effect, for Marx as for Hegel, creative work allows persons to know one another by externalizing themselves in an existence oriented towards others. Such an existence, which is the condition for individuation, can occur in industrial-market society, but in that context it takes the form of competition for recognition comparable to the competition for goods, while in communist society the creator's pleasure in considering his or her objectified individuality converges with the pleasure of having 'satisfied a *human* need' and of having 'objectified *man's* essential nature' (Marx, *Comment on James Mill*, cited in Elster 1985, 87).

This sketch of a communist polity presents many features that have often stirred up doubts about the degree to which it corresponds to reality. In particular, let us consider the expectation of abundance, the abolition of the division of labour, and the absence of rewards for individual contributions; these are treated at once as necessary conditions for the development of the creative faculty and as consequences of the liberation of this faculty. In a communist polity, the abolition of the division of labour frees the creative capacities of all persons. In so doing, it engenders an abundance that, through a rebound effect, ensures the full abolition of the division of labour. Elster's work has the merit of taking the communist polity seriously, and thus of opening it up to rational discussion. Barely sketched out in Marx's work, and relegated to an indeterminate future, this polity is often treated as a utopia or as a mobilizing myth that is unworthy of detailed analysis.

The arguments Elster develops to show the particularly unrealistic character of Marx's second principle and its corollaries will help highlight the feature that seems to me to distinguish the state of peace in a communist polity from justice properly speaking. Elster's critique bears first of all on the connection Marx establishes between communism and abundance, which Elster sees as completely utopian. This connection is made through the abolition of the division of labour. In Marx's construction, the division of labour is what stifles the creative capacities of persons and thus limits the development of productive forces; hence its abolition, by liberating these capacities, inaugurates an era of abundance. The connection with creative forces suggests that this abundance must be conceived first and foremost as an abundance of industrial goods. To be sure, if one follows the theory of need in Marx (Heller 1976), access to abundance does not signify an unlimited multiplication of goods on which desires in an industrial-market society are focused. As we have seen, freedom to act on the need to create, by opening up to persons the possibility of self-realization and self-knowledge, transforms the nature of desires, which are detached from the acquisition of goods and redirected towards externalization through creation. Elster argues that this reorientation of desire towards need does not eliminate scarcity. In fact, depending on the object towards which it is directed, creation presupposes reliance on resources that are very different in nature and present in very unequal quantities (Elster 1985, 51). According to Elster, the free choice of means of self-realization may well be directed spontaneously towards activities that require the most resources. The focus on creation thus does not eliminate the problem of how to allocate scarce resources. It does not abolish the need to coordinate and supervise, which inhibits individual creative freedom. Elster's second argument is that it is also completely utopian not to take into account the unequal distribution of natural capacities (Rawls [2005] does not deny this unequal distribution, but he neutralizes it behind a veil of ignorance), so that the opening towards creation does not suffice in itself to neutralize competition among persons. It is thus impossible to maintain that there is a necessary connection between the appearance of abundance and the disappearance of the need for a principle of distributive justice. In fact, certain persons will have to sacrifice certain forms of self-realization in order to make the self-realization of others possible; this runs counter to Marx's vision, according to which, in a communist

135

society, full self-actualization would spontaneously go hand in hand with the full realization of the community as a whole. It is not self-evident, then, that the objective of full self-realization would produce the technical efficacy that is its precondition. To ensure the equilibrium of the communist model, Elster considers it necessary to introduce the idea that persons could develop new forms of 'altruism' that would lead them to sacrifice to society not only their material well-being but also their personal development; he judges this idea improbable (Elster 1985, 525–6). His arguments, which cannot be reproduced in full here, all subject the validity of the model of the communist polity to criteria that are industrial in nature. This claim is legitimate, since Marx links his model to the question of production. Yet the compromise that Marx seeks to build does not lead to equilibrium, according to Elster. Either one has to give up industrial requirements, in which case the preconditions for self-actualization are no longer guaranteed, or one has to give up free access to self-realization, in which case the model regresses towards socialism as a simple realization that is just and thereby in conformity with Marx's theoretical and ethical presuppositions about the industrial order.

This justified critique nevertheless raises a question: why did Marx – who cannot be said to have been unaware of the nature of the industrial order, since, when he gave up philosophy for economics, he chose that order, perhaps reluctantly, as the principal object of his research – persist to the last in looking for a compromise between creation and production? The answer can be found only in his obstinate refusal to abandon an ethical position that he had adopted and maintained from the beginning. As I see it, however, that position is not a position of justice, and it is precisely in this respect that the irony Marx always manifested with regard to justice is not in contradiction with the normative tendency of his work. What commentators identify as Marx's second principle does not bring us back to justice, because it does not constitute a principle of justice; on the contrary, it is directed towards the abolition of justice. It can be shown, I believe, that Marx's ethical position is characterized by a rejection of factors that produce equivalence. This rejection, which might even be characterized as disgust, is expressed particularly clearly in his critique of money, which is used, he says, as a tool of prostitution, since through it the diversity of persons and goods is abolished and in it everything is equal to everything else. The rejection of the source of equivalence is thus what justifies the disappearance of rewards in the communist polity, and accounts for Marx's preference for a state in which the activities of persons would be motivated solely by the satisfaction drawn from them, or by the lack of any hierarchy among tasks.

But Marx's resistance to calculation is manifested especially in his stubborn determination to see the division of labour abolished. This is a central point, because the communist model depends ultimately on the abolition of this division, which subtends the industrial order as a whole. Here is the point of departure for the deployment of the communist model. Indeed, in the communist polity sketched out in *The Gotha Program*, persons are no longer defined by the exercise of a profession, by a trade, or even by their occupation of a determined state. The same persons exercise at will the various activities towards which they are drawn by their desire to create – that is, to realize their full potential and to know themselves through self-actualization in the world, passing in no predetermined temporal order from manual to intellectual activities, mixing, as did the 'virtuous citizen' to whom Rousseau 'owe[d] [his] birth', the 'work of his hands' and the contemplation of 'the most sublime truths'.[11] This is how they realized their essence as 'generic beings' (Haarscher 1980). Now, Marx's critique of the division of labour does not depend solely on his critique of the way certain persons appropriate – sometimes to the detriment of the majority – the creative activities that allow people to realize their full potential. It is tied more fundamentally to his rejection, already expressed in *The German Ideology*, of difference in natural talents (Marx and Engels 1964, 428–32). The refusal to recognize any inequality of talents is inscribed in Marx in the framework of the relation he establishes between power and act. This relation is determined by his insistence on maintaining a radical uncertainty about the powers invested in persons: since these powers become apparent only when they are accomplished through acts, they are never completely revealed, because the possibility of acting is never foreclosed. Yet the division of labour, which rests on a differentiation and a hierarchization of competencies, implies predetermination and stabilization, which support the reciprocal expectations of persons established in different positions. The architect who does not build, to use Aristotle's classic example (Aristotle 1933, IX.iii.1), nonetheless does not cease to be wholly defined by his power to build. Now it is fundamentally important, in Marx's anthropology, to maintain the most radical uncertainty about the powers of persons, precisely to prevent them from being the object of a calculation. If we actually know what humanity in general, and each person in particular, has the potential to accomplish, we reduce the gamut of what is possible; this opens the way to strategy and calculation, and it reinstitutes relations of interest among persons. The abundance of communist society refers to this lack of interest in calculation. It is characterized less by an exceptional accumulation of material goods than by a lowering of competition, allowing attention to be detached not from goods themselves but from the foreclosure defined by scarcity, which had previously been the focal point of all desires. Thus abundance refers first and foremost, here, to the absence of limits.

12.3 The paradoxes of gifts and counter-gifts

Marcel Mauss's theory of the gift was inspired by indigenous conceptions borrowed from very different cultural and historical configurations – a sign of their universalizing aim – and particularly by the perspective of a Maori sage, Tamati Ranaipiri, as reported by the anthropologist Elsdon Best (see *The Gift*, Mauss 1990). Mauss's theory contains a tension that has constituted the main impetus behind the debate over this construct (probably one of the most important in anthropology). The stakes go beyond the problems that serve as the essay's premises, to the extent that the concept of the gift Mauss develops here is linked to a more general theory of reciprocity (see, for example, Racine 1986), which touches on many domains – kinship in particular – and also to the extent that it can be connected to attempts to establish objective indicators on which the opposition between the economies of traditional societies and those of market societies can be based (see especially Polanyi 2001 and Dumont 1983). The definition of reciprocity supported by *The Gift* can be associated with philia, which I have described briefly above. Just as philia applies without distinction to relations between persons and relations between polities, for Mauss the reciprocity of gift-giving is a notion directly linked to political philosophy, as Marshall Sahlins has shown (1972). Starting, on the same grounds as Hobbes, from an 'original condition of disorder', Mauss 'saw exchange as a form of political contract' that constitutes the alternative to violence and war; rather than taking, as Hobbes does, the path of the 'classic contract' and the state as a 'structure of submission', Mauss viewed exchange as a relation between two terms, one in which 'the gift ... would not organize society in a corporate sense, only in a segmentary sense' (Sahlins 1972, 169–70).

The difficulty presented by the notion of reciprocity in the exchange of gifts has to do, as Mark Rogin Anspach (1987) shows, with the tension between 'the gratuitousness of the gift' and 'the requirement of exchange'. The 'gift exchanged' incorporates a 'paradox', and 'the very expression "exchange of gifts" constitutes a contradiction in terms'. In fact, either the emphasis is placed on the gift itself – that is, precisely on the 'gratuitous' character of the gift – and one loses sight of the exchange, or the exchange is emphasized, and the gratuitousness of the gift can no longer appear except as an illusion or a deception. As Anspach remarks, 'Mauss himself seems to suggest at the outset that the gift is a fictive form taken on by the obligation to exchange, which is the only "reality" in archaic societies' (Anspach 1987, 260). And, indeed, Mauss writes: 'In Scandinavian civilization, and in a good number of others, exchanges and contracts take place in the form of gifts; in theory these are voluntary, in reality given and reciprocated obligatorily' (Mauss 1990, 3). According to Anspach, Mauss formulates his research project in the form of two questions that for him constitute a single 'precise question': 'What rule of legality and self-interest, in societies of a backward or archaic type, compels the gift that has been received to be obligatorily reciprocated? What power resides in the object given that causes its recipient to pay it back?' (ibid.). Remaining very close to the Maori tradition, Mauss proposes a solution supported by the Maori concept of *hau*, the spirit of the gift, a power in the gift that obliges its return.

This construction is challenged by Claude Lévi-Strauss, who accuses Mauss of letting himself be fooled by the 'informant': 'Are we not dealing with a mystification, an effect quite often produced in the minds of ethnographers by indigenous people?' (Lévi-Strauss 1987, 47). In fact, Lévi-Strauss says in the introduction he wrote in 1950 for a new edition of Mauss's most important essays: '*Hau* is not the ultimate explanation for exchange: it is the conscious form whereby men of a given society, in which the problem had particular importance, apprehended an unconscious necessity whose explanation lies elsewhere' (ibid., 48). While Mauss's reasoning started from 'three obligations: giving, receiving, returning', which were supplied by 'empirical observation' (ibid., 46), Lévi-Strauss for his part sees 'exchange' as the common denominator, a 'synthesis immediately given to, and given by, symbolic thought', so that it is useless to invoke 'some emotional-mystical cement' (ibid., 58) that would connect the 'discrete operations' among which social life is divided (ibid., 47). Thus it is precisely the truth of exchange that the concept of *hau* would have the function of concealing from the Maoris. Lévi-Strauss's position may legitimately be called objectivist: what is real for him is exchange, insofar as it obeys rules. But these rules are not conscious. Recourse to the notion of the unconscious allows him to dismiss what he calls the 'indigenous theory' (that is, here, the ideology of *hau*): 'whether they be Fuegians or Australian Aboriginals, the interested parties' beliefs are always far removed from what they actually think or do' (ibid., 48). He thus abolishes the tension that inhabited Mauss's formulation and undoes the paradox with an unveiling: in fact, the so-called gift is only an exchange. But one can reproach this vigorous reduction for being unable to explain why the natives deceive themselves on the truth of their exchanges by grasping them in the mode of gift.

This critique was first formulated in 1951 by Claude Lefort in 'L'Échange et la lutte des hommes', an essay that challenges Lévi-Strauss's objectivism by turning to phenomenology for support (Lefort 1978, 15–29). Comparing Mauss to the early Marx, inasmuch as they both take 'total man' as their object and 'attack every theory that would treat society as an abstraction', Lefort, even as he acknowledges, with Lévi-Strauss, the inadequacy of the explanation by way of *hau*, reproaches the latter, with his ambition to reduce the social to a universe that can be calculated according to rules, for missing 'the intention immanent to behaviours' (ibid., 17). In fact, what matters to Lefort is grasping 'the meaning of the gift exchange' (ibid., 19) and, beyond this, the signification of the gift itself. For if interpretation through the reciprocity of exchange accounts for the obligation to give back, Lefort says, it does not account for the obligation to give as it is manifested in the 'opening gift', the gift as act, unless it treats every donor as a debtor. Lefort's argument is oriented here by the intention to substitute a sociology of action for the Durkheimian sociology of social phenomena – based on a critique of experience – with which Lévi-Strauss is associated.[12] Lefort is intent on revealing in the gift 'not only an act but the act par excellence through which man conquers his subjectivity' (ibid., 25), by demonstrating that man is not what he gives. The gift thus becomes, for Lefort, 'the act through which man reveals himself *for* man and *through* man'. . . . The gift is thus at once the establishment of difference and the discovery of likeness': 'the idea that the gift must be returned implies that the other is another I who must act as I do; and this gesture in return has to confirm for me the truth of my own gesture, that is, my subjectivity.' This means that '*one does not give to receive; one gives so that the other will give*'; persons who give confirm 'for one another that they are not things' (ibid., 27).

In *Outline of a Theory of Practice* (1977), first published in 1972 and reissued in France in 1980 (*The Logic of Practice*, 1990b), Pierre Bourdieu reopened the debate by seeking to surmount the opposition between the two preceding positions, defined as 'objectivist' and 'subjectivist'. *Outline of a Theory of Practice*, directly connected with anthropology, is of particular relevance to my project. It aims to renew the social sciences and to strengthen their scientific character by liberating them from a narrow conception of what it means to be scientific, a view according to which one's work is done when one has come up with an algorithm that makes it possible to characterize the world by means of calculations. Social science, as *Outline* reminds us, is first of all the science of the social science of actors. What it must account for in the first place, by reformulating it in the language proper to social science, is thus the practice of actors and their ability, in the face of routine or novel situations, to produce actions that are consistent with those situations and thereby endowed with meaning. Now, the actions of persons do not obey the rules of calculation that are used in the construction of models.[13] *Outline* thus seeks to reconstitute the relevant logic in the order of *practice* (a concept stemming as much from Marxist tradition as from phenomenology), and this leads Bourdieu to stress the dimensions of behaviours that cannot readily be represented by reductionist, mechanistic models. These dimensions are not unfamiliar: I have already pointed them out, for the most part, in sketching the opposition between agape and other notions of love. To a concept of behaviour as execution of an external rule in a legalistic framework, Bourdieu thus opposes the internalization and incorporation of schema that allow people to act with discernment without falling back on injunctions, prescriptions or taboos destined to be followed to the letter. Similarly, he insists on the gap between the precision of an economy subjected to a constraint of rigorous calculability and the fuzziness of ordinary practice. These properties of practice, especially when they are developed with regard to traditional societies, are associated with weak instrumentation, and particularly with the absence or scarcity of the instruments needed to support general equivalences, for example money or law, and of those needed to objectivize and apprehend simultaneously relationships that are scattered in space or time, such as writing, and graphic schematization more generally (Goody 1975). The analysis of temporality as actually experienced, in contrast to the homogeneous time in which calculable relations are immersed, plays a central role here, because, as we shall see in the case of gifts, it underlies a major part of the demonstration intended to explain the preference for approximation that characterizes the 'economy of practices'.

In the pages he devotes to gifts and counter-gifts, Bourdieu begins by critiquing Lévi-Strauss's objectivist approach. Lévi-Strauss seeks to define the *rules* that must be recorded in order to account for observable properties, and his aim is to integrate these rules into a model. He is not interested in the internalized constraints that weigh upon the behaviours of actors or on the way the latter operate to construct the meaning of their own actions. Bourdieu's goal is to integrate the contributions of Durkheim's work, Marxism and phenomenology into a new synthesis. He does not give up the concept of social phenomena or the cartographic ambition associated with it. But he also means to construct a theory of action that will account both for the practice of actors and for the meaning that actors confer on their practice. In relation to the problem that interests us, this project leads Bourdieu to recentre his interrogation on the practice of actors who, countering the expectations of Lévi-Strauss's objectivism, persist in considering the object of exchange as a gift; the object is thus exempt from simple 'reciprocity', so that 'the exchange of real gifts does not take place with the mechanical certainty that the structural model possesses' (Anspach 1987, 268). Bourdieu bases his demonstration on temporality, which is not a relevant dimension in models that aim solely to build the objective structure that would permit completion of exchanges. 'The temporal structure of gift exchange', he says, 'is what makes possible the coexistence of two opposing truths, which defines the full truth of the gift' (Bourdieu 1977, 5). He thus sets about to analyse everything that makes the gift exchange irreducible to economic exchange in the strict sense, as it operates in a marketplace.

> In every society it may be observed that, if it is not to constitute an insult, the counter-gift must be *deferred* and *different*, because the immediate return of an exactly identical object clearly amounts to a refusal (i.e. the return of the same object). Thus gift exchange is opposed on the one hand to *swapping*, which, like the theoretical model of the cycle of reciprocity, telescopes gift and counter-gift into the same instant, and on the other hand to *lending*, in which the return of the loan is explicitly guaranteed by a juridical act and is thus *already accomplished* at the very moment of the drawing up of a contract capable of ensuring that the acts it prescribes are predictable and calculable. (Ibid.)

Bourdieu grants central importance to the 'lag':

> the *interval* between gift and counter-gift is what allows a pattern of exchange that is always liable to strike the observer and also the participants as *reversible*, i.e. both forced and interested, to be experienced as irreversible. . . . To betray one's haste to be free of an obligation one has incurred, and thus to reveal too overtly one's desire to pay off services

142

rendered or gifts received, so as to be quits, is to denounce the initial gift retrospectively as motivated by the intention of obliging one. (Ibid., 6)

The 'interval of time' is treated as a necessary condition for distinguishing an economic exchange, which is accomplished in an instant, and an exchange of gifts; to a large extent, it is also perceived as a sufficient condition, since the immediate exchange of the same object, which no longer deserves to be called an exchange, is excluded, and since the fact that the objects exchanged are different is not fully taken into account by the analysis, because that would presuppose a theory of value which is not present in this passage. But why does the 'interval', the 'lag' or 'delay', suffice to restore the dimension of gift? The question does not come up, because, as in Lévi-Strauss's analyses, the gift exists here only in the illusions of the actors and in the false theories that the informants deliver to the sociologists. Now the analysis – if it indeed is intended to take into account 'the subjective experience of the practice of exchange' (Bourdieu 1977, 5) – is not meant to stop there, inasmuch as it aims to establish the objectivity of the exchanges in terms of a more complex, more sophisticated, and thus more robust construction, by constituting the actors' commitment to the gift as a belief – that is, here, as a necessary and effective illusion presumably based (although this is not stated explicitly) on the forgetting made possible by the passage of time that separates the gift from the counter-gift. This belief is solidly integrated into the model, because it is presented as the condition of possibility of objective exchange: 'the operation of gift exchange presupposes (individual and collective) misrecognition [méconnaissance] of the reality of the objective "mechanism" of the exchange, a reality which an immediate response brutally exposes' (ibid., 5–6).

Let us note that such a construction demands an external observer capable – unlike the actors – of plunging the entire set of observations into a homogeneous space and time treated as a space of calculation. But this space of calculation must also be, in a way, that of the actors; otherwise there is no reason why the observer's objectivity would allow him to identify a 'reality'. This problem is of little interest to Lévi-Strauss, because it is not situated in the framework of a theory of action. In the paradigm of social phenomena, reference to the notion of the 'unconscious' suffices to fence off a world of objective phenomena independent of the actors' justifications. The same claim cannot be made in the framework of a theory designed, as is the case here, to account for the way in which persons' actions are engendered. 'Self-deception', which is substituted here for the unconscious, integrates

143

the opposition between the observers' realism and the actors' beliefs. It allows persons to be characterized as agents who are not 'entirely unaware of the truth of their exchanges' (Bourdieu 1977, 6) and who are thus in a position to shape – but in bad faith – the reality that the objective observer reveals. In this construction, time, the time that passes, thus intervenes only as a condition of possibility of bad faith and self-deception:

> the lapse of time *separating* the gift from the counter-gift is what author-izes the deliberate oversight, the collectively maintained and approved self-deception without which symbolic exchange, a fake circulation of fake coins, could not operate. If the system is to work, the agents must not be completely unaware of the truth of their exchanges, which is made explicit in the anthropologist's model, while at the same time they must refuse to know and above all to recognize it. (Ibid.)

This analysis, which uses ethnographic observations to illuminate the procedures people use to turn away from calculation, nevertheless does not say why bad faith, introduced in an effort to provide a solid grounding for the realism of the system, would be necessary in order to carry out objective exchanges. The tension between the obligation to give, which by its very structure turns away from calculation and does not seek equivalence, and the obligation to give in return, which is inconceivable outside a space of calculation that makes it possible to establish equivalence between a counter-gift and a gift, remains intact, even if an element of approximation is introduced by the vari-able length of the time lapse between the two.

— 13 —

TOWARDS A SOCIOLOGY OF AGAPE

13.1 The model of pure agape

To pursue my project, I must now try to specify both the extent to which the notion of agape might be deployed in the field of sociology and the nature of the actions on which it might shed light. Unlike other conceptions of love (attachment defined as natural and rooted in biology, desire for possession or sublimation, or relations of reciprocity between persons who hold each other in mutual esteem), conceptions that have been amply exploited by the various social sciences, agape possesses singular properties, as we have seen, such as a preference for the present, the rejection of comparison and equivalence, the silence of desires, and the absence of anticipation in interactions, all of which set it apart from the models on which our social disciplines – economics, sociology and psychology – customarily rely. An obstacle stands in the way of research here, and it has tripped up a number of those who have tried to break away from a concept of social relations based on interest. This stumbling block is romantic sociology as it has been developed, for example, by members of the Collège de sociologie (Hollier 1988), in texts bent on highlighting the affective dimension of human behaviours, even their Dionysiac or orgiastic aspect. Ensnared in the opposition between the rational and the irrational, romantic sociology is readily paired with utilitarianism, whose power of conviction it paradoxically reinforces. My first task here thus consists in developing somewhat further than I have done so far the utopian vision of a world in which everyone is immersed in a state of agape. As a thought experiment, I shall try to spell out the sort of equilibrium towards which this world might tend if, however far it may be from reality as we know it, such a world is not simply absurd. Without repeating the description of agape that I have gleaned from certain theological texts, Kierkegaard's *Works of Love*, and *Little Flowers*, I propose to focus on specific features of this form of love in order to draw out their consequences and explore their interesting properties.

1 In a world under the law of agape, in which persons keep desire at a remove and know nothing of justice or worth, each one is, in turn and thus in circular fashion, the protector of anyone he or she encounters. But, given that agape addresses itself in the singular and that one gives to anyone whose path one crosses, to anyone one sees, such a world requires that persons have eyes with which to see one another and also the possibility of coming into contact, which implies a vagabond use of space. Persons have to move about in order to cross paths and to avoid confining themselves to narrow circles of acquaintance.

2 This world is sheltered from anxiety, as Kierkegaard notes, since on the one hand all persons, renouncing judgement, protect others from the tests from which they themselves are exempt, and, on the other hand, not anticipating any response, each person is spared the anxious expectation of a return. In the absence of tests, no one knows his or her own strength or weakness. In this world I can thus treat others without distinction as weaker than I am, in order to protect them, and also as stronger, in order to receive from them whatever they have to give. Here, my weakness is a necessary gift, for, as Benveniste shows (1973, 159–62) in connection with the Latin notion of *gratia*, gratuitousness, I 'thus do the giver . . . the favor of having to give' (Taieb 1984). This world may entail a temptation, however: precisely the temptation of the test, which would bring back into the foreground the reference to equivalence, which agape sets aside.

3 Everyone in the state of agape gives to anyone he or she meets. But the one to whom the gift is addressed demands nothing, since he or she too sets aside the thought of desire. How does the gift find its place between indifference (it is asking for nothing; I ignore it) and the excess that stalks it since it is limitless by its very structure? This is where self-reference comes into play: its presence, in the injunction to 'love others as oneself', which seems to promote the self-love that is nevertheless foreign to agape, has been the object of many commentaries in theological literature. The reference to the self and to the needs of life[1] is in fact necessary, in the absence of a rule of general equivalence, in order to give everyone a basis

for discerning and meeting the need of the person whose path one is crossing.[2] But it is true that this presupposes, if not self-love, at least love for what is on the side of life, and thereby implies assent to whatever is animated in oneself.

4 Since in agape each person anticipates the needs of others by referring to his or her own needs, and since the scope of these needs can be viewed as closely linked to the amplitude of the means available to meet them (and this depends in turn on gifts received), mutual giving must lead fairly quickly to an equalization of possessions, even under the hypothesis of significant inequality in the distribution of goods in the initial state. In fact, those who have more, and whose needs are thereby greater, give more because they see the needs of the persons who benefit from their gifts as if those needs were their own. Those who have received, and who thus have more, give more in turn for the same reasons, and so on.

5 This equalization must go hand in hand with a stabilization of goods at a fairly low level corresponding to the satisfaction of vital needs, although equality in impoverishment does not result from calculation or even from an ascetic determination to satisfy an ideal of poverty. In fact, all persons in agape impoverish themselves in response to the impoverishment they encounter. No one keeps more than what is immediately needed. No one keeps reserves, for themselves or for others. No one takes thought for the morrow. But no one projects giving into the future, either. What the person I encounter has not received from me just now, because it was not in my possession, cannot be expected later on. A different person, encountered at another moment, will supply it, perhaps, but that thought itself is at an outer limit, unlikely to occur to someone in a state of agape.

6 Similarly, production must be limited to what is needed to cover immediate vital needs. If the person I encounter is cold, and I myself am feeling cold, I give away what warm clothing I have. The recipient, equally sensitive to cold and consequently capable of perceiving the meaning of my shivering, will spare me the pain of giving away too much. Or, to take another example, if I am struggling at work and working alongside someone else, the other person will without a word take on the task that is exhausting me. But if I have nothing warm to give the person who crosses my path and who is cold, I will not spend the night weaving a cloth to offer that person the next day. If a thought for the morrow should cross my mind, it will involve another passer-by who will present the gift that I was unable to make for want of material. For

production presupposes anticipation and sacrifice of the present for the future; these have no place in the temporal dimension where agape is located.

7 For the same reasons, preference for the present and refusal to judge, no one totalizes. The search for totalization would immediately take us out of the state of agape, and, as we shall see, if just one person exits from that state, everyone else has an equal possibility of doing the same. The free play of forgetting favours implicitness, because being explicit would presuppose access to forms of generalization aimed at the apprehension of totalities. The inhibition of the capacity to judge and to totalize is such that identification is problematic. Persons thus limit the work of biographical reconstruction through selection and retotalization that would allow everyone to be provided with the density of a past (Mesure 1988, 23). In fact, the permanence of persons is essentially ensured by the constraint of retrospective judgement passed on actions previously accomplished and by the concern for reducing uncertainty about the future by conferring a predictable character on behaviours; in agape, these factors do not count.[3] The same thing holds true for the reidentification of others at different moments, when circumstances bring people back into presence; this reidentification cannot depend on a synthetic totalization of the person, stylized in a typical form (on this mode of social recognition, see Boltanski and Thévenot 1983), still less on a contractual relation or on the memory of a debt. Recognition can have meaning in agape only through reference to gratitude, which reidentifies the donor only to reconsider him or her with affection and not, obviously, to reward him or her for the trouble taken, as would be the case in a spirit of justice; for, if the spirit of justice is to be achieved, it must have access not only to means for calculation but also to a memory that can retain what is subjected to calculation. Simone Weil is right when she says that the verse 'and forgive us our debts, as we also forgive our debtors' implies renouncing 'the whole of the past in a lump', and especially 'the principal claim we think we have on the universe' – that is, 'that our personality should continue' (Weil 1973, 223).

As these remarks suggest, a world ensconced in the regime of agape could no doubt achieve forms of self-organization from which a stable state would emerge, with one peculiar feature: equilibrium could be achieved only provided that it not be anyone's explicit aim. In fact, persons in this state do not have access to the instrumentation – in particular, a homogeneous space – that would allow the measure, the totalization and the calculation they would need to ground strategies that would lead, moreover, if deployed, to a series of gaps with respect to the point of equilibrium, and these gaps would lead in turn to the collapse of the regime. Thus if the regime of agape is to be maintained, all persons must be inhabited by the same lack of interest in calculation, and all must have access to the same resources, the ones necessary to do the work – on themselves and on others – that ensures the inhibition of the calculating capabilities naturally present in human persons. This is to say, too, that the economics of a world operating under the regime of agape can never be constructed in that world. Equilibrium can be achieved only by a *laissez-faire* outlook that excludes even its own theorization. In fact, because agape is not an interactionist model in which all persons incorporate anticipation of the responses of others into their own behaviour, in order to behave according to the logic of this regime people do not need to know that the others behave in the same way. Moreover, any totalization aiming to bring to light an economics of exchanges and their completion around a point of equilibrium would lead to the denunciation, in agape, of a false appearance made possible by bad faith, as we have seen in analysing the tensions that inhabit the passages Bourdieu's *Outline of a Theory of Practice* devotes to the problem of the gift. This is to say too, then, that a world operating under the regime of agape can be governed by economics only in the eyes of an external observer who is foreign to the regime and does not communicate with those inside it (for, if the observer can communicate with them, he or she will end up making them all shift out of agape).[4]

Rather than spend more time on the regime of pure agape, let us turn to less utopian situations in which persons are not wholly or permanently ensconced in the state of love. While in the regime of pure agape all persons are in the same state, I shall concentrate on describing the kind of relations that can be instituted between persons immersed in agape and persons subject to a different regime. I shall leave aside, at least for now, the relation between beings immersed in violence and persons imperturbably rooted in love who appear, as a result, to be condemned to martyrdom; instead, I shall look at the relation that may be instituted between persons in a regime of love and persons in a regime of justice. For reasons that I am about to indicate, I shall make a special effort to understand how, in this quite particular relation between persons who are not in the same game, one of two outcomes may occur: either those who had been in love up to that point will shift to justice, or else those who were previously committed to justice will shift to love.

13.2 Access to the states of agape

The methodological decision that consists in not losing sight of justice while studying love has to do with the special difficulties encountered by sociology when it focuses on the states of agape, one of whose distinctive features is its inaccessibility to a direct approach. Even if justice relies on the presence of things for support, it can never completely dispense with argumentative means; at some point it has to fall back on arguments in order to succeed in its test – that is, in order to propose imputations and justify them through reference to general forms. Unlike justice, as we have seen, love does not need to turn back to itself in the reporting mode for its full accomplishment. When love speaks, it is to pass into action, as a gesture is prolonged in words. But it never uses speech to refer to itself; it never takes itself into consideration by exposing itself in a discursive form.[5] Sociology, whose methods are derived for the most part from the analysis of texts – either written or transcribed oral indigenous discourses or else reports in which observers record their remarks – turns out to be lacking in this regard. Kierkegaard noted the difficulty that love encounters in speaking about itself without shifting into another regime; this difficulty cannot be avoided except by relying on a structural opposition one of whose terms is justice, as we have already seen in connection with parables. It is only in the tension that it maintains with justice that love in the sense of agape can carve out a path towards expression.

This observation dictates my research strategy. To gain access to agape, I shall have to pay particular attention, on the one hand, to the inventory of a phenomenon that, while it does not appear to be in contradiction with a norm of legitimate justice, does not accompany its accomplishment with a discourse aiming to relate action to general forms, and, on the other hand, to the exploration of the processes that are at work at the moment when persons on the verge of shifting from one state into the other come into contiguity, as it were (as sketched out in sections 13.3 and 13.4, below); finally, I shall have to seek any traces that may have been left behind, in modes of expression oriented towards justice, by the persistence of states first engaged in the regime of agape (the possibility of which we shall examine in section 13.5).

Agape, as we have seen, is unacquainted with desire. We have to keep this fundamental property in mind in order to recognize the dimension of agape in the presence of what we know cannot be asked of it. Agape does not question, since it believes everything. The constraints that weigh on questioning, in all regimes and in all cultures (Goody 1975), are manifested here with the greatest possible force. But agape makes no requests, either. In the state of agape, persons lack the possibility of requesting what is not given them, or of relying on an earlier gift in the expectation that it will be renewed and requiring this renewal, or of protesting because they are no longer getting something they had once been granted. If requests were possible, they would draw persons out of agape, since asking for something implies actively engaging desire in situations that bring persons together.[6] Thus one of the pathways granting access to the states of agape consists in considering what is not requested or what is irremediably modified in its nature by a request. My criterion will be that of the non-request and the absence of justification. Let us take as an example – a trivial one, but one that corresponds to a familiar experience – the action that consists in holding the door for a stranger in a public place. Quite particular conditions of validity are required for this act to be requested (for example, the person making the request has both hands full), but, even if the request is accompanied by a justification it will qualify the situation with reference to justice or even orient it towards dispute ('you really could have held the door for me'). For one can only validate the request by treating the act as something that is due, and, if this action due is deemed to be self-evident, it may seem difficult to have to request it without losing face (Goffman 1967, 5–45), so that the absence of the action is always treated as an offence. The orientation towards justice will depend largely on the degree of generality granted to the act; this can be limited to the singular, thus disallowing the expectation of a return, since nothing guarantees that the encounter will be reproduced under the same circumstances, between the same persons, or it can be related to a general rule of reciprocity, which implies, among strangers, that, for the particular persons who find themselves in each other's presence, one must substitute beings defined by general properties such that the act accomplished in favour of one of them can be paid back by an act accomplished elsewhere, and later on, by another person who does not know the first one any more than does the one who is already expecting the same thing of him.[7] It is on such expectations, supported by common knowledge (Lewis 1969), that civility or politeness are based, inasmuch as they are universalizable

151

conventions that are independent of the state of persons and that, from the viewpoint of agape, can be denounced as conventional signs simulating a non-existent love.

So the very properties of agape are indeed what impel me to adopt a structural method like the one clearly exposed, for example, in the work of Georges Dumézil, especially in the works in which he sets up, by a systematic use of comparatism, the tripartite structure associated with his name ([1948] 1988; also 1949, especially pp. 34–5), while never losing sight, with regard to each of the regimes I propose to examine, the relation of opposition and complementarity that they maintain with the others. I hope in this way to avoid the utopia of a world in which everyone would be immersed in agape, but also the no less fallacious utopias – although these are more readily accepted by contemporary social science – in which all relations among persons are based, in the final analysis, on one form or another of violence, or else on opposing theories that know only justice, or finally on constructs that want to know nothing about persons except that they are entirely subjected to the authority that brings to bear on them the state of things as they are. I shall hypothesize that, in the concrete situations of life, persons may be engaged to varying degrees in each of the regimes, and that there is no situation, however stabilized it may appear, that does not offer the possibility of acceding to a regime that is not the one in which the situation seems to be involved. This hypothesis seems to me to be necessary in order to understand the incessant shifts from one regime to another. For if each of the regimes includes, according to its own law, a tendency to persist and even to extend itself through dissemination of the state that is associated with it, none of the regimes is eternal; love may not last, but violence, too, comes to an end. As I suggested at the beginning of this study, it is not enough to keep disputes removed from violence by engaging them in justice in order to bring them to an end, and justice itself, which like the other regimes is animated by an internal tendency to dissemination, also poses the question of how to achieve closure. I suggest that each of the regimes ceases to follow its own course only by shifting into a different regime. Thus if the shift to justice is indeed in a position to bring violence to an end, still another bifurcation has to be invoked if we are to understand that an end can also be brought to a dispute carried out in a regime of justice. Seeking to sketch out a model of the way in which these shifts might occur, I shall start with situations in which the various protagonists do not appear to be in the same state and thus are not playing the same game. I shall limit myself here to model cases in which one of the partners is in the regime of justice and the other in the regime of love, while trying to spell out certain of the processes through which justice can get the upper hand and place each of the parties under its control, or through which, on the contrary, love can win out.

13.3 From love to justice

How can we conceive of an exit from the state of love? It cannot be spontaneous and voluntary. No one can exit first and of his or her own free will from love, just as, presumably, no one can take the first step in the cycle of violence, for violence, as has been demonstrated for crises of aggression in witchcraft (Favret-Saada 1990), is always constituted as a response to a prior act of violence. Thus in order to account for an act of violence it is necessary to invoke something that originated with the person to whom the act is addressed. The difficulty stems here from the non-interactive character of the state in which persons ensconced in the regime of agape find themselves. One cannot explain the shift away from love by invoking the disappointment that would be gradually engendered by the absence or the modesty of what is received in return, or the progressive frustration of desire. This mechanism suffices to account for the decline in friendships according to philia, since they are based on reciprocity, but it is inoperative in agape. We have seen that the person in a state of agape holds the thought of desire at a remove, and that a gift made in this state does not call for or anticipate a counter-gift. The fact that this latter is non-existent or insufficient does not affect the permanence of love, which has no interest in counter-gifts; as Kierkegaard emphasizes, love is tireless, so that we do not see at first what there is in the behaviour of the person on whom love is bestowed that could make this incessant flow dry up. The problem finds a solution only on the condition that we make a slight correction to the principle, one generally acknowledged as true in a first approximation, according to which desires are entirely absent in agape. For, in the states of agape that are accessible to us, one desire that cannot be completely set aside is firmly maintained on the boundaries: this is none other than the desire to give. Present in a latent state when it is satisfied, this desire cannot keep from returning to the foreground if it is thwarted. The only obstacle it may encounter is refusal of the gift, at the very moment when the gift is made. As we know, this refusal can manifest itself in various ways that are not always easy for the person who is initially plunged into the carefree state of agape to recognize

153

as such. The refusal can be expressed in formal terms, but also by the immediate return of the gift to the giver, or else – and these possibilities have been envisaged in studies devoted to reciprocity – it can be manifested by the rapid offering of another strictly equivalent object, which annuls the very possibility of an exchange. Finally, as in a *potlatch*, rejection of the gift can be demonstrated through the ostentatious display of an overwhelming abundance of wealth, which 'the author of the potlatch destroy[s] in order not to receive' (Lefort 1978, 26); this gesture, intended to deny the very quality of gift attributed to whatever is circulating, may be rightly considered as a form of violence.

Only refusal of the gift has the power to lead desire to reintroduce itself into the situation; this abolishes the gap between eros and agape, through the breach that the re-engagement of the desire to give has opened up. In order to account for the re-engagement of desire, it is thus not necessary to invoke the indignation aroused by the unequal character of the exchange, as will be the case once everyone is back in a competition governed by reciprocity and equivalence – in other words, in a dispute arbitrated in the regime of justice. Such a dispute is inconceivable as long as one of the partners remains in the regime of love. But the process is already under way when the giver is confronted with the test of seeing the offered gift rejected. For, once the gift has been refused, the desire to give can no longer remain simply present as a tacit precondition for the offering. Thwarted, it is compelled to manifest itself in what drives it and thus to appear as desire – that is, in its self-centred dimension. For it can no longer be constituted simply with reference to the needs of the person to whom it is directed; it now has to reckon as well with a self-satisfaction that becomes real as soon as an impediment presents itself in opposition. The giver, however, still lodged in agape, cannot lay claim directly to a self-centred desire of which the regime on which he or she depends is unaware, and which can henceforth accede to expression only in the form of a desire to receive and to obtain according to what is due; thus the giver tilts into the regime of justice. In fact, the obstacle that stands in the way of the gift reactivates a memory that had remained dormant in agape – that is, the memory of benefits granted – and it frees means of calculation that were previously inhibited. Attention then turns away from the rejected gift towards the absent counter-gift. Now the return of memory suffices to bring a person out of the regime of agape; as we have seen, if it is to persist, agape presupposes collective use of a faculty of forgetting. It is enough for one of the partners to entertain once again the possibility of remembering benefits and faults, and thus to reconstitute a space of calculation, for the operations guaranteeing the stability of the regime to grind to a halt.

Once desire is engaged anew, it finds itself confronting the bifurcation between violence and justice. Desire as such does not encompass the validity of its own satisfaction, which can be sought at any cost, even by force. I shall not explore that eventuality here, although nothing rules it out. But if we acknowledge that persons try to keep themselves at a distance from violence, and thus try to keep their disputes within the limits of justice, they must validate their desire and obtain from their partners the recognition of this validity by looking for an equivalence capable of justifying their claims. If we reject the path of violence, the re-engagement of desire includes the need for justification. In fact, to validate a demand, one must be able to justify it as something that is due, and this implies reference to a general equivalence, one that is external and superior to the parties in presence and thereby has a universal character. Reference to a general law, legitimated in a construction that has the properties of a metaphysics (*OJ* 65–82), is necessary, then, to support the claim of equality of the exchanges in a reciprocity that takes into account the unequal value of the different parties and of their contribution to the common good. This operation defines the shift to justice.

The movement towards justification, which accompanies the exit from agape and the shift into justice, puts an end to the silence of love and reopens access to the resource of a discursive and even argumentative use of language. For in justice, as we have seen, language is necessary to bring to trial, ask questions, cast in doubt, make reproaches, constitute complaints, bring back remote facts from the depths of forgetting and confront each person with them. Language is there to give reasons, validate requests, have the last word. As a result, the shift to justice is accompanied by a rise in generality, and this process is the form in which a dispute is disseminated when it occurs in the regime of justice. In order to support their claims, all parties will look for arguments validated by reference to general forms, but they will also seek out persons to serve as witnesses or objects to serve as proof. In the process that interests us here, the shift from love to justice, the reappearance of a request is marked by the return of questioning. But the sole question that is pertinent to the dividing line between love and justice – 'Why did you not anticipate my request?' or 'Why did you not spare me the request?' – cannot be raised in either register. In pure agape, nothing allows it to surface, and, in justice, it is immediately covered over by the canonical question of this register: 'Why have I not received my due?'

13.4 From justice to love

The question of the entrance into agape – which I shall approach here by interrogating a hypothetical example in which a person under the empire of justice shifts into a state of love, the state in which another person with whom the first is in contact abides – is important for my project because the classical theories of agape take for granted the capacity of love to spread according to a law of its own. This theme is amply developed in Kierkegaard; it even inspires the title of the book the philosopher devotes to the problem that concerns us here: *Works of Love*. Without being deliberately driven by the intent to operate conversions into its regime, love works surreptitiously, in Kierkegaard's view, and through this silent toil it brings in turn those towards whom it is directed into the kind of state that defines it. Kierkegaard excludes constraint from the outset (love cannot be 'forced', even in a 'charitable' spirit), but he also excludes voluntary action more generally: it is impossible, he maintains, to deposit love in the heart of a person purely by a decree of the will (Kierkegaard 1995, 216). He also refuses to invoke imitation, which suggests comparison, want and desire, which we know to be foreign to the state of agape (ibid., 27). On these grounds, the shift into love is, indeed, 'essentially [a] by-product', in Jon Elster's sense – that is, an effect that 'can only *come about* as the by-product of actions undertaken for other ends'; it 'can never . . . be *brought about* intelligently and intentionally' (Elster 1981, 431). The 'edification' of love thus cannot be accomplished by inspiring in others a wish for love, or even by setting an example, but only by creating conditions such that others can allow themselves to be grasped by a state they can all attain, on the sole condition that they do not resist it actively. So how is the spread of love possible? According to Kierkegaard, 'the one who loves presupposes that love is in the other person's heart, and by this very presupposition he builds up love in him – from the ground up, provided, of course, that in love he indeed presupposes its presence in the ground' (Kierkegaard 1995, 216). One must thus suppose that love already exists if it is to manifest its presence and grow. While a teacher, to bring about an increase in the knowledge of the person he is teaching, 'presupposes that the pupil is ignorant', a person 'who loves and builds up' – that is, contributes to the dissemination of the regime under which he is operating – 'has only one course of action, to presuppose love'. 'Love that edifies has nothing to point to, since its work consists only of presupposing.' The work of love is thereby invisible ('love humbly makes itself inconspicuous just when it is working the hardest') and passive, since that work seems to consist in doing nothing, which constitutes, as Kierkegaard rightly notes, the hardest work of all (ibid., 216–17). This construct accounts for the spread of love through unconditional and immediate adherence ('love believes all things' [ibid., 235]) or, alternatively, by a creative supposition which, like a 'self-fulfilling prophecy' (Merton 1936), would bring about what it presumes to be already in existence, without having intentionally aimed at this outcome and thus apart from any instrumental or strategic orientation. The interest of this construct lies first of all in the fact that it treats agape as one of the states that people can attain by liberating capacities that belong to the ordinary competence of human persons. But Kierkegaard does not pursue the analysis of the way in which the passivity of the person who supposes love in another can lead the first one actually to shift into that state.

This is the missing link that I should like to try to develop here, while restricting myself to the situation already evoked in the preceding paragraph involving the relation between two persons, one of whom is in a state of love and the other in a state of justice. More precisely, I shall try to treat this relation as if it were not merely a game of tacit coordination in which the two partners communicate only through acts (love, which does not construct arguments, does not accompany its action by a report), in such a way that the response of each depends on an interpretation of the actions of the other, as in the examples explored by Schelling (1960), but also a game in which the partners follow different rules, so that their expectations cannot find support, at least in the initial state, in common knowledge. Such a situation is characterized, more precisely, by an asymmetry between the players, since one of them – the one who is in love – unlike the one who is under the regime of justice, expects nothing in return, and consequently not only does not anticipate the other's response but is unaware of the very possibility that the other player can anticipate the partner's responses. It is not a question of radical foreignness here, as it would be, for example, between animals of different species endowed with different genetic programmes, since the two persons in question are human and as such can shift into different regimes in which they have competence; it is a matter of a temporary difference that generates misunderstandings, as we often observe in daily life. I shall consider, finally, that the object of cooperation is an exchange of gifts and counter-gifts that cannot appear clearly as such, for reasons we have seen, except to the partner operating under the regime of justice. The game can be treated as an apprenticeship exercise that can be won following an indefinite number of moves.

The two partners – let us call them X and Y – direct their actions towards each other and transmit gestures and things back and forth; these gestures and things can be the object of differing interpretations on each side. X, who is in a state of agape, gives with no concern for getting anything back, then forgets. Y, who is in a state of justice, interprets the gift in the logic of gift/counter-gift and, incorporating into X's gesture an expectation of getting something in return, tries to make the appropriate response while satisfying the rule that pertains in this case (observation of a delay and choice of a different object of approximately equal value). Y expects something in return. X accepts the offer as a pure gift, not relating it to what was given in the previous move, so that there is no obligation of a counter-gift. X's behaviour may take one of several forms that all have the same effect. X may give nothing, or give something that is not in proportion to the gift received, or (if Y is no longer present) allow a long time to pass, and so on. When Y, operating in the regime of justice, receives something once again, the gesture is interpreted as a return of what is due. But, in Y's eyes, the rules of exchange have not been respected, and this is upsetting. Y may seek to pursue the operations according to the same programme as before, but after an indefinite number of moves Y will no longer be able to ignore X's erratic behaviour; as we know, there is no reason for X's strange attitude to change at this stage in the game, since, whatever the response, X is imperturbably pursuing the work of love. Thus it is Y whose behaviour must be modified. Y then reaches a turning point, and may decide to refuse any gift offered from this moment on. We find ourselves in the hypothetical situation examined in the previous paragraph, and there is every chance that Y's attitude may lead X, for the reasons set forth earlier, to shift from love into justice. Y may stop accepting gifts for reasons such as the following: considering that X is not expecting any counter-gift in the form of material or immaterial goods detached from Y's person, which are only acceptable in the regime of justice, and considering that, being in the regime of agape, X is incapable of suspecting that Y expects nothing, Y may conclude that X's expectations bear upon Y's very person. X wants to be endlessly obliging, wants to impose a debt impossible to repay, and thereby to take possession of Y's person. As we know, it is indeed by means of this sort of argument that gifts are often denounced as a sort of abuse. The gift will then be interpreted in a logic of violence that only refusal can bring to a halt. The giver will thus give up the expectation of receiving. In fact, installed in justice, this player (Y) cannot readily be resigned (even though this possibility cannot be completely dismissed) to adopting the predatory attitude that would consist in accepting the gifts of the irrational partner (X) without worrying at all about giving something in return and deliberately renouncing all forms of reciprocity. But another path remains open. Y may, through love of justice, refuse to shatter the reciprocity engaged in the previous stages and, put on notice that there are to be no returns, may continue the game by redirecting the impetus in a way that liberates the intention to give. Y will then be able to achieve 'the shift from object to gift' that marks access to agape (Di Sante 1991, 50). The manoeuvre may consist in detaching oneself from what is circulating in the exchange – and which, resistant to equivalence, can offer only the support of calculation – and attaching oneself to the giver in seeking a return, for Y, no longer able to match the gift received, has to turn towards X and take that person's needs in their singular aspects into account. In this example, then, renunciation of giving back but not of receiving ensures the possibility of a shift into the logic of agape. This shift can be conceived as the outcome of a gradual process. Just as the path of strict reciprocity, which, if it is taken, brings the game to a halt through a refusal to receive, can be marked by a gradual reduction of the lapse between gift and response, and by a growing and always disappointed effort to give back the same thing by approaching the strictest possible equivalence, in the same way the path that leads to the apprenticeship of the faculty of giving can be characterized by a gradual increase in response time and by more and more approximate returns in terms of equivalence to the initial gift.

13.5 Agape and emotion

I do not propose to explore the empirical applications of the construction presented here; I would simply like to suggest some of the problems on which this brief sketch may shed some light. They include two related issues in particular: disputes that go on and on, and disputes that justice does not suffice to settle, since, in justice, persons can always (although to differing degrees, depending on how the situation is arranged) find support in new objects in order to repeat the test (*OJ* 215–36).

Disputes that are pursued in the register of justice and sometimes go on for years without reaching a conclusion caught my attention when, as part of an effort to shed light on processes of accusation, I undertook to study public denunciations of injustice and public accusations (see chapter 1). The problematic character of these affairs, which have often been addressed in the register of psychopathology (for instance, when their principal protagonists are qualified as 'paranoid'), lies in the actors' apparent inability to converge towards an acceptable agreement that would allow them to bring the dispute to a close. In these affairs, the main effect of the various operations aimed at obtaining justice is to start the dispute up again and to ensure that it spreads, with each party striving to involve still more new objects and to mobilize new persons or new institutions to support his or her cause. The intransigence of persons who find themselves in the position of victim is particularly striking. (These may be different persons, depending on the standpoint of the observers, for the latter, lacking access to the affair if they do not establish privileged ties to one of the actors, most often find themselves conscripted.) The victim accepts no friendly deals, refuses all compromises – denouncing them as compromising – and, when the affair is brought to justice (or brought before an entity that can play the role of arbitrator), repudiates the judge if the verdict does not recognize all the wrongs of which the victim accuses his or her adversary. As the original affair extends over time in this way, other complaints are grafted onto it. Some, such as conflicts with lawyers or with the judicial administration, seem connected with the refusal to accept any form of arbitration; others may antedate the principal affair, which seems to have served as a trigger for bringing up old grievances that victims associate with the actions of their persecutors. The result is an immense population of apparently disparate beings – employers, administrative services, family members, rules, colleagues, parties, lawyers, politicians, businesses, judges, machines, police officers, experts, support groups, doctors, municipalities, laws, notaries, neighbours, pamphlets, unions, houses, lands, nations, and so on – among which the victim's testimony (letters to the editor accompanied by a thick dossier or a lengthy interview) establishes complex connections. Taking these into account necessitates a detour via forms of equivalence that compel the construction of such long and tenuous links to associate the particular case with a general principle valid for all that the very efforts to make the victim's story acceptable in terms of justice often have the effect of revealing his or her abnormal character and thereby disqualifying the grievance. (For an analysis of such affairs, see Part III of this work.)[8]

My hypothesis, then, is the following: the interminable character of 'chronic' affairs may originate essentially in the heterogeneity between the regime of justice, the only one in which a grievance can achieve expression, and the regime of agape, in which the parties

160

involved were ensconced when their activities encountered the obstacle that made them fall out of that state. It is the incommensurability between the object of the loss and the means employed to try to repair the situation, and not only an excessive attachment to what is right (David-Jougneau 1988) or desperate efforts to avoid losing face (Goffman 1959), that account for the impossibility of ending the dispute in justice and for the victims' apparent indifference to the price – often disproportionate, in the eyes of an observer – they must pay to pursue an affair that in many cases becomes the major affair of their lives. For intransigence here has to do with the impossibility of establishing equivalence between what could be rendered in the regime of justice, bent on consolidating fairness, as revealed by a test, and what has been lost in the regime of agape, where persons give of themselves – as people sometimes say when they are speaking about their actions, and even also in the workplace – without counting and without calculation, setting equivalence aside. This is why, in such affairs, the grievance, associated without regard for costs and sometimes in a preposterous way with the most general cause, if it is to satisfy the constraints that bear upon justice, is always also addressed, indirectly, to the particular person whose refusal – in the form, for example, of a reminder of the rules, or the application of a test according to a formalized procedure, a form apt to provide acceptable objectivizations for all – has caused the plaintiff to fall out of agape. There has been a fall from a high place. In these cases, reparation in justice, which pursues the test in different forms, cannot stop the protests of innocence that only an action capable of overthrowing the validity of the equivalence could halt – for example, a gesture signifying that the aggrieved party has forgotten what has taken place, a sign of letting go, of abandonment, as if nothing had happened (an unthinkable condition in justice). Lacking this recourse, intransigent maintenance of the accusation, stubborn persistence in the grievance, is the only means victims can use to maintain themselves in the presence of those who have outraged them and who, however reluctantly, are obliged to go along, to argue, to respond, to present themselves or have themselves represented at the trial. Thus they will not be dismissed, and only the pursuit of an action in justice can ensure the prolongation in justice of a dispute whose interruption appears unbearable (see chapters 21 and 22).

We know nothing of the regime under which the parties were operating previously, and, once they are in the regime of justice, these persons say nothing about it. But we can identify it through the traces that it leaves in the protest presented in the regime of justice and that help disqualify that protest. In chronic affairs, the act of accusation often bears marks that point up the singular character of the denunciation, marks related to the person of the persecutor that predate the general cause invoked to bring out the legitimacy of the case. These signs of oddness in written texts – scribbles, overwriting, elaborately drawn letters, underlining in colour, cross-outs, and so on – do not fool readers, who usually see them as confirming their suspicions of mental illness. They appear intended to bring back, indirectly and in the register of emotion, the singularity of the relation that the accuser had maintained with the persecutors. It is in fact through emotions that the traces of one regime are manifested in another – more precisely, here, the traces of love in justice. In both of these regimes, when they are operating on their own terms, emotion is absent. This is obvious for justice, but it is also the case for love. The absence of emotion is what is signified, moreover, by the reference to peace, a quality intrinsically associated with states of agape, for agape, by definition, excludes the anxious tumult of emotion. Emotion here is not only the product of the conversion of behaviours that is associated with the shift from one regime to another, but also the product of the efforts made to stay as close as possible, as long as possible, to the axis around which these two regimes pivot, as if to maintain them in contiguity. Emotion is indeed, in this sense, to use Paul Ricoeur's expression, an 'unmoving evocation' of something that is 'absent', something that 'is distinguished from simple intellectual anticipation by its host of organic concomitants' (Ricoeur 1966, 257). This ambiguity confers on emotion its troubled and transitory character (as when one speaks of a 'fleeting emotion'). Dissociated from the reference to a different regime, emotion is calmed, and we speak of the peace of love, serene justice, placid things or cold violence.[9]

It is indeed the bodily character of emotion that makes it the support of memory traces. A thing of the body, exempt from deliberation and will, it can preserve the memory of a state that is no longer the one in which the person is installed and which grips or overwhelms the person unbidden. Thus, in justice, emotion is at its peak when, on the occasion of an incident in a trial, the protagonists find themselves face to face once again. It comes as no surprise, then, that the mediation of the emotions can also lead the persons in presence to abandon a dispute in the regime of justice. I shall borrow this last example from research under way in an educational establishment within which particularly difficult working conditions maintain an elevated level of tension between the teachers and the students and between the administration and the teachers, even while these same conditions encourage altruistic behaviour that goes beyond the ordinary requirements of the job.[10]

The first phase of the dispute is characterized by the unification of local or limited discontents or conflicts. The persons involved do the work of associating dissatisfactions with specific complaints – for example, a problem of prolonged shut-downs of the heating system during the winter, a conflict bearing on the use of time, a disagreement about internship hours, and so on – and bring them together as a cluster, in the present.[11] The second phase is a moment of crisis, marked by a spreading of the dispute from which no one escapes, not even the students.[12] The phase of unification of local crises and generalization of the dispute, often at an improvised meeting in the teachers' lounge during a recess that lasts longer than the regulation fifteen minutes, with the students waiting in the courtyard, gives rise to 'a terrible explosion'. A woman I interviewed about one such crisis described her fear: 'I had a moment when I pulled back, I was afraid, really frightened, like a bird going into a trap. Mostly, they were angry. It lasted twenty minutes in the faculty lounge, I was trembling in my chair, telling myself "they're coming in". Then what I was expecting happened – I mean, I had a howling mob in my office.' In a third phase, the various protagonists attempt to shift into justice. Each person seeks a rule to fall back on, a code, a principle of equivalence from which a legitimate action in the particular case can be derived, in order to set violence aside and pursue the dispute in the regime of justice. To do this, the teachers have to give form to their discontents, consolidate their denunciation by basing it on acceptable justifications. They do it most often, it seems, by turning to union resources. These resources allow them to generalize their protest by shifting from singular traumas to a demand that purports to be valid for everyone. This demand also serves to curb anger, and thus to give shape to the emotions that have provided the energy necessary to transgress the school rules – by deciding, in the case in question, not to return to the classroom after the break. The school principal is feeling her way, too, trying to get hold of a rule she can use to regain control of the situation in the register of justice. This is a difficult passage. It depends on anger in order to get away from anger. One of the techniques perfected by the principal to exhaust her own anger (she recognizes that she, too, has 'a somewhat lively temperament') consists in channelling it into a written document. Then she files this text away and prepares a second draft, to be posted in the teacher's lounge, in which she takes care to avoid a polemical tone and to justify her position by relying only on facts and legitimate arguments. (She kept copies of all these documents and I had the opportunity to read several versions of the same story.) The shift towards justice presupposes that the protagonists in the situation are redefined in a register apt to bring out the principle that makes for equivalence among them.[13] The dispute goes on, but the identities change. In a notice posted by the faculty, Mme A., the principal, becomes 'the administration'. In a notice posted by Mme A., the angry teachers become 'the unions'. However, such changes are fragile. Representatives can always fall back into the state of ordinary persons.[14] The institutionalization of the relationship, the definition of meeting times and places, the separation of spaces to avoid chance meetings that could turn out badly, all these tactics are aimed at channelling the test, keeping a lid on uncontrollable outbursts of anger.[15] In the trial that follows, and that here takes the form of a general assembly, or a board meeting, the test initiates a shift into justice.[16] But violence has not been completely set aside. Anger is still evident in tones of voice, in the bitterness of people's remarks. In the description given to me, it was finally the impossibility of completely suppressing emotions that provided the resource for the return to peace. Emotion was indeed, in this case, 'an involuntary which *sustains* voluntary action, which *serves* it in preceding and limiting it' (Ricoeur 1966, 251). In fact the trial, as often happens, short-circuited. It did lead to reconciliation, but without going through a convincing test capable of supporting a solid agreement. The emotions aroused in the face-to-face contacts among the actors, in the antagonists' confrontation during a trial whose thread they were losing, hastened the reconciliation that had been made possible by the shift into justice: 'In the end ... there were people who cried, in the room, some of my most vociferous detractors. And from that moment on, at the end of the meeting we practically fell into each other's arms.' Peace is re-established, then, for a period of variable duration; the participants all give themselves over, illogically, to forgetting, taking care of their own business, letting themselves be guided by the state of things as they are, as if the dispute had not taken place; peace is manifested only in the superficial register of 'small gestures'. But these marks of affection could conceal instrumental aims. Thus the principal truly attached value only to a sign manifested in her absence. Some teachers sang her praises in speaking to the inspector general:

> That was a supreme gift for me, it really was. An extraordinary gesture, all the more so because it wasn't calculated, wasn't anticipated, because no one told me about it, because I didn't hear it from the teachers

164

afterward. I found out about it in a very indirect way, because they could have set things up so I would learn about it as a booby-trapped gift, as it were. This time, no, it was a gift without the expectation of any particular return.

Part III

Public Denunciation

Five days after routing [the] two armies [set against him], Kohlhaas reached Leipzig and set fire to the city in three places. In the manifesto which he had distributed on this occasion he termed himself 'an emissary of the Archangel Michael, come to punish with fire and the sword all those who join the Squire's cause in this dispute, as well as the deceitfulness into which the whole world has fallen'. Then, from Castle Lützner, which he had taken by surprise, and in which he had set up his headquarters, he called upon the people to join forces with him to establish a better order of things. The manifesto was signed, in a kind of deranged way: 'given under our hand at the headquarters of our provisional world government, Castle Lützen.'

Heinrich von Kleist, *Michael Kohlhaas*

— 14 —

THE AFFAIR AS A SOCIAL FORM

The distinction between individual and collective action is one of the fundamental oppositions on which the sociology and social history of modes of protest rely – often implicitly, given its self-evidence. These disciplines recognize as legitimate objects only demands associated with a social movement. They reject as outside their universe of competence manifestations of revolt or grievances whose authors act alone and in such a way that their actions cannot be associated with economic patterns or with a series presenting repetitive features; they dismiss such manifestations as abnormal, better addressed by historical psychoanalysis or social psychiatry, for example. In the pages that follow, I seek to move beyond this opposition by outlining a problematics; more precisely, I shall try to construct a system or 'grammar' of transformation that will allow me to account for the variations that affect acts of protest and the way they are perceived by others, according to the degree to which they are presented and received as 'individual' or 'collective' acts. In doing this, I shall use the same rules to analyse 'normal' cases (the ones with which sociology and social history are concerned) and 'abnormal' ones (those that ordinarily fall within the purview of psychology or psychiatry).

To construct this problematics, I shall take denunciation as my object, and more precisely public denunciation, playing on the variations that affect the meaning of the term – for the word denunciation can designate, at one extreme, a social critique that points out an injustice in its most general aspect without necessarily calling for reparations of a repressive order and, at the other extreme, an individual critique that targets an individual, in the sense of denouncing someone to the authorities for the purpose of having a sanction applied. In the cases examined here, denunciation of an injustice presupposes the designation of a guilty or responsible party. According to a casuistics whose logic I shall try to demonstrate, this party can be represented by a synecdoche of abstraction (for example, 'capitalism', in a union pronouncement intended to protest against layoffs), or it can be identified and designated by name. The denouncer has to persuade other persons, associate them with the protest, mobilize them; in the process, the denouncer must not only convince the others that he or she is speaking the truth, but also that it is right to speak out, and that the accusation designating a being (individual or collective) for public retribution is equal to the injustice denounced. Vengeance pursued by means of direct violence, whether physical (blows) or verbal (insults), can always be achieved, even if the results are not always predictable. In contrast, denunciation may not reach its aim – it may fail – if a denouncer who has rejected the possibility of personally administering the desired punishment does not encounter people who are inclined to offer support.

The author of a public denunciation is asking, in effect, to be followed by an indefinite – but necessarily large – number of persons ('all', 'all those who count', 'all men of good will'). The cause the author is defending entails a claim to universality. Starting from a particular yet exemplary case, it concerns everyone; thus there are no natural limits to the dimensions of an affair, as we see in the legal and political jargon used to designate the processes of signing on to a problematic and litigious case where the issues and their resolution are bound up with manoeuvres of argumentation and proof where each camp strives to mobilize support. A vocabulary of size is used to express these struggles: some parties strive to extend them, to make them 'grow', 'swell', 'come out', while others seek on the contrary to 'cut them down to size, 'deflate' them or 'nip them in the bud'. The operations performed by affairs, which contribute, in their way, to creating and dissolving groups, are thus always associated with shifts between the 'particular case' and the 'general interest', the singular and the collective. In order to pursue an affair and submit it to the verdict of public opinion, one has to test the capacities for generalization contained in an incident of purely local origin. But generalization is not animated simply by the intent to inform. It is also designed to draw on the weight of opinion so as to obtain reparations that, aside from any material or legal sanction, may consist simply in the rehabilitation of an unjustly accused victim and, as a result, in the moral condemnation of the person at fault. It follows that disputes arising around an affair have honour or dishonour at stake first and foremost; the goals for which the recognition of others is sought

170

are simultaneously restorative and repressive. In this sense, public denunciation is indeed, as Bayle puts it, a 'civil homicide'.[1]

The analyses that follow are based on a set of 275 letters received by the Service des informations générales [General News Service] of the newspaper *Le Monde* in 1979, 1980 and 1981. The letters were sent for informational purposes and with a view to publication (although very few were actually published); they vary in length from two to forty pages. Some were sent directly to the service, while others were addressed to the publisher, to the editor in chief, or to *Le Monde* without further specification (in which case they were forwarded to the service by the receiving departments). In this newspaper, which publishes 'miscellaneous incidents' only in a purified – that is, generalized or, as it were, sublimated – form, the Service des informations générales deals with matters involving the police and the legal system, but it also handles the 'Society' page. This section is devoted to problems, phenomena, individuals and groups that do not belong in the 'Domestic Politics' section (which provides information about the government, politicians and political parties) or under the 'Current Labour Issues' rubric (which deals with matters directly related to the major national unions: labour conflicts in big companies, strikes, national negotiations, agreements, and so on), but that are nevertheless deemed relevant to the understanding of French society and its evolution. The anecdote form (which, as we see from the definition of anecdote in the Robert dictionary, 'sheds light on the underside of things'), and even the parable or fable forms, may be used to report singular events that happened to ordinary people in ordinary circumstances, while bringing out the exemplary value and general import of these events. The position that the Service des informations générales occupies in *Le Monde* determines and limits the field covered by the body of letters I undertook to analyse. Strictly political letters (from the head of a major political party writing about legislative reform, for instance) are excluded as well as letters directly related to 'social' (that is, labour) issues defined in terms of institutions (for example, a letter from the general secretary of a major labour union concerning an agreement with the government about the retirement age). In contrast, the set includes many letters about groups that are in the process of organizing, or about associations, causes and problems that are beginning to be politicized; these letters deal with feminism, regionalism, ecology, racism, prison reform, the death penalty, homosexuality, young people, drugs, poverty, crime, police actions, and so on.

All these properties mean that the body of letters I chose to examine lent itself remarkably well to a study of the way causes are constructed around the denunciation of an injustice, and to an analysis of the relationship between the construction of causes and the formation of groups (Moore 1978). Causes constituted in this way are always associated with groups, and a large number of groups can crystallize around a single cause. In the end, the procedures used to constitute and objectify collective persons and those used to associate individual persons with collective ones are quite similar (Boltanski 1987a). The interest of my corpus lies in the fact that denunciations associated with causes recognized as collective are present (owing to the position of Le Monde in the French press as the newspaper of record, and to the position of the Service des informations générales within the newspaper) in a single set of denunciations associated with unevenly constituted causes. The corpus is thus a product of practice, not a set shaped by a sociologist to suit a particular demonstration. As it happens, it contains denunciations associated with causes recognized as collective (such as a letter from a university professor taking up the defence of a political prisoner, and letters from party and union headquarters), among them causes that are in the process of being constituted and that have very uneven chances of success (regionalism, homosexuality, opposition to vaccinations, and so on); thus it also offers an opportunity to investigate the conditions that ensure the success of a given cause (Gamson 1975). Finally, the corpus includes denunciations that seem to be associated with individual interests or with causes that might be characterized as singular (for example, when an individual writes about a conflict that has set him against a colleague, a neighbour or a member of his own family), if there were not something paradoxical in the association of the two terms 'cause' and 'singular' that brings out its strangeness.

I had access to all the letters received and archived during this three-year period. My analysis bore on those that included a denunciation of injustice, whether explicit or not (76 per cent of the whole). Within this corpus, I identified those in which a victim was designated, an individual or collective person with the capacity to bring civil charges before the courts or in whose name someone else could be authorized to do so. In contrast, someone who writes to stigmatize the wrongs perpetrated by 'consumer society' is carrying out an act of denunciation, but without explicitly designating a victim. There is an implicit victim here, but one that remains indeterminate and generic (society, man, modern man, France, and so on). The situation is different when a mother writes in favour of her son, a conscientious objector in prison, or when a suburban Catholic Workers Action Group writes to denounce the efforts of the local residents' association to prevent

172

the Islamic Association from building a mosque in the same locality. The work presented here bears only on letters in which a victim was identified (43 per cent).

An error that was introduced into the reply to one of these letters will make it easier to grasp the difference between the cases in which the author wrote in the name of a general cause and the cases in which the author wrote in the name of a particular victim (possibly the author himself or herself). The head of the Service des informations générales responded to most of the letters received (80 per cent). In 33 per cent of these cases, the secretary in charge of the mail chose among several standard formulas. One of these ('Thank you for letting us know your point of view on . . . but the press of news is such that it will be impossible for us to publish . . .') was to be used in responding to letters presenting a general denunciation. Used by mistake to answer a letter in which a mother denounced the unjust imprisonment of her son, the same formula produced the following sentence: 'Madame, you were kind enough, a few weeks ago, to let us know your point of view on your son Jean-Pierre. We would have very much liked to be able to share it. Unfortunately, the press of news prevented us from doing so. We sincerely regret this.' A son, a personal object of investment, does not belong to the series of beings on which it is legitimate, for a mother, to have 'a point of view'.

Journalists read these letters, but without too many illusions, they report; they have a professional obligation to read them, in the hope of coming across some interesting piece of information whose authenticity they will then have to verify. But questions about the statements' interest or veracity are subordinated to a prior question, raised implicitly or explicitly about all the letters received: whether or not the sender is 'normal'. Some letters of denunciation may have non-trivial consequences, especially if an individual is identified by name. Le Monde subjects these immediately to a tacit screening in which readers rely on their ordinary sense of normality. Brought into play in an implicit and often seemingly unconscious fashion, this ordinary sense can be made at least partially explicit in an interview situation. Thus the journalists I questioned declared that they recognized mental illness by certain signs, often formal ones such as handwriting, the way the text was laid out on the page (cramped or widely spaced, for example), the form of the signature, the presence of several signatures by the same person, the use of rubber stamps, the presence of multiple underlinings, and reference to worthless or less than credible titles ('President of the [City] Bowling Association', 'Treasurer of the [City] Veteran's Club', and so on); more generally, readers note a contrast between marks of importance and signs betraying solitude or poverty. However, the journalists say that there is no clear-cut way to determine normality. While certain letters are 'undoubtedly' sent by 'normal' persons, whereas others 'obviously' come from 'unbalanced' persons, there are many cases in which it is hard to tell. Evidence of this uncertainty is found, for example, in a letter addressed by a representative of the service to a correspondent in the provinces: 'A woman from Toulouse recently sent us a sort of call for help; from Paris, it is hard to judge whether this appeal is genuine or whether it comes from a paranoid individual. I am taking the liberty of sending it to you so that you can see whether or not it warrants an article. Cordially yours . . .' But the ambiguity and diversity of the letters account in large part for the interest of this corpus, which can be distributed along a continuum from the particular to the general, from singular individuals to collective persons. The characteristics of the corpus justify the search for rules that would make it possible to establish correspondences between the properties of a given text, the author's self-representation, and the feeling of normality or abnormality that is aroused in the reader. Texts from political or labour union sources would not serve this purpose, nor would a set of letters by individuals perceived as unbalanced. I might have compared a pair of 'sample' sets constituted according to this same principle of opposition, but, in the absence of clearly delimited mother populations,[2] such samples would have to be based on the authority of experts – political scientists on the one hand and psychiatrists on the other; this would entail falling back on the same mode of categorization that these experts use in their professional activities. I would then be taking on two discrete and non-intersecting populations completely foreign to one another, distinguished according to the worldviews of two distinct professional groups. But I would be giving up all hope of reducing the disastrous gap between the disciplines that focus on groups and those concerned with individuals, a gap that deeply divides the human sciences, as it does the institutions these sciences help to illuminate.

In the pages that follow, I shall draw on the selected corpus as I attempt to specify what conditions a public denunciation must meet to be judged normal, and what features signal a denunciation's abnormal character along with the oddness of its author. My goal is to construct a system of rules that will make it possible to determine in what cases the attitude that consists in speaking out and protesting in a public way has any chance of being recognized as valid, even if it is contested, and in what cases it is ignored or disqualified. In this way,

I hope in particular to extend certain of the models Albert Hirschman established when he identified the constraints of normality – which are very narrow, as we shall see – to which protests and public denunciations are subject (Hirschman 1970). To analyse displacements on the particular–general axis, it will also be useful to take into account the constraints of normality that help define what can legitimately be critiqued in private or denounced in public (Hirschman 2002).

Undertaking to use a single set of instruments to deal with the 275 texts, which are remarkably disparate in most respects, I sought to reduce their diversity by applying a set of codes in a uniform manner – that is, by submitting them all to the same examination without regard to the characteristics of their authors, objects, contents, dimensions, formal properties, and so on. Like questionnaires, with which they share many properties, codes exercise a double constraint on objects: they apply a standard form to different entities and at the same time they impose the limits of the underlying theory on the questioning. In the present case, the constraint of codes on content analysis and especially on statistical analysis is more visible than when the taxonomic operation is applied to objects whose manner of classification appears self-evident because it is already used in the ordinary world – for the purposes of administrative management, for example – and because it thereby helps to generate the form in which the phenomenon studied presents itself to sociological discourse (classification by age, sex, place of residence, profession, and so on). But this does not necessarily mean that the constraint is more powerful (Desrosières and Thévenot 1979). The same can be said about the factorial analyses of the correspondences on which my descriptions of the texts and their conditions of normality are based to a significant degree. The results of these analyses depend essentially on prior coding. The analyses also extend the work of unifying the raw material by requiring the reader to discover and identify stronger principles of relevance – that is, principles endowed with a higher power of generalization than any of the codes taken separately.

The codification of the letters bore upon the following aspects.

1 *The description of the affairs* I recorded the duration of each affair, the presence of one or more interconnected affairs, the milieu in which the affair developed, the nature of the injustice suffered by the victim, the number and type of incidents of harassment or persecution inflicted on the victim (for example, exclusion, swindling, falsification of documents, threats or violence), the institutional resources that were mobilized in an effort to seek reparations (the

175

assistance of a lawyer, recourse to the courts, articles published in the press, the support of an elected official, a political party, a union or an association, and so on), the number and nature of symbolic gestures made to mobilize support (the distribution of pamphlets, the refusal to follow rules, hunger strikes, and the like), the instruments of mobilization used (for example, a support committee or petitions) and, finally, the presence in the affair of well-known personalities or of statements mentioning the existence of a conspiracy.

2 *The description of the content of the letters and the files that often accompany them* I noted the presence of one or more 'open letters', addressed, for example, to politicians or to other newspapers, and supporting documents intended to serve as proofs (most often photocopies): trial records, financial statements, tracts, personal letters, receipts of registered letters, and so on.

3 *The graphic properties of texts* I observed the accuracy of the typing when the letters were typewritten, the legibility and other characteristics of the handwriting when they were drafted by hand, the presence of supplementary markings (for example, the use of rubber stamps, underlining, or more than one ink colour) and spelling mistakes.

4 *The stylistic and rhetorical quality of the texts* Thus I noted the titles authors used to qualify themselves, the characteristics of the heading (for example, whether it was printed on a corporate letterhead or handwritten with only the name of the sender), the way authors manifested their presence in the statement ('we', 'I', 'I', 'the undersigned', and so on), the stylistic manoeuvres used (legal, literary or scientific flourishes), the procedures for generalization and association with collective causes (reference to 'the rights of man'), irony, invective, threats, statements regarding additional revelations to follow, personal confessions (including sexual elements in particular), neologisms, incomplete sentences or statements ending with suspension points, markers of distancing ('I will not go so far as to say that ...', 'they will object that ...'), stereotypical repetitions, stylistic inconsistencies (a mix of elevated and vulgar styles, or of intimate details and general propositions), logical inconsistencies, syntactic peculiarities, denegations (especially concerning mental illness) and, finally, the general properties of the report (was it a chronological narrative, or an account of events without reference to the date of the incidents reported or to the order in which they occurred?) and the presence or absence of information about the context in which the events in question took place.

5 *The properties of the response* I also studied the responses sent
   by the editors of *Le Monde*, observing the degree of 'personaliza-
   tion' (as opposed to the use of standard formulas), the presence in
   the dossier of correspondence between journalists about the affair,
   and so on.

I introduced additional codes into the factorial analysis of correspondences in the form of supplementary variables. The first ones
inventory the properties firmly attached to the letter's author: sex,
age, profession, place of residence. The second record judgements of
normality. I asked six people to read the letters rapidly and to rate
the authors' degree of normality on a scale of 1 (completely normal)
to 10 (completely insane). The judges were instructed to assign their
rating immediately after reading each letter, and they were forbidden
to change the score (for example, by comparing the letters later): 43
per cent of the letters were given, on average, a rating of 1 or 2; 23 per
cent earned a 3 or a 4; 26 per cent scored between 5 and 8; and 8 per
cent were rated 9 or 10. The time required for the task of reading and
judging the 275 letters (some of which were very long) was roughly
forty to sixty hours. In the absence of funds that could have been used
to remunerate the judges, I had to limit their number (all volunteers)
to six and to select them from my own circle of acquaintances. There
were two men and four women ranging in age from twenty-five to
seventy, all engaged in intellectual professions. I am clearly unable
to assess the bias introduced by the fact that the judges belonged to
a relatively homogeneous intellectual milieu. I cannot tell whether
judgements of normality vary according to social milieu, and to what
degree, or whether they are, on the contrary, relatively independent
of the judge's profession. A certain number of indications actually
suggest another possibility, which would be that the appreciation of
the degree of normality varies relatively little, since each individual
possesses the necessary competence to distinguish between normal and
abnormal appearances by adjusting his or her judgement in anticipation of the judgement of others, or with reference, as George Herbert
Mead puts it, to a 'generalized other'. But this first estimation could be
modified quickly by the appreciation that the individual brings to bear
on the common-sense judgement that he or she has just made, inasmuch as the individual making the judgement recognizes this as the
internalization of the judgement of others. However, the way in which
individuals reaffirm the singularity of their own position-takings
(in the ethical or political sense) with respect to what they think is
common sense unquestionably varies with the social milieu.

— 15 —

THE ACTANTIAL SYSTEM OF DENUNCIATION

A final series of codes, introduced in the form of supplementary variables, characterizes the actantial system of denunciation. These codes define, on the one hand, the characteristics of each of the actants, and the various modalities in which they may present themselves, and, on the other hand, the various modes of relations that can be established among them. The term actant, borrowed from semiology (Greimas 1982), has been used in sociology by Bruno Latour (1988b) in the sense I am giving it here. It is useful in that it designates the beings that intervene in a denunciation by a single term, whether these are individual persons, beings constituted (or in the process of being constituted) as collective persons (for example, 'Corsicans' or 'women'), or collective bodies figuring in utterances where the referent is problematic and open to question, in the sense that it can be at stake in disputes because the groups have not been constituted in an institutional form apt to confer on them an objective character ('men of good will', 'all those who suffer', and so on). One of the interesting aspects of the concept of actant lies in its capacity to replace discrete oppositions that refer to differences treated as substantial (for example, between 'individuals' and 'groups') by continuous variations in size (Callon and Latour 1981).[1]

A denunciation institutes a system of relations among four actants: (1) the one who denounces; (2) the one in favour of whom the denunciation is carried out; (3) the one to the detriment of whom it is directed; (4) the one to whom it is addressed. To simplify the exposé that follows, I shall adopt a convention allowing me to designate these four actants by the terms *denouncer*, *victim*, *persecutor* and *judge*. We should not lose sight of the fact that this mode of designation describes the system from a particular perspective – that of the

178

letter-writer; one of the stakes in the crisis in which the denunciation is inscribed is precisely that of fixing the referent for each of the terms associated with the different positions that characterize the system. In my description, each of the four actants is qualified by the position it occupies on a continuum that goes from smallest to largest, from the most singular to the most general. Let us take, first, the being to whom the denunciation is addressed. This may be a singular individual (for example, when someone informs a wife about the behaviour of her husband, who is trying to deprive her of an inheritance in favour of his mistress) or, at the opposite pole, a collective person authorized to represent humanity as a whole (for example, when 'the genocide of the Armenian people by the Turks' is denounced on the floor of the United Nations). A multitude of instances occupy intermediate positions between these two extremes. Denunciations addressed to an undercover or secret police force are thus more singular, for example, than those addressed to a judge in charge of an investigation, as the latter are subject to confirmation in a public trial. Similarly, denunciations addressed to the leaders of a political party can be considered more singular than denunciations addressed to the general assembly or the annual meeting, and so forth. In the case of the letters analysed here, which were sent to a newspaper of record that tacitly acts as an agency of civic judgement, and which were for the most part intended by their authors for publication, the being to which the denunciations were addressed (identical in each case, so that it was not necessary to identify this feature by means of a code) occupies an elevated position on the singular–general axis, since *public opinion* is involved.

The same remarks apply to the other three actants – the denouncer, the victim and the persecutor – each of whom also occupies a determined position between the singular and the general. Thus the author

1 may not give a self-endorsement, which is the case when the letter-writer does not mention his or her own name (*anonymous individual*);[2]
2 may write in his or her own name and only in that name (*singular individual*);
3 may write in his or her own name while indicating that he or she represents something more – for example, by invoking a profession that authorizes its practitioners (doctors, priests, sociologists, lawyers, and so on) to speak for others, or by bringing out connections with others, using a company letterhead, for instance, even in a denunciation not explicitly made in the name of the collective person designated by the letterhead (*authorized individual*);

179

4 may speak in the name of a collective person without managing to induce the belief that he or she is actually supported by others, which is the case, for example, when the denouncer is at once the victim and the president of the defence committee in the name of which he or she claims to be intervening (*dubious collective person*);

5 may speak in the name of a collective person whose existence is attested and collectively recognized (even if its representativeness is contested, in particular by competing agencies, which is practically always the case) but whose area of specialization is limited – for example, the Society of Certified Teachers, the Organic Farmers Association, the Consumers Anti-Noise Association, and so on (*restricted collective person*);

6 may intervene in the name of a collective person whose existence is undeniable and whose field of activity is extensive, as is the case, for example, with large labour confederations such as the Confédération générale du travail or the Confédération française démocratique du travail, or major political parties (*extensive collective person*).

Victims also occupy a determined position along the same axis, depending on whether they present themselves as individuals or as collective beings. The victim may be

1 a single private person whose case is not connected with a recognized cause (*victim = singular individual*);

2 an individual who as a person does not embody a cause but whose denunciation can be associated with a collective cause – a conscientious objector, for example (*victim = individual with the potential of becoming a cause*);

3 an individual who is, in his or her singularity and indissociably, inasmuch as he or she embodies a collective interest, a cause for others.

This last was the case with Captain Dreyfus, who remains the often invoked and stereotypical example of the series. We know indeed that Dreyfus, stripped of his own affair to the extent that he became an object and an instrument of mobilization, existed for his defenders only inasmuch as he was the support for a cause, and thus was the binding element of a group, although the cohesiveness supplied was relatively supple as compared to the rigidity introduced by criterial and legal modes of constitution. This is clear from the episode of his pardon, reported by Pierre Vidal-Naquet. When Dreyfus accepted the pardon that was offered him, which granted him freedom but not collective and official recognition of his innocence, he no longer represented anyone but himself: in other words, he represented nothing at all, as was noted by a radical Dreyfusard, the lawyer Fernand Labori.[3] In my corpus, I identified IRA hunger strikers as individuals-who-became-causes, but also, for example, Philippe Maurice, a prisoner condemned to death, and Roger Knobelspiess, another prisoner condemned 'by common law'; these men embodied the struggle against the death penalty and maximum-security confinement (*victim=individual-who-becomes-a-cause*). The victim can also be

4 an acknowledged collective person: an association, a political party, an institution, and so forth (*victim = acknowledged collective person*); or, finally,
5 a group nominally designated in its generality, and not through its agencies of representation, without reference to membership criteria or to sharply drawn boundaries, as when one speaks of the proletariat, victims of racism, the poor, the disabled, and so on (*victim = a group with fuzzy contours*).

Persecutors can be characterized in the same way. A persecutor can be

1 an unknown individual, which is the case, for example, when a letter denounces an attack carried out in a public place (*persecutor = unknown*);
2 a private individual whose name and identity are known (*persecutor = identified individual*);
3 a private individual acting nevertheless as a representative of an institution or group – for instance, when the persecutor is qualified as the head of a business, a judge, a superintendent of schools, and so on (*persecutor = authorized representative*); or, finally,
4 an institution or group designated in its generality (*persecutor = collective person*).

Two other coding arrangements describe the relation between the actants and, more precisely, their degree of proximity – that is, as we shall see later on, the degree of singularity of the relation between the denouncer and the victim and between the victim and the persecutor. The denouncer can

1 know nothing at all about the victim, which is the case, for example, in testimony that reports street violence (*victim–denouncer = no link*);
2 be associated with the victim in a relationship of militancy (for example, be a member of the victim's support committee);
3 maintain either a *professional relationship* with the victim (for example, when colleagues from the same institution are involved) or a *friendly relationship*; or, finally,
4 belong to the *same family*.

But the denouncer and the victim may also be one and the same person, as for example when the author of a letter writes to expose his own case and submits the injustice that he has suffered to public opinion. This relation of self to self comes closer to identity when

5 the denouncer-victim is a *private individual* than when she is already recognized by others as a cause, so that the victim can speak about herself not in her own name but in the name of a collective interest, and, as it were, with distance, as if she were a stranger to herself (*victim-denouncer = a single individual who becomes a cause*).

As for the victim,

1 he may have had no prior relationship with the person who did him wrong – who aggressed him, for example (*victim–persecutor = no link*);
2 she may be situated in the same universe as the persecutor, one in which, for example, the persecutor has power over her, though without having any personal relationship, as when an employee is led to denounce the conduct of the head of human resources in her company (*victim–persecutor: impersonal link*).

But the victim may also maintain, or may have maintained in the past, close personal relations with the persecutor, who may be

3 a colleague (*victim–persecutor = professional link*);
4 a neighbour (*victim–persecutor = link of proximity*), or
5 a relative (*victim–persecutor = family connection*).

The factorial analysis of correspondences distributes the properties of the corpus that were subjected to codification according to a structure isomorphic to that of the actantial system (see figure 1). The first axis, which represents 8.71 per cent of the total inertia (see Appendix 1), contrasts the letters in terms of the degree of proximity between the actants – that is, in terms of the degree to which the relation that links them is personal. This applies to both the victim–denouncer and the victim–persecutor relations. Thus cases in which the denouncer and the victim are the same private person are opposed to cases in which they have no link. Between these two extreme positions, we find relations that are less and less personal as we move towards the right side of the figure: family relations (for example, a wife writes on behalf of her husband), friendly or professional relations and, finally, militant relations (for example, a member of an association or a support committee defends an individual inasmuch as that individual represents a cause). The relations between victim and perpetrator are ordered along the same axis and according to a similar principle. Thus at one pole we find cases in which the victim and the persecutor maintain the most personal relations, since they are linked by family ties, and at the opposite pole we have cases in which their encounter was random and fleeting: they entered into interaction inasmuch as they belonged to different social categories, so that any actor in the denunciation could be replaced by any other member of the same category with no modification in the structure of the relation uniting the parties. Between these two extremes, moving towards the right of the figure, we find a continuum going in the direction of disinvestment and distancing of the relation between victim and persecutor; in order of proximity, these actants may be close neighbours or in a direct relationship within the same community, or in a relationship within the same professional community or the same institution, or, finally, they may be situated in the same universe, linked by institutional dependencies or relations of subordination, but without knowing each other personally. Further on in the same series we find cases in which the persecutor is not an individual but a collective person, group, institution or even a state (a modality that is equally pertinent on the second axis).

The second axis (4.27 per cent of the total inertia) depicts the position of the actants between the singular and the collective, and the degree to which collective resources have been brought into play. Here, cases in which the principal actants are private individuals who have not mobilized collective resources are opposed to cases in which the principal actants are collective persons or their representatives, and in which numerous collective resources (associations, courts, journals, and so on) have been used. Letters in which the author

183

Figure 1

The structure of the actanfial system

NB The numbers represent the projection of normality ratings.

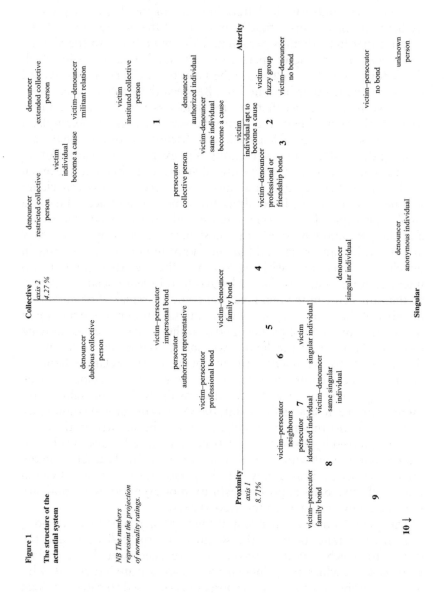

writes in his or her name alone (and, still further on in the order of singularity but with a weak factorial weight, those in which the author remains anonymous) are thus opposed to letters in which the author writes in the name of a collective person. Between these two poles we find a series of intermediate cases, in which, for example, the author writes in her own name but points out the connection that links her with others, or those in which the author carries out his act in the name of an unknown collective person and without guarantees. These differences are manifested in the very way in which the author's identity is set forth: for instance, in the choice between plain paper and letterhead, between a handwritten header and a typed header, and, finally – closest to the collective pole – the use of a printed letterhead that includes the writer's name and titles or, for collective persons, the corporate name.

Different modes of denunciation correspond to the different states that the actantial system can take on, as I shall try to show by briefly describing figure 2. For easier reading, I have divided this figure into four parts defined by the intersection of the first two axes.[4] In the first zone (A), characterized by a high level of singularity on the part of both the actants and the relations that unite them, the victim herself denounces the injustice of which she claims to have been the object, and she designates a persecutor who is close to her, to whom she is linked by relations of geographical proximity or even family ties. The affair is not taken over by collective agencies. The victim alone writes long letters, pages saturated with text or overwritten with graphic or syntactic signs or singular features: underlining, more than one ink colour, capital letters, marks of hesitation (for example, a sudden break in the middle of a sentence), 'paradoxisms' (associating words that are ordinarily opposed), and so on. She lists in no particular order the many persecutions she has suffered, often over a long period of time, and mobilizes figures of speech best suited to express despair and vehemence, such as insults, nicknames, sarcasm, repetitions and neologisms.

In the second zone (B), collective resources are used. But these are resources which have as their principal feature (as would be the case in the legal system) the fact that they operate in the name of the group, managing controversies between individuals who remain designated by their own names, as persons, and not as personifications of historical and economic forces (as would be the case in political discourse): recourse to the courts (strongly represented on both axes) or to a lawyer (well represented on axis 2), intervention (however brief) by the police, and so on. Here we find in particular economic conflicts

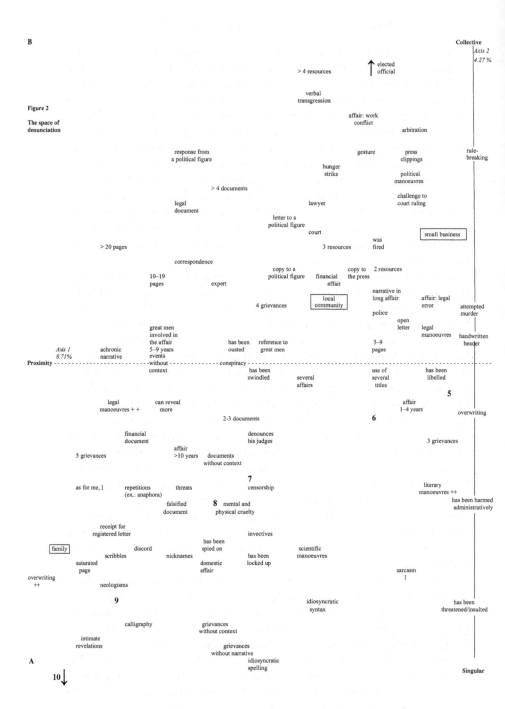

B

Collective

Axis 2
4.27 %

> 4 resources — elected official

verbal transgression

Figure 2

The space of denunciation

affair: work conflict

arbitration

response from a political figure — gesture — press clippings — rule-breaking

hunger strike

political manoeuvres

> 4 documents

challenge to court ruling

legal document — lawyer

letter to a political figure

court — was fired — small business

> 20 pages — 3 resources

correspondence

10–19 pages — copy to a political figure — financial affair — copy to the press — 2 resources

expert

narrative in long affair — affair: legal error — attempted murder

4 grievances — local community — police — open letter — legal manoeuvres — handwritten header

great men involved in the affair — has been ousted — reference to great men — 5–9 pages

Axis 1
8.71%

achronic narrative — 5–9 years events

Proximity - - - - - - - - - - - without - - - - - - - - - - conspiracy -
context

has been swindled — several affairs — use of several titles — has been libelled

5

legal manoeuvres + + — can reveal more

affair 1–4 years — overwriting

2-3 documents

6

financial document — denounces his judges — 3 grievances

5 grievances — affair >10 years — documents without context

7

as for me, I — repetitions (ex.: anaphora) — threats — censorship — literary manoeuvres ++

has been harmed administratively

falsified document — **8** mental and physical cruelty

receipt for registered letter — invectives

family — discord — has been spied on — scientific manoeuvres

scribbles — nicknames — has been locked up — sarcasm I

saturated page — domestic affair

overwriting ++ — neologisms

9

idiosyncratic syntax — has been threatened/insulted

calligraphy — grievances without context

intimate revelations — grievances without narrative — idiosyncratic spelling

A

10 ↓

Singular

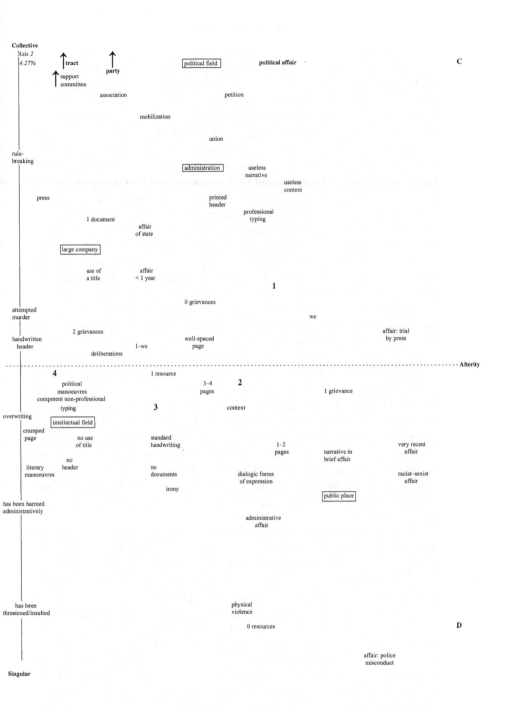

(for example, over the sale of goods or real property, or involving dishonest competition) in which the victim is often a farmer, a tradesman, an artisan, or a small business owner who makes the denunciation himself or has it handled by a family member or friend (these are the social categories in which the denouncer is most often linked to the victim by family ties). Moving towards the right (lesser proximity) or towards the top (increased collective character), we find modalities that, for different reasons and to different degrees, correspond to modes of constitution and shaping, and to strategies. More particularly, they involve controversies situated inside businesses or government agencies in which the victim and the persecutor belong to the same professional milieu without necessarily knowing each other. These affairs may take shape, for example, around a firing deemed unwarranted. They may include recourse to an arbitration board (well represented on axis 2). Letters in this set report affairs that are in the process of being constituted as collective, characterized by the occupation of an intermediate position between, on the one hand, personal controversies involving individuals linked by a tissue of relations, especially affective ones, and, on the other hand, union or party conflicts that are presented as involving not only individuals but also groups; among letters in the latter category is a narrative constructed in chronological order and presented straightforwardly ('here are the facts'). The use of stylistic devices with a political flavour is inscribed in this part of the factorial grid along with the other manoeuvres by means of which individuals who lack the support of political organizations can attempt to confer a collective dimension on their affairs by undertaking an individual effort to mobilize support (for example, making gestures with symbolic value such as openly breaking rules, taking the floor in public, distributing pamphlets, or going on a hunger strike).

To these individualized protests (often linked to recommendations by dubious collective persons) are opposed, in the third quadrant of figure 2 (C), the modalities that refer to the universe of politics properly speaking, characterized at once by formalization and normalization of the relations among the actants and by a collective acceptance of responsibility for the denunciation. The author writes in the capacity of representative and uses the first person plural ('we'); the victim is associated with a constituted cause (conscientious objector, regionalist political militant, and so on). The victim is persecuted by a state in the name of 'the right of the state', or by an individual, but only inasmuch as the individual represents an institution or a group. The denouncer, linked to the victim by a militant relation,

188

Table 1 Resources and persecutions (in percentages)

Universe	Resources							Persecutions							
	Union	Labour board	Political party	Association	Elected official	Court	Lawyer	Firing or layoff	Exclusion	Libel	Swindling	Falsification	Spying	Ordinary violence	Hidden violence
Big companies, gov't agencies	19	14	5	5	10	43	24	48	14	10	24	10	10	5	19
Political world	6	6	28	56	11	33	11	11	6	28	–	–	11	28	–
Artists, intellectuals, teachers	8	13	–	4	4	25	13	33	29	21	25	8	8	13	13
Small businesses	–	10	–	5	5	67	24	24	10	43	62	19	–	5	14
Villages, small towns, rural areas	6	13	10	6	6	55	42	13	13	42	48	16	16	23	6
Families	–	–	–	10	5	65	55	5	30	45	50	40	25	20	45

Note: This composite table, like the ones that follow, presents figures drawn from various matrices. It reads as follows: in 19 per cent of the affairs that have occurred in a large company or government agency, union resources have been used.

refers to a mobilization from which the victim has already benefited, and uses this as the chief argument for mobilizing public opinion. The denouncer invokes the support of collective and political resources – associations, unions, parties, defence committees – and supplies material proof in the form of petitions, photocopies of tracts, or press clippings (all indicators of collective mobilization have a very high factorial level in the determination of the second axis). The dimension of the actants shrinks as one moves down axis 2, which represents the factor characterized by the opposition between private persons and collective persons. Thus in the part of figure 2 close to axis 1 we find letters in which the denouncer expresses herself vigorously in her own name, but only inasmuch as she possesses a personal authority that authorizes her to speak for others (as attested by the alternation between ' I' and 'one') in favour of major humanitarian causes (important doctors or lawyers, well-known intellectuals, cadres in public agencies, artists who write on letterhead and mention their titles, and so on).

The fourth quadrant of figure 2 (D) is characterized, like the third, by the absence of singular and invested relations among the beings present in the denunciation, but it differs in the size of the actants. The upper part of the schema represents collective persons that are more or less legally constituted; the lower part represents individuals endowed with bodies (they may have exchanged blows). In this part of the factorial schema we find letters of denunciation referring to brief, incidental affairs characterized by the lack of prior links among the participants, these actants having been brought inexorably into relationship by the affair itself. This is especially the case with clashes, often accompanied by physical aggression and brutality, that take place in anonymous sites, such as city streets, department stores, supermarkets, car parks, train stations, and the like. An individual is aggressed by police officers (in numerous cases), by security guards, by a petty criminal, because he is black or of North African origin (*racism*), because she is a woman (*sexism*), and so on. Both victims and aggressors are defined by their membership in a category. Another individual who happens to be on the spot – often, reportedly, by chance – and who does not know the actors or the reasons for the dispute, becomes associated with this incipient affair and constitutes it precisely as such, either by intervening or simply by observing passively and then testifying in public, as a journalist might. There is no relation between the victim and the persecutor or between the denouncer and the victim. They did not know one another before the encounter and were not until that point objects of investments, negative or positive, for one another. Nothing lasting – debt, gratitude or desire – associates them with one another.

— 16 —

THE REQUIREMENT OF DESINGULARIZATION

The normality ratings are ordered along a diagonal trajectory on figure 2. They rise steadily as we move from affairs that were taken in hand by a collective agency, and in which the participants maintained no personal relations, to affairs that associated individuals already linked by affective relations (especially family ties) and that had to be entirely managed by the victim without the help of collective resources, and without recourse to the minimal form of accompaniment that would entail transferring the burden of the denunciation onto someone else, perhaps a close friend or family member. My first hypothesis concerns the rules on which the competence to pass judgements of normality is based. The reader's composite judgement regarding the normality or oddness of the testimony submitted depends on the relation between the relative worths of the four actants and on the respective positions they occupy between the singular and the collective, the particular and the general. There is nothing abnormal about denunciations in themselves. Injustice and scandal can be proclaimed, and indeed are constantly announced, in a variety of registers: in political or union discourse but also on a daily basis, and more or less casually, by one person to another, among friends, on the telephone, in families, on the bus, among colleagues, in whispers or out loud, in the lunchroom, discreetly, in the elevator, by persons alone, in endless rehashings ('then I told him . . .' 'do you know what he had the nerve to answer . . .', 'it's really unbelievable', 'it's shameful', 'can you imagine, if the word got out . . .', 'you have to see it to believe it', and so on). In our societies, all actors possess critical capacities and can mobilize the critical resources they use in the course of their everyday lives, although they no doubt do this more or less

191

effectively depending on the situation. This is the sense in which our societies can be qualified as critical.

What constitutes abnormal behaviour for actors is thus not that they use their sense of justice to point out instances of unfairness, humiliation or offence, or even that they try to get others to share the indignation these instances arouse, for these ordinary activities are part of our daily routines. The abnormality consists simply, in these cases, in denouncing an injustice suffered in situations that do not lend themselves to denunciation, and in addressing protests to inappropriate persons, whether individual or collective. In this sense, the origin of the abnormality can be said to be first of all cognitive. In sum, a denunciation is abnormal if it is produced in a situation that does not allow the harmonization of actants of the same size. There is discordance, for example, when a victim, attested in his or her most *singular* aspects, designates for *public* reprobation an equally singular persecutor, identified by name and qualified as a person and not as a representative of a collective. A denunciation is not judged abnormal (although it still may not be judged morally justifiable or legitimate) when the actants occupy roughly homologous positions on the singular–collective axis. It is not abnormal for someone to denounce publicly, in the name of the leadership of a major national union, the destruction of Palestinian camps by the Israeli air force; it is not abnormal for the residents' association of Boissy-Saint-Léger to denounce to the municipal authorities the expulsion of the inhabitants of a poor neighbourhood by a real estate development firm. Here we recognize two modalities of 'political action', and political action itself can be situated at different levels of generality. Thus particular and circumstantial denunciations can be opposed to a political programme oriented towards the definition of a common good. In such cases the denunciation may remain implicit, precisely because it is immersed in the general, in such a way that certain of the actants, and most notably the victim, no longer need to be explicitly qualified.

It is not abnormal, either, for an ordinary individual to denounce injustices committed towards him by his department head to someone in his entourage – a relative, friend or colleague – in a private or what might be called a *domestic* relation. He will do this by word of mouth and in the mode of gossip, which can be communicated without need for the sort of justifications valid across the board that a public denunciation requires. Gossip is in fact the way in which the singular makes itself known without being articulated in a public context; it begins in discourse produced by an individual and transmitted serially in singular relations from one private person to another. Its main feature is that it lacks a subject as its source, since each person only reports to another the information that has been transmitted by a third party; it is available for new investments only to the extent that the question of its relation to reality can be suspended. One can spread gossip without being subjected to a requirement of justification and, consequently, without having to use procedures of proof. The interlocutor is free to believe it or not. For gossip is simply a matter of belief, in the sense of an unforced adherence that one does not have to legitimize by clarifying its reference to an object through a series of testable mediations. In gossip, one can say anything, because one's speech only passes through relations where nothing intervenes to solidify it. Thus, as Max Gluckman has noted (Gluckman 1963), one can only collect gossip incidentally, by inserting oneself in one of the chains where it circulates; one can never do so in a systematic or explicit way. A sociologist cannot undertake an interview campaign, for instance, by asking an informant: 'Tell me the gossip that's going around in your professional circle.' The same person who was ready to keep you in the register of gossip for hours will now remain silent – not in an act of self-censorship, but because she finds nothing more to say in the speech situation created by the interview with a social scientist and because, owing to the very fact that the situation includes taping or note-taking, it implicitly refers to a public space that extends beyond the immediate context.

Thus, in the register of civic action, denunciation brings together actants who are all large-scale collective persons or their representatives. It is quite easy to see this in the case of a political critique focused on the common good that submits the injustice suffered by one group at the hands of another to the judgement of public opinion – that is, to the judgement of the sovereign people. At the opposite pole, a denunciation can bring together actants whose references are to singular individuals, provided that the speech situation is of the personal or private order. In both cases, the critique can be carried out in a perfectly acceptable way without shocking our ordinary sense of normality. But the larger the gap between the position occupied on the singular–collective axis by the various actants brought together by the act of denunciation, the more the denunciation risks being perceived as abnormal. It is not normal, for example, for the father of a family to write a political programme destined solely for his children (unless of course he is a king who embodies in his lineage the generality of the common good). It is not normal to send a letter to the police denouncing the behaviour of the ruling class in general. It is not normal, either, for a private individual to use a letter to the editor as a means to denounce before public opinion a son guilty of lacking respect for his parents. These things are not done – at least not in democratic republics – that is, in a political order in which domestic relations are completely detached from civic relations. But they were possible in France under the Old Regime, where the generality of the common good was constituted in terms of filiation, and subjects could appeal directly to the king to resolve family problems, as we can see from the *lettres de cachet* published by Arlette Farge and Michel Foucault (1982). As this example shows, if my analysis is correct, the constraints of normality that weigh on denunciation must depend fundamentally on the way in which each political order constructs the relation between the particular and the general, between private interests and the common good.

For the same reasons, the chances that a denunciation may be perceived as normal or abnormal seem to depend as well on the degree to which relations between the individuals engaged in the affair are close or distant. Knowing that a public denunciation calls for the punishment of a guilty party, it understandably appears more suspicious if the one whose wrongdoing is denounced is close to the denouncer – if he belongs to the same family, institution or community. The act of public denunciation in fact puts at risk not only the individual designated but also the entire community to which the denouncer and the persecutor belong, a community whose reputation with respect to the outside world is tarnished and which is also threatened with internal disruption through the polarization between opposing camps that is inherent in the logic of mobilization at work in affairs. The suspicion that weighs upon the denunciation increases even more when the denouncer acts alone and intervenes in public to take up his own defence. For in this case it is easy to denounce the denunciation in return by unmasking it not as an act oriented towards justice but as an act of individual vengeance designed to serve purely personal interests.

This is where it becomes necessary, if a denunciation is to be able to claim validity, for its weight to be supported by two different actants – that is, both by the victim who suffered from the action denounced and by the denouncer who made the injustice known to public opinion. The doubling of the victim and the one who puts the accusation before the public in the victim's place (and who often plays the role of spokesperson or master of ceremonies with respect to a silent victim) guarantees that the interests involved are not purely individual. The greater the degree of 'otherness' between victim and denouncer, and the longer the chain of mediations between them, the more credible the guarantee of disinterestedness will be. The supporting power that one individual can place at the service of another thus depends not only on his or her own value (credibility, honourableness, and so on), and in this way on his or her power of mobilization, but also on the degree of distance between victim and defender. Those close to the victim – friends, neighbours, acquaintances, co-workers, and especially, of course, those who belong to the same family – are not completely other. This is a classic argument; it is the one Aristotle used to exclude problems stemming from 'the internal order of the family' from political law governing relations of justice within a polity (Villey 1975, 36–43): 'For the law-maker would be able to determine a proportion only between persons who are different but equal in certain respects. Members of the same family, united by love, sharing in the same economic life, are not sufficiently other with respect to one another – "the son is something of the father"' (Villey 1983, 58–9). Those nearest to the victim – members of the same family, community or group – share their singularity with the victim, and the way they make one body with the victim is suspect because it always tends to reduce otherness to unity through the bias of hidden interest. Apparently double, they are only one since they are 'in cahoots', as it were. If support for a victim is to exercise a mobilizing effect on other persons, there must be nothing in the situation that could hint at a connection between the denouncer and the victim that could support a common interest. These partners must be united solely by a shared goal, which is the common good.

In conformity with this principle, in the course of affairs there are only two ways to reduce the effect of a denunciation and to disqualify an act of support. The first (which might be called sociological disqualification) consists in diminishing the otherness of the partners by revealing, through interpretation, that they are connected by a hidden interest, that they are concealing a common attribute powerful enough to override other determining factors, especially the motives they invoke to justify their actions. What connects the victim and his or her defender is that, 'in fact', they are both Jewish, or freemasons, or members of the bourgeoisie, or communists, and so on. The public support these sidekicks offer one another is paralleled by a secret agreement or a tacit alliance. One can then hypothesize that the power of a mobilization – that is, its power to enroll new individuals (although not necessarily its cohesive force and the resulting capacity to resist adverse blows over time) – depends on the degree to which it appears as unpredictable – in other words, the degree to which the ruptures to which it leads or the alliances that it inaugurates seem

195

irreducible to pre-existing divisions that are recognized as such and inscribed in texts, nomenclatures or the law (for example, ethnic or religious divisions, social classes or political parties). In short, the associations created by an affair are all the stronger to the extent that, when tested, they prove to be irreducible to any other form of association. This is why, in the Dreyfus affair, for example, the actors supporting Dreyfus emphasized the unpredictable character of the support received by those who were struggling for a review of the trial, while their adversaries, conversely, were trying to unveil the bonds that secretly linked all the Dreyfusards. 'I was young', Léon Blum wrote in his recollections of the affair,

> and there was something that experience had not yet taught me: that the most fallacious operation of the mind is the advance calculation of the reactions of a man or a woman to a truly unforeseen test. One is almost always wrong when one claims to be making this calculation by applying already-acquired psychological data, through a sort of logical extension of known character and past life. Every test is new and every test finds a new man. Among the stars of anti-Dreyfusism, and even of Dreyfusism, certain ones did not occupy their logical place, their logically foreseeable place, and these tangled misplacements troubled my innocence. (Blum 1935, 74)

But the fact remains – and this is the second available procedure – that, when an act of denunciation or support cannot be disqualified by reference to an underlying interest, one can still try to reduce it by emphasizing its arbitrary and therefore irrational, absurd or insane character (psychiatric disqualification).

I still need to specify the sense in which I am using the term *proximity* to qualify the bond that can unite the individuals involved in an affair. What characterizes those 'near' to the actants is not, or not only, the respective positions they occupy in space, but the degree of singularity of the relation that unites them. This is a function of the nature and strength of their mutual investments, affective investments in particular – that is, the 'costs' each one has agreed to bear in order to establish a 'stable relation [with the other] over a certain period of time' (Thévenot 1983) and – by that very token, as we shall see more clearly later on – in order to establish, by means of this external constraint, a stable relation to his or her own identity. These investments may themselves be very unequally singularized according to the degree to which the instruments used to establish the relation, to achieve equivalencies and to constitute a common interest are incorporated and thus bound to the uses made of bodies, or, on the contrary, the degree to which the instruments are standardized and objectified, as for example when two persons are associated by belonging to the same institution or by having the same title (Bourdieu and Boltanski 1975). Depending on the nature of the instruments to which they can turn in order to bond with others, individuals in fact have very unequal access to institutional resources that permit them – especially in cases of crisis or conflict – to put 'distance' between themselves and others – that is, to manage their relations in an impersonal, rule-governed way, in terms of a legally defined identity and with reference to a collective interest. We may say that a relation is capable of being *desingularized* when one of the individuals involved can be treated, according to the circumstances, as a member of a category for whom any other member of the same category could be substituted without any resulting modification in the structure of the relation.[1] On the contrary, in a singular relation, the relation defines the objects that it connects, and there is no more powerful principle for identifying these objects than the relationship itself. What characterizes the relation between those 'close' to an individual is precisely the fact that the structure of the relationship depends on each of the terms inasmuch as they cannot be assigned to classes. My hypothesis is that collective work is required – the deployment of particular social procedures and the construction of specific institutions (Boltanski 1987a) – if people are to refer to a general interest and establish principles of equivalence that allow them to bring together in the same category individuals whose associations had previously been difficult or unlikely, and, by the same operation, to put distance between individuals who are close in other respects and desingularize their relations by distributing them among different classes. However, this collective work is very unevenly accomplished in the various worlds in which persons enter into relationships: instruments of desingularization are less accessible, for example, in the universe of family relations than in that of work relations. Thus adolescents can speak among themselves of 'parents' in general in a way that is never quite the same as when union members speak of 'bosses'. In fact, in the case of kinship bonds, the institutional desingularization of invested relations is not a normal recourse. It is still difficult today, despite the work done since the nineteenth century (Boltanski 1969) and the recent development of psychoanalytic and legal resources, to manage the relation that one maintains with one's mother or brother as if it were a generic relation to mothers or brothers. The fact remains that, even in the case of work relations, the possibilities of desingularization remain very uneven depending on the space taken into account. The differences

197

in this regard are once again quite considerable; they depend in particular on whether one is dealing with large organizations that have a formal hierarchy of positions, a significant union presence, collective bargaining agreements, and so on, or with small businesses in which work relations, and in particular relations of subordination, are not easily distinguished from domestic relations among persons.

— 17 —

THE DIFFICULT DENUNCIATION OF
KITH AND KIN

The presence of collective resources affects denunciations in that it allows offended individuals to externalize their grievances by organizing them in a narrative and even, under certain conditions, by making them public in generic and therefore acceptable forms. But it does more than this: it also helps define the very object of the victims' complaints. The persecutions mentioned in the corpus are distributed along the second axis as a function of the degree to which the victim can appeal to collective resources in order to obtain reparation. Thus insults or threats, which affect elderly persons and women in particular, and which are taken into account by the courts only under certain very limited circumstances (when they are in writing, for example), are opposed to firings, which are probably the easiest of all forms of damage to manage collectively, because they can be addressed both by unions and by the courts. But persecutions are also pertinent on the first axis, where they are distributed according to a continuum that follows the degree to which the relation between the actants is objectified. Here we see an opposition, for example, between *firing*, which is a particularly frequent motif in big companies and in public administrations, and which presupposes a clear (that is, legally constituted) boundary separating belonging from non-belonging, and *exclusion*, often invoked in artistic and intellectual milieus, where belonging depends essentially on recognition by others and where obtaining such recognition is never guaranteed or achieved for all time. Following the same logic, *libel*, which refers to an objectifiable and legally sanctioned act, is opposed to *spying*, which presupposes physical proximity of the persecutor and causes all the more suffering in that the offence is virtually impossible to prove or even to make credible in the eyes of others.

The statistically clear relation between the nature of the persecutions suffered and the universe in which their author is embedded (a relation that is particularly strong when the victim is also the denouncer) depends essentially on the degree to which collective resources are available in each universe, and on the nature of these resources. Those that exercise the strongest power of desingularization – namely, the support of a political party, an association or a union – are available in practical terms only when the affair arises in the space of political struggles explicitly defined as such (in regionalist conflicts, for example), in a large company or in a major public administration. The work of the union, and more precisely the work of the union delegate, consists largely in selecting from among the multitude of everyday clashes those that can be raised to the order of a collective demand. For this purpose, personal conflicts in which the actors are fully immersed, along with their multifaceted commitments and investments (for example, their sexuality, which could not have been taken into account in union discourse before the feminist movement constituted collective linguistic resources),[1] have to be transformed into *categorial conflicts*. This transformation presupposes a vast work of stylization, mobilization and shaping, simultaneous explicitation and implicitation that makes it possible to convert 'dirty' conflicts that bring together the most disparate beings in indescribable disorder – men, interests, things, passions, bodies, women, money, attachments, acts of treachery, and so on – in 'clean' conflicts that recognize only fitting, impersonal and, above all, homogeneous beings such as rules, agreements, groups, representatives, and so on.

But even in contexts where unions exist, the fact remains that even the most apparently detached relations still have to rely on repressing the bonds of proximity, attachment and investment towards which they can always regress. This is particularly apparent in the professional milieus that demand a high degree of investment and loyalty on the part of individuals. In these universes, union constructs are particularly fragile because the alterity of the union members and their adversaries can always be undone by the revelation of what everyone knows in a different state of relations: that the collective person of the union and the collective person to which the union is opposed (the company, the bosses, the administration, and so on) consist of the same individuals and the same resources. These situations are very costly because they oblige individuals themselves to attend constantly, and without the possibility of relying on habitual routines, to the way the positions they occupy in different collective

200

persons are interrelated. Thus, for example, to return to a paradigmatic figure, individuals may have to state publicly in whose name they are speaking ('here I'm putting on my union cap'). Explicitly or tacitly, everyday practices thus continually raise the same questions. As a union member, for instance, how am I to use information that would be useful to me but that I cannot acknowledge having because I have gained access to it by non-union means?

In contrast, in small businesses, where resources that would permit a regulated management of reciprocities in the categorial mode (that is, by means of institutionalized systems permitting individuals to be viewed as equivalent) are not very well developed, conflicts have to be managed as they arise. One approach involves turning to an arbitration board (Cam 1981), an institution whose power of desingularization is relatively weak since it deals with each case precisely in terms of what is singular about it, and according to jurisprudence that can remain implicit, without associating each of the actors in the clash with more general classes ('the proletariat', 'management', 'wage-earners', and so on). In universes subject to the logic of personal relations, in which individuals are connected by a common past and often caught up in networks of mutual obligations, making clashes explicit and, especially, making them known to the outside world always threatens to affect the entire set of relations within the group in every respect. In the case of conflicts between neighbours, to take another type of community as an example, denunciations are most often made public by the victims themselves, at their own risk. These conflicts are sometimes taken up by a political agency, an association, or local elected officials who are individualized political representatives occupying an intermediary position between the most generalizing resources – unions or political parties – and resources who, like lawyers, manage singularity institutionally. But in most cases the legal system constitutes the only recourse, and this is especially true when the clash has an economic dimension (as in conflicts over real estate).

Where families are concerned, the high degree of singularity of the bonds among individuals makes the use of institutional resources virtually incompatible with the maintenance of the relation that these institutions have to manage. This is the case not only for resources constituted in the political mode in the form of associations centred around a cause (an association of divorced fathers, for instance), but also for the judicial resources accessible only when victims manage to transform their family dramas into legal affairs (divorce, conflict over an inheritance, and so on). Moreover, this process does not always suffice to make explicit a grievance that escapes the logic of the instituted forms; by that very token, it may not suffice to bring the affair to an end. Finally, external collective resources are least numerous and most difficult to mobilize in artistic milieus, which recognize no law but the judgement of peers (a judgement often confused with the verdict of the market, which may consist – as it does in the art world – of a tight network of buyers, museum conservators and private collectors), but also in intellectual circles and, to a lesser degree, in universities; because the victim in these contexts is very often connected, and for the same reasons, to the persecutor (whose judgement the victim internalizes), the circumstances make it very difficult to objectify the trauma.

The less access victims have to collective resources that would allow them to objectify their grievances and desingularize their relations with the persons who are the cause of their distress, the more the persecutions they suffer tend to take bodily forms, as we see in cases of complaints that refer to physical or mental violence, or to various manoeuvres targeting vital forces. The wounds and injuries inflicted on the victim sometimes take on objectified forms whose instruments and effects are physical and, most importantly, whose agent is an external individual, as is the case when a blow is struck; in other cases, wounds and injuries take on internalized or even incorporated, invisible, insidious forms that even more surely destroy the individuals that they are secretly attacking from within. Here we find an opposition that is common in ordinary discourse about illness, which distinguishes sharply between exogenous illnesses produced by an external agent, objectified in a fever and limited in time, such as infectious diseases, and endogenous illnesses, essentially forms of cancer, which belong to and are incorporated within individuals, ravaging and destroying them from the inside (Boltanski 1971).

In fact, the closer persecutors are to their victims, the more the wounds and offences that are inflicted – and that cannot be formulated in normal discourse in the absence of collective support – are made endogenic, and the more they have the effect of attacking the victims' integrity and, as it were, separating them from themselves. Thus along the first axis (structured according to the degree of proximity between the actants) we see how incidental and exogenic physical violence (for example, a blow from a policeman's club) is opposed to the insidious, endogenized violence that acts unbeknown to others, and often even to the victim: withholding of care, poisoned food or water, electric shocks during sleep, lasers, constant intolerable noise, whispered insults, and so on. Such acts are not so much

202

aimed at killing victims as at driving them to suicide. These crimes are brought to fruition only when victims take on the intentions of their persecutors and carry out the sentence in spite of themselves; in so doing, they are in a way confirming the singularity of the relation between the actants by conferring a character of quasi-identity on the proximity between victim and persecutor. These acts are thus distinct from ordinary attempted murders, as it were, in which the criminal intent remains clearly external; the latter occupy an intermediate position on the first axis between incidental physical violence, which leaves only bruises, and internalized violence, which takes hold of the victim and does not let go.

The same thing can be said about plagiarism, that intellectual quasi-murder whose victims of predilection are intellectuals and artists. In this particular form of outrage, the persecutor appropriates the sentences, the words, and even the mind of the individual harmed, who is then forced to denounce, in the person who wishes her ill, precisely what is closest to her, what makes the two alike, what they have in common. She is compelled to denounce the other, paradoxically, not for his ideas, to which she can only subscribe, since they are her own, but for the very fact of having made them public, having delivered them over to others, and, by publishing them, having shattered the community property – the community of thought – that they had previously shared. The individual who has been plagiarized, looted, is destroyed through and in her own thought. Her own words, not yet objectified, words that until then rested silently in her mind and are now exposed under the name of another, are killing her. They reduce her to herself – that is, to nothing – because they abolish, perhaps forever, her capacities for externalization, her opportunities to build something sturdier and larger than herself, an arrangement by means of which she could ally herself with others and enlarge herself by obtaining their consent to her speaking in their name and 'sorting out' for them the 'truth and the secret relationships of things', as Paul Sérieux and Joseph Capgras, two eminent specialists in paranoia, put it at the beginning of the twentieth century to characterize the 'delirium of interpretation' (Sérieux and Capgras 1982, 105).

The duration of affairs also depends on the intensity of the bonds that unite victims with those against whom they clamour for justice. The length of time the grievances have been harboured increases with proximity to the designated persecutor, who is sometimes so intimately involved with the author of the complaint, with his investments and his identity, that no manoeuvre seems powerful enough to destroy that interest. Denunciation is yet another means, in this case,

for securing the continuity of the relation. Through his public proc-
lamations, the victim holds onto hope for a remainder, an account
not closed, a response to which to respond, an exchange of blows or
counter-blows capable of ensuring the prolongation of a dependence
whose interruption is the one thing that appears insurmountable.
Indicators concerning repetition and duration play a particularly
important role in the determination of the first axis. This holds true
for the various forms of repetitions of stereotyped arguments, stylistic reiterations in which ritual phrases, pregnant words, often in the
form of anaphora, are used to obtain an effect of reinforcement or
symmetry, presumably by analogy with legal discourse. But this is
also true of the size of the missive (the number of pages it includes),
the number of affairs it presents, and especially the duration of these
affairs, which is noted in order along the first axis with the opposition
between incidental affairs and those that have gone on for a decade or
more, often after having been taken over by the courts. The working
of the legal system, and especially the use made in it of time – a fundamental resource that allows the actors to absorb and specialize the
conflicts that are perpetuated in the form of legal battles and not, for
example, by exchanges of blows – tends to drag out the affairs by
regularly supplying the parties (who might have worn themselves out
in an ordinary struggle) with new expectations, new stakes, new rules
to follow and, by the same token, new occasions to keep an exchange
alive, if only through the intermediary of their lawyers.

In major denunciations that can go on for years and years, even
decades ('I am establishing a general complaint concerning the last
thirty-five years of my life' [letter 596]), the dimension of time seems
to have been abolished. Complaints about events from the distant
past can be found alongside current grievances, and the human
ability to forget does not seem to have played the role often attributed to it in the calming of disputes. The way time is treated in
denunciations will be clearer if we examine the way persecution
stories are told. On the one hand, the presence or absence of a narrative, including a chronology or at least a temporal orientation,
and, on the other hand, details about the context in which the events
related are inscribed express the relation that the author maintains
with the intended recipient of his or her discourse. The narratives
are addressed to recipients who presumably know nothing about
the affair being recounted, for they are completely foreign to it. By
multiplying the details, ordering them in a scrupulous arrangement,
writers show awareness of the recipients' otherness (Labov 1972a,
359–71). In the analysis of the letters in my corpus, the various ways

of recounting an affair or of dispensing oneself from doing so are thus opposed to the achronic narratives and the disorderly sequences of grievances or documents in the corpus according to a continuum that appears to be a function of the degree of proximity between the actants. The absence of narrative and of context increases as the singularity of the relation between the denouncer, the victim and the persecutor increases, with one exception that confirms the rule. The exception involves cases in which the context is not reconstructed because major affairs that have achieved a high level of support and publicity are at stake, affairs that may be legitimately supposed to be known to all, or at least to journalists. They figure, like the intentionally contextualized missives, on the pole of the first axis characterized by a high degree of alterity between the various actors in the drama. Because these affairs have landed in the public domain, it seems pointless to recall them in full detail.

But this explanation does not account for the often impenetrable opacity surrounding narratives of affairs that have remained in the private domain. To understand the seemingly contradictory reasons that lead someone to utter a denunciation destined to become public without giving the recipient the means to grasp it in order to make it known and transmit it to others, we have to return once again to the relation that the victim – the letter-writer – has with the person against whom he is lodging the complaint. The closer his persecutor is to him, the less he has managed to break the bonds in which he still finds himself tied up and the more his discourse dispenses with narrative. There is no point in telling the story. What good does it do to recount an affair to the one person who knows it better than anyone else, to the one who knows (and with good reason!) what the others will perhaps never know? For, behind the fiction of public opinion, the writer is still addressing himself to an individual who is not the unknown or anonymous journalist to whom the message is sent, but rather precisely the private individual who is the cause of the difficulty and who must be defied yet again in an attempt to obtain a response. Thus, in the dimension of the narrative, the presence of another actant is always made manifest, but not the same one every time. With the completion of a narrative, the restoration of the context, the writer recognizes the existence of the person from whom he is demanding justice and to whom he means to provide the necessary information so that the latter can put her capacity for judgement to work. In the absence of a narrative, it is no longer the judge who is designated as the recipient but the persecutor himself. Made manifest by means of negative traces, implications, silences, threats of revelations, suspension points, and so on, his crushing presence is no less patent.

These different ways of treating narrative are associated with different types of figures of speech that are distributed in similar fashion along the first axis. On the side of proximity between actors, we find sarcasm, invective, threats, neologisms, nicknames, idiosyncratic discourse that does not demand recognition or even comprehension by others, because it is produced for just one person; on the side of alterity, we find deliberations or dialogic forms that entail a goal of legitimacy. By manifesting the attention paid to others and to their 'point of view', these latter are acts of homage rendered by the author to the normal good sense of the intended recipient (Bakhtin 1973). Irony, which is a marker of distance (Recanati 1987, 233–5), and which expresses here more particularly a distance from oneself and the fictional adoption of a point of view towards oneself that could be that of an impartial observer, occupies an intermediate position in this rhetorical structure. While it may never be used to denounce wrongdoing of which a foreign individual is the victim (one does not describe with irony, distance or humour the beating of an immigrant worker by three armed guards), irony is in contrast very often put to work for defensive purposes (Berrendonner 1981, 175–239), when letter-writers perform the denunciation on their own behalf (even though they are not connected to the person or persons against whom they are lodging a complaint) and use irony to try to depict as normal – and to get the recipient to accept as normal – an undertaking that always risks showing too much complacency towards its author, always threatens to appear 'disproportionate'.

— 18 —

MANOEUVRING TO INCREASE ONE'S OWN STATURE

Being considered normal is the minimal condition that a denunciation must meet to have any chance of succeeding – that is, of being taken up by others. Individuals engaged in denunciation who have the same sense of normality as their judges (even if they are led to perform acts judged abnormal, as we shall see) will try to give their gesture the most normal form possible. When they do not benefit from the support of a collective agency capable of accomplishing the work of generalization on their behalf, they have to carry out the necessary task of desingularization and aggrandizement themselves, in a denunciation addressed to public opinion, in order to adjust the dimensions of the other actants to that of the judge. I shall now try to show that the operations through which they seek to normalize their denunciations, by emphasizing associations between their singular case and collective bodies, are the very ones that, for others, constitute signs of abnormality.[1] In the course of everyday life, individuals quite often make associations of this type, but in ways that make them acceptable, either because the gap between the singular and the general is narrow enough so that the *bridges* intended to span it can go unnoticed or, where the gap is considerable, because the individuals in question benefit from the support of an institution. This is the case, for example, when people draw upon an institutional title to associate themselves with a collective body ('Professor X, PhD') or when they use certified competence to relate an anecdotal element to a diagnostic chart, as doctors do (Cicourel 1981). To bring out the difference between 'normal' associations and those found in certain letters of denunciation that we perceive as foreign or unacceptable, here is an example of ordinary associations borrowed from an interview with the head of a technical school conducted by Bernard

207

Urlacher. The interview focused on conflicts that had taken place in the institution. At one point the conversation took a delicate turn when the interviewee had to speak to one of his former subordinates, himself a union member (with whom he had maintained friendly relations that had made the interview possible), about his tense relations with the union. The head of the school suddenly began to speak of himself in the third person, designating himself by the title 'director', before specifying that he was not acting in his own name and in his own particular interests but in the interest of management in general, whatever his incarnation in a physical person might be; in other words, he was speaking in the interest of management as a representative of the institution, and in this way in the interest of the institution:

> Listen, in the union, in my life, I've refused three things. First, the takeover of my room. You know, I had a room next to the dining hall, and they asked to have it for the union. I said no, I prefer to put it completely out of service. That room is always available at any time of day so the director can receive people, so the director can do X or Y, not me, you know! not me . . .! [silence] The head of the school.

Each of us performs countless operations of this sort on a daily basis, and they generally go unnoticed.

In contrast, in the situations that we shall examine next, the operations intended to associate particular cases with examples having a general value and to connect individuals to collectives are so forceful that they stand out sharply, and strangely, against the continuous weave of ordinary actions. These manoeuvres are especially remarkable when the letter-writer is a single individual who is also the victim and when the persecutor is someone close to the victim. To establish an association with collective bodies and adjust the dimensions of the actants, the writer has to inflate the importance of the denouncer, the victim and the persecutor. I have identified three principal devices aimed at increasing the importance of the denouncer. First, writers may increase their own importance as denouncer by indicating their titles and qualities (using a letterhead, for example). Second, they may focus on the relations they maintain with prominent people. Denouncers increase their own importance indirectly by placing themselves on an equal footing with individuals endowed with a high level of generality, whether this generality is related to a representative capacity of the civic order, guaranteed by a mandate, or recognized in these persons apart from any institutional support for the traits of genius or the inspired works that have made them known. Finally, denouncers can increase their own importance by manipulating the forms by means of which they manifest their presence in the text. With respect to the neutral position of the subject who speaks in the first person ('I'), an author may thus align us with those who are presumed to be supporters, by using, in part of the letter or throughout, the first person plural ('we'), a customary usage in discourses produced in the name of a group. In contrast, writers can increase their importance, but this time as singular subjects, by multiplying the marks of their presence – that is, by giving themselves a stature that conforms to the way in which the inspired worth of prominent figures is manifested (for example, major writers, who need no mandate to translate the aspirations of others whom they embody in their very persons). In this latter case, a variety of procedures may be used, but they are all based on the doubling of the sign that designates the author ('I, X', 'As for me, I', and so on) or on the doubling of the signature.

Let us look at two examples of multiple signatures. The author of letter 712, a 46-year-old man who heads an elementary school in southwestern France, has been pursuing – on his own, in court, relying on legal resources after dismissing his lawyers – various quarrels connected with a divorce (he wants custody of his children). In this thick file of more than forty pages we find several open letters addressed to the president or the minister of justice. Handwritten, in a rounded calligraphy, these letters resemble legal decrees and bear the same signature twice – the first time in the same ink as the text (blue), the second time in black ink and preceded by the conventional notation 'Read and approved'. The author is doubled: on one side, there is the denouncer who draws up the act of accusation; on the other, the victim who approves it. Letter 594 is of particular interest because the conflict of persons that is at the origin of the affair is carried to a high degree of desingularization and because, by the same token, the operations of aggrandizement take a particularly surprising form. The author writes in the name of a professional association and on a letterhead. His denunciation is drafted in general terms, the way a spokesperson would write. But he is very probably personally involved in the affair for which he is mobilizing himself. He denounces a journalist who 'cast discredit' on 'a legal decision' in a controversy opposing dentists to a dean of the faculty over the establishment of the list of candidates qualified to be appointed to professorships. The letter bears three juxtaposed signatures ('the co-signers of the present document'). But the same signature, written in the hand of the same individual, appears twice: once, followed by the name in typescript

Table 2 Techniques of aggrandizement (in percentages)

Denounces . . .	Mentions one title	Mentions two or more titles	Printed letterhead with title indicated	The author says 'we'	Shift from 'I' to 'we'	The author says 'I'	The author insists: 'as for me, I . . .'	'Important' persons are mentioned	Weak generalization: specialized cause	Strong generalization: e.g., rights of man
In the name of one large collective person	60	10	40	80	20	–	–	–	40	40
In the name of one small collective person	57	13	52	57	26	13	4	21	35	48
In the name of one dubious collective person	36	7	7	50	36	–	14	57	14	56
In his/her own name with ties to others	61	20	39	39	45	11	5	2	25	53
In his/her own name alone	14	6	5	21	34	32	13	25	17	64

(Mr X), and again, followed by the typed indication 'President of the Association . . .' These figures, and especially the doubled signature, appear only when the victim and the denouncer are one and the same individual, who finds here a way to reconstitute, by doubling himself, the complete set of actants. The figures recall legal rhetoric: 'I, the undersigned, X', with a signature at the bottom of the page and initials repeated in the margins for authentification purposes.

These assorted manoeuvres, although they are based on ordinary operations of social life, discredit their author when their use is exaggerated. Thus, as we have seen, a title, which designates one's membership in a class of agents constituted as equivalents, is an ordinary way of making an association with other persons. Mentioning a title creates an association with the collective pole (and thus with normality), as we can see by examining the first factorial grid; this is particularly true when the title appears on a letterhead. A printed title is more convincing than a handwritten one for at least three reasons: (1) because a printed letterhead, which in certain cases is governed by legal considerations, occupies a higher position than handwriting in the continuum of judicial objectification; (2) because the production

Table 3 Relations among the actants and techniques of aggrandizement (in percentages)

	The author says 'we'	Shift from 'I' to 'we'	The author says 'I'	The author insists: 'as for me, I …'	'Important' persons are mentioned	There is a conspiracy
Denouncer–victim						
No connection	62	31	8	–	12	15
Militant relation	68	27	5	–	19	27
Professional tie or bond of friendship	38	57	–	5	19	29
Family tie	25	50	21	4	8	33
Denouncer and victim = same person	8	28	43	21	36	61
Victim–persecutor						
No connection	29	58	13	–	–	6
Hierarchical or technical dependence	30	41	30	–	11	30
Professional tie	9	39	35	17	34	74
Bond of proximity (e.g., neighbours)	7	7	50	36	43	71
Family tie	4	19	46	31	50	77

of a letterhead presupposes an investment in money and time; and (3) because printing, by multiplying writing in a standard form, embodies the principal property of a title, which is to be at once stable and collective, guaranteed – that is, indifferent to the properties of the relation in which it is engaged.

The use made of a reference to a title nevertheless has to be controlled in order to stay within the limits of normality. Thus, for example, when there is too wide a gap between the singular character of the denunciation and the general properties of the title, the denouncer may try to control the effect of usurpation by a denegation, by writing on stationery whose letterhead, still legible, has been crossed out ('I am not expressing myself in the name of the title that gives me the right to express myself').

If the use of a title can be a guarantee of normality, mentioning two or more titles, particularly when each of them is of little value, or augmenting the title by a supertitle, as it were (president, director, president-director, and so on), pushes the denouncer slightly towards abnormality. The titles, if they are indeed intended to serve as proofs here, nevertheless do not add up in the way medieval legal scholars practised the calculation of proofs, for example, by constituting a whole proof out of quarter-proofs. The accumulation of disparate titles discredits the sender and exposes him to suspicion ('why is he piling it on?'). Similarly, showing that one is speaking in the name of other persons by saying 'we' is the most normal way of carrying out a public denunciation. But to aggrandize oneself by using a whole array of stylistic manoeuvres ('as for me, I . . .', multiple signatures, and so on) to stress one's presence in the text (as in low-budget theatre productions where each actor plays several roles) clearly inclines the denunciation towards abnormality.

The manoeuvres used by writers to aggrandize themselves are particularly numerous in the letters sent by singular persons to denounce injustices they have suffered. Denouncers who operate in the name of a collective person, and whose great size thus goes without saying, do not need to pursue these costly manoeuvres. It is enough for them to mention a title – that is, to signify on what basis they are legitimately authorized to express themselves – and, in the name of this 'hard' title (printed on a letterhead), to say 'we'. Thus, for example, three militant feminists (letter 430) write about an attempted rape. Each one mentions a title, and just one ('lawyer', 'sociologist', 'teacher'). The three signatories write in defence of a victim but almost immediately rise to the level of the general ('we wish to specify our position concerning the affair and the phenomenon of rape in general'). Expressing themselves collectively and in the name of all women, these militants are personally absent from their denunciation, in which the victim herself figures only as an example and as a way to introduce the arguments.

The authors of letters who have only themselves on their side, or who claim to represent a collective person whose existence is uncertain, and who do not inspire confidence are led in contrast to try to increase their authority by doing more, going too far, and this discredits them. They mention several titles, stress their own presence by strange stylistic markers, or drop the names of well-known public figures, saying or suggesting that these people might well be involved in the affair. Thus, for example (letter 540), a resident of a small town in central France, who sends the newspaper an 'open letter to the Minister of Justice' lists the following titles: 'Degree in applied PSYCHOLOGY; Lecturer at the INSTITUTE; President of the ASRA: International Committee for the Defence of Human Rights; President of the Departmental Union of Penal Judges'. Similarly, the degree to which the manoeuvre of aggrandizement in which one places oneself

212

on equal footing with important public figures can inspire belief obviously depends on the self-representation that the writer manages to produce, for this determines in turn the social value the reader recognizes in him or her. Thus, for example, Philippe Simonnot (an economist and journalist who commented on economic issues for *Le Monde* and was fired for allegedly stealing a document from a ministry)[2] is credible when he includes both supportive and threatening messages addressed to him by important political figures in the work of denunciation devoted to his affair.[3] Conversely, a retiree from a small town in southwestern France (letter 601) is not credible when he challenges President Valéry Giscard d'Estaing and Minister of Justice Alain Peyrefitte 'to agree to a televised debate with me where I promise to produce only official documents to prove that the Rights of Man, Justice, and Morality were odiously trampled under foot in France', and when he accuses the well-known persons he has challenged of having 'shrivelled' – that is, of having lost the qualities that had made them great. The challenge to the 'great' is a particularly appreciated way of aggrandizing oneself because it implies – unilaterally – that the relation with the person challenged goes both ways. In fact, in the logic of honour, a challenge, calling for a response, presupposes a certain equality between the partners (Bourdieu 1977). A device often used in denunciations, an open letter to a prominent figure such as a political leader, is also a way to establish a relation of familiarity via a challenge, as Marc Angenot remarks in the book he devoted to pamphlet writing (1983).

To be aggrandized, the victim, like the other actants, has to be associated with a collective: the victim's affair has to be tied to a constituted and recognized cause. An affair worthy of the name is 'exemplary'. It deserves to be raised to the order of public denunciation, not for itself, but only to the extent that it constitutes a remarkable case within a series characterized by its best example. The effect of normality depends, here again, on the degree to which the bridge required to build the relation to the general is visible. Affairs taken in hand by a collective person are most often associated with an already constituted cause, which makes it possible to carry out the operation of generalization without having to build overly powerful connections. Causes, which are always associated with groups, in fact occupy an intermediate position between pure singularity (the case of Mr So-and-so) and the greatest generality (humanity). The deployment of political rhetoric (especially when it is borrowed from the tradition of workers' movements) is the exemplary way of attaching oneself to a group and engendering collective discourse. But the very

213

generality of this form tends to limit the possibilities for its use. Its universalizing power is so great that it obliges denouncers either to give up the expression of the singular altogether or else to construct very cumbersome connections, associations that are hard to establish and hard to conceal. These constraints of normality are themselves a function of the denouncer's degree of singularity. Thus an abrupt shift from a general declaration to a particular case is entirely tolerable when the denouncer is a collective person, but it makes the denunciation suspect when the denouncer and the victim are one and the same person, even when the author is speaking in the name of a recognized institution.

A first example that can serve to illustrate this opposition is an open letter (719) addressed to several ministers and signed by important figures in a labour union, the Confédération générale du travail (CGT) in protest against the dismissal of the president of an institution in which responsibility is supposed to be shared between management and the relevant unions. The very heavy singular–collective connections nevertheless remain acceptable, because they are achieved in the rhetoric of the workers' movement and underwritten by a major organization:

> The Confédération générale du travail considers that on the occasion of the attacks made against the person of the CEO, it is at bottom the entire orientation of the Institute that is being challenged ... This achievement must not be turned away from its initial objective and turned into an instrument at the service of Management ... The CGT considers that a new and serious attack against workers' rights is being mounted ... Management is in a hurry, because hidden behind a problem of 'one person' there is a much larger operation that touches the institution ... The true dimension of the problem raised is such that the highest authorities in the CGT have not hesitated to intervene at the highest level.

In contrast, the author of letter 533, a psychiatrist dismissed by the institution that had been employing him, writes to denounce the injustice of which he himself was the victim. But he does this – a rare instance – in the name of a large collective organization by means of a tract on a CGT letterhead (he himself had been the union's elected representative on the board of arbitration). The discourse constantly shifts between collective denunciation, where the writer uses the language of class struggle ('the employers') or speaks of himself as if about someone else ('the psychiatrist'), and personal conflict, where he mentions proper names:

214

This affair illustrates how, in the current context where there is a policy of austerity and unemployment on the part of Power, in response to the aggravated economic crisis, employers do not hesitate to get rid of their employees . . . By eliminating the psychiatrist, the employer, at the request of the production department, X [the collective title is followed by the last name of its holder] believed he could eliminate the conflicts that were arising under new forms in his 'association'. These conflicts, formerly reduced to the settling of accounts between individuals, led to the inevitable elimination by Management of any [female] employee or user resistant to the arbitrariness of his methods. Over time, these conflicts took on a more collective expression, in which groups of workers were directly directly or indirectly opposed to their supervisors.

The composite character of the forms used, perceptible in this last example, is even more clearly visible in letters in which the authors speak for themselves, in their own names and without the support of an institution. Denouncers must then, to escape singularity, produce very strong connections and harmonize themselves with others at a very high level of generality (for instance, by invoking great humanitarian principles, justice in general, human rights, and so on). The manoeuvres required to aggrandize the victim can be based, in practical terms, on a number of different procedures.

1 The author can invoke exemplarity with reference to the most general principles of validation: 'Because my Sincere "story" unhappily in History.[4] Because that what I suffered leaves indelible bruises, I would desire that you give me the opportunity to say so through this communiqué' (letter 547; the writer is a female employee treated roughly by the police). 'It is my duty to make known the incredible truth about this affair and I am really determined to do this . . . I am fighting so that other french people will not be victims of such odious abuse and will not suffer like me undeserved moral and physical torment' (letter 718; this man, a 'cement technician' living in the Paris region, is the author of a vast denunciation dozens of pages long that includes various affairs muddled together: divorce, a clash with the police following an accident, and so on. He says he is waging a hunger strike.) A gang is threatening the life of a 76-year-old woman (letter 400), a retired chemical engineer living in the Paris region. She generalizes her affair by referring to the interests of the nation ('I think that you will understand the interest of not disappointing the expectation of an old woman, not for her own sake of course . . . but because of this Country that will not die with me . . .'), and

215

also, in what is a common practice, by associating the persecutions directed at her with attacks suffered during the same period by the newspaper *Le Monde* (against which the Ministry of Justice had brought libel charges). To shore up this association, she uses two operators: 'in the same boat', which establishes equivalence, and 'on different scales', which aims to normalize the operation of aggrandizement. 'On different scales we are thus, you and I, in the same boat, scum to be muzzled and eliminated.'

2 The writer can associate his case with a series that has a collective dimension by invoking major historical and political examples (THE rights of man, fascism, THE Gestapo, and so on): 'As in Russian affairs of the Léonid Plioutch type' (letter 704: an engineer who had been fired). 'I think it is high time to make the french aware that everything about them is being recorded from foetus to death ... which constitutes a danger and a serious infringement on Human Rights' (letter 433: a woman, sixty-one, president of a retirees' club). 'I inform you moreover that I'm doing my second year in the Gulag for DOING NOTHING AT ALL' (letter 510: a man, in jail in a small town in the south of France). A father speaks of his son's arrest following a demonstration: 'Seeing him leave in good-natured company, I could not keep myself from seeing other images, those of my Resistance comrades ..., images of Jewish friends taken to Drancy.'

3 The writer can also aggrandize the victim (who, in most of the cases analysed here, is none other than himself) by establishing an equivalence with a famous individual who typically embodies the series with which he is trying to associate his own affair. These connections are achieved by means of operators of the type 'I am thinking of ...', 'I am comparing [this] to ...', 'after the X affair we now have ...', 'as in the X affair', 'the X-style affair', and so on. In certain cases, writers can also attempt to normalize the association that they have introduced by distancing themselves through rhetorical means – for example, by showing that they are not unaware of the difference in scope between their affair and the one they are invoking so as to aggrandize themselves as victims, either by denegation ('I am not X, but an unknown person') or by direct reference to effects of scale ('at my level', 'relatively speaking', and so on). Individuals who embody causes and who can be invoked in order to insert the affair into a series themselves have highly unequal degrees of generality, as do the causes themselves. Dreyfus is undoubtedly the paradigmatic figure of an individual who becomes a cause.

216

The Dreyfus affair, often evoked and so famous that one can designate it implicitly by means of a single word or a proper name ('J'accuse ...'; 'Zola ...', and so on), is not associated with a particular cause. It occupies a paradigmatic position in the series of affairs in general, independent of their content: 'This trial has been distorted. I ACCUSE' (letter 515); 'I am thinking about Dreyfus and Watergate' (letter 714: a man employed in a provincial real estate agency, in prison for swindling); 'Zola, Labory, L'Aurore ... are no longer with us, but this is of no matter to History and the record' (letter 712: the director of a primary school in southwestern France). But recalling the figure of Dreyfus is not the only way to link one's own affair with a more general cause. The letter-writers can also refer to victims of affairs featured in French newspapers in the 1970s and 1980s (Aranda, Bidalou, Boulin, Lucet, and so on). 'After the famous affair of Captain Dreyfus, after the famous Gabriel Arada affair – the State caught in a trap – once again the State is trapped by a mere "civvy", by me' (letter 735: a male surveillance agent, former non-commissioned officer, writing from Paris). 'All shook up as it is by the spasms of the "Poniatowski–De Broglie" affair, public opinion is often unaware that there are even more scandalous but alas unrecognized judicial anomalies' (letter 711: a mid-level cadre in the Paris region). The example of Robert Boulin (a government minister who committed suicide – according to the police version, which was challenged by the family – following an accusation judged libellous) is often invoked, for example by a small business owner ruined by taxes: 'Yes, I STOOPED SO LOW as to ask for JUSTICE, like ROBERT BOULIN, but I too would die in my poison' (letter 507). In letter 618 (from a retired officer in Belgium), the affair hinges on an inheritance. The notaries assigned the victim's property to other family members: 'The suffering I have been enduring for five years has made me feel, in the way I am depicting, the drama of the Boulin affair ... I have known moral hell for five years. I posit in this letter to the notaries that Robert Boulin died of such a hell.' In letter 445, which also deals with the Boulin affair, the process of generalization is reversed: the denouncer (a male psychological counsellor in a medium-sized city in the south of France) wrote to the newspaper to propose a 'Point of View' column on Robert Boulin's death, in the form of a four-page typewritten article. At the end of the second page, the writer shifts abruptly into his 'personal case', which has not been mentioned previously ('my personal case is

Table 4 Relations among the actants and stylistic manoeuvres (in percentages)

Victim–persecutor	Weak generalization: specialized cause	Strong generalization: ex. rights of man	Legal stylistic manoeuvres ++	Overwriting ++	Intimate revelations	Thematic dissonance	Nicknames	Neologisms
No connection	26	6	–	–	–	6	–	–
Hierarchical or technical dependence	7	11	15	–	–	19	7	–
Professional tie	13	17	22	4	13	26	22	13
Bond of proximity	14	28	21	21	29	50	36	14
Family tie	8	23	27	31	38	54	19	15

both exemplary and common'). At stake is the history of a family conflict following a divorce with an accusation of homosexuality, corruption of a minor, and so forth.

The manoeuvre that serves to aggrandize the victim can also be used to aggrandize the persecutor, as for example when the police are compared to the Gestapo. But when the persecutor is a singular individual, and especially when he is someone close to the victim, a frequent solution consists in associating him with a conspiracy. Reference to the existence of a conspiracy, which is correlated with a high degree of proximity between the actants (a case in which the victim and the denouncer are the same person and in which the persecutor is close to that person), comes into play with increased potency in the determination of the first factorial axis, where it is opposed to the mention, in the name of the persecutor, of a singular individual, a modality that is itself opposed, but this time on the second axis, to cases in which the persecutor is a collective person designated by a generic name (a country, a political party, an association, and so on). In a conspiracy, a particular persecutor is indeed designated, but as someone who acts in accord with others to whom he is linked by a secret pact or by an invisible property. He may occupy different positions in that coalition: he may be its leader or, as is often suggested when the persecutor belongs to the family, he may be only a passive instrument manipulated by others who possess him and

218

act through him. In fact, in cases of conspiracy, the victim's relation with the persecutor becomes less personal, and the denunciation is consequently less difficult to assume. The persecutor no longer acts in the capacity of a person defined by his relationship with the victim. In coalition with individuals external to the network of familial or friendly relations, he operates in affairs in which leading personalities are involved. Under the influence of other persons, and even often manipulated from abroad, he acts to the benefit of interests that surpass him. When the victim manages to discover a hidden principle accounting for the secret alliances she had suspected, her persecutor may be denounced, no longer as an individual family member or as a close friend, but as the representative of a group that acts secretly and can be characterized in a discrete way by the existence of a common criterion, as for example when someone denounces a conspiracy on the part of Jews or freemasons.

WHAT NOT TO DO BY ONESELF

There is no procedure for generalization, whether it entails explicit association with a cause, or with another affair viewed as exemplary, or the use of stylistic means associated with genres or institutional jargons that cannot be interpreted as a sign of abnormality when actors are led to perform alone, relying only on their own powers. Such manoeuvres must be carried out by collective bodies to be recognized as acceptable. I shall try to demonstrate this by examining the third factorial axis (3 per cent of the total inertia), and especially the projection of points in figure 3 constituted by the intersection of the second and third axes. The third axis contrasts different ways of emphasizing, underlining or overloading the act of denunciation in order to augment its weight, to increase its presence to others, to make it more remarkable, more durable, more solid than the everyday actions of ordinary life. The various devices used for emphasis are normally associated with collective resources whose orderly use is subject to institutional control. But they owe their particularity here precisely to the fact that they are used outside of their institutional conditions of validity, by singular individuals, acting independently and on their own behalf.

By themselves, and most often for themselves, these isolated denouncers, defenders of desperate causes, perform operations on symbolic forms subject to collective control, and they reappropriate general forms for a singular use. The more the denunciation diverges from the social conditions of normality, the more likely it is that these devices for emphasis will be used. This is why we find at the centre of the axis the modalities (they have not been noted on figure 3 to make it easier to read) corresponding to causes that are easy to defend in the public space (for example, denouncing an act of racist aggression) and the actantial conditions most favourable to the utterance of a denunciation considered normal (the least severe judgements of normality are located in the same part of the figure). Conversely, the more one moves towards the outer poles of the axis, the more the modalities encountered suggest the denouncer's appropriation for personal use of a general form associated with a collective resource. The axis is structured by the opposition between argumentative devices that rely on the inscription and deployment of means of proof according to standardized procedures, as in the legal system (Perelman and Foriers 1981), and devices aimed at convincing others and gaining their adherence by the strength and vehemence of an assertion of innocence, by the extraordinary character of the actions accomplished, and by the risks that the victim deliberately agrees to run in order to bring the truth to light. Among the most powerful factors determining axis 3 are, on one side, the presence of numerous documents together with recourse to a lawyer, a court or an expert, and, on the other, the assertion that the affair has given rise to a mobilization, the presence of a support group and/or of a petition, the accomplishment of symbolic gestures, and denunciation in the name of a dubious collective person. But this opposition itself can take different forms according to the degree to which the means deployed presuppose access to collective resources. This becomes clear in the structure of the factorial schema formed by the projection on a single diagram of the third axis and the second axis (defined, let us recall, by the opposition between singular acts and actants on the one hand and collective acts and actants on the other, as is shown most notably by the alignment on this axis of the number of collective resources utilized). Denouncers, who are all the more often spokespersons for their own cause as we move towards the outer limits of the third axis, are thus distributed on the factorial schema according to a triangular structure characterized by the oppositions among three positions that can be described as follows.

1 Negatively on the third axis (inscription), and positively on the second axis (collective resources), one finds denouncers who on their own behalf perform operations of a legal nature normally accomplished by judicial institutions. These denouncers strive, for example, to discredit their judges. They declare that they are operating in place of their lawyers (this implies the use of institutional resources of the judicial order at an early stage of the affair). They try to obtain acknowledgement that they are in the right by administering 'material' proofs of their innocence, as legal scholars say

221

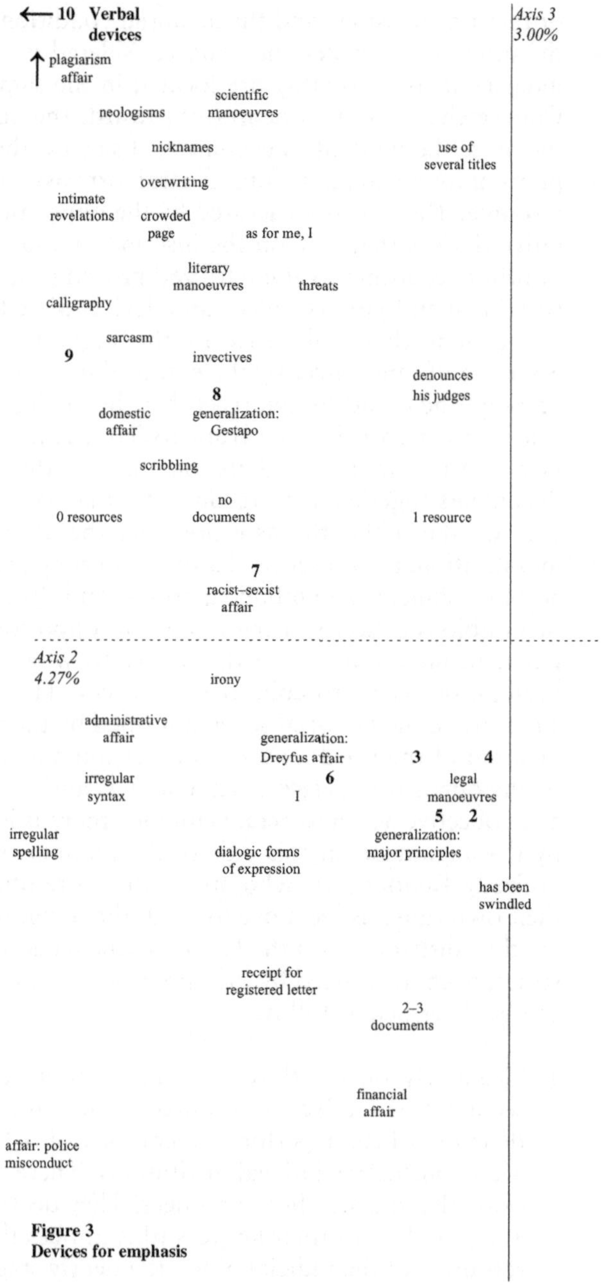
10 Verbal devices
Axis 3
3.00%
plagiarism affair
scientific manoeuvres
neologisms
nicknames
use of several titles
overwriting
intimate revelations
crowded page
as for me, I
literary manoeuvres
threats
calligraphy
sarcasm
9
invectives
denounces his judges
8
domestic affair
generalization: Gestapo
scribbling
no documents
0 resources
1 resource
7
racist–sexist affair
Axis 2
4.27%
irony
administrative affair
generalization: Dreyfus affair
3
4
irregular syntax
6
legal manoeuvres
I
5
2
irregular spelling
generalization: major principles
dialogic forms of expression
has been swindled
receipt for registered letter
2–3 documents
financial affair
affair: police misconduct

Figure 3
Devices for emphasis

Axis 3
3.00%

Political devices

↑ affair of state   ↑ petition

                                        support committee

political manoeuvres

generalization rights of man   rule-breaking   mobilization

great men are involved in the affair   political affair

open letter   copy to political figure   professional typing   association

                                                                          → tract

we   verbal transgression

copy to press   generalization: various causes   gesture

police   1 document   union

---------------------------------------hunger strike--→

2 resources **1**

affair: judicial error   press

I–we

challenges the judgement   → party

affair: work conflict

has been swindled   3 resources

court

expert   lawyer   > 4 resources

legal document

press clipping   elected official

correspondence   > 4 documents
arbitrator

letter to political figure

financial document   response from political figure   **Legal devices**

(Levy-Bruhl 1964), in the form of documents, photocopies, traces of all sorts.

2 Positioned positively on the third axis (affirmation) and positively on the second axis (collective resources) are denouncers who carry out denunciations of a political nature on their own behalf and try to bring others into their protest by saying that they have supporters and by conferring on the mobilizations around their person – mobilizations whose existence they assert – an institutional, durable and explicitly political character.

3 Finally, the position defined positively on the third axis (affirmation) and negatively on the second axis (collective resources) is occupied by denouncers whose demonstrations of innocence cannot find support either in the rhetoric of proof or in the deflection or modellized reproduction of collective resources. They then affirm their conviction and proclaim their protest by an act of parasitism with regard to the only resource they have at hand, one that seems to be available for singular appropriation even though it too is under institutional control – namely, the resource of language. In effect, they perform operations of the linguistic order on their own behalf, and they fabricate language on their own, as others do politics or law on an individual basis. These producers of neologisms, sarcasm, invective and nicknames, who aggrandize themselves in solitude by multiplying the traces of their presence (signatures, rubber stamps, 'I, the undersigned', and so on), by associating the persecutions to which they are subject with emblems endowed with a very high power of generalization (the Gestapo, the rights of man, and so on), or by blending together in the same intimate sphere the events that have disturbed their own bodily selves and others that have modified the course of the world – these writers receive the most severe judgements on the normality scale. This is probably because, among all the ways one can singlehandedly carry out actions subjected to certain collective constraints of production and validation, they have opted for the most ambitious one: the one that consists in modifying, by their own will, by a radical assertion of self and by a 'rupture in the system of language' (Lacan 1993, 55), the social form that is most strongly exempted from the arbitrariness of an individual will, as Saussure declared, and which is situated 'outside the individual who can never create it nor modify it by himself'; language 'exists perfectly only within a collectivity' (Saussure 1966, 14).

224

In denunciation, as in science, neologisms designate something never before designated, something inconceivable, unheard of in ordinary language, something that the creator of the new syntagma is the first to experience and to perceive. Better than any other device, neologisms express the enormity of the injustice suffered by the victim, an enormity that victims attempt to make manifest in the strongest conceivable way: by contriving to inscribe in the generality of the common language the singular thing that has happened to them, precisely in its inconceivable, unnameable aspect. For by delivering it to others in an indecipherable formulation, victims are still keeping it for themselves alone. The same thing applies to nicknames, which, by singularizing a word whose referent is unique, push the logic of proper names to the limit: a nickname designates the other publicly by a name that belongs only to the self. This singular appropriation is itself suspended between ciphering and deciphering. The nickname, which associates an essential and hidden particularity of the bearer with the phonic form belonging to the family name, unmasks, under the apparent neutrality of an arbitrary sign, the necessary relations between the being and the name. For nothing in the person of the persecutor is there by chance, and word play plagues the hidden secret – as Jean Starobinski says about Saussure's anagrams (Starobinski 1979) – that lies buried at the heart of the persecutor's name and entire being. But in the subtlest nicknames this secret still remains hidden, at least for a reader external to the affair. Refusing to reveal its meaning, the letter-writer withholds the key that would make its deciphering possible and that in its singularity may be accessible to no one – except of course the interested party, the only person in a position to recognize the concealed reference.

What has just been said about neologisms and nicknames can also be applied, to a lesser degree, to denouncers who try to solidify their cause in solitude by mobilizing a stylistics and other resources that have a scientific tone, without benefiting from the support of scientific institutions (Boltanski and Maldidier 1977). The manoeuvres by means of which these autodidacts claim to establish scientific proof of their innocence occupy a position close to neologism on figure 3 constituted by the second and third axes. Thus, for example, in letter 605, a cadre in computer science, an autodidact who has been fired by his company, is the self-described victim of a plot to suppress one of his inventions through a *conspiracy of silence*. He presents a seventeen-page denunciation in which he lays out his case in the form of a series of algorithms intended to demonstrate in a rigorous way the reality of the injustice he has suffered: 'Analyses 2 and 6 describe inconsistencies that increase with time. They create a negative field that provokes by a counter-effect the logical reactions of I-H.S. 7.5.-24061978 to the sole end of extending the NEGATIVE FIELD. But why this programme solution and not another? The answer will be found in document HS-7.5.21101980.' The signature follows, plus a note in red: 'BY ALLOWING THE LAWS YOU HAVE APPLIED TO ME TO APPLY TO YOURSELVES, YOU WILL SUFFER A SLOW AGONY, THE BIG GUNS ARE GOING TO GO OFF AT FORCE 2. . ., 3. . .'

Flight into the universality of science is not unfamiliar to us. We may recall that this is the device used by President Schreber to make his revelations public; in particular, it allowed him to desingularize the relation he maintained with Professor Flechsig, in relation to whom he asserts, in the presentation of his book, that he does not 'harbour any personal grievance' and whose 'integrity and moral worth' he has 'not the least right to doubt' (Schreber 1955, 33–4). But Schreber also, and especially, invokes religion – and what is more universal, more general and greater than reference to the sacred? Now, for reasons that would be difficult and time-consuming to elucidate and that probably have to do, at least in part, with the relation of substitution that has been instituted between the powers of the great beyond and the sacredness of the state, none of the authors of the letters analysed here has followed Schreber's path and fabricated a personal mythology, and none attempts to prove that he is right by asserting that the gods are with him.

Manoeuvres of the legal type are ordered along axis 3, from the centre towards the lower pole. They are often carried out by farmers, tradesmen, artisans, small business owners or members of liberal professions in affairs in which they are in conflict with the internal revenue service or with other individuals to whom they are linked by economic relations, for example in small companies. These manoeuvres include, first, recourse to a court (institutionally controlled and entailing legal risks), then a lawyer's services (more readily accessible), and finally reappropriation by the denouncer himself of the work of gathering proof and developing a legal case. These affairs, in which an interpretation has to be validated and others have to be made to acknowledge it, often borrow devices that are juridical in tone even when they have been developed entirely outside of the legal system. And this is especially the case when the writer gives up the attempt to make it clear that she is right by showing that others support her, and undertakes instead – often after dismissing authorized specialists such as lawyers or judges – to establish the material proof of her innocence and to set up, on her own, a trial in which she appears at once as the unjustly accused victim and as the witness for the prosecution in relation to the persecutor.

The first task consists in establishing grounds for the arguments by putting together a dossier. The letters in my corpus are often accompanied by a large number of texts that look like legal documents and, more generally, by a file including all sorts of photocopies, even receipts from registered letters. Photocopies have become indispensable instruments in the development of an affair. The collection and accumulation of the most disparate documents intended to serve as proof in a future test are probably among the most clear-cut signs by which one can tell that an affair is being grafted onto the course of everyday life, and interrupting it. For, when everything is going well, it is taken for granted that ordinary life will keep on following its course. Proofs are of no use, since no one has any reason to ask that they be presented. The first action marking a break with the ordinary routine carried out by someone who feels threatened in the workplace – facing a possible layoff, for example – and who is undertaking, very anxiously and with an eye to self-defence, to *make it an affair*, consists in collecting, photocopying and preserving, as proofs and means of pressure, documents that had until then been circulating, passed from hand to hand, misplaced, abandoned in dusty archives or destroyed without being the object of any particular interest. Persons who feel threatened accumulate their own 'secret file', as individuals often say under interrogation. This overinvestment in written documents, a kind of idolatrous over-objectivization fixated on texts as things, has some affinity moreover with the logic of building a solid legal case; it confers a new significance on the documents that have been copied and preserved, one that arises precisely out of their association in a collection. Receipts for registered letters – documents that it seems particularly odd to photocopy and forward – thus appear to have the same relation to legal documents, properly speaking, as improvised or cobbled-together legal expressions have to the rhetorical means that conform to the practices of the legal system. The formality of registration constitutes one of the most accessible quasi-juridical acts and one of the simplest ways to obtain a document – a receipt, an official, standard printed form that can be reproduced at will by photocopying. At the post office, for a relatively small sum, anyone can solidify a piece of mail, can fabricate proof and generate law.

The accumulation and publication of documents can be pursued over a long period of time, even when, after a judgement, the cause appears to have been heard and the affair settled. It happens fairly often, in fact, that denouncers whose cause has been judged in a way they deem unjust do not resign themselves; instead, they reject the sentence and set out to relaunch the affair by seeking new elements of proof intended to shore up their arguments. The work of proof does not contain any principle of closure in itself. As is suggested, for example, by the obligation to judge to which magistrates are subject, trials might go on indefinitely if judges were not invested with an authority that not only allows but commands them to bring the affairs brought before them to an end, by an 'act of sovereignty whose goal is to establish judicial peace' (Perelman 1972, 212). Moreover, this is why Henri Levy-Bruhl (1964), seeking to determine the nature of judicial proof, gives up all substantive definitions and acknowledges that, in the category of proof, any arrangements that make it possible to bring a dispute to an end, from ordeals (probatory measures to which we no longer grant credit today) to reports by experts in hand-writing, ballistics, and so on (whose arguments are currently treated as acceptable), are nevertheless the object of numerous challenges.

But letter-writers can also create legalese on their own with words: they can borrow the vocabulary of the law and produce prose over-flowing with terms like 'notwithstanding', 'whereas', and so on; they can even manufacture a language that resembles legal terminology without being completely authentic, for example by forming deriva-tions in the mode of false etymologies (Bally 1951, 32–40). They can also produce utterances that recall legal discourse simply by having recourse to very general forms that can be used, as Lacan says about capital letters (1993, 37), 'whenever one is obliged to provide signs that are supplementary to what language offers', forms from which properly legal terms are themselves derived. Legal writing, destined to become an act, is characterized in fact by a high degree of rituali-zation. It uses fixed forms that preclude variation; indeed, variation is treated as transgressive, as threatening to abolish the effectiveness of the speech act (a 'technicality'), and the user is thus constrained to repetition. Every device aiming to emphasize and solidify dis-course through repetition, reinscription, ritualization, reiteration, and the like, thus confers properties on the text that relate it to legal documents, even if the denouncer's means cannot be credited with a juridical genealogy.

GENERALIZATION AND SINGULARITY

Denouncers best escape the rigours of the judgement of normality by resorting to political modes of emphasis – that is, by accomplishing acts that solicit interpretation in the register of politics and by referring to collective persons in the name of whom they purport to be authorized to express themselves. This is particularly true, once again, when the victim's case is taken up by formally constituted collectives. Thus, starting from the centre of axis 3, we find an ordering of different forms of actions belonging to the register of political motivation; these become less and less satisfactory as proofs as we move towards the upper pole. First we find references to highly institutionalized and very large collective persons, such as big labour unions or major political parties. It is not just anyone who is authorized to invoke these collectives, and the authorized spokespersons may resist attempts at appropriation by singular individuals: for example, they may contradict an assertion that their organization would defend the victim officially. Next, we encounter support by specialized associations, which are smaller and more easily manipulated, and support by collective persons lacking in institutional guarantees – for example, defence committees that may have been constituted by the victim or by someone close to him (and that can thus be accused of being a total set-up). Finally, there are symbolic gestures of protest and mobilization – for example, the distribution of pamphlets, public acts of insubordination or rule-breaking, and so on – that an individual, the victim or a spokesperson, is always free to accomplish alone, without the assistance of others, and sometimes also without obtaining the support that these acts are designed to generate.

For one can perfectly well engage in politics on one's own by using mobilization procedures that normally require participation by several persons; however, in so doing one exposes oneself to disbelief or to accusations of abnormality. One can create one's own political organisation, for example, although this seems to be a relatively infrequent occurrence. Letter 629 is presented in the form of a lengthy confession (thirteen pages). The author, who writes in the name of the FLP (Front de libération prolétarienne [Proletarian Liberation Front]) and the TULIPE (Tribune universelle pour la LIBERATION de l'INTELLIGENCE PROLÉTARIENNE EXPANSIVE [Universal Tribunal for the Liberation of Expansive Proletarian Intelligence]) claims the following titles: 'Companion of the pro-humanist liberation, antifascist war cross, Commander of the anti-imperialist legion of honour'. A butcher's apprentice at age fourteen, a nurse at twenty-one, in 1963 the writer took the special entrance examination for admission to the faculty of science. Eight years later, having entered medical school, he failed an examination and, when the administration refused to grant him the right to review his examination papers, he took one of the professors hostage:

In the name of the Proletarian Liberation Front with the support of a twenty-page evolutionist text with a print run of 900 copies, I took Dean X, doctor and legislator whose very functions produce the image of a man of the far right, reactionary, alienating for the people and proletarian intelligence. Pistols in hand and in holsters, my goal was to compel my papers to be brought to me by force by topping that black flagpole with a death's head. But not wanting to shoot down Jean-Marc, a maintenance worker who had intervened, the affair turned out badly and, helped by his doctors in law and doctors in medicine, the political environment stifled the affair so that it would not be given a fair trial in the eyes of the people and the workers.

The author struggles henceforth against 'the UNIVERSITY SEGREGATIONISM OF THE SOCIAL CLASSES', and for 'EVOLUTION AGAINST CEREBRO-SOCIAL INVOLUTION' ('No social class must be society's brains – the people are at once body and social brain').

It is more common to create one's own support committee. In letter 593, which takes the form of a tract (titles in large capitals; slogans: 'JUSTICE! Equal for all?', and so on) and announces a hunger strike, a saleswoman 'ruined following a legal error' thus launches 'an appeal for a support committee to all those who are for the respect of human rights'. She presides over the support committee that she seeks to constitute in favour of her own cause. She adds to her denunciation an open letter to the minister of justice:

Dear Minister [NAME], I have the honour of making you aware that before doing me justice I ask you one last time that you be so kind as to grant me an appointment to speak with you before 30 October, the date on which I shall end my last hunger strike begun today to save the person to whom I owe [my] life and that of my children. After that date, the 'Legitimate Defence' committee (JO n° 180,05.03.78) will go into action.

In letter 515, the author writes under the title 'Co-founding member of the P... C... Defence Committee', in the name of an engineer accused of rape and imprisoned. The text is entirely handwritten, but punctuated, as in a tract, with slogans in capital letters (P... C... IS INNOCENT', 'I ACCUSE'). No indication, no sign of any officially constituted collective, no list of names makes it possible to attribute a body to the defence committee and confer on it an objective existence distinct from the person of the denouncer, who situates the committee's headquarters at his own personal address. Suspicion obviously begins to arise in the reader's mind: Is this a 'real' defence committee? Isn't the denouncer connected with the victim, a relative or a friend? We might also consider letter 536, which refers to a defence committee constituted around the case of J. H., also accused of rape, even though in this case the existence of the committee has somewhat more solid support in that it is said to have been set up 'under the auspices of a priest'. To make the fragility of these improvised support committees more perceptible, we can contrast them with letter 420, written in the name of a committee in support of P. L. (a judge in a juvenile court who had been subject to sanctions); this letter presents all the signs of normality. The committee was created at the initiative of an 'inter-union' body that brought together 'the judges' union, the interdepartmental unions CGT and CT, the national union of personnel in supervised education, the CSF, the Federations of the PS, the PSU, and the LCR, along with several municipalities of the union of the left'.

Another form of manifestation – petitions – invites similar remarks. These parades of names, whose power to convince is all the higher to the extent that they bring together major public figures for whom the granting of the name may have a cost (X is 'devaluing his name'), tend towards abnormality and are thus rendered null and void if the alterity between the signatories and the beneficiary of the petition is not guaranteed. In a letter published by *Le Monde* in February 1983, a television journalist threatened with dismissal wrote in response to an article: 'I read with indignation in this article that I am said to be the instigator of the petition that some forty intellectuals have signed in my favour.' Letter 455, sent by a university professor, is perfectly normal. It presents an appeal in favour of a Russian dissident, about whom the sender, who speaks in the name of a collective, expresses himself in the first person plural, declaring that the letter has been writted by physicists: 'We are in the process of collecting signatures of physicists . . . but we have also contacted certain persons outside the field of physics.' The personal letter, written by hand and signed with a name and a title, is accompanied by a mimeographed letter that includes about 200 signatories, among them several well-known personalities from the academic world; these ensure the credibility of this standard petition. The same thing cannot be said about letter 411. This handwritten letter is accompanied by a typewritten text that presents numerous typos; it is titled 'NOCTURNAL BEATING'. The text denounces police intervention, on the pretext of excessive noise, during an evening event attended by friends. It is signed by four of the participants.

Even without creating institutions out of whole cloth, one can still fabricate politics by carrying out *gestures* – that is, acts accomplished individually in order to attract attention, mobilize others and perhaps lead them to repeat the gesture inaugurated by the solitary individual, for example by associating themselves with a hunger strike, by turning in their military papers in a sign of solidarity, by resigning from their jobs, and so on. To be seen, the gesture has to stand out in striking fashion from the weave of ordinary behaviours and demand an interpretation from others. When the gesture becomes sufficiently striking, a work of interpretation is always necessary to manage it, whether one means to identify its symbolic value – that is, its generality in view of the common good – or whether, on the contrary, one means to devalue it, either by reducing it to the flow of ordinary practices dominated by interest or by rejecting it as marginal or insane. Almost anything can be used to make a gesture, and in particular any act of transgression – for example, in the cases studied, the theft of a document or an art object, or simply silence in a situation that requires speech[1] – provided that the gesture can be detached from the satisfaction of personal interest so as to reveal the gratuitousness of a transgression accomplished for the sake of transgressing – that is, carried out as a protest against the arbitrariness of the interdiction that it brings to light. But, to attract attention, the gesture must not only be gratuitous, it must also entail risk. Because disinterestedness is manifest if the personal costs are higher than the personal profits that might accrue, the riskiest gestures, the most insane, the ones most apt to be explained away in psychiatric terms, are also the most effective operators when they encounter, in others, interpretations capable of revealing – or, more precisely, capable of constituting – their collective dimension. Public betrayal, which can be a form of denunciation, is of this order. An individual exposes publicly, to the outside community, secrets of the community to which he belongs – family, church, party, company, and so on – and does this alone, in the name of the very values of the group, which he accuses the other members of no longer respecting.[2]

Letter-writers thus strive to stir up mobilizations around their affair by sending back their decorations (letter 441), by refusing to appear in court and making their refusal known (letter 614, whose author is an unemployed cadre, aged fifty, involved in a divorce case), or by chaining themselves to a television camera in order to deliver an address to the president during a public meeting (letter 768, written by an actor). One of the gestures most often used today, and among the most spectacular, is the hunger strike.[3] The tactical interest of the hunger strike – as opposed, for example, to self-mutilation or suicide, which are all-or-nothing affairs – is that the degree of risk is a function of time, and this makes it possible to adjust both the rhythm according to which the gesture is accomplished and the rhythm according to which information is transmitted and mobilization occurs. The argument based on an increase in risk over time is a weighty one in the quest for mobilization. It goes without saying that the degree to which a hunger strike can arouse the interest of others and enlist their adherence depends primarily on its duration. Today, simply announcing a hunger strike seems to have almost no effect, and the effectiveness of this device seems to diminish as the practice spreads. Some hunger strikers complain that a long fast is no longer enough to attract attention to their denunciation. Thus the reminder or the announcement of a hunger strike has to be dramatized, as is the case in the two examples that follow. In letter 749, an unemployed engineer, who since 1968 has been denouncing the 'incredible abuses' to which he has been subjected, says he went on a hunger strike in 1973: 'In 1973, to raise a call of alarm, I put my life in danger for 25 days in a dramatic hunger strike, on the fiftieth birthday of a man who was already ill. Panic-stricken by the conclusion that threatened, the authorities succeeded in interrupting this hunger strike by pretending to grant me some satisfaction and making some promises quickly forgotten.' The open letter, addressed to a number of public political, union or legal bodies, and sent by the writer to the press, is identified as number 14 and has the dateline '4538th day of resistance of a Lorraine family to oppression'. In letter 560, a farmer from northern France writes a thirty-page confession denouncing the injustices committed towards him by his in-laws, prefacing his account with an open letter announcing a hunger strike:

> Dear all of you, I launch this appeal to all persons for whom I have been able to work, either in France–Belgium or abroad, all the farmers, independents, artisans, citizens, friends, family . . . I am going to undertake a hunger strike, I appeal to all of you for moral support, demonstration in view of seeing justice, public denunciation, and truth break out in broad daylight take place in this country my Fatherlands: of so-called of democracy, of republic . . . France and Belgium . . .

It is indeed their sense of normality that leads the authors of letters judged least normal to give their writings a strange form, for at least two reasons. First, to establish a connection with groups, as we have seen, they have to attain a certain level of generality and carry out, on their own, operations that are normally accomplished with others or in the name of others. But, secondly, the rise in generality does not satisfy the feeling that impels them to denounce the persecutor(s) responsible for the injustice and to let the world know the intensity of the suffering that they have endured. Normalizing the denunciation through procedures of generalization – substituting a group representing a collective body for a person designated by his or her own name, for instance – requires a sacrifice that can leave the victim unsatisfied. The victim may well denounce the 'dominant class' and thus maintain the denunciation within the limits of normality. But doing this says nothing, or next to nothing, about the pain that has been caused by the person(s) who deprived the victim of something that cannot be given up for lost; it says nothing about the trauma experienced, about the expectations that have been discouraged or disappointed. The object of the victim's indignation is not the 'dominant class', or even an individual who is qualified in that he or she would be the representative or the 'personification' of that collective being, but the most singular of persons and often the closest.

It follows that the closer the persecutor is to the victim, the more difficult it is to designate the persecutor publicly without suffering and shame, and the more the suffering caused by that persecutor will be difficult to repair in the only register where it can be publicly expressed, that of collective action. The author of the denunciation will then be moved to bring his or her suffering to the surface by indirect means; the suffering is all the more shameful and intense in that it cannot be legitimately expressed in the constituted forms of public denunciation, either legal or political. For the denunciation to have meaning, for it to be authentic and thus salutary, the writer has to use allusions, signs and traces to bring out the singularity of the case, the story and the person, a singularity that the victim first had to renounce in order to try to gain support from others and to be recognized as innocent. What incites victims to reintroduce into their texts the singularity that they have tried to banish depends on forms that may bear no direct relation to the explicit theme of the denunciation, or even to the properties of the designated persecutor(s). To accomplish the impossible task that consists in communicating to others, to the public at large, what is least transmissible about suffering, any singularity is good provided that it betrays, as if by accident, the disguise introduced by the work of generalization. This singularity may be manufactured by parasitizing and subverting any form endowed with a minimum of regularity. It is thus manifested at the smallest cost when it is lodged within the most general, most standardized forms (Thévenot 1983) – that is, in places where small deviations suffice to introduce remarkable perturbations. In the texts analysed here, this is the case, for example, with writing, spelling and syntax.

Let us take handwriting, for example. A standard form of general validity, it is also considered, at least since the second half of the nineteenth century (Tajan and Delage 1981, 37), as one of the supports in which what is the most singular in the individual can be inscribed. It can reveal what distinguishes her; it can betray what she conceals from others and from herself. Unlike printed characters, which are impersonal and mechanical, owe nothing to the particularities of the typist and retain no memory of his work, the trace of the writer's hand is open to a search for identification (Ginzburg 1980). This opposition is found on the second axis. Towards the collective pole, we find typewritten letters produced in a professional, impersonal way (use of an electric typewriter, absence of typos and erasures, respect for the normal forms of presentation, and so on), as is fitting for texts signed by a collective or sent in the name of a group, in which the writer reveals nothing but his or her technical competence. In contrast, towards the singular pole, we find handwritten letters in which the author makes something of himself available to interpretation by the receiver (who might, for example, submit the missive to graphological analysis), although the author does this passively, as it were, without taking deliberate steps to increase the formal singularity of the text. Letters competently produced by a non-professional typist fall into an intermediate position close to the centre on this axis. Their degree of singularity is heightened, even in the absence of mistakes, when they have been produced on a manual rather than an electric typewriter. Especially in the case of portable typewriters, we know that the irregularity of the characters makes it possible to identify the source of a text. But this irregularity never betrays the sort of bodily presence that handwriting reveals.

The distribution of the forms along the first axis expresses a difference of another order. The more the relation between the actants is singular, and the more the letter-writer has therefore had to construct strong connections so as to ensure the tie to collective bodies (by invoking 'human rights' in general, for instance, instead of referring to a smaller constituted cause associated with a special-interest group), the more the incitation to singularize the general forms is heightened. It is then manifested by typos, left visible even after they have been corrected by overwriting (as with 'XXX'), which retains the trace of the work required by the denunciation, its hesitations and its reticences, in the form of cross-outs or corrections in a different ink, and especially by means of particular graphic features that do not offer themselves up to free interpretation but rather assert with authority the way in which they differ from ordinary handwriting. Disorderly, hasty, messy writing, almost or even totally illegible, with irregular, confused and contorted strokes, produced under the influence of indignation, vehemence or other emotions, is, in the realm of graphology, what insults, threats, neologisms and nicknames are in the realm of stylistics. Such extravagant deviations indicate how the writer has appropriated a general form and made it eminently personal, in order to assert as emphatically as possible the injustice the victim has suffered. And these excesses are precisely what serve as proof. But the same impulse to personalize may also be satisfied by other, more complex graphic means. Thus calligraphy, with its letters fully drawn in printed capitals or in old-fashioned quill pen strokes, its heavily slanted script in a network of traceries, carries out two contradictory operations at the same time. It solidifies the written form and enlarges it. It brings it closer to the status of an official document, a printed text, a legal document, a notarized act, but at the same time it breaks completely with the ordinary modes of writing and restores the singularity of the writer, who can no longer pass unnoticed by anyone under any circumstances. Thus the writer manages to inscribe the unique, unprecedented and unqualifiable character of the affair in question within the neutrality of standard forms.

The same analyses can be applied to additions, underlinings (often in colour, preferably red, as in old seals), rewriting in the same ink in the margin, often perpendicular to the body of the text, oversize capitals intended to enlarge and emphasize the terms deemed important (which sometimes include almost all the words of the denunciation), rubber stamps, and so on. These striking additions are, in the realm of graphic presentation, the equivalent of legal manoeuvres in the stylistic realm. Their purpose is to produce an 'act' and to imbue the denunciation with the feel of a text that has the value of law and the capacity to constitute proof; they aim to make the document look more authentic, more credible, more solid, more durable than an ordinary text. A text overloaded in this way is, as it were, more inscribed, more profoundly anchored in the texture of a support that can itself be overloaded: stamped or watermarked paper, for example (whose controlled – and high – price indicates its symbolic value), firmer and more official than ordinary paper ('a scrap of paper'), like paper money, more profoundly tied to a collective body that ensures its durability by granting it recognition. Filling up the entire surface of the paper, sometimes saturating it with lines so close together that they touch in some places, is another way of alluding to legal writing. We know, for example, that the rules for notarized acts in France require that they be drafted in a single sitting, without blanks or spaces between the lines. But, as in the case of different types of calligraphy, these simulacra of instituted forms achieved by any means at hand inevitably express the writer's singularity. This singularity, which letter-writers courageously dare to put on public display – for it constitutes their greatness, they say – authorizes them, by aggrandizing them, to accomplish in person, and all by themselves, acts that require institutional authority in order to be carried out in a normal way. For one must already be great and possess a considerable power over others if one is to aggrandize oneself while confronting a test that consists in accomplishing symbolic gestures and acts – speech acts and especially performative speech acts – publicly and effectively without regard for their institutional conditions of validity. Nevertheless, as we shall see, this is precisely the desperate operation attempted by the letter-writers whose denunciation is the most difficult to accomplish and the easiest to disqualify.

When the singularity of the system of actants increases and when, as a result, the operations necessary for fabricating collective material – if only with words, for want of the power to do it with persons – are too hard to accomplish, the manoeuvres of generalization become scarce or disappear entirely. The letter-writers then seem to give up trying to bring about associations between the singular and the collective, the particular and the general, which demand so much ingenuity, as we have seen, on the part of the more or less desperate denouncers. In these borderline texts, we find utterances that refer to the singular dimensions of the writer's identity: allusions to sexual preference alongside utterances tied to contexts that are very strongly constituted collectively or endowed with very broad, even planetary generality, such as political programmes, observations about major international crises, and so on. But, in the latter case, no manoeuvre is attempted to connect the elements that belong to the two series. For the authors of these strange texts can immerse themselves totally in the group without believing themselves obliged for all that to give up the expression of their own most singular aspects. However, this suspension of the opposition between the singular and the collective, which certainly constitutes one of the most pronounced signs of delirium from the reader's standpoint, is nothing but the adoption by ordinary individuals of a discursive conduct that can succeed if the person who accompanies it is a major public figure: precisely someone who, unlike a representational spokesperson, can not only represent others without a mandate, but who can also, in the mode of prophecy, make an argument of his or her independence and singularity ('I speak in the name of no one', 'I represent only myself') to demand explicitly or tacitly to be followed, to be listened to and heard. The 'great man', in fact, mobilizes a group of which he is the binding agent and of which he constitutes in a way the criterion of belonging, since he means to represent, precisely in what is singular about him, the unlimited set of those who have found an instrument of knowledge and recognition in the expression of that singularity.[4]

— 21 —

DIGNITY OFFENDED

I shall now try to describe the series that leads individuals whose own sense of normality is not altered – since, as we have seen, the efforts they make to correct the abnormal character of their acts is precisely what signals the strangeness of those acts to others – to make gestures of public denunciation whose conditions of validity have not been met and whose principal effect is most often to disqualify those who have carried them out. Let us begin with the most objectivizable properties of the letter-writers (their sex, age or profession, for example) in order to forestall interpretations that might tend to eliminate the troubling aspects of the denunciatory activity by attaching them irrevocably to a marginal condition.

In almost all cases we know the letter-writer's sex and place of residence. The profession is known in just under 80 per cent of the cases. Moreover, I relied on a certain number of indicators that allowed me to distribute them among three loosely defined categories (lower, middle and upper), even when the profession was not explicitly mentioned; this increased the usable information by about 10 per cent. It is obviously impossible to know with any precision what margin of error may affect this estimate. The exact age is known in 30 per cent of the cases. When the age was not indicated, I proceeded, as I had done for social class, to produce an estimate designed to grasp in particular the proportion of authors aged sixty and above; this allowed me to take age into account in about 80 per cent of the cases. I have not tried to code the level of education systematically, but numerous letters include information about the author's studies and the presence or absence of academic titles (often mentioned in the header). It was thus possible to identify a number of self-educated cadres who established a relation of cause and effect between the handicaps that had prevented them from undertaking higher-level studies and the injustices of which they were later victims in the course of their professional lives.[1]

The distribution among the writers' socio-professional categories makes it clear that the higher categories are significantly overrepresented. Conversely, blue-collar workers are decidedly underrepresented, with the middle classes occupying an intermediate position. To explain these divergences, it is not enough to invoke the effect of selection exercised by the newspaper to which the letters were addressed, as is shown by comparing the distribution of the letter-writers among the various socio-professional categories with the distribution, according to the same principle, of a sample of *Le Monde*'s readership.[2] Hourly wage-earners and salaried employees are relatively more numerous in the readership of *Le Monde* than among the letter-writers. In the upper classes, the proportion of members of categories close to the public sector or exercising intellectual professions (liberal professions, cadres in the public sector and especially professors, writers and artists) is much higher among the letter-writers than among the newspaper readers. Conversely, industrialists, big businessmen and upper-level cadres in the private sector are less well represented in the correspondence than in the readership. In contrast, in the middle classes, the independent categories – farmers, artisans, tradesmen, small business owners – appear relatively more numerous in the corpus of letters than in the sample set of readers. To understand these variations, we must take into account the effects of selection inherent in the act of denunciation, which are exercised in different ways depending on the properties of the actantial system.

To carry out a normal denunciation, characterized in particular, as we have seen, by alterity between the denouncer and the victim, one has to possess the authority necessary to take up the defence of another individual, to rush to his aid and especially to designate a third party for public condemnation in that individual's name. This authority is a function of the dimension into which the denouncer has managed to raise herself – that is, of the degree to which people have acknowledged her ability to embody other persons, either explicitly by means of a legally guaranteed mandate, as is the case for representatives of collective persons, or implicitly (and in this latter case rather in the manner of 'great men') in her very person. Now the stature of which an individual can boast and which is likely to be recognized by others is not independent of the properties that define identity in its most official and most easily objectivizable aspects (for example, in

Table 5 Professions of the authors of the letters of denunciation (in percentages)

	Authors of letters	Readers of *Le Monde*	French population*
TOTAL	100	100	100
Inactive	8.5	12.5	31.5
Labourers, workers in the service industries	7	15	30
Employees		7.5	8.5
Middle-level cadres	19.5	20	8.5
Professors and teachers	8.5	–	
News media, fine arts, performing arts	18.5	7.5	
Cadres in the public sector, advertising	8	6	8.5
Liberal professions	6.5	3	
Entrepreneurial cadres, engineers	9	16.5	
Industrialists, big business owners	3.5	7	
Small business owners	9	4	6.5
Farmers, salaried farmworkers	2	1.5	6.5

Note: *Socio-professional classification of heads of households in the 1975 census.

Table 6 Properties of denunciation according to profession (in percentages)

	Four or more persecutions	Age sixty or above	Women	Small towns, villages	Paris and surrounding region	Victim = individual without a cause	Victim and persecutor = in same community	Speaks in his or her own name	Marks a connection with others	Speaks for one collective person	Victim and denouncer = same individual	Victim = individual ≠ denouncer	Victim = group
Workers, employees	43	28	43	–	48	79	42	93	7	–	71	18	7
Farmers, artists, tradesmen, small business owners	41	16	25	29	45	84	38	84	3	13	78	19	3
Intermediate professions	22	7	15	27	53	56	17	51	27	22	41	44	12
Cadres in businesses	37	10	11	5	84	74	52	84	11	5	69	26	5
Liberal professions	7	7	29	14	38	50	14	21	71	7	43	49	7
Cadres in the public sector	6	13	13	12	57	38	18	38	6	56	31	44	25
Professors and teachers	16	–	18	13	62	33	24	44	44	13	41	36	23
News media, fine arts, performing arts	12	6	33	6	41	56	23	50	44	6	22	61	11

'identity papers') and thus not independent of age, sex or profession. Certain professional states provide access to mastery more readily than others, often with the legal sanction of titles. Such resources can be mobilized as a basis for the aspiration to speak for others or to represent them. To embody others, one has to be able to rely on a political apparatus, on an administrative or judicial body, or else, as in the case of members of intellectual professions, on collective institutions that are also specialized languages.

Thus we see the opposition taking shape on the first factorial grid (axes 1 and 2) between, on the one hand, the categories in which the proportion of those who write to take up the defence of someone else is highest and, on the other hand, the categories whose members write especially for themselves. Cadres in the public sector, who often express themselves in the name of collective persons, professors and teachers, who share with public-sector cadres the tendency to take up the defence of an entire group; artists and intellectuals; members of liberal professions, chiefly doctors and lawyers who express themselves in their own name (often a well-known name) but use multiple signs to mark the ties that associate them with collectives: these groups occupy an almost identical position on the first axis and are distributed along the second precisely as a function of their importance, their worthiness, which authorizes them to represent or mobilize other persons and to take a public stance on worthy causes. Closer to the individual pole on axis 2, we find mainly professors and teachers, for the most part from the secondary level. Writers and artists, whose notoriety is often high, are located on the same axis, but closer to the collective pole (the differences would probably be sharper if the small size of the sample had not led to a relatively high level of aggregation). The former defend human rights by testifying in favour of ordinary individuals who have been assaulted or otherwise harmed, and by standing up for unknown persons. The latter rush to the aid of famous personalities, illustrious martyrs embodying worthy causes, groups, and sometimes entire peoples. The dimension of the victim is thus directly linked to the stature of the defender.

In contrast, the individuals who carry out the act of denunciation on their own behalf are more often cadres in large companies, small business owners, artisans, tradesmen, farmers, and even more often employees or service personnel; they are often self-educated. They write in their own name alone and set before public opinion complaints that are particularly hard to associate with collective causes. 'Altruism' seems to be more characteristic of members of

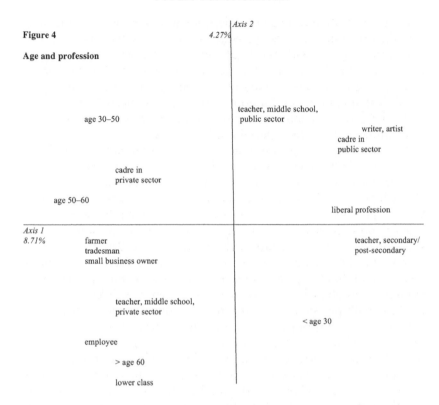

Figure 4

Age and profession

Axis 2
4.27%

age 30–50

teacher, middle school,
public sector

writer, artist
cadre in
public sector

cadre in
private sector

age 50–60

liberal profession

Axis 1
8.71%

farmer
tradesman
small business owner

teacher, secondary/
post-secondary

teacher, middle school,
private sector

< age 30

employee

> age 60

lower class

the public sector and government employees. 'Egoism' seems to be associated, conversely, with the private sector and the ownership of material goods. These correspondences seem to go without saying, since they are based on ethical and political oppositions that are deeply rooted in the 'republican idea' (Nicolet 1982, 371–5) and that are also present in sociological discourse, especially in Durkheim (Filloux 1977, 55–7). But moral self-evidence once again conceals effects of worth or size. In fact, to take up the defence of others before public opinion, to speak in the name of the public good, one must have access to an identity defined with reference to the civic forms on which the construction of modern states is based, such as nationally recognized diplomas, legally guaranteed professional titles, administrative or political mandates, and so on. This is not the case for industrialists, tradesmen or farmers: having easier access to the possibility of moving to a higher level of generality by relying on domestic resources, they often prefer the play of personal relations to the mobilization of public opinion. In these categories, public

244

denunciation constitutes a last resort, for oneself or for one's family or close acquaintances, when all other means have failed.

The various professions are distributed along the second axis according to the degree to which they offer resources allowing those who exercise them to mobilize other persons and, indissociably, to accredit their capacity to formulate utterances of general validity. We thus find along this axis, close to the singular pole, individuals who have to rely on themselves because they do not have access to collective resources and because they do not have access to the worth required to represent others or to be their spokespersons. This is often the case for women, and even more so for the elderly of either sex. Elderly denouncers, who are most likely to lack ways of making themselves heard, write most frequently to newspapers to point out injustices from which they themselves have suffered. The impulse to demand justice seems to increase over time and appears to reach a peak among the elderly. The reason may lie in the writers' proximity to death, which establishes a horizon on the basis of which one's past life can be the object of a calculation. This same retrospective attitude is already manifested in the desire, frequent towards the end of life, to bequeath an inheritance, to write an autobiography or memoirs, or simply to recount one's past to children, family and friends. But the autobiographical position is not exclusively retrospective. It is also placed in a perspective of justice and, more precisely, in that of a final judgement (see chapter 9). At the end of life, the requirement of justice becomes more pressing as a tacit promise of the uncertain future, the hope that redemption or revenge will be provided by life itself, fades away. At that point we draw up our balance sheets and demand from others the reimbursement of the debt that life will not acquit. The proximity of death solidifies the demand, makes it more violent and more urgent.

But it is often at the same time of life that the resources needed to obtain satisfaction become scarcer. The elderly denouncers whose letters appear in the corpus have seen their resources – physical strength, money, relationships – diminish with time. Most of them appear in fact to have enjoyed higher status in the past. The writers are often small-scale local personalities whose authority is no longer recognized. In a number of cases, the affair they mean to make public seems to hinge on a scene in which their honour has been tarnished. The appeal to public opinion thus becomes one of the last means available to them for obtaining reparations and restoring what they have lost. Low in status, incapable of ensuring their own defence (not to mention that of others), these people and their small-scale stories seem out of place in the correspondence of Le Monde, a quasi-official newspaper devoted to worthy causes whose readers include everyone whose opinions 'count'. But it is precisely their lack of resources that leads these elderly persons to address themselves to all the major newspapers as a last resort, and thus to Le Monde among others, in endless, repetitive letters that often display an accumulation of infallibly disqualifying signs of abnormality.

Let us take for example letter 568. This is a dossier of thirty-six pages consisting for the most part of photocopied documents. The author of this letter, honorary chief treasurer of a medium-sized city in the south of France, aged seventy-seven, denounces the 'abuse of power of the person in charge of road repairs', who seven years earlier had destroyed the hedge walling off his garden; the writer also denounces the 'demigod judge' who did not take into account the 'lies noted' during the trial and 'inappropriately' declared the suit 'null and void: condemning the victim to pay all charges and expenses without recourse'. All this, says the writer in the letter addressed to the chief editor of the newspaper (accompanied by an open letter to the minister of justice), is 'sickening and revolting owing to the age of the victim, honourably known in X and treated like a criminal'. He demands support so that the 'debate' can be brought to 'public attention' ('and I dare to hope that voices more powerful than mine and with much more authority will get involved in the debate'); he hopes this will lead to a 'reform of justice'. The duration of affairs generally increases with the victim's age, as if aging had the effect of reinforcing the petitioner's stubborn determination, probably because it increases the attachment to past identifications whose maintenance through doggedly repetitive operations absorbs an ever-greater share of the energy available.

The decline of which numerous writers complain in order to ensure their own defence is not attributable to age alone, however. It seems that the cadres whose letters appear in the corpus are most often self-educated individuals who have been victims of a process of exclusion and dismissal (this is frequently the case for cadres who lack credentials [Boltanski 1987a, 247–64). Similarly, many indications suggest that most of the small business owners, artisans, tradesmen and farmers whose letters are in the corpus have experienced a crisis that led not only to the decline of their businesses but also a weakening of their social positions. Finally, with salaried employees and blue-collar workers we find traces of family history on the decline but also, in other cases, of personal failures that have interrupted the rise in social mobility of the individual or the family.

Suffering, indignation and vehemence are manifested most force-fully in the letters whose authors belong to the lower classes and often have an imperfect mastery of written language. Sending a letter to a major newspaper constitutes a particularly meaningful and chal-lenging act for these writers, so that the threshold of suffering on the basis of which this undertaking is carried out is probably higher in these cases than it is for better-educated denouncers who have a stronger command of written language. These texts also present numerous features that are interpreted by their judges as signs of abnormality. Among the representatives of the lower classes in our corpus, manoeuvres of self-aggrandizement indeed stand out. Their letters are notably lacking in stylistic devices such as irony, which would make it possible to control and temper the effects of the denun-ciation on the reader, at least to a limited extent. Either the writers are unacquainted with such devices, in which case their statements appear exaggerated and violent, their careless language suggesting the absence of self-control, or else they make an effort to adopt a noble style, in which case their errors or hypercorrections (Labov 1972b, 141) give their discourse a borrowed feel that makes their efforts to aggrandize themselves through their writing more obvious and even more ridiculous.[3]

The fact remains that the relation between the act of denuncia-tion and the properties most readily objectivized and most durably attached to the person of the denouncer is neither foreordained nor mechanical. Thus the letter-writer's socio-professional category does not make a strong contribution to the determination of any of the axes, and the actantial structure is always more clearly linked to the relevant characteristics of the denunciation than are the properties of the denouncer. It would be still more misguided to seek to account for acts of denunciation by invoking the relation between one's social sit-uation and one's objective chances of being the victim of an injustice. If an injustice is to lead to a legal or political response, it must still be identified as such (Felstiner et al. 1980–81) – that is, as a particular form of offence that elicits reparations, unlike a multitude of other misfortunes such as the death of a loved one, an event with which one simply has to come to terms. Moreover, a recognized injustice can be handled by a variety of means: for example, it can be avenged in secret, compensated on different grounds, or simply forgotten, so that a public denunciation must be considered as one manoeuvre among others, one that, while it is never totally lacking in the pos-sibility of success (we shall see this more clearly in what follows), unquestionably entails risks for the denouncer.

For a firmer grasp of the situations in which persons engage in acts of public denunciation, we need to recall briefly the different ways in which a social identity can be acquired in a more or less durable manner or – and this amounts to the same thing, since all individuals are assured of their own continuity to the extent that they are recognized by others as having stable identities[4] – the various ways in which an individual can be connected with a group, a category or a collective body associated with a specific form of generality. The establishment and maintenance of a durable self, without which any investment in oneself is impossible, can be accomplished in at least three different, although not mutually exclusive, ways, corresponding to three ways of connecting the self with the self through the intermediary of others (Elster 1985). Belonging may be defined in terms of criteria and be legally guaranteed by a title – in particular, today, by a diploma or a professional title. In such cases, social identity, guaranteed by a convention, possesses weak elasticity in the sense that its permanence is affected relatively little by the title-holder's professional and social behaviour. One of the effects of the legal guarantee associated with a title is that it partially relieves individuals from the continuous work of identifying self with self (Bourdieu and Boltanski 1975) and frees them for other tasks, but it also allows for possible divergences with respect both to the most official and most stereotypical definition of identity – what Erving Goffman calls 'role distance' (Goffman 1961, 83–152) – and to the title-holder's past behaviour, which does not always have to be consistent in order to satisfy the expectations that others have placed in the title-holder.

Belonging can also be acquired and preserved, in the absence of any legal instrumentation, by means of ongoing efforts to identify with a collective body (for example, it can be marked by the use of signs and emblems); this work is carried out from day to day by the individual who benefits from it. In this case, the permanence of identity, always fragile, is obtained at the price of a considerable expenditure of energy, and especially at the price of great rigidity in behaviour, since the adjustment to the group referenced is achieved at every moment by self-consistency – that is, by ensuring, to the greatest possible extent, the conformity of one's present behaviour with a behaviour that succeeded in the past and that is used as a schema for producing new behaviours.

Finally, association with a collective body may be achieved through the intermediary of identification with a person. One's connection with a group and the acquisition of a permanent identity are accomplished in this case through a relationship with an individual who is an object of investment both inasmuch as he or she is singular – that is, characterized entirely by the reversible relation through which one relates to that person (and, consequently, in a way irreducible to any other mode of classification resting on a principle endowed with greater validity), and also inasmuch as the person embodies a group to which he or she can be connected in a lasting and powerful way, by means of a title, for example; through the intermediary of the other person, this group is inscribed at the heart of the relationship itself. When no legal instrument is present to consolidate an identity that must be perpetually repaired by using the relation maintained with others, any significant disturbance, especially when it affects privileged relations with the privileged individuals who carry out the connection with a group, can introduce a threat to the maintenance of identity and brutally raise the level of uncertainty about the environment and thus raise the anxiety level of the person whose protections have suddenly fallen away.

Let us take the example of an elementary school teacher, P., who took up the teaching profession somewhat late, after working for a British company.[5] A few years after he began teaching, he was promoted to a position as an English teacher in a middle school. But in 1966, following an evaluation by an inspector, he was sent back to teach at the elementary level. He then resumed his studies, earned a university diploma in modern literature, and over several years made a series of approaches to the school administration, which finally offered him a position as an adjunct instructor of English. He refused, demanding a reversal of the negative evaluation delivered in 1966. In 1974, he published and delivered a pamphlet in the form of a sixteen-page brochure in which he insulted, by name, certain inspectors and school principals in his district. Dismissed, he appealed to authorities in the national Department of Education and filed a demand for redress with the minister of education. In 1975, now fifty-one years old, he started a hunger strike. A support committee was organized, under the leadership of Maoist militants for the most part. Granted amnesty by the administrative tribunal in January 1976 but not reinstated, P. pursued his hunger strike, which went on for ninety-two days. Manifestations of support were multiplied. For example, on 16 February 1976, Jean-Paul Sartre appealed to the president. On 17 February, four young people chained themselves to fixtures in the lobby of the Saint-Lazare train station. Shortly after stopping the hunger strike, while he was still in a weakened condition, P. began what he called a 'tour de France', and became a prominent figure in the teachers' movement against inspections, a movement supported by a teachers' union and by certain factions of the National Education Federation such as l'École émancipée [Free School]. In some places, he attracted several hundred listeners; he marched at the head of demonstrations, held press conferences surrounded by famous academics and intellectuals, and on several occasions met Jean-Paul Sartre and Simone de Beauvoir, who continued to support him. Then the movement's intensity diminished. P. rejected all the administration's offers and doggedly insisted, as he had from the start, on a full retraction of the first inspection report. Still fighting almost twenty years after the beginning of the affair, he wrote memoirs in which he denounced the omnipresence of freemasonry, attributing to that organization a preponderant, secret and injurious role not only during his affair (whose principal protagonists – inspectors, administrators, judges, and so on – were, as if by chance, freemasons) but also throughout his earlier life and, more generally, throughout French history.

P.'s perseverance, his dogged determination to obtain total annulment of the first inspection report as opposed to any other form of reparation, doubtless has something to do first of all with his anxiety at having to provide proof of his competence in English, the way one brings irrefutable proof during a court trial – which is different from demonstrating one's capacity to speak and write English correctly in situations that require it. P. knew that he knew English, but he was not sure he could 'prove' it in a perfectly objective and absolutely irrefutable way before judges whose criteria of judgement were partly opaque. He thus worried about the quality of his accent, which he acquired while he was working for a company in a British colony and which may not have conformed to the standards of Oxford. And how could he be sure that he possessed something as vague and uncertain as knowledge, particularly in the case of a foreign language, when his mastery had not been certified by an irreversible legal action? The action of the inspector representing the institution to which P. belonged – an institution that had accepted him, acknowledged him (at least P. thought so) and promoted him, an institution with respect to which P.'s identity was henceforth defined – abolished at a single stroke the very thing that had given him the possibility of linking the past with the future without radically modifying his self-definition and thus ensured the permanence of the self. This permanence made it possible for P. to invest in the profession, in his students, in the language, in his colleagues, in his career and, more generally, in the multiplicity of daily enterprises through which consciousness of social honour is maintained (Sabel 1982). P. could not rest until he could demonstrate that his persecutor, the abusive inspector (about whom he would come to believe twenty years later that he was simply the instrument of a conspiracy of freemasons), did not know English or, rather, that he himself was not a specialist in English and was not legally qualified to pass administrative judgement on a professor of English. P.'s mistrust of the tests that were offered to him, his fear that they would be rigged against him, led him to refuse one of the available procedures for recovering his status, a second inspection on appeal; he was apprehensive about its outcome, because the second inspection could not be appealed. The changes in professional life that accompanied P.'s return to elementary school teaching took on the character of a veritable exclusion (change of place, of task, of colleagues, and so on) to which he could not resign himself. He could not accept the loss of the promotion that had been granted him and then brutally withdrawn. He thus tried to restore the former state of affairs by clinging to a line that consisted in treating the act that had abolished him as a simple *error*. The administration was supposed to proceed as if the inspection that led to his demotion had never taken place, or was not valid because the conditions under which it was carried out, the conditions that established the effectiveness of this act of authority, had not been respected. It was then necessary to win acknowledgement of the technicality – a *vice de forme*, in French legal language – that would make it possible to invalidate the test.

When he spoke about the inspector who had persecuted him, P. characterized him sometimes as an agent of the administration, a mandated representative of a collective person for whom no other agent furnished with the same mandate could be substituted, and sometimes as a singular person, with his own passions, diction, tics, and so on. Inasmuch as he was mandated by the institution, the inspector was authorized to deliver sanctions. P. recognized the validity of the institution to which they both belonged. Thus he had no a priori reasons to challenge the principle of inspection or the values on which inspections were based, or any reasons to constitute inspection, as the organizations that supported his cause would do later, as an abusive 'power' exercised over him from the outside, against his will, in a 'report' in which 'forces' confronted one another. Thus it was as a person that the inspector had failed, and the injustice he had committed was moreover no less harmful to the institution than it was to the victim. But this division between separate roles is difficult to sustain. The inspector, always designated by name (Mr X), was most often manifested in an ambiguous way: he had the features of a singular individual, a person like any other, with whom one could argue, whose judgement one could contest, and so on, but he also had the features of an institutional agent. For, if the inspector was only a human being, passionate and fallible, why was his judgement without appeal? And if he was an institution, why was his judgement not impartial? Thus the inspector had to be a deceitful agent – an agent whose institutional attributes concealed singular intentions and who acted not as an agent – that is, for the sole good of the institution and within the limits of the powers conferred on him – but as an individual, and with reference to a hidden interest, which was not that of an institution; it was even contrary to the institution's interest, and it was defined as individual before being assimilated to that of a clandestine group. Only after trying in vain to have the inspection annulled by the academic administration did P. gradually come to see the two sets that until then had been partially separate as one and the same: the conspiratorial group that acted in underhanded ways and the official institution whose façade remained respectable. The form of the inspector was then inscribed in salient fashion in the victim's memory, precisely inasmuch as that form singularly embodied a collective person. The identification of singularities was stabilized by means of nicknames, which abound in the pamphlet P. devoted to the affair: 'the Mastodon', 'Monsieur le Baron', 'the Coryphaeus of these ladies', 'Guiguite', 'Hi-han', 'the human Sacrophyte', 'the Suborner', and so on. This invested form was to be used as a cognitive instrument for social identification (Boltanski and Thévenot 1983) in this universe, that of the National Education Department, which had been familiar up to that point but whose dangerous strangeness was gradually being revealed. This form makes it possible to identify the others, to classify them (for example, as good or bad), and to recognize, among those who may appear friendly and peaceful at first, the hidden bad side, what they will do to you later if you are not careful, what they have in common with the persecutor-inspector, the way in which they could secretly 'constitute a mass' against him (Favret-Saada 1990, 204) – something they may already have been doing, as P. saw it.

— 22 —

CONFIDENCE BETRAYED

In the case we have just examined, the violence of the crisis was attenuated by the existence of a formalized relation between the persecutor and the victim, and by the presence of a large number of institutional resources (unions, administrative tribunals, and so on) that could be mobilized to constitute the injustice in a public way. But the deficit of identity, tied to the rupture of a privileged relation that served as an operator for achieving the connection with a group, can take much more brutal forms when the relation between the actors is more singular and when the resources making it possible to manage the crisis collectively are scarcer or less accessible. In these cases, the betrayal of the one who is to be designated in the discourse of denunciation as the privileged persecutor can lead to reactions of high intensity. The crisis often starts, it seems, with a scene during which the victim, who gives himself over unstintingly to the service of his protector, is accused of 'going too far'. He is reminded of his hierarchical position, the bureaucratic rules that limit his task, the legal forms in which the task is to be carried out, and so on. The effect of these interventions is a brutal desingularization of the relationship, which shifts from a state of disinterestedness based on personal affinities to an asymmetrical and anonymous hierarchical relation.[1] This change, which leads to the rupture of the singular relation by means of which the individual could cement his permanence by binding himself to himself through the mediation of others, casts suspicion on the whole social environment, which tilts into uncertainty. When the figure of the authoritarian superior – autocrat, traitor, ambitious climber – under the mask of a friend is unveiled to show the true face, and when one perceives that one has been played for a fool, devoting oneself in the name of an affection that has not been returned, then nothing else can be taken as certain. For if the world that has been unveiled is genuine, then both the happiness that preceded it and the way in which the self was presented in it were illusory. Only at the price of this doubt can a stable identity be maintained, and a deceitful world is the price paid for safeguarding a self that is not deceptive.

But this is not enough. To restore the minimal permanence without which nothing can be reinvested, not even another relationship, the victim has to bind himself to himself once again through his determination to 'struggle' – that is, to refuse to recognize the degradation. To confer the fatal character of an objective necessity on his own determination and ensure that there is no turning back, the victim has to bind himself anew through a sort of oath that is initially tacit, then more and more explicit as the resistances encountered and the fatigue experienced affect his will and especially his faith in his own cause. The work of rerooting most often follows the path of a continuum anchored below the level of language; it moves from the simple dramatization of a gesture (as when one weeps) to a formulation for oneself alone in the murmuring of one's inner language. The next step is a formulation for someone else, in a confidential mode, in a singular relation and with a requirement of secrecy, and then a statement intended for a larger audience, chosen in increasingly distant circles, with the tacit acceptance of the circulation of the statement in the form of gossip. These steps are followed by more intentional and more explicit undertakings, in the sense that they are decided on in advance and not triggered by a passing lapse that one thinks one can retract because the ties it creates with others have no official status: examples might include ambiguous letters to third parties, requests to friends, or to friends of friends, consultations with experts but on a 'private' basis, or 'unofficial' solicitations of holders of collective resources (unions, representatives of associations, and the like). Then, as the victim's determination is reassured, timid public protests can take shape, discreet ways of arousing the attention of others without explicitly asking for it, ways of obtaining from them a spontaneous adhesion that opens the way in turn to more explicit appeals for mobilization, whose scope depends, as we have seen, on the degree to which the particular interests of the defence can be dissociated from the generalized interests of the victim. At each moment along this continuum, new instruments have to be deployed to give the protest a more and more objective form – that is, a form more and more independent of the very person of the one who is expressing it and of the one to whom it is addressed, as the number of individuals taken into the victim's confidence increases along with their alterity. This is the case, for example, with legal rhetoric, which is understood, along with scientific rhetoric, as the language of truth; indeed, it constitutes a privileged form which can be used to prove indisputably that, given the deceitfulness of the world, the victim is not mistaken in presenting him- or herself as such.

This very general process can take especially sudden and violent forms when the intensity of the crisis and the panic that follows the collapse of identity call for rapid and desperate measures of reparation, and also, since the two things often go hand in hand, when the victim is not supported by others and when the efforts corresponding to the first stages of the work of rerooting meet only indifference in the victim's surroundings – or, worse, when they arouse forms of hostility or concern among those close to the victim and thus increase the victim's isolation (Goffman 1969, Lemert 1967). In these cases, an appeal to public opinion – that is, an appeal for the unconditional and undifferentiated support of all the others, whoever they are, close or distant, known or unknown – becomes one of the only ways to re-establish objectivity, or what some would call reality. 'Are you with me?' Jacques Lacan used to ask his students (Lacan 1988, 104). 'If you are with me, we will be able to go a long way. The question is not so much one of knowing up to what point one should go, the question is more one of knowing if one will be followed. In fact that is an element which allows one to discriminate what one may call reality' (ibid., 274). For being followed constitutes a way of restoring the social bond which, through the attachment of others, can again link individuals to themselves. Followed, they can 'realize' themselves once more. In the case of P., that link was restored at least temporarily when he received the endorsement of Jean-Paul Sartre, a singular embodiment of the collectivity of intellectuals; by supporting him as a friend, and especially by encouraging him to write, Sartre could re-establish P.'s relation to the authentic universe of pure and true knowledge.

The appeal to public opinion, even when it is carried out under unfavourable conditions, is thus never a completely desperate manoeuvre. Its chances of success depend on the degree to which the others can recognize in the victim's protest a gesture, and, more precisely, a political gesture – that is, an act destined not to compensate an individual loss but to reveal an arbitrary act that had been previously unknown, and thereby to make its constraint felt. For this, the victim's interests have to meet the expectations of an already existing group, at the price of a work of homogenization centred on an interest constituted at its most general level, and this requires new operations that establish equivalence permitting mutual recognition to occur. We see this clearly once again in the case of P., whose solitary struggle is incorporated, after nine years, into a protest movement led by young teachers in the secondary system; these supporters, many of whom had diplomas entitling them to teach at the university level, sought to increase their margin of professional autonomy before falling back, a few years later, into silence and isolation.[2] What led P. to give a new meaning to his action was the contact with the spokespersons of organizations endowed with a high level of academic legitimacy, and especially perhaps with a certain public – that of the meetings during which he tirelessly recounted his affair – a public whose spokespersons told him that they identified with him, thus justifying his own identification with his listeners. He discerned political dimensions in his protest which had escaped him earlier (and which outstripped him thereafter). These new dimensions further reinforced his determination not to give an inch, not to abandon a fight that he would not have had the courage to pursue to the end if he were not doing it for others, as he put it – as if he had become a cause foreign to himself.

To rehabilitate those who have exposed themselves by their own denunciatory activity to suspicions of abnormality, or even insanity, does it suffice to denounce psychiatry as an institution in turn, and to unveil, borrowing the arguments and weapons of the denouncers, the arbitrariness of the labelling of which the mentally ill person is the victim? Similarly, does it suffice to denounce the psychological or psychiatric illusion to establish the validity of an analysis that offers an inverted sociological interpretation in support of the claims of self-described victims? I believe that the sociological analysis of persecution is not complete if it does not go beyond showing that this feeling of victimization, far from being illusory, is indeed well founded, at least in its origins. In an important article that made a frontal attack on a terrain over which psychiatry had had a monopoly, Edwin Lemert (1967) opposes the 'reality' of the conspiracy to the conspiratorial 'pseudo-community', to borrow Norman Cameron's expression (Cameron 1943, 1959). This approach helps in spite of everything to reproduce the opposition between sociology and psychology, conceived as the opposition between the real and the imaginary, the objective and the subjective, and so on. As Charles W. Lidz remarks (1978), 'taking seriously' the viewpoint of someone who is labelled as ill (labelling theory) is a methodological decision that consists in analysing, by means of the same instruments, the behaviours and utterances that are socially defined as normal or abnormal, instead of, for example, explaining the former by the constraints of the situation and the latter by a permanent, hidden disposition on the part of the subject. But one obviously becomes locked into the very logic of the process that one has taken as one's object of study if one means thereby, as is often the case, at least implicitly, to take the side of the persecuted individual (as, for example, in Mirowski and Ross 1983). In fact, the individuals whose protest one seeks to belittle by accusing them of not thinking straight themselves use all available resources, including scientific ones, to demonstrate their lucidity and, in the struggle that opposes them to their enemies, their judges, and especially their doctors, they often invoke arguments with a sociological flavour, or even, when they are acquainted with it, the authority of sociology. The denunciation of institutional violence does not suffice, either, to ensure the protection of the interested parties. The interests of these parties are certainly more urgent than those of knowledge, because the indignant critique of social control and labelling has, at best, the power to repress, in bad faith, the ordinary judgements of common sense, without which the verdict of institutions would not carry much weight. But, because it does not seek to understand the logic of the practices it denounces, this critique does not reach them in their principle. It thus shows itself to be incapable of loosening the constraints of normality that limit, in daily life, the expression of pride, distress or dissidence. It is still just as difficult to revolt, or even to demand justice.

To understand these constraints, one must first try to establish the grammars that generate ordinary judgements, and perhaps on occasion the verdicts of experts as well. The configurations of the medico-legal vulgate (see Bantman 1979 for an excellent bibliography), which are taught today to all those who practise the helping professions and professions of social control, often have the self-evidence of good form because they are undergirded by pre-existing knowledge. Scientific psychology parallels in this case, and confirms, 'naïve psychology' (Heider 1958). And it is perhaps in this way that these configurations are valid and effective. But the conditions of their use do not require making explicit the adjustment – however problematic it may be – between the most improbable deviations and the expectations of common sense, which is able to recognize these deviations as if it had created them. The same thing can be said about the ever-so-familiar affinity between persecution, demands for reparation, worth and interpretation, which, to be deployed, has to be constructed with the requirement of not changing rationality when one moves from cases in which the reference to these figures seems justified to cases in which it seems aberrant.

257

As we have seen, denunciations in our corpus take the most vehement forms, and, from the vantage point of common sense, the most pathological forms, in cases in which the letter-writers have stabilized their identity and ensured the permanence of self by linking themselves with a collective person through the intermediary of identification with a person, a concrete individual person, closely connected to the group, bearer both of a singular body and objectivized signs of belonging to a group. It is when the crisis of identity is rooted in a rupture of the relation with 'the person ... at one time loved', as Freud put it in connection with President Schreber (Freud 1993, 116) – a person whose identity, legally guaranteed, has operated as a binding agent – that recourse to the manoeuvre that consists in trying to re-create something durable through the intermediary of 'public opinion' seems most frequent. Normality's tacit respect for common sense, and especially for the rule according to which the various actants have to occupy a similar position on the singular–collective axis and to be thereby perceptibly of the same size,[3] is thus what forces the denouncer to aggrandize both himself and the designated persecutor – for example, by invoking the existence of a conspiracy – in a manoeuvre whose effect is also to desingularize the relation between denouncer and persecutor. As the foregoing analyses suggest, the axis that leads from the singular to the general probably constitutes one of the privileged dimensions used by the cognitive operations destined to think about, and work on, the always problematic and difficult relation between individuals as singular beings and individuals as they are endowed with an identity defined at the highest level of generality by reference to collective bodies. It is also this axis that must be explored to analyse the constraints confronted by the hope of being a little more than oneself. Access to the general is also a privilege, perhaps the greatest of all. One form of insanity, in the sense in which one opposes the wise to the insane, consists precisely in the attempt to conquer, in solitary fashion and by an act of pure will, this tangible salvation to which recognition by others gives access.

Appendix 1

BUILDING THE FACTORIAL ANALYSIS

The data used here have been addressed by means of a factorial analysis of correspondence. This method of data analysis, developed by Jean-Paul Benzecri in 1979, takes the results of a survey and produces cartographic diagrams on which the individuals or variables included in the survey are projected. These maps supply representations of the social space. Two individuals whose responses and/or properties are similar will be situated close to one another on the map; two variables that classify individuals in a similar way will likewise be in proximity. The interest of this method is that, using the notion of *inertia*, it reveals and makes visible the groupings and proximities according to which the data gathered during the survey are organized. Inertia measures the distance between an individual and the centre of gravity of the cloud of points formed by the projection of the numerical data set in a space with N dimensions. The inertia of an individual is large when it is far from the centre of gravity, small when it is close. The total inertia of the cloud is small when the individuals are clustered close together (they resemble one another), large in the contrary case (when they are dissimilar). Factorial analysis consists in projecting the different axes of the cloud (factorial axes) onto planes. The analyst seeks to identify a small number of axes (ideally two, which can then be represented on paper) that have the property of maximizing the inertia of the cloud – that is, of preserving a maximum amount of information from the initial cloud of data points. The breakdown into factorial axes thus makes it possible to determine the proportion of the total inertia of the cloud that can be attributed to each of these axes and, consequently, to each of the explanatory factors taken into account in the analysis.

In the case of the analysis that underlies the work presented here, the initial approach to the data involved 140 variables with a total of 803 modalities that could be used. The first univariate analyses made it possible to eliminate certain variables and to group together categories that were too weakly represented to stand alone. In all, 106 variables were retained, with 385 possible modalities. These variables are not all of the same nature: 87 variables in 227 modalities describe the nature of the affair, the contents and appearance of the letter or dossier; 7 variables in 52 modalities describe the actantial system; 6 variables in 32 modalities are devoted to the description of the letter-writer; finally, there are 6 indicators of normality in 13 modalities. The 227 descriptors of the affair and the dossier constitute the active data in the factorial analysis of the correspondences; the other groups of variables count as supplementary elements. In the case of variables that concern the writer's social properties, this decision is explained by the relatively weak reliability of the data and the considerable number of non-responses.

As far as the judgements of normality are concerned, it seemed obvious that these exogenous elements could not intervene in an active way in the factorial decomposition. Six judges were charged with rating the 275 'affairs' on a scale of 1 to 10, with 1 being the most normal and 10 the most pathological. The operation of disjunctive coding then created, for each of the judges, ten variables coded as present or absent: in other words, sixty variables in all. For judge 1, for example, we obtained the following results:

$$
\text{JU1, 1 score} \begin{array}{ll} = 1 & \text{yes} \\ = 0 & \text{no} \end{array} \qquad
\text{JU1, 2 score} \begin{array}{ll} = 1 & \text{yes} \\ = 0 & \text{no} \end{array} \quad \ldots \quad
\text{JU1, 10 score} \begin{array}{ll} = 1 & \text{yes} \\ = 0 & \text{no} \end{array}
$$

If we want to simplify the factorial representations and retain a single summary of the values attributed to the letters while neglecting information about 'who judged', we are led to reason about the scores. We then count, for each dossier, the number of times it was scored 1, 2, and so on, up to 10. We thus obtain the distribution of grades assigned to the affair, and keep them as ten new variables, named SC1, SC2, SC2, ... SC10.

For example, letters 462 and 769 were scored as follows:

	JU1	JU2	JU3	JU4	JU5	JU6
462	4	3	2	3	2	7
769	1	1	1	1	3	1

They were then recoded:

	SC1	SC2	SC3	SC4	SC5	SC6	SC7	SC8	SC9	SC10
462	0	2	2	1	0	0	1	0	0	0
769	5	0	1	0	0	0	0	0	0	0

At the end of this recoding, the variable SC1 is associated with all the dossiers that earned a score of 1 at least once, and it is weighted by the number of agreements. Summing up the six judgements in this way retains all the information about the scores that was originally available; only the information about the judges is lost. If I had chosen to summarize by using the average of the six judgements, we would have obtained less precise results. An average of 5 may represent perfect agreement (5 5 5 5 5 5), partial agreement (5 5 3 7 6 4) or considerable disagreement (9 1 4 2 8 6); and in the last case the average corresponds to none of the scores actually awarded. In this case we are no longer associating scores and dossiers, but dossiers and average judgements that can sum up extremely diverse configurations in exactly the same way.

In its definitive representation, the factorial analysis bears only on 155 active modalities and 68 supplementary elements, after the elimination of irrelevant modalities. For a detailed description of the procedure followed and the statistical results, see Schiltz 1983; this article includes in particular the various states of the first factorial map, the histogram of the singular values and the table of the ten variables that contribute the most strongly, positively or negatively, to the first factor for the three successive analyses. Given that, in the case of a disjunctive table, phi^2 cannot serve as an indicator of associations among the variables, the information has to be found in the decrease, rapid or not, of the singular values and in the numerical importance of the first of these. The first two singular λ values, $\lambda 1 = .3736$ and $\lambda 2 = .1832$, allow us to conclude that there is a strong association between the active variables and the dossiers.

Appendix 2

A SAMPLING OF TYPICAL LETTERS

These texts are excerpted from twelve letters chosen because of the typical positions they occupy on the first factorial map (see figure 5). All the information (names of persons, places, dates, and so on) that might have permitted the writer to be identified has been omitted or changed. The original spellings and syntax, left unaltered in the French edition, are reflected insofar as possible in the translation.

1 Letter no. 615

Pursuant to the violations of private life, thefts and abuse of authority on the part of the prosecutor's office in M 1960–1979. I take the liberty of pointing out to you that, if one were to consider my reference to B. (the name only, I am no judge) in the doctoral Thesis, three typed volumes, 950 pages, written between 1969 and 1971, 49 X Street, 10th floor, apartment rented to Mr X, 750, then 1,000 f per month, type F5, on investigations carried out by myself, on my project and my ideas, with index cards purchased and paid for by myself, with my salary, X Street Paris XIV, or on paper belonging to me (scraps or purchases), 66 X Street in M., typed by two ladies who had answered an advertisement, paid at my expense, about 8,000 f total, bound in A., la Pensée Universitaire, at my expense, 500 f, illustrations printed in M., place de la Bourse, at my expense 1,200 f. Defended in Paris, on X date, round trip Paris-M. at my expense,

as if it were a collective effort that a shitty Swiss reserve officer had manipulated, ordered or had a right to use, update, plagiarize, you will be so kind as to inform, via Mme the Minister of Universities,

Figure 5

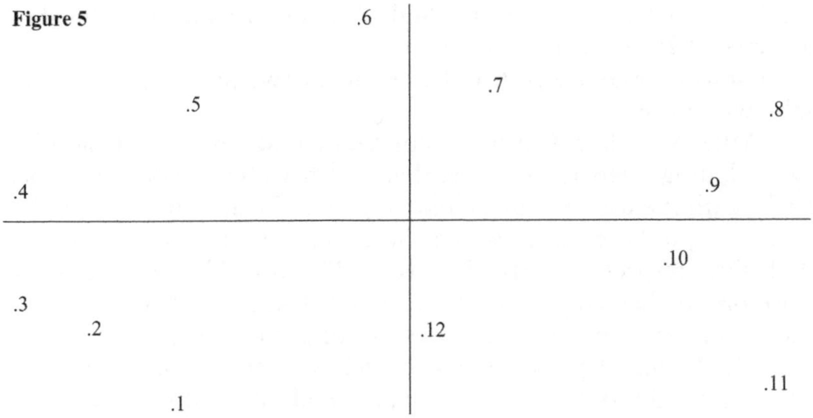

the General Prosecutor of the Seine district, to be forwarded to the jurisdictions concerned.

In particular, I have nothing to do with the Swiss, despite the fact that I was invited with my wife and my children on New Year's Eve by local protestants, including Mr X whom I had met when he was a cadet and I rank and file. We have not had a falling out, but all those guys think they have the right to give orders to the local illiterates and the kikes and make them do anything at all to show off. I am not a Voltairean, best regards.

2 Letter no. 531

FOR MY CHILDREN IN PHYSICAL AND MORAL DANGER

pursuant to the administration's deficiencies in the 'divorce' process, which allows any bandit to seize children with impunity, a process that has nothing to do with the cliché of a clash between man and woman.

Pursuant to my letter of approval, concerning the Police, whose behaviour you denounced in S., and about which I pointed out that it did not behave better in P., the last straw being that the 'police force' which takes itself for a 'STRIKE FORCE' is at the service of JUSTICE, you were so kind as to inform me that you were preparing an article about 'DIVORCE', and its catastrophic consequences for children. My testimony being apt to retain your attention, according to what you informed me, I am sending you, attached, as a first reaction to the

263

receipt of the text of the second 'SOCIAL' survey,which I obtained by a decree of 20 November 1970:

– photocopies of excerpts of letters by the two principal unmarried false witnesses:

– Mlle X, called Corinne, representing all by herself sleeping around, drugs, department store thefts – left with three dresses on her back, with the use of young children giving the appearance of a fine mother – , in hotels after which she collects the sheets embroidered with their respective coats of arms, and even on the premises of at least one of her employers, from which I succeeded in extracting them; unmarried mother; her son with the grandmother.

– Mr X, unbalanced, unmarried 42 X avenue, where my children ages eight and seven were sequestered and badly treated after School.

– Mr X, widower at the time of the kidnapping, which he used to force me to re-establish my home 250 km. away from Paris, according to the answer I received from my demand for reinstatement; my presence impeded him from remarrying.

3 Letter no. 560

It is a young man, who needs to speak from the heart, to a man who he thinks is understanding and represents what he considers the highest in justice.

After events that happened recently. I am especially determined to inform you about things that appeared suspicious to me, and about the persecution that they call imaginary, but that was in fact relative. After a struggle that has been going on since the age of 15, to eat, to educate myself, and to get myself into a position to meet the needs of my mother and a home. This year our business picked up again and before perhaps capability and will had reawakened the jealousy of some who owing to that fact played a role of detractors through arguments and sabotage. If there were only a few private persons interested in these machinations, it would be nothing, but when government and society, . . . gets involved in this game what do you want a young man, exhausted by work and his mother worn out and continually ill, to do . . . complaint for one or the other? In this case one would have done only that. But! When one was doing it some people found clever ways to abort the investigation or turn it around (cancel). Such were the rumours, that the heifer 18 months old dead in pasture, had been killed by me (with a knife). Whereas I had not been over there for five or six days. Who? let my dogs loose at night, made complaints, sent me to court, how many times and why? . . . Locked up my dogs without drinking or eating, took away the stools from my hunting spot, took down markers or tried to destroy them (burning while clearing the meadows . . . etc.) summoned to court for grazing on others with defective fencing (why did Mister X prefer to read my depositions himself). And these last woods steal destroyed, electric fence sabotaged, set his dog on my cows (interest in aborting) finding himself on the path with dogs running free when I was taking them to the fields, not to mention the provocations . . . etc. there would be too many, I would have a book to write . . .

4 Letter no. 729

Having had Mr X on the telephone this morning, Mr X being the President of the Defense Committee, having himself been the victim of a crooked property manager in C, and which put him behind bars for several years; the same swindlers rule in F. R., and of course everywhere in France. But in R. they've run into a stone wall, because for me the swindlers and accomplices won't get away with it, so taking advantage of the upcoming elections Mister X asked me if you couldn't report the Facts in your Newspaper, for what I am writing is very serious for as that Asshole Prosecutor used to say when he was in R., and who got moved thanks to me if at least W. [the author of the letter] did something stupid I would have that piece of shit locked up for Shame, but W. hasn't done anything stupid, he's pursuing the swindlers in their machinations and it isn't pretty, they've gone to the township of P, and the Mayor of that township is to contact me this evening; for after going to M. they came, no X king of the swindles and Director of Family Benefits of I. went to Look for them in A. I have all the details and I propose to make them known to you when you wish but as soon as possible for I would be grateful if really you could publish articles on the Corruption that Reigns in R. and everywhere in France, right now so that the french would vote in full knowledge for proper People and not for protectors of Corruption, swindlers for as I had said to my Lawyers on March 2 or 3 there will be more about this soon they were septical but now they are astonished at what I know and when the hateful Minister X came to R. after passing through L. and N. it was simply to throw people off the track, for he would have been very embarrassed if he had had to and say to the Press that he had come to find out whether I was telling the Truth about the Corruption in the Court, the Judges, the Cops of the Judicial Police who made false documents to protect the swindlers like X Notary and X king of the Swindlers notary at G. and others.

5 Letter no. 711

My father being victim of a swindle of 150,000 (one hundred fifty thousand francs) and of a serious injustice, I am taking the liberty of writing you this letter.

I am of course quite aware that a newspaper of such importance as yours must receive hundreds of letters of this sort, but I judge that my father's case is deserving of interest. If I write to your newspaper rather than to another, it is because at the present time 'Le Monde' remains the only press organ that has dared to criticize the inconsistencies of the French judicial system and that apart from 'Le Canard Enchaîné' which published three articles (copies enclosed) on this subject, the press has made a total 'black out' on this scandal – as happens every time a politician is the source of a scandal. In order to inform you summarily of the precise nature of the problem, I am enclosing a copy of a letter that I tried in vain to have published in the press more than a year ago. The facts described there already constitute a scandal in themselves. The affair becomes more complicated when one knows that my father has been condemned to compensate X, president of the X company, and social security for the affair of assault and battery, that the appeal for the vehicular property resulted in a rejection (decree of 12 X 81), that my father has sent two registered letters to the Honourable Keeper of the Seals without receiving an answer, a registered letter to the Honourable President of the Republic which received, for its part, a negative response. But what remains most staggering in my father's case are the anomalies – or the incompetencies – that have marked this affair from the beginning of its settlement in court. Hoping that you will deign to grant your full attention to this letter and remaining at your disposal for any further information, I assure you of my very best regards.

P. S. I must point out to you that, in order to obtain justice, my father began a hunger strike last Thursday evening and that since Friday evening he has been in front of the Ministry of Justice, Place Vendôme.

6 Letter no. 583

Not despairing of getting support for my point of view (it is horrible, what people think of others) I beg you to find enclosed, to this end, my latest memorandum to the Administrative Tribunal of A., authorizing you to transcribe it in 'Le Monde' in particular for the ways and means belonging to public opinion in our country.

The real question, given the seriousness of an arbitrary revocation of Government Services (accompanied by an attempt at homicide by suggestion) is whether the law of 1 July 1972 on discrimination is not itself discriminatory – and whether it does not implicitly violate (at the very least) – the Constitution: does the law on discrimination imply reservations? This is the question that I am also asking you.

7 Letter no. 559

The Instructional Teams of S., gathered in general assembly on 12 October 1980, in the name of the attachment to public schooling and to the gospel of Jesus, declare that they are called by all the phenomena that are calling into question schools, justice, the rights of man and by all individual and collective suffering.

They are deeply moved by the trial and condemnation of their colleague X, an elementary school teacher in the region, a woman committed to the education and instruction of particularly underprivileged and troubled children (in Special Education and in Medical and Pedagogical Services for the Handicapped).

Her summons came during a period of peace for our country whereas the Court for State Security was set up during a period of war. Its status does not give all those who are brought before it guarantees equivalent to those that are offered by other jurisdictions: even though these latter have to rule on criminal affairs all of which include appeal procedures. Famous judicial errors compel us – for the safeguard of the rights of the accused and public peace – to ask the Supreme Court of Appeals to re-examine the formal conditions of X's trial.

8 Letter no. 632

The C. Section of the PCF [French Communist Party] denounces the lamentable anti-Communist provocation of the leadership of the

PS [Socialist Party] in C. Indeed, in the Monde of X/X/80 and through tracts, the PS explains to whoever will listen that two Socialist militants have been attacked by Communists. There is no proof for this assertion. May be it is a question of a provocation from the right? the PS pretends to wonder, what does it matter in any case the PCF is behind this act because of its campaign with respect to the PS. The dishonesty of this underhanded political manoeuvre is reinforced by the fact that the investigators themselves, after identifying the owner of the aggressors' car, declared that nothing allows them to assert that the authors of this violent act are members of the PCF. The truth is that there is no longer anything but slander and misdirection among the PS leadership to get out of the difficulties in which they have been placed by the Communist proposals for saving jobs and the future of C., while demanding that the Socialist municipality stop going along with the rightists and favouring the departure of businesses: being unable to answer as to its real responsibilities concerning the departure of X company, the leadership of the PS chose to move ahead without looking back. The Communists of C., for their part, will not lose their cool in the face of this irresponsible provocation and will continue as in the past to act for the defence of jobs and the future of our city.

For the leadership of the section, X First Secretary of the C. section of the PCF.

9 Letter no. 511

X, sculptor, age 35, Breton, whose works have been selected by the salon of young sculptors, the fall salon, the European salon of Strasbourg. Invited to exhibits in New York, Montreal, Lausanne, Geneva . . . holder of an honoris causa from the European Academy of Fine Arts, is in prison in B. He will be judged by the court of T. on 16 January 1980 for theft of art objects.

If I write to you, it is not to justify the theft, but to inform you and to focus the spotlight on an incident that is highly meaningful and consequential. If X, a fundamentally honest, humble, and courageous individual, has committed this offence, it is for two reasons: the first is the deplorable situation in which, like most young artists in France, he had fallen. The second is that he had been aware of the existence, in the practically abandoned second residence of a doctor, Mr X, of a huge pile of art works – paintings by great masters, Greek and Egyptian sculptures, Russian icons, tapestries – that would make many of our museums grow pale with envy. Revolted at seeing such an artistic patrimony confiscated, abandoned, overwhelmed by a hopeless material situation, indignant at the fate reserved to creative and artistic forces in our country which sees itself as the standard-bearer for culture and ART, he took on this theft alone, out of defiance and despair. It is not a matter of declaring X innocent, he pleads guilty and JUSTICE will judge. He asks personally neither for help nor for indulgence. He assumes full responsibility for his act and its consequences. Through this incident that affects a friend today, it is the general situation of young artists that I wish to expose . . .

10 Letter no. 405

We cannot remain silent about the incident that took place last November 19 at 10:40 p.m. in Café X on the Champs-Élysées. The facts are the following: We had both decided, after seeing a movie, to have a drink at this café, on the enclosed terrace. We ordered herbal tea and fruit juice. The waiter came back after a few moments to inform us that it was not possible for him to serve two women alone. We asked for an explanation and one of the maîtres d'hôtel came over to specify:

– that in fact management orders were not to serve women alone.

– that we were undoubtedly engaged in solicitation.

– and in response to a question from us, he did not hesitate to reply that he took us in fact to be whores.

Very shocked by this attitude, we left the establishment without provoking a scandal, surely a mistake.

We believe that this behaviour constitutes a serious challenge, on the one hand, to the dignity of women, and, on the other hand, to the legislation governing sales. We have written to the director of the establishment and we obviously expect a reply which we shall not fail to pass on to you.

We thank you in advance for sharing our REVULSION in the face of such treatment and we remain of course entirely at your disposal for any supplementary information you might wish to have.

11 Letter no. 454

Living in V., I go to I. to select my books at the library. It is located on the third floor of a building. The police headquarters are on the

269

first floor. Today a crowd was waiting. All immigrants needing to take steps to renew their residency permit for one year according to the new 'Stoleru' law (for North Africans). Before going up to look for my books, a big commotion caught my attention. 'Only ten people; all the others go outside and come back tomorrow', a policeman yelled. The people who had been waiting a long time immediately shouted out their indignation: 'But', one cried out, 'I've already lost three hours of work. I can't lose three more tomorrow.' 'Shut up and piss off – out!' People rebelled. Three policemen come to the rescue. They shove people out with all their might. A woman falls. Her husband shoves a policeman, seeing his wife on the ground. The policeman hits him hard, on the head. The immigrants are terrorized. A blind, elderly Arab man accompanied by a little boy six or seven years old is struck in turn. Another man is beaten by two policemen. He cries out that he is already injured and that he is ill. The beating continues, harder than before. The man falls and stops moving. The panic-stricken people rush outside. I find myself with other people. The three policemen yell at us: 'You too, outside.' 'But we're going to the library" I say. '"Outside," I said.' They grab us violently and shove us brutally outside. An ambulance arrives and takes the injured man away. I hear a Policeman say 'we're in France and we make the law. They can go rot in their own country.' Indignant, I went back home. I decided to go to the library in my own town now. But I am ashamed of the policemen's attitude; I am ashamed to be French.

12 Letter no. 501

I take the liberty of writing you to let you know the following facts: my niece mother of two children aged 6 and 3 and currently seven months pregnant sought shelter in my home and has been there since Saturday 22 March 1980 to escape from repeated beatings by her domestic partner, who has confiscated her identity documents, her keys, and her personal belongings in order to force her to leave the apartment that they acquired both together in A. . . . Since she left A. my niece has been attacked in the street several times by her ex-partner who took from her each time her handbag containing duplicate copies of the various papers that the relevant authorities have been willing to prepare for her after much lengthy effort.

On Friday 4 April 1980 my niece's ex-partner called me in my office to find out whether he could come visit his children in my home? Finding no obstacles to that we thus made an appointment to meet at my house on Wednesday 9 April at 6 p.m. Unfortunately, upon leaving my visitor made off discreetly with my niece's handbag containing her papers, money, and a complete set of keys to my apartment. Which is very serious, since I myself have three children aged 8, 6, and 4 months, and I work at night. At police headquarters in B. and in A. they declared that it was not in their mandate to find a solution to the problem and that is why I am writing personally to you for a rapid resolution of this matter that could take a very bad turn at any moment.

CC the honourable Commissioner of A.; the honourable Commissioner of B.; the Assistant for Social Affairs of the City of A.; Le Canard Enchaîné; RTL [a radio station]; Le Monde; France Soir; Le Meilleur; the Association for Battered Women; Assoc. Let Them Live; Mr X, my niece's ex-partner; the honourable Minister of the Interior.

NOTES

1 The most interesting interviews were carried out according to an arrangement condemned by textbook methodologies, because it appears to break
with the requirements of exteriority, neutrality, objectivity and non-involve-
ment that have long been viewed as criteria of the scientific approach in the
relation between investigator and subject. These interviews took place during
meals or at evening gatherings where the mutual friends who had arranged
the encounter between the sociologist and the managers being interviewed
were present. This arrangement, which could be qualified as *domestic*
according to the classification established in *On Justification* (Boltanski
and Thévenot 2006; hereafter *OJ*), presented many advantages for research
purposes – notably that of ensuring an atmosphere of trust between investigator and subject that is rarely achieved when the person being questioned
is contacted directly in the workplace, and especially when the sociologist is
introduced into that context by members of the hierarchy, since that exposes
him or her to suspicion of complicity with 'management'. This atmosphere of
trust facilitated the recital of injustices that had been experienced and made
it easier for the informer to adopt a critical attitude. In addition, the presence of mutual friends brought to bear a constraint that favoured a search
for solid justifications in support of the denunciations articulated. For, if a
denunciation was to be viewed as legitimate, it had to rise above the victim's
individual case and be generalized to the company as a whole. The presence
of friends also gave rise to an expectation of biographical coherence that
is often difficult to fulfil. As it happened, the long-time friends involved in
these encounters had in most cases known the cadres being interviewed at an
earlier point in their careers, when, far from criticizing their company, they
had felt at home and had often been unstinting in their praise for their
employers and working conditions. The question that was then asked of the
victims, explicitly or, more often, tacitly, was essentially the following: how
had they been able to remain blind for so long to the brutalities and injustices being perpetrated around them, and, furthermore, how could they be
sure that they themselves had not been involved in some unseemly business?

Under this constraint, which weighed upon quite a number of 'penitents' or 'dissidents', victims had not only to justify their accusations, they also had to exculpate themselves from the tacit accusation of complicity with those they were now accusing. For how could one avoid thinking that the victims opened their eyes only when unjust behaviour customary within the institution was turned against them?

2 Lemert used ethnographic methods to study cases in which persons under psychiatric care had been diagnosed with paranoia following affairs that had originated in their work environment. By reconstituting their history and making inquiries in the companies in which the affairs had begun, Lemert traced the stories back to the offences to which the victims had been subjected, and he established 'in reality' what the psychiatric approach addressed as fantasy ('the pseudo-conspiratorial community'). Under the auspices of what is known as labelling theory, Lemert's research opened the way to a sociological approach to phenomena that had been viewed earlier as purely psychological or psychiatric. The drawback of this work was its polemical stance on psychiatry, whose position it simply reversed.

Texts published around the 1980s in *Law and Society Review* (*LSR*) in the context of the American Civil Litigation Research Project adopted a more radical position. This project dealt primarily with 'middle range disputing': it excluded, on the one hand, personal disputes that remained entirely outside the judicial realm and, on the other hand, major conflicts that had an explicitly collective or political dimension. The project is interesting for its reliance on a method that sought to grasp the logic governing the evolution of disputes over time. Felstiner, Abel and Sarat describe three distinct phases: in a first phase ('naming'), the harm is identified, named, and constituted as such under the heading of 'perceived injurious experience'; in a second phase, responsibility for the harm is imputed to another actor against whom a complaint is formulated ('blaming'); finally, in the third phase, the accusation is made known to other persons, and particularly to the one who caused the problem, accompanied by a demand for reparation ('claiming'). The principal interest of this approach is that it applies the perspective and methods of constructivism to objects that had previously been addressed either in a legal or a sociological framework, and whose specificity was defined to a great extent in opposition to law. The use of the constructivist perspective had an impact on this field similar to its impact on the sociology of political crises (Dobry 1986) or in scientific controversies (Latour 1982). In the case of the *LSR* articles, this perspective is limited by the fact that it posited, at the start of every dispute, the existence of an 'unperceived injurious experience' prior to any awareness or characterization of that experience; it is limited, too, by the search for a method making it possible to define, record and take into account these experiences of harm that were not identified by the actors (Coates and Penrod 1980; Miller and Sarat 1980–81). Preoccupations linked to an essentialist conception of conflicts and their causes thus tend to be reinscribed in constructivist studies. It is precisely to escape from this form of essentialism that in his study of consumer complaints, which was partly inspired by the methods applied in the *LSR* texts, Jean-Yves Trepos speaks of the 'crystallization' of an affair, using a concept that refers both to the solidification accomplished by the formal recording of an affair and to the mobilization that accompanied its unfolding in time (Trepos 1988). This concept makes it possible to dispense with unverifiable conjectures relating to the 'first' causes of the affairs under consideration.

3 Another example can be found in the analysis carried out by Vinoli Delamourd (1988) of a corpus of 300 letters sent by unemployed individuals to the president of France; the writers explained their situation and sought presidential intervention so that they would have priority in the allocation of jobs. Delamourd's analysis dealt with the cognitive operations that were marshalled in this epistolary test, especially the justifying manoeuvres made by the petitioners in order to convince their reader of the validity of their undertaking. The study of this corpus makes it possible to recapture the constraints that a letter demanding presidential intercession must satisfy if it is to be acceptable. These constraints, functioning like a grammar, constitute an example of shared knowledge, as attested by numerous dialogic expressions referring to the objections of an interlocutor: 'I know very well that . . .', 'I am well aware that . . .'). These constraints apply to the construction of arrangements for addressing the president (with tension between the republican and kingly characteristics attributed to him), to the establishment of a relation between the specific demand in favour of a particular individual and a common good valid for all, and also, among other things, to the self-presentation purporting to justify the request for priority employment. There can be tension between some of these manoeuvres. For example, to support a request, the petitioner often uses the argument of urgency: the request has priority because the condition of unemployment leads to a loss of skills – these will wither without exercise – and to a progressive destruction of one's personality. But writers who use this argument also have to show that they are still capable of holding a job and that they still possess the traits needed to fill the position they might be offered.

4 To my knowledge, there is still no systematic history of the notion of *cause* as a specific social form. In the work available, the notion of cause is the object of varying constructions depending on whether it is approached in terms of the problematics of public space (Habermas 1989), the birth of critiques (Koselleck 1979) or the history of public opinion (Baker 1987). The interest of Élisabeth Claverie's work on the constitution of causes as a social form, in the eighteenth and nineteenth centuries and in particular from the Calas Affair to the Dreyfus Affair, lies in the tight connections it makes between judicial and political history, between the emergence of affairs as a form and the construction of the republican concept of citizenship (Claverie 1987).

5 One indication of the salience of the categories of singular and collective can be found in the efforts of Edward Palmer Thompson – author of *The Making of the English Working Class* (1963), a historian very well informed about the processes by which collective beings were constituted – to demonstrate that the anonymous eighteenth-century letters he was analysing (Thompson 1975) could not be attributed to singular, isolated or even demented individuals (this, in his mind, would have stripped them of all interest), but rather that they were thoroughly embedded in collective movements.

6 Studying complaints that had arisen within the Société nationale des chemins de fer (SNCF [French National Railways]), Philippe Corcuff (1989) gives examples of affairs that arose from similar situations but that were either relegated to the level of individuals or else generalized in such a way as to take on a collective character. He also brings to light the role of psychologists

and union leaders in these operations and, indirectly, the role of the disciplines on which they rely, at least in part, for the legitimacy of their actions: psychology and the sociology of labour, respectively. Let us consider, first, two affairs that started out as work stoppages, in which two train engineers refused to work (temporarily, in one case) and which led to reassignment. In each case, the decision to stop working had come in the wake of 'nerve problems' experienced by the employee in question. Medical and psychological intervention allowed the affair to be relegated to the realm of the singular after some initial protests and appeals to the unions. The success of the interventions seems to have stemmed from the establishment of personal ties and of a relation of trust between the sanctioned workers and their therapists. The employees chose not to construe their work stoppages as part of a 'collective struggle'; instead, they represented them as 'personal decisions', apparently in order to avoid the costs of a break in personal relations with the therapists who had been working with them. Here is how one of the engineers explained his story, after the fact: 'Then, well, then I was starting to be confused about what was happening, then obviously I threw criticisms around. I was critical of the union structure, the management structure, and so on. Whereas in fact that wasn't it, it was my own structure that was the problem.'

A third case, in which a contract worker assigned to a ticket window in a station was fired for 'inaptitude' after a psychiatric examination, had a completely different outcome. This case became the occasion for the union to construct a collective cause by denouncing 'the use of medicine and psychology to repressive ends'. In support of this cause, the union mobilized the registers of collective will and public opinion: press conferences, appeals to well-known personalities (for example, Félix Guattari, a pioneer in the anti-psychiatry movement), and so on. There was even an effort to recruit a sociologist whose principal access to the affair was through the unions. As it took on this collective character, the affair led management and the doctors and psychologists involved to commit themselves in turn more energetically than ever to accumulating proofs of the employee's mental illness and crediting it with a degree of irreversibility. But the psychiatric motive for the firing did not become official. The union then attempted to attack the irreversibility of the diagnosis of abnormality by undoing the links among the employee's various instances of medical leave in order to endow them with a contingent character, after which it lodged an appeal with the administrative tribunal.

Chapter 2 The Political Basis for General Forms

1 In certain cases, I had access to a series of protest documents: fliers, tracts that appeared at different phases in the development of affairs calling into question work relations within a company. Thus I could follow the changes in the way the principal actors were designated as the affair grew in scope and shifted from the stage of individual protest to that of protest orchestrated by collective agencies, especially unions. The persons against whom the protest was directed were designated in the early texts by their first names or by nicknames; as the affair progressed, they were identified by their titles or

by entities representing quasi-personages (as, for example, 'the bosses'). On this point, see Bernard Urlacher's thesis (1984).

2 The question of personal dependency is found at the heart of Rousseau's political writings as well as in his intimate texts. In this sense, his political works offer a general solution to a singular problem. Conflicts between worths – and especially the tension between civic worth, which recognizes only desingularized relations, and domestic worth, which recognizes only personalized relations – are addressed with the resources of political philosophy in *The Social Contract*, but they also come up in many passages in Rousseau's *Confessions*, where they are developed in the register of emotions and sentiments. To a great extent, what has been called Rousseau's malady (Starobinski 1988) could probably be interpreted as the result of an untenable tension between incompatible worths (on this point, see *OJ*, 107–17).

3 The French electoral code makes a point of detaching the civic bond from the domestic bond. Thus we know that, according to the code, 'in communes of more than 500 inhabitants, ascendants and descendants, brothers and sisters, cannot be members of the municipal council simultaneously.' Similarly, the law enumerating incompatibilities specifies that providers of municipal services and salaried employees of the commune who might be linked to sitting judges through a relation of personal dependency or in a commercial context are not eligible to serve on the municipal council. (On denunciation of domestic relations from the standpoint of a civic polity, see *OJ*, 251–9). More generally, the definition of a citizen as a 'man without qualities' and the difficulty of representing interests politically in the political construction of the French nation after the Revolution – which had abolished the officially recognized bodies, or *corps*, around which society had previously been organized – constituted a major political problem that led to a search for new solutions such as corporatism or 'plan-ism', especially between 1930 and 1950 (Boltanski 1987a).

CHAPTER 3 ORDINARY DENUNCIATIONS AND CRITICAL SOCIOLOGY

1 What needs to be noted instead, I think, is, on the contrary, the ease with which ordinary persons accept the explanations proposed by sociologists. In this regard one can apply to sociology the reversal that Wittgenstein operated for psychoanalysis: 'Freud in his analysis provides explanations which many people are inclined to accept. He emphasizes that people are *dis*-inclined to accept them. But if the explanation is one which people are disinclined to accept, it is highly probable that it is also one which they are *inclined* to accept. And this is what Freud had actually brought out' (Wittgenstein 1966, 43).

2 In classical sociology, the asymmetry that is required to ensure the coherence of the paradigm of unveiling is supported by very powerful instrumentation. The large quantity of data gathered in France between the late 1950s and the early 1960s was made possible, for instance, by the establishment of what could be called a standard chain of sociological and statistical production (Desrosières and Thévenot 1979): definition of the problem (often in relation to a social demand and, more specifically, to a demand by the state bearing on issues of distribution of goods and services); open-ended interviews

serving as pre-investigations; establishment of a questionnaire; completion of the questionnaire by a representative or logical sample; codification; data processing; analysis of the statistical data (double-entry tables, correlations, and so on); identification of regularities; description of these regularities in statements associating words with numbers; and drafting of a final research report. Beyond the gains in time and the economies of scale that go along with the standardization of operations, this chain made it possible to establish a strict division of labour – for instance, between those who came up with the overall design and the investigators, or between coders and statisticians; in many cases, significant numbers of operators were interposed between the 'technical collaborators', who were in contact with the persons affected by the investigation, and the researchers responsible for the interpretation of the data, who often remained behind in their laboratories or institutes. This production chain is used in units modelled on laboratories in the natural sciences or on administrative groups, or else created in a mixed form (designated fairly aptly by the terms 'institute', or 'centre for the study of . . .') that developed in the late 1950s and especially in the mid-1960s (Pollak 1976), often in the wake of interventions related to the Marshall Plan (Boltanski 1987a, 130–1). These administrative research units became important sites of contact among academics, managers from the public sector, planners, business owners, union leaders, and so on – that is, among the various actors who were defining the 'social demand' for social science.

3 See Bruno Latour's analysis (1990) of Steven Shapin and Simon Schaffer, *Leviathan and the Air-Pump: Hobbes, Boyle, and the Experimental Life* (Princeton, NJ: Princeton University Press, 1985). This book describes the invention of the laboratory as a place separate from the space of political or theological quarrels, a place where it is possible to engage in controversy under the control of observable facts, and thus to avoid violence, or to reach agreements according to reason, apart from any arbitrary domination. What interests Latour in this example is that it allows us to put ourselves back in the historical moment when the division that still prevails today was instituted, the division between politics and science, between what is attributed to the bond among persons and what is attributed to the bond among things.

4 The theoretical paradigm that underlies a great deal of research carried out in France in the 1960s, 1970s and 1980s is grounded to a large extent in a compromise between Marx's thought and that of Durkheim. The instruments deployed by this paradigm are derived from techniques of a different origin, borrowed for the most part from American social psychology of the interwar period (techniques for conducting investigations by means of surveys, for example). In the late 1950s, Durkheim's ideas resurfaced in French sociology by way of anthropology, and especially structuralist anthropology through the work of Claude Lévi-Strauss. As for the importance attributed to 'Marxism', a vague term that, at the time, designated roughly as many different constructs as there were commentators, it obviously has to be understood in the context of the political debates that were concentrated, in the social sciences in France, around a large contingent of communist intellectuals.

Why Marx *and* Durkheim, Marx with Durkheim? The two are often opposed, in the sense that Marx is said to have insisted on the conflictual dimensions of the social order and Durkheim on the consensual aspects. But Pierre Ansart (1969) made an important contribution when he showed in detail all that Marx owed to the new conception of *reality* that had taken shape in the early nineteenth century in France and was presented systematically early on in Saint-Simon's work. In opposition to the old philosophy, according to Saint-Simon, one had to seek the true laws of society, which was conceived as a natural organism. As Durkheim was to say in 1887 in the very enlightening lecture that inaugurated his social science course in Bordeaux (Durkheim 1970), this positivist extension of natural law opposed the 'natural laws' of society to the 'civil laws made by princes'. The invention of *society* as an organism with its own reality, independent of the individuals who comprise it, found powerful support throughout the nineteenth century in statistics and particularly in the notion of the average (Desrosières 2008): the average, whose value belongs to no single one of the elements, is charged with establishing the empirical proof of the existence of a group as a supra-individual reality. Now, this schema, explicitly present in Durkheim, can also be attributed to Marx, at least when one is giving a holistic presentation of his work, to borrow Louis Dumont's terms. (For interpretations that bring to light, in contrast, the place Marx attributed to the singular, see Part II of this volume, chapter 12.2). If we rely on these two bodies of work, the schema allows us to construct a space of unveiling defined by the opposition between infrastructure and superstructure. On one side, a conscious but artefactual superficial knowledge: law, the state, pre-notions, ideologies; on the other, a deep reality, opaque and external to consciousness, whose mode of existence is comparable to that of biological realities, which obey their own specific laws. The unveiling of this deep reality requires going beyond the motives of persons, which are suspect a priori; it presupposes the use of specific methods, especially the statistical method charged with discovering objective realities that take the place of natural laws.

5 The role played by the memory of the French Revolution in the development of sociological thought has been noted by many scholars; see especially Aron 2008, Dumont 1977 and Nisbet 1966.

6 The paradox of nihilism is expressed by Nietzsche as follows:

> A nihilist is a man who judges of the world as it is that it ought *not* to be, and of the world as it ought to be that it does not exist. According to this view, our existence (action, suffering, willing, feeling) has no meaning: the pathos of 'in vain' is the nihilists' pathos – at the same time, as pathos, an inconsistency on the part of the nihilists. (1967, 318 [aphorism 585A])

7 This is clear, for example, in Erving Goffman, especially in his early works, where he sets up the principal concepts – actor, public, representation, stage, wings, and so on – that allow him to unfurl his vision of the world as 'theatre' and thereby to renew a tradition that includes in particular such seventeenth-century French moralists as La Rochefoucauld, La Bruyère and, in certain respects, Pascal. For to show the world as theatre is also necessarily to apply to it a strategy of suspicion (Boltanski 1973) and to reveal its inauthenticity. The Goffmanian actor is inauthentic even when he is not seeking to dissimulate or to deceive, because for him the register of expression always has primacy over that of action. We see this especially clearly when Goffman borrows Sartrean paradigms such as the 'attentive pupil who wishes to *be* attentive', or the no less famous 'waiter in a café' who conforms – too closely – to the concept of a waiter in a cafe (Goffman 1959, 33, 75–6). But the

description of an inauthentic world can only be achieved by relying, at least implicitly, on the ideal of authenticity – that is, in Goffman's case, the ideal of congruence between the 'outer world' – that of representation – and the 'inner world' – that of lived experience (Habermas 1984, 90–4), in a relation of perfect mutual transparency.

8 The same observation can be made about many works by historians who, through their archival investigations and their publications, help revive the past disputes that they have taken as their object of study, or who pursue in the present the historical affairs on which their research has focused. This is certainly true for the French Revolution, as François Furet has demonstrated (Furet 1981), but also no doubt for many other affairs, in particular the Dreyfus case.

9 The relations between the scientific constructs of sociology and the competence on which ordinary persons call to orient themselves in the social world was clearly established by experimental research conducted between 1980 and 1982 when I was collaborating with Laurent Thévenot. Our goal was to use a series of tests and games to grasp our subjects' ability to carry out specific tasks: first, to classify people by comparing questionnaires excerpted from the census that presented not only a person's profession but also information such as sex, age and degrees earned; second, to agree, through negotiation, on a taxonomy of professions that would be acceptable to all and consequently considered valid across the board; finally, to discover a person's profession on the basis of other information – related, for instance, to cultural activities, life patterns or objects owned – that is, by exploring the network of the most probable juxtapositions (Boltanski and Thévenot 1983). When we analysed the results of these exercises, we found, on the one hand, that the social classifications – especially the socio-professional ones – used both by the major agencies that produced statistics such as INSEE [the French National Institute of Statistics and Economic Studies] and by the field of sociology were also in widespread use by non-specialists, and, on the other hand, that ordinary persons have the capacity to do the sort of inductive reasoning that guides sociological knowledge of the social world when sociologists set out to relate behaviour reputed to be contingent to attributes considered more stable or more durably attached to individual identity. Clearly, one cannot deduce from these results that ordinary persons would mobilize this type of competence, which can be related to a determinist sociology, in all situations in which they might find themselves, but only that, under the specific constraints of an experimental situation, they are most often fully capable of mobilizing it, although to unequal degrees depending on the person. These inequalities in the ability to deploy a determinist schema seem to be a function, in particular, of the degree to which persons, in order to acquire practical mastery of their environment and make predictions about the future, need to develop interpretations about the people around them, and especially about those on whom they depend directly, instead of simply relying on rules or conventional habits. This is probably the reason why such competence seems especially prevalent in persons who are frequently confronted with situations in which they depend personally on someone else – that is, in domestic situations; this is often the case with women (in their roles as wives, secretaries, and so on).

10 At the beginning of my study of cadres, knowing nothing about this milieu,

I intended to inform myself by talking to highly placed persons – union leaders, heads of personnel, officers of associations, and so on – whom I saw as 'native informants'. But these not very exotic natives responded to my questions with questions and sent me back to my discipline of origin; they were astonished to see me question them, mere amateurs, on matters that were supposed to have already been settled by one sociologist or another whose works they had read on the subject of 'cadres', 'classes' or 'social structure'. They often knew these works better than I did.

11 For example, advertisers today excel in pushing a product by choosing actors who fit the target mould: that is, they know how to link the target group for whom the product is intended with a bodily habitus (*hexis*) defined with reference to groups that have been recognized and studied by the social sciences, such as social classes, professional or religious groups, and so on. The capacity to supply stylized representations of social types, once the privilege of naturalist novelists, would probably not be possible in its current form without the apprenticeship that specialists in 'communications' and the media owe to their assiduous attention to the social sciences and to the spread of a new form of characterology based on sociology rather than psychology. This ironic representation of the world, grasped in its most immediately current form by advertising and by the media more generally, contributes in itself to the diffusion of a critical stance. If the critical position is given its broadest definition as a position of exteriority on the basis of which it is possible to disengage from the world so as to contemplate it as an outsider, the stylized reproduction of fragments of the world that are thus pinpointed creates an effect of detachment, distancing and irony. One can use the same operation both to develop a critique, by showing that nothing can nor should in principle escape it ('nothing is sacred'), and to neutralize it, by pulling it towards relativism – that is, by stressing the possibility that it can be turned against itself, through a free exchange among all possible viewpoints, which are all equivalent.

12 In the 1960s, the notion of the unconscious served to unify the human sciences. It is obviously central in psychoanalysis, but also in anthropology, which claims to have imported it from Saussurian linguistics ('anthropology draws its originality from the unconscious nature of collective phenomena'; Lévi-Strauss 1963, 1:18), in sociology ('unconsciously accepted presuppositions on the basis of which spontaneous sociology generated these preconceptions'; Bourdieu, Chamboredon and Passeron 1991, 15) and in history, where it arises from the opposition between 'the history of events', which 'registers from day to day the so-called history of the world as it is happening' and 'the history of the *longue durée*', or 'structural history' (Braudel 1980, 74–6). The links among disciplines, which these multiple uses of the word 'unconscious' have woven, have turned out to be fairly solid, even though they have most often been based on a misunderstanding. The reference to unconscious or 'non-conscious' objects may in fact designate (1) the existence of repressed material connected with prohibitions and censorship, both (a) in the stronger, psychoanalytic sense and also (b) in a weaker sense, in sociology, with the reference to 'unconscious interests'; (2) the actors' inability to gain access to the true meaning of their actions, because they act according to forces beyond their grasp. This second meaning, which always refers to some form of ruse on the part of reason, is specified differently

depending on whether the milieu in which the action is totalized – and from which the action thus takes its hidden meaning – incorporates temporality or not – that is, whether the context for the action is (a) the invisible hand of the marketplace (absence of temporality), (b) history conceived, eschatologically, in the form of a tribunal passing ultimate judgement (temporal unity) or (c) society (which may be considered in both dimensions, whether this is specified or not). In addition, the reference to unconscious or 'non-conscious' objects may designate (3) the actors' inability to become acquainted with certain objects to which the researcher may have access; the actors cannot totalize, either (a) because the object is too big (for example, a 'social structure') or (b) because, engaged as they are in practice, they cannot turn away from the action to consider it and grasp it from the outside (these two meanings seem to me to be close to what linguists mean when they assert that language is 'unconscious'); or it may designate (4) the fact that, as Paul Ricoeur suggests (1966, 380), all our actions produce unintended effects that escape our attention and develop their own logic (the reference to 'perverse effects', for example, combines this meaning and meaning 2[a]).

The way researchers can gain access to unconscious objects will obviously be conceived differently according to the definition adopted. Examples: the occupation of a neutral position according to definition 1(b) ('the intellectual without attachments'); a strong capacity to totalize associated with powerful instrumentalization in 3(a); and so on.

CHAPTER 4 THE SOCIOLOGY OF CRITICAL SOCIETY

1 Comparative analysis of the critical resources available in different types of societies and of the forms of critiques available to these societies could constitute an object common to sociology, anthropology and history. Thus, for example, while the denigration of the lofty by the lowly, and notably of men by women, when the latter are alone among themselves, is attested in many of the traditional societies studied by anthropologists, we do not know to what extent this calling into question that has a domestic flavour presupposes – on the same basis as the critiques for which the *OJ* model seeks to account – the possibility of finding support in incompatible polities and worlds. Let us note that, for Jürgen Habermas, the totalizing character of mythic thought is what prohibits the deployment of the type of rationality that supports the forms of critical action we can observe in our own society (Habermas 1984, 45–8).

2 This possibility depends first of all on the researchers' ability to free themselves from the temporal constraint that bears on the spoken chain, for if 'language enunciates relations, it does not enunciate many, because it unfolds in time' (Weil 1957a, 32 [translator's note: here and elsewhere, where French source texts are cited, the translations are my own]). To the extent that speakers can rely on common conventions, language can function while at the same time surmounting the temporal constraint. But, unlike persons engaged in the act of speaking, researchers take these conventions as their object and have to make them explicit if they are to render the utterance comprehensible while bringing out the relations that have remained implicit in it.

3 In the fieldwork on which I am drawing, the question of the researcher's latitude to clarify utterances is vexed. When the constraints of the situation, and especially the influence of a critique, have led the actors to raise the level of generality and to make the principle of justice on which their argumentation rests more or less explicit, clarification by the researcher has a good chance of looking like a trivial paraphrase. Conversely, when the actor's utterances are ambiguous or highly unspecific, a clarification that aims to go back to first principles may seem abusive and arbitrary. Let us take for example the exclamation 'Praise God!'. Do I have the right to identify this utterance as a way of engaging the inspired nature of the situation? Just as poetic style must achieve balance between the platitudinous and the enigmatic, according to Aristotle, if clarification is to succeed it must be positioned at a proper distance from the object so as to avoid redundancy even while remaining in the sphere of recognition. Its validity is in effect subject to its capacity to be recognized by the reader, whose critical sense may accept or reject the proposition of intelligibility being presented.

4 The 'Prothèse' software program developed by Francis Chateauraynaud and Gilbert Macquart under the auspices of the Centre d'étude de l'emploi [Centre for the Study of Employment] uses the tools of artificial intelligence to process the textual data provided in the multiple reports collected on a given affair. The software is capable of identifying consistencies or inconsistencies between objects of different worlds; it can bring to light itineraries, networks or branchings of relations among objects. In particular, the software makes it possible to 'carry out quickly and in a logical way itineraries that the user could only discover with much difficulty by means of a lengthy work of interpretation'.

CHAPTER 5 A MODEL OF COMPETENCE FOR JUDGEMENT

1 What are we to do with ideals? This question, while it no longer comes up very often in these terms, is nevertheless a central one in the problematics of the social sciences as constituted in the nineteenth century. In most of its manifestations, the question encompasses the opposition between the ideal and the real. This opposition itself enters into various combinations with the character of the motives – conscious or unconscious, voluntary or involuntary – that guide action. By combining the opposition between the ideal and the real with the opposition between the conscious and the unconscious, one obtains a matrix that is interesting to explore because it allows us to identify various theories of the social bond and distinguish among them. The theories of unveiling thus contrast a voluntary action aiming at an ideal, treated as pure illusion, with the reality of an action dominated by unconscious motives and aiming at the realization of a particular interest. Utilitarianism also recognizes the interested character of actions, but it does not need to repress this character and attribute it to an unconscious, because in the tradition of liberal economics it allows itself the possibility of reconstituting a common good by means of a ruse of reason, the contention that individual interests taken together will have a beneficial effect (Hirschman 1977). Durkheim's position on this point is complex and not entirely consistent. Without being too presumptuous, one could probably attribute to Durkheim an option

according to which under certain conditions individuals can seek an ideal by involuntary actions, because inasmuch as they belong to a group they harbour an altruistic tendency. But I find no construct intent upon developing in a consistent way the possibility for persons to seek an ideal by voluntary action, although that possibility underlies certain of the uses Max Weber makes of the concept of legitimacy. In constructs that take the ideals espoused by actors into account, even while maintaining a clear opposition between the ideals asserted and a reality based on the unconscious pursuit of particular interests, the central question becomes that of the relation between these two instances (on this point, see below, chapter 12.3).

2 This tension maintains the connection between our model and a Durkheimian framework. In fact, as Dénes Némedi has shown (1990), Durkheim's theory of knowledge accepts the 'Kantian distinction between categories and empirical impressions', constituted according to the opposition between the contingent and the necessary. But if these categories have an a priori character, and if they cannot be derived from experience, they have to be treated as transhistorical constituents of action, which tends to remove them from empirical control. Conversely, adherence to the empiricist thesis leaves reason without any character of necessity, so that Durkheim tends to reduce empiricism to a form of irrationalism. Durkheim manages to surmount the opposition between transcendentalism and irrationalism by constituting a space with two levels, of which the first is occupied by persons and the second by social conventions that make it possible to qualify persons and to establish a justifiable connection between them.

3 The ambiguity of the uses associated with the concept of 'legitimate order' is found in its earliest occurrence in the arsenal of classical sociology with Max Weber himself. In *Economy and Society* (1978), Weber juxtaposes two very different definitions of legitimacy without trying to reconcile them (Corcuff and Lafaye 1989). When he defines a 'legitimate order', Weber designates first of all the 'validity of an order' whose stability would not depend only on an orientation of individual actions towards the maximization of 'self-interest' ('expediency'), or on the strength of 'custom', so that it could not be reduced to 'the mere existence of a uniformity of social action determined by custom or self-interest' (Weber 1978, 31). This last remark is important because it allows us to distinguish clearly between what stems from *norms* and what stems from *ideals*, a distinction that post-Weberian sociology has striven to abolish in order to remove all reality from *ideals*, attributing these dismissively either to 'ideologies' or to 'objective regularities' (as, for example, when, in a more Durkheimian perspective, the genesis of explicit rules, and particularly rules of law, is conceived as an operation in which the state takes charge of what is already present, inscribed in custom or morals, when the actual state of things is attested by the presence of statistical regularities). But in the same work, in passages devoted to 'domination', Weber modifies the way he uses the term 'legitimacy' (213–14). Nietzsche offers a theory of justification as deceit expressed in almost the same terms. 'Whatever his situation, man needs value judgements owing to which he justifies in his own eyes, and especially in the eyes of those around him, his acts, his intentions, and his states; in other words, it is his way of glorifying himself. Every natural morality expresses the satisfaction that a certain type of men experiences with itself' (Nietzsche 1967, 1: 324). In this second definition, the legitimate

character of an order, always essentially arbitrary – that is, ultimately based on some form of violence, will to power or *ressentiment* – depends on its capacity to make people believe that it is really based on the ideal to which it lays claim. Legitimacy, a pure matter of *belief*, is then a collectively maintained illusion. Classical sociology, which for the most part has retained this second definition, will speak in this case rather of 'legitimation', abandoning 'legitimacy' to law and political philosophy, disciplines reputed to be 'naive' (Lagroye 1987).

Chapter 6 Principles of Equivalence and Admissible Proofs

1 As an example likely to be familiar to readers of this book, we might consider a dispute over the worth to be attributed to a book published by a researcher. One can emphasize the fact that the book is very well *known*, that it has *sold* very well; conversely, one can contend that the research on which it is based is not truly *systematic*, or that the work is rather pedestrian, not very *imaginative*, and so on. All such arguments can be related to different principles of equivalence stemming from different polities.

2 The continuity between the type of problem addressed by political philosophy and the kind of questions sociology has sought to answer has often been blurred in the work of sociologists. We see this especially at difficult moments in the history of sociology in which, confronting powerful competition from philosophy, our discipline has been led to stress the break with philosophy in order to defend its own identity as a scientific discipline. The polemic against philosophy, already present in Saint-Simon, who chastised 'metaphysicians' and 'phrase-making legal scholars' (in other words, in his view, philosophers of the social contract) in the name of social science (Saint-Simon 1869, 67, 189), is also clearly present in Durkheim, where it is associated with the critique of spiritualism. It underwent a vigorous renaissance a century later, in France in the 1960s, when sociology reconstructed itself as a discipline and developed its own apparatus. The fact remains that, at these different periods, the sociologists most committed to solidifying the break with philosophy came primarily from the philosophical disciplines; this inclined them to nourish their work with questions and concepts borrowed from the philosophical tradition, though they often dispensed with explicit references and failed to undertake the analyses that would have been necessary to make clearly visible the reinterpretations that accompanied their borrowing (Héran 1987).

3 The reference to tradition has to be inserted within a framework stemming from social anthropology if a hermeneutic conception of the sociologist's activity is to be sustained. By relying on the relation – mediated by the dual reference to tradition – between the categories they deploy and the actors' activities, sociologists can gain some advance understanding of those activities and posit a horizon of meaning that can be modified by successive operations of clarification, as the researchers gradually approach this horizon and put it to the test with the tools at their disposal. The anthropological framework imposes a constraint on the traditions that can reasonably be put to profitable use. Thus, while it is not impossible that, starting from the tradition of Zen Buddhism, we might be able to clarify some phenomenon

stemming from the ordinary competence of persons in our society, it is more reasonable to rely on traditions for which we can verify the institutional and historical mediations that allow us to comprehend the transmission of this competence by means of a practical apprenticeship and to grasp the degree to which it is commensurate with the world of objects. For the fields that concern us here, then, we can turn to Western political philosophy, which was used to construct the *OJ* model, but also to the Christian tradition that is the basis for my attempt to clarify the possibility of a social bond founded on love (see Part II of this volume).

4 The polities taken into account in *OJ* can be characterized as follows:

   1 The *inspired polity* is based on St Augustine's *City of God* and on the treatises Augustine devoted to the problem of grace. In this polity, worth is conceived in the form of an immediate relation to an external principle that is the source of all worth. Defined by access to a state of grace that thus does not depend on recognition by others, this worth is revealed in the body itself, prepared by asceticism; the inspired manifestations of the body (sanctity, creativity, artistic sense, authenticity, and so on) constitute the privileged form of expression.

   2 The *domestic polity* stems from a commentary on Bossuet's *Politics Drawn from the Very Words of Holy Scripture*. In the domestic polity, people's worth depends on their hierarchical positions in a chain of personal dependencies. In a formula of subordination established on a domestic model, the political bond among beings is conceived as a generalization of the bond of generation combining tradition and proximity.

   3 The *polity of fame* is based on Hobbes's *Leviathan*, especially the chapter devoted to honour. Whereas in the domestic polity worth is inscribed in a hierarchical chain, in the polity of fame it depends solely on the opinion of others. Linked to the constitution of conventional signs that condense people's power and their esteem – and this makes it possible to establish equivalence and to calculate value – worth depends solely on the number of persons who grant their credit; by virtue of this formula of equivalence, it is abstracted from any personal dependency.

   4 The *civic* (or collective) *polity* is analysed in Rousseau's *Social Contract*. The formula of subordination to the common good does not depend on divine grace, on submission to the paternal principle or on acceptance of the opinion of others. Sovereignty, embodying the higher common principle, is no longer tied to the person of a prince; it consists of all persons, when each renounces the individual state. Civic worth is thus established both in opposition to the personal dependency on which domestic worth is based and in opposition to the opinion of others, on which the worth of fame relies.

   5 The *market polity* is derived from Adam Smith's *The Wealth of Nations*. This work sets forth the elements that ensure the foundation of a *polity* on the basis of a market bond. The market bond unites persons through the intermediary of scarce goods, subjected to the appetites of all. These goods can govern disagreements, as the competition among desires for goods subordinates the price set for the possession of an item to the desires of others.

   6 The *industrial polity* is drawn from the work of Saint-Simon. Here worth

285

is based on efficiency, and it determines a scale of professional capacities. Associated with the production of material goods, it is oriented, by organization, programming and investment, towards the future.

5 In constructs that endow individuals with a strong capacity for resistance to the situation, the repetition of identical or similar forms of response to different situations and at different moments in life is related to the corporeal or quasi-corporeal character of the responses, conceived on the model of habit; precisely because they escape considered action by persons, these responses ensure exceptional qualities of constancy and thus establish conditions under which persons can remain true to themselves. At the opposite pole from ethical conceptions that construe persistence as the result of a determination to be faithful to values that allow people to resist the anarchic and changing demands of the appetites ('flesh is weak'), constructs that base identity on incorporation view the displacement from *ethics* to *ethos* – that is, the inscription of morality in the body (achieved at the price of remaining implicit) as the mechanism ensuring agents a stability that allows them in all circumstances to find the behaviours through which they can reach agreement among themselves (according to this schema, these are often behaviours that serve their own interests) while betraying their superficial adherence to surface 'values' ('flesh is strong').

6 These two approaches correspond to two different ways of construing free will and defining its limits. In our model, people have a fundamental freedom: they are subjected not to internalized determinations but to external constraints that depend on the repertory of resources available in the situation. Conversely, in constructs that endow individuals with powerful internal armour and subject them to incorporated constraints, people can lean on these constraints as a way of removing themselves, at least in part, from the requirements of a given situation and as a way of maintaining their personalities or their integrity in all situations (I owe this observation to Paul Ladrière). But, in the logic of our model, people who maintain their integrity in all circumstances come close to abnormality: inscribed once and for all in a world that they cannot leave and that they carry around with them, in a sense, they cannot help but be perpetually tempted to rely on that world to denounce situations structured according to the different worlds into which they are plunged by the vicissitudes of life.

CHAPTER 7 TESTS AND TEMPORALITY

1 As an example, let us consider a case analysed by Claudette Lafaye, in which a worker with seniority was denied the opportunity for retesting after failing an initial test.

A foreman assigns a young agent, a recent graduate, to operate a complicated modern machine. A worker on the team protests, invoking his seniority. The foreman replies that the worker does not have the competence required to operate the equipment correctly, but agrees to test him by letting him try. And then, wouldn't you know, the worker makes a mistake in handling the machine and breaks a part. 'That can happen to anyone', he says in his own defence. Some time later, the foreman sets a new test with a different machine, which the worker damages while putting it back in the garage. The foreman uses these two consecutive failures as his argument for refusing to assign the worker in question anything but low-level tasks, and he reserves the use of complex machinery to those who have the requisite competence, no matter how much seniority on the team they may have. (Lafaye 1989, 209)

2 One of the problems raised by the empirical use of the *OJ* model is how to determine what is to be registered as a test. Should any operation that establishes a relation between things and the persons that valorize them count as a test? If the answer is yes, the routine operations of office workers at their desks are just as much tests as the use of complex machinery by a neophyte. But the first cases tend to be straightforward and go unnoticed, while the second situation is highly problematic: it focuses the attention of the participants, who await its outcome so they can pass judgement on the applicant's capabilities and make predictions about his or her future acts. The attention paid to the concept of test in the model thus leads to lumping together situations that are not treated as tests by the actors and situations whose properly probational nature the actors are prepared to recognize. Let us go back to the example of an office worker. Let us suppose that in the accomplishment of his daily routines there are failures, and that these failures are repeated on several occasions, a fact that makes it difficult to write them off by invoking the circumstances. One may suppose that sooner or later the worker will come in every morning in the state of mind in which one confronts a test – that is, he will be experiencing uncertainty and anxiety, calling on will power, and so on. The same thing will hold true for the other actors, who pay more attention than usual to what the worker in question will do, how he will cope, and so on. We may suppose that after some time a formal test will be set up, something like the psycho-technical tests used by the SNCF and analysed by Philippe Corcuff (1989). This example suggests that one can shift gradually from routine situations that are not treated as tests by the actors to testing situations identified as such. The shift appears to be linked, on the one hand, to an explicit reckoning with uncertainty and, on the other hand, to a changed perception of the act in question, which is no longer apprehended insofar as it impacts and modifies the world, but insofar as it can reveal the presence or absence of some power in the actor, and thereby support predictions regarding his or her future actions.

3 The diversity of modes and degrees of inscription is inscribed in language. Thus we say that someone *is* 'a high school graduate' or *is* 'a Nobel Prize winner'. And this remains true for the duration of that person's life; in the absence of fraud, no agency can undo what was done when the title was awarded. In contrast, we say that someone *has won* the Booker Prize, and we normally specify the year, especially if the award was made a number of years earlier. In this case, the power revealed by the test still retains a more or less durable presence, but it tends to be called back into question if it is not reaffirmed by new tests. An anecdote of which Romain Gary was at once the instigator, the hero and the victim (the incident preceded his suicide) is particularly interesting in this regard. Gary had won the Prix Goncourt some years earlier for *Les Racines du ciel*; to reassure himself that he still possessed the power to obtain it and to avoid the risk that the test might be affected by

287

the memory of his prior successes, he came up with the idea of attributing the authorship of his next-to-last work, *La Vie devant soi*, to a nephew (Émile Ajar), who in fact won the prestigious prize.

4 According to Hannah Arendt, this is why the hero, in order to be 'master of his . . . greatness', has to perish in the act that reveals his power:

> whoever consciously aims at being 'essential', at leaving behind a story and an identity which will win 'immortal fame,' must not only risk his life but expressly choose, as Achilles did, a short life and premature death. Only a man who does not survive his one supreme act remains the indisputable master of his identity and possible greatness, because he withdraws into death from the possible consequences and continuation of what he began. What gives the story of Achilles its paradigmatic signifi-cance is that it shows in a nutshell that *eudaimonia* can be bought only at the price of life and that one can make sure of it only by foregoing the continuity of living in which we disclose ourselves piecemeal, by summing up all of one's life in a single deed, so that the story of the act comes to its end together with life itself. (Arendt 1958, 193–4)

5 'There are some, *e.g.* the Megaric school, who say that a thing only has potency when it functions, and that when it is not functioning it has no potency. *E.g.*, they say that a man who is not building cannot build, but only the man who is building, and at the moment when he is building; and simi-larly in the other cases' (Aristotle 1933, IX.iii.1, p. 435).

6 Let us consider, for example, the results achieved by department heads in a company. Their supervisor may take into account solely their latest bottom line in determining the bonus each is to receive, and rank them according to this principle. However, this approach can be challenged, on the grounds that is it unfair to reduce the bonus of a manager with a certain amount of seniority even if her results have not been as good as those of younger col-leagues, because acts of value that she has accomplished in the past must be taken into account. Conversely, one can call into question the validity of a contemporary test by pointing out that acts accomplished in the past have been taken into account, whether those acts enhanced the person's worth or diminished it. But the question can also be put differently: for example, in a case of the type just described, an argument may arise over whether the evaluation must bear only on acts or whether it should also include a judge-ment on the person. Questions of this sort will often come up towards the end of a career (whether to impose early retirement, whether awarding an honorary position is legitimate, and so on).

7 I refer here to the study that Paul Ladrière (1989) devoted to the history of the notion of person in philosophy, theology and the social sciences. In this study he sought in particular to formulate clearly the relation between three terms often wrongly conflated in sociology, anthropology and political science: individual, person and self. This conflict is apparent even in Marcel Mauss's impressive attempt to gain access, through a wide array of exam-ples taken from societies broadly divergent in space and time, to a synthetic grasp of the sense of individuality as a universal category in the human mind (Mauss 1979). To understand the position occupied by the notion of person in the ordinary metaphysics of members of our own society, we must first go back to its origins, not so much in the Latin metaphor of mask (*persona*)

that is often invoked in social science, and especially in the theory of roles, but rather in the theology of hypostasis, which recognizes God as a single nature (*ousia*) in three persons (*hypostasis*). In this sense, the term 'person' designates an individual being, not only inasmuch as this being is not susceptible either to sharing or to division, and inasmuch as he exists in the singular unity of all his components, but especially inasmuch as he is in a state of *persistence* apart from the accidents in which he manifests himself, as an incommunicable substantial reality (Aquinas 1947, 1: 156–7 [Part 1, question 29, article 2]). This tradition thus refers us to a view of persons conceived not only as absolute singularities but also as impenetrable powers irreducible to what is revealed by their self-realizing acts.

8 The polity model does not integrate time as such because it is inscribed in the cyclic conception of Greek time, which identifies events with contingency and reduces history to a simple chronicle of events lacking in necessity and thereby exempt from philosophy. The world has neither origin nor end; its rule is the eternal return, so that the relation of the past to the future does not suffice to form an oriented temporal vector. Conversely, in the Christian construct, time is not cyclical but directional. The world of men has been created, has fallen into sin, has been ransomed, and is oriented towards the last days, which present the last judgement and the inauguration of the kingdom of God. What can be said of this world thus takes the form of a history. It is from the standpoint of the history of salvation that contingency and necessity can be distinguished: what may seem contingent from the narrow viewpoint of the present appears as necessary when the mind moves to a higher vantage point in order to grasp the history of humanity in terms of the history of salvation. Political history and the history of salvation thus tend to merge. The perspective of the history of salvation is what confers meaning on the seemingly contingent events of political history, on the succession of empires and on wars among men, while it makes visible the necessity of these events for the salvation of the world (Puech 1978, 1: 217–33). These two different ways of conceptualizing time are associated with two ways of constructing generality. The architecture of the polity model is based on a conception of the relation between the particular and the general that takes the most general principle as the measure of particular objects. It is by going back to the general principle that one can establish equivalence among particular objects and consider them in their reality by exempting them from contingency. In this framework, justice is itself conceived as a process of going back and forth between the particular and the general. This is not the case with the Christian construct. For the event on which the whole history of salvation hinges, the crucifixion, is a perfectly singular event, located at a specific point in time and space. It is through the intermediary of this singular event, which divides history into two parts, that eternity is inscribed in human time. The relation between the particular and the general thus finds itself overturned. From this point on it is in the particular, in particular persons and in particular events of human life, that the presence of God must be deciphered, a presence that confers their generality upon persons, events and objects (Guitton 1971, 399–405). In Part II of this book, I shall try to show how the ideal of love as *agape* is substituted for the ideal of justice in this construct.

9 These remarks owe a great deal to the work on school testing carried out with Jean-Louis Derouet during the winter of 1987–8.

10 To avoid being confined within the framework of a theory of argumentation, the *OJ* model anticipates that certain situations, including the possibility of tests, are set up in advance according to an arrangement of relevant
objects in a world. The consistency of the situation, and thus its capacity to
bring to bear a constraint on critique, depends in fact on the coherence of
this arrangement. But, however meticulously a situation may have been set
up in advance in the coherence of a world, the presence of objects treated
as irrelevant, yet whose relevance is capable of being identified, during a
dispute, with reference to the coherence of a different world, cannot be
excluded. Let us take, for example, a computer technology laboratory that
has openings onto the outdoors. What could keep one of the actors present
from noting the marvellous sunset illuminating the window frame (a phenomenon irrelevant to the goal of technological efficiency) and from turning
for support to an inspired world in order to denounce the inhumanity of the
industrial arrangement in which her colleagues are confined? In the absence
of any explicit denunciation, what are the objects that I must point out in my
description? If I take 'irrelevant' phenomena into account, the list of objects
to be included is unlimited, and I will never be able to complete the work of
recording. If I am content, on the contrary, to register the objects on which
the cohesion and coherence of the situation seem to depend, I will no longer
be able to account for disputes to which the situation might give rise.

CHAPTER 8 FOUR MODES OF ACTION

1 'It is this durability', Hannah Arendt writes,

> which gives the things of the world their relative independence from men
> who produced them and use them, their 'objectivity' which makes them
> withstand, 'stand against' and endure, at least for a time, the voracious
> needs and wants of their living makers and users. From this viewpoint,
> the things of the world have the function of stabilizing human life, and
> their objectivity lies in the fact that – in contradiction to the Heraclitean
> saying that the same man can never enter the same stream – men, their
> ever-changing nature notwithstanding, can retrieve their sameness, that
> is, their identity, by being related to the same chair and the same table.
> (Arendt 1958, 137)

According to Arendt, this is why 'the objectivity of the world – its object- or
thing-character – and the human condition supplement each other; because
human existence is conditioned existence, it would be impossible without
things, and things would be a heap of unrelated articles, a non-world, if they
were not the conditioners of human existence' (ibid., 9).

2 These remarks on professionals were suggested to me by Francis
Chateauraynaud.

3 This is why we cannot follow Hobbes here when he makes 'equality of
ability' between men the basis for violence, which is, for him, a war 'of every
man, against every man' in which men 'endeavour to destroy, or subdue one
another' (Hobbes 1996, 83–4). For the equality of which Hobbes speaks, and
which he presents as equality in nature pre-existing any relationship, has to
be constructed. It has to be established in a relationship, which presupposes

the reference to equivalence on a second level. But then one exits from disputes in violence and from pure violence, shifting towards the possibility of a dispute in justice whose reference to equivalence allows arbitration. What characterizes violence is thus not the existence of a pre-existing equality but, quite to the contrary, the shift towards a world of unknowable forces, or else towards a test of other no less unknown forces that are revealed in the resistance they oppose to their adverse counterparts. In contrast, Hobbes brings clearly to light the internal constraint of violence once it is engaged: 'the invader again is in the like danger of another. And from this diffidence of one another, there is no way for any man to secure himself, so reasonable, as anticipation; that is, by force, or wiles, to master the persons of all men he can, so long, till he see no other power great enough to endanger him' (ibid., 83). The analysis of this dynamics leads Hobbes to introduce a factor of duration into his model:

> For WAR, consisteth not in battle only, or the act of fighting, but in a tract of time . . . and therefore the notion of *time*, is to be considered in the nature of war . . . the nature of war consisteth not in actual fighting; but in the known disposition thereto, during all the time there is no assurance to the contrary. All other time is PEACE. (Ibid., 84)

4 As Raymond Aron's analysis of the first chapter of Book I of *On War* (Aron 1985, 61–7) makes clear, Clausewitz abandons a first definition of war, as pure violence, in favour of a second definition, corresponding better to real wars, in which war is connected with politics. In the first definition, Clausewitz relies on a model of pure violence conceived as 'a duel' between 'a pair of wrestlers', in which 'each tries through physical force . . . to *throw* his opponent in order to make him incapable of further resistance'. According to this first definition, then, war is an act of force through which 'each tries . . . to compel the other to do his will'. Force is understood here solely in the sense of 'physical force', 'for moral force has no existence save as expressed in the state' (Clausewitz 1976, 75). War is thus a violent act, 'an act of force, and there is no logical limit to the application of that force. Each side, therefore, compels its opponent to follow suit; a reciprocal is started which must lead, in theory, to extremes.' In fact, 'the worst of all conditions in which a belligerent can find himself is to be utterly defenseless. . . . It follows, then, that to overcome the enemy or disarm him – call it what you will – must always be the aim of warfare' (ibid., 77). The 'overthrow', as Raymond Aron says, thus 'constitutes the true objective of the struggle as a trial of strength' (Aron 1985, 62). The test is sustained by the reciprocal character of the action: 'As long as I have not thrown the enemy onto the ground, I must fear that he will throw me to the ground. In effect, only the "overthrow", the disarmament of the adversary, gives me security; but he reasons as I do. Security for the one implies that the other loses the means to defend himself.' This form of interaction necessarily includes the necessity of going to extremes, because 'if each reasons in the same way, each outdoes the other until they come to extremes' (ibid., 63). But there is another more fundamental reason that has to do, in this first model, with the unknown, and thus incalculable, character of the forces involved. Clausewitz distinguishes two components in force: 'the *total means at* [the opponent's] *disposal* and *the strength of his will*' (Clausewitz 1976, 77). But while 'the extent of the means at his disposal' can

be estimated, the same cannot be said of 'the strength of his will', which can be assessed only in very approximate terms (ibid.); the latter consequently remains unknown until it is revealed in the outcome of the trial. The need to go to extremes stems chiefly from this radical uncertainty. Reducing the uncertainty permits a shift towards the second definition, which Aron calls 'threefold', because alongside blind violence and chance it introduces a 'political' component. Real war is accompanied by a calculation of 'the political situation' (ibid., 78), and this calculation can reduce uncertainty about the strength of the opponent's will. But here we are exiting from pure violence and returning to a complex world into which human conditions as various as motives, emotions and character have to be reintroduced, along with institutions and laws of the state; these bring conventions and equivalences back into the assessment of strengths. Reduction of uncertainty about the opponent's intentions substitutes human forms for forces of nature, sets limits on going to extremes and leads to a search for the point at which it is appropriate to 'reduce [one's] efforts' (ibid., 80).

5 'So that *injury*, or *injustice*, in the controversies of the world, is somewhat like to that, which in the disputations of scholars is called *absurdity*. For as it is there called an absurdity, to contradict what one maintained in the beginning, so in the world, it is called injustice, and injury, voluntarily to undo that, which from the beginning he had voluntarily done' (Hobbes 1996, 88).

6 In this sense, the operation of desingularization I mentioned earlier is always fragile and never completely achieved. The legal error consists precisely in believing that projection onto the plane of justice and reference to one of the equivalences that sustained legitimate principles of justice would make it possible to transport the debt generated by a loss in another regime, especially in the regime of agape, and to exhaust it.

7 In justice, where the term is associated with ideas of reciprocity and contract, recognition appears as recognition of a debt that bears upon things that can be the object of an evaluation, a debt that can thus be reimbursed. In agape, the term has an entirely different meaning, because it concerns not the thing exchanged but the person of the giver. It departs from reciprocity, knows nothing of contractual limits and constitutes itself as 'infinite recognition' (see chapter 13.4).

8 This expression, cited by Paul Thibaud (1988), is used by Ricoeur in connection with the events of May 1968 to characterize the attitude of his left-wing interlocutors at the University of Nanterre, where he was dean at the time. Such a demand is obviously impossible to satisfy, and in this respect it can be characterized as delirious. For either the recognition of a debt is instituted in justice, where by definition it cannot be infinite, or it is instituted in agape, and the question of 'regulation' and 'payment is definitively set aside.

9 In Part II, I formulate the hypothesis according to which emotions are particularly intense when persons keep themselves on the dividing line between two regimes, or shift from one regime to another, in such a way that forms stemming from several regimes are maintained in contiguity in immediate memory. Moments of great emotion can thus be analysed as situations in which persons shift in quick succession from one regime to another, as in the case of lovers' crises, where recriminations in justice ('I'm always the one who fixes dinner') follow outbursts of violence and abandonment of agape. Are emotions not said to be 'fleeting'?

CHAPTER 9 BELOW THE THRESHOLD OF THE REPORT

1 In a regime of agape, an actor can of course make a report, but only one: this is what happens when someone says 'I love you'. But such a report does not touch on the reasons for the affirmation; to clarify those reasons, one would have to accumulate proofs, launch the possibility of a test, and thus bring back, through a series of comparisons and juxtapositions, the equivalences that this regime excludes. In this sense, the report in agape has certain properties of the performative, since 'the uttering of the sentence is, or is a part of, the doing of an action, which ... would not *normally* be described as, or as "just", saying something' (Austin 1975, 5). It can be assimilated to a gesture that accompanies and accomplishes the act. To say 'I love you' is not to say 'I walk' (an utterance that can very well accept questions of the sort 'Why do you walk?' or 'How do you walk?' Rather, it is to accomplish the act by saying it. As with 'I swear', analysed by Émile Benveniste, 'the utterance ... is the very act which pledges me, not the description of the act that I am performing ... The utterance is identified with the act itself.'). In both cases, it is the re-engagement of the person of the speaker that confers on the verb a character of accomplishment. For, in the case of 'I swear',

> this condition is not given in the meaning of the verb, it is the 'subjectivity' of discourse which makes it possible. The difference will be seen when *I swear* is replaced by *he swears*. While *I swear* is a pledge, *he swears* is simply a description on the same plane as *he runs, he smokes*. Here it can be seen that, within the conditions belonging to these expressions, the same verb, according as it is assumed by a 'subject' or is placed outside 'person', takes on a different value. This is a consequence of the fact that the instance of discourse that contains the verb establishes the act at the same time that it sets up the subject. Hence the act is performed by the instance of the utterance of its 'name' (which is 'swear'). (Benveniste 1971, 229–30)

To be sure, the utterance 'I love you' may be true or false (I may be lying). But if the actors undertake to validate this assertion (for example, by asking 'Is it true that you love me?'), which leads to 'Give me proofs of your love', then they are slipping from 'pledge' to 'description', to use Benveniste's terms, and exiting from the regime of agape. Similarly, in agape, one cannot say 'You see, I am in the process of loving you', for an assertion of this type refers on the one hand to the possibility that I can imagine an observer watching me love ('he loves'), and thus that I can put myself in the fictional situation of describing my acts, and on the other hand to the existence of proofs of love that could give rise to a calculation by identifying those elements among the objects of the situation that could be the focus of a relevant description.

2 This opposition cannot be reduced to the opposition set up between spontaneity and reflexivity, as constituted by Alfred Schutz, to distinguish what belongs to 'action', defined as conduct which is devised in advance, which is based on a preconceived project', from 'working' – that is, 'action in the outer world, based upon a project and characterized by the intention to bring about the projected state of affairs by bodily movements' (Schutz 1970, 125–6). The opposition I am seeking to identify does not contrast 'stream of

consciousness' with 'reflexive consciousness', or 'action as it is being carried out' with 'action carried out' (Isambert 1989); it refers rather to more specific constraints. In effect, in the regime of agape, the production of utterances aiming at totalization from a position of overview does not merely imply taking one's distance with respect to the action being carried out; the utterances in question actually have a self-refuting character and thus trigger a slippage outside of the regime.

3 It is this uncertainty inherent in the present action that the sociology of political crises is currently seeking to recapture, against the historiographies of the 'after the fact' and the 'it was written . . .' schools (Dobry 1989).

4 Élisabeth Claverie is thus renewing the sociology of religion by observing what people do on pilgrimages, and by comparing what they are capable of in this arrangement with what they say upon their return, immersed in different arrangements – familial, professional or even religious – in which they lose the possibility not only of reporting their actions but even of retaining them in memory, except in the mode of nostalgia and absence.

CHAPTER 10 DISPUTES AND PEACE

1 Anthropologists who have studied the way violent reciprocity is brought to an end make similar observations. To end a dispute, one has to look for an additional element that does not involve reciprocity: for example, a sum of money, in the case of cycles of murder (Coppet 1970).

2 In 'Homeric phraseology', Emile Benveniste writes,

> the notion of *philos* expresses the behaviour incumbent on a member of the community towards a *xénos*, the 'guest-stranger'. The xénos, a 'guest', who is visiting in a country where, as a stranger, he is deprived of all rights, of all protection, of all means of existence . . . finds no welcome, no lodging and no guarantee except in the house of the man with whom he is connected by *philótēs* . . . The pact concluded in the name of *philótēs* makes the contracting parties *phíloi*: they are henceforth committed to a reciprocity of services which constitute 'hospitality'. (Benveniste 1973, 278)

3 This is why the literature on love produced by sociology and its cousins will be of little use in my endeavour. Sociologists, like many other people, have shown particular interest in passion-love. The most solid recent work on the topic is Niklas Luhmann's *Love as Passion* (1986). Combining historical analysis and systems theory, Luhmann deals with the emergence of a semantics of passion-love, first outside of marriage and then within it. The work is inscribed within his theory of society as 'a social system that consists solely of communications and therefore as a system that can only reproduce communications by means of communications' (1986, 3–4). Through the study of passion-love, Luhmann examines the shift from traditional 'stratified' societies to modern 'functional' societies insofar as this shift is ensured by a differentiation among means of symbolic communication (ibid., 4–5). His book is thus principally devoted to the way 'passionate love' has been codified (ibid., 48), especially in French and English fiction of the seventeenth, eighteenth and nineteenth centuries. This focus is also what makes the book easily

accessible and appealing to educated persons whose ability to talk about love owes much to the reading of novels. In this respect, Luhmann's book can be juxtaposed to the elegant work combining introspection and literary references that Roland Barthes devoted to the discourse or 'code' of love (1978). But Barthes says practically nothing of use on the subject that concerns us here. An older work by Denis de Rougemont, *Love in the Western World*, originally published in 1938, deals with a closely related subject, the birth of passion-love in medieval courtly literature, and it has one advantage, at least, even though it is based on a less weighty theoretical apparatus: it acknowledges the opposition between *eros* and *agape* (Rougement 1974, 61–71), which Luhmann ignores. But de Rougemont does not develop this opposition; he too abandons it in favour of analysing the rhetoric of passion through literary works. The curious book by Pitirim Sorokin first published in 1954 seems closer to our topic (Sorokin 1982). But while he is initially attentive to the notion of agape, Sorokin does not seem to have truly penetrated its meaning, since he blends his discussion of it with considerations on 'creativity' that do not belong in this context. Finally, the scattered essays by Georg Simmel (on prostitution, the family, coquetry, and so on) that were published in France under the misleading title *Philosophie de l'amour* (1988 [Philosophy of Love]) make no significant contributions to my effort. These remarks also apply to the posthumous text that concludes Simmel's volume (in English in Simmel 1984); it consists of notes visibly thrown together in haste aiming at a sort of phenomenology of the experience of love, in which promising views (for example, on the relation between the generic character of the erotic object and the use of money in prostitution) are mixed in with disastrous confusions (for example, between the unmerited character of grace and feelings that degrade [ibid., 190]). These confusions are no doubt inherent in the project of grasping 'the unity of experience' (ibid., 173) by apprehending love synthetically in 'the diversity of the many phenomena that language designates by means of the concept of love' (ibid., 157).

4 Here we can follow the analyses of Hans-Georg Gadamer, when he shows how the double opposition hinges on the notion of 'prejudice', from which it takes its ambiguous character. Observers in effect strive either to use their knowledge to unveil and rectify an actor's prejudice, inasmuch as it is traditional, or to rehabilitate the popular prejudice, inasmuch as it is rooted in the poetic, mythical, originary, authentic aspects of the tradition. If these two apparently contradictory positions can be found combined in a single author and in a single text, it is because 'the paradoxical tendency to restoration, ie the tendency to reconstruct the old because it is old, the conscious return to the unconscious' (Gadamer 1982, 242), is the result of the 'romantic reversal of this criterion of value of the enlightenment' (ibid., 243) and its 'fundamental prejudice', which is 'the prejudice against prejudice itself, which deprives tradition of its power' (ibid., 239–40). The rejection of this double opposition brings my undertaking closer to a 'historical hermeneutics' aiming to abolish 'the abstract antithesis between tradition and historical research' (ibid., 251) and to rethink the notion of prejudice, through which the presence of tradition is manifested in action and its interpretation, while defining it not as 'the opposite pole from a reason without presupposition' but as 'a component of comprehending', linked to the historical character of actors and interpreters (Ladrière 1986).

5 It seems to me that one must posit the existence of capacities that allow for a preconception of agape, as it appears in the New Testament, in order to maintain the interface between anthropology and theology. Nevertheless, following this path leads me to a theological option (to which Charles Fredrikson has drawn my attention) that is an object of controversy. The question of pre-comprehension lies at the heart of a debate that is summarized most luminously in Kierkegaard's *Philosophical Crumbs* (Kierkegaard 2009). As Paul Petit remarks in his preface to the French edition (Petit 1967), the response offered to the question of pre-comprehension is linked directly to the way the problem of the relation between *nature* and *grace* has been approached. Kierkegaard's demonstration is built around the opposition between Socrates and Jesus. To elucidate the difficulty raised in *Meno*, according to which a man 'cannot inquire about what he knows ... nor again can he inquire about what he does not know', Socrates introduces the idea that 'research and learning are wholly recollection', so that an ignorant person, 'without anyone having taught him, and only through questions put to him, ... will understand recovering the knowledge out of himself', by recollection (Plato 1924, 80e, 81d, 85d). The work of the master can consequently be described as a work of midwifery; through interrogation, a teacher enables an ignorant person to discover knowledge that he or she had possessed, unwittingly, all along. According to this conception, which makes truth the result of an effort at *clarification*, 'every temporal point of departure is *eo ipso* contingent' (Kierkegaard 2009, 89). Kierkegaard contrasts this analytic concept of truth as recognition with the concept of an introduced truth, access to which would not depend exclusively on the activation of a pre-existing capacity. It is thus through the concern of the god, who 'loves the learner' (ibid., 103), that the possibility of a relation of comprehension is established. But this concept entails a different construction of time. For what counts then is the *instant* of revelation, and that instant has both historical and eternal value, in keeping with the Christian understanding of the relation between time and eternity (see Guitton 1971; Ricoeur 1976; Puech 1978).

6 Rudolf Bultmann opts, it seems to me, for the hypothesis of pre-comprehension:

> If the neighbour is the one who is always there already, then all men have always had their neighbours. And in so far as human life together has never completely misunderstood itself, it has always in some way or other seen the demand of love. The demand of love, therefore, does not arise in Christianity as something completely new in spiritual history; rather, the self-evident nature of the demand of love in Christianity reckons with the fact that everyone should really know what love is, and that everyone knows who his neighbour is when he is told, *Thou shalt love thy neighbour as thyself.* (Bultmann 1947, 48)

Bultmann defines the capacity that ensures the pre-comprehension of love as agape and characterizes it as 'practical': 'love does not denote the result of an action, not an end or ideal. . . . It is rather a definite *understanding* of the solidarity of connexion of *I* and *Thou*, and moreover not a theoretical but a practical understanding' (ibid., 47–8).

7 This property is posited by Rudolf Bultmann: 'Actually, one cannot speak

about love at all unless the speaking about it is itself an act of love. Any other talk about love does not speak *about* love, for it stands outside love' (Bultmann 1987, 53).

CHAPTER 11 THREE FORMS OF LOVE

1 Among the various terms analysed by Ceslas Spicq, I shall leave aside those associated with the form expressing attachment 'in its spontaneous, natural, and almost instinctive aspects'; these are used primarily, according to Spicq, to designate 'familial love, that of a mother for her children' and 'the attachment of animals to their offspring' (1955, 1–6).

2 'People who enter into friendly relations quickly have the wish to be friends, but cannot really be friends without being worthy of friendship, and also knowing each other to be so' (Aristotle 1926b, VIII.iii.9).

3 Friends have to 'have the disposition to be so. For separation does not destroy friendship absolutely, though it prevents its active exercise' (ibid., VIII.v.1).

4 'Each party therefore both loves his own good and also makes an equivalent return by wishing the other's good, and by affording him pleasure; for there is a saying, "Amity is equality", and this is most fully realized in the friendship of the good' (ibid., VIII.v.5). The theme of equality is particularly well developed: 'The forms of friendship of which we have spoken are friendships of equality, for both parties render the same benefit and wish the same good to each other, or else exchange two different benefits, for instance pleasure and profit' (ibid., VIII.vi.7).

5 'Friendship is most lasting when each friend derives the same benefit, for instance pleasure, from the other, and not only so, but derives it from the same thing, as in a friendship between two witty people' (ibid., VIII.iv.1).

6 'The affection rendered in these various unequal friendships should also be proportionate: the better of the two parties, for instance, or the more useful or otherwise superior as the case may be, should receive more affection than he bestows; since when the affection rendered is proportionate to desert, this produces equality in a sense between the parties, and equality is felt to be an essential element of friendship' (ibid., VIII.vii.2).

7 'To take vengeance on one's enemies is nobler than to come to terms with them; for to retaliate is just, and that which is just is noble; and further, a courageous man ought not to allow himself to be beaten. Victory and honour also are noble; for both are desirable even when they are fruitless, and are manifestations of superior virtue' (Aristotle 1926a, I.ix.24–5).

8 Max Scheler stresses the proximity between *eros* and *agon*: 'Too little attention has been given to the peculiar relation between this idea of love and the principle of the "agona", the ambitious contest for the goal, which dominated Greek life in all its aspects – from the Gymnasium and the games to dialectics and the political life of the Greek city states' (Scheler 1998, 65).

9 On the treatment of desire in eighteenth-century social theory, and on the way the selfish appetites manifested in warlike competition might be turned towards commerce in order to domesticate the violent passions by subordinating them to the calmer passions, see Hirschman 1977.

10   After the stage of heterosexual object-choices has been reached, the homosexual tendencies are not, as might be supposed, done away with or brought to a stop; they are merely deflected from their sexual aim and applied to fresh uses. They now combine with portions of the ego-instincts and, as 'anaclitic' components, help to constitute the social instincts, thus contributing an erotic factor to friendship and comradeship, to *esprit de corps* and to the love of mankind in general. How large a contribution is in fact derived from erotic sources (though with the sexual aim inhibited) could scarcely be guessed from the normal social relations of mankind. But it is not irrelevant to note that it is precisely manifest homosexuals, and among them again precisely those that struggle against an indulgence in sensual acts, who distinguish themselves by taking a particularly active share in the general interest of humanity – interests which have themselves sprung from a sublimation of erotic instincts. (Freud 1993, 164)

11   What is needed if social order is to reign is that the mass of men be content with their lot. But what is needed for them to be content, is not that they have more or less but that they be convinced that they have no right to more. And for this, it is absolutely essential that there be an authority whose superiority they acknowledge and which tells them what is right. For an individual committed only to the pressure of his needs will never admit he has reached the extreme limits of his rightful portion. If he is not conscious of a force above him which he respects, which stops him and tells him with authority that the compensation due him is fulfilled, then inevitably he will expect as due him all that his needs demand. And, since in our hypothesis these needs are limitless, their exigency is necessarily without limit. For it to be otherwise, a moral power is required whose superiority he recognizes, and which cries out: 'You must go no further'. (Durkheim 1958, 200)

12 For Durkheim, selfishness and altruism are opposed as the personal to the impersonal, the particular to the general: 'These two forms of our activity and our thought are turned in two different directions. The appetites derived from our senses are necessarily selfish; their object is our individuality, and that alone. Moral activity, by definition, pursues impersonal ends ... Between these two aspects of our psychic life, between these two halves of ourselves, there is thus the same opposition as between the personal and the impersonal' (Durkheim 1975, 31).

13 This is equally true for the love human beings have for God. According to Nygren, the thematics of separation from God and the desire for God that permeates mysticism so deeply (for example, in Theresa of Avila [1997]) results from a compromise with eros, which from the earliest centuries of our era has reinvested the Christian theory of love through the intermediary of neo-Platonic thought, Alexandrine in particular (Nygren 1953). Similar observations are developed by Rudolf Bultmann: 'Christian [agape], of course, is just as strictly distinguished from the concept of love in *mysticism*', which, through its 'quest, an outgoing towards an object desired', is on the side of eros. But Bultmann introduces a distinction (absent in Nygren) between eros and mysticism: 'In distinction from [eros], mystical "love", however, is characterized by its "longing" and its fulfilment being regarded

not in respect of their character of intention . . . but as a state of feeling; it . . . remains in itself as a feeling' (Bultmann 1947, 50n.1).

14 Anders Nygren addresses the same critique to Max Scheler (Scheler 1998), who follows Nietzsche (Nietzsche 1990; also 1967, e.g., the critique of disinterestedness, 211–14 [Book II, aphorisms 394, 395, 396]) in an attempt to unveil a morality of 'ressentiment' behind the 'altruism' and 'love of humanity' that inspire 'modern philanthropy', a morality originating in the notion of agape (Nygren 1953, 72–5). To be sure, Scheler, who expands on Nietzsche's theory of ressentiment, tries to correct it by detaching it from conceptions proper to primitive Christianity. But in his many discussions of the 'decadence' of the 'West', which 'represents the rule of the weak over the strong' (Scheler 1998, 143) and which he associates with the development of Christianity and its perpetuation in socialism, he manifests his own adherence to the Nietzschean vulgate in its most fiercely ideological – biologist and elitist – forms. These tendencies gained purchase in the German university system during the first half of the twentieth century; see, for example, Karl Löwith's account of the German university in the 1930s (Löwith 1994).

15 With his two books (1955, 1958) and particularly the second, Ceslas Spicq offers – after Nygren (1953), with whom he strongly disagrees – the essential sources for a study of agape. In the three volumes of the monumental work published in 1958 (*Agapé dans le Nouveau Testament: analyse de textes*), which were intended as prolegomena to the construction of a theory of agape, Spicq identified and analysed all the references to the term or concept that appear in the New Testament.

16 After reviewing a considerable body of literature in anthropology, psychology and sociology, Alvin Gouldner concludes that the principle of reciprocity has a universal character, comparable in his view to the prohibition on incest (Gouldner 1960).

17 The opposition between the *new law* and the *old law*, a theological commonplace that interests me in particular here inasmuch as it supports a critique of formalism, must not lead us to overestimate the differences that separate the ethics of the Old and the New Testament. The reference to 'loving one's neighbour' is present throughout the Old Testament, which manifests familiarity with the notion covered by the term agape without giving it the 'extraordinary novelty' that it will take on in the New Testament, 'when a complete reversal of the notion of neighbour comes about', in particular with the prescription to 'love one's enemies' (Légasse 1989). One could say exactly the same thing about the liturgical expressions of agape which, in Christian liturgy, extend the Jewish forms (Di Sante 1991).

18 It would not be going too far, it seems to me, to speak here not only of internalization but also of incorporation. In fact, we find an association between body and temple first of all in St Paul and, in his wake, in Tertullian. With the internalization of the new law, the body becomes a tabernacle.

19 The most literal formulation of this faculty of forgetting, because it connects pardon with the rejection of equivalence, including equivalence with oneself, is provided by Simone Weil in her commentary on the passage 'and forgive us our debts, as we also forgive our debtors'. What this text asks us to renounce, she says, are

all . . . the rights that we think the past has given us over the future. First there is the right to a certain permanence. . . . Then there is the right to a compensation for every effort, whatever its nature, be it work, suffering, or desire. . . . Every time we give anything out we have an absolute need that at least the equivalents should come into us, and because we need this we think we have a right to it. . . . We think we have claims everywhere. In every claim we think we possess there is always the idea of an imaginary claim of the past on the future. That is the claim we have to renounce. (Weil 1973, 222–3)

Starting with the permanence of the self as equivalence to self, Weil goes on: 'The principal claim we think we have on the universe is that our personality should continue.' She concludes: 'To remit debts is to renounce our own personality' (ibid., 223–4).

20 The first rule of the Friars Minor does not preclude work, but it forbids jobs that presuppose either commandment or calculation (they should not be 'administrators', 'managers' or 'supervisors' – all jobs that involve money (Francis of Assisi 1982, 115–17) or law (Michel Villey writes that 'St Francis requires that his monks abstain from using the law, that they not get mixed up in this guaranteed distribution of temporal goods which is the specific object of law' [Villey 1975, 192]). Thus we read in St Francis's 'Testament' (dictated in 1226, during his final illness):

we were simple and subject to all. And I used to work with my hands, and I [still] desire to work; and I firmly wish that all my brothers give themselves to honest work. Let those who do not know how [to work] learn, not from desire of receiving wages for their work but as an example and in order to avoid idleness. And when we are not paid for our work, let us have recourse to the table of the Lord, seeking alms from door to door. (Francis of Assisi 1982, 155)

21 Ultimately, the relation to violence is what constitutes the criterion here for existence maintained in a state of agape. For, to the question whether existence in a state of agape can be distinguished from *idiocy* (a question Nietzsche answers in the negative), it seems to me one possible response is the following. To be sure, a person in a state of agape resembles an idiot, especially in the sense that he or she abandons all concern for calculation. And one cannot say, a priori, whether a person who does not calculate, who does not anticipate, who does not strike back, is an idiot or a saint. Here we have a particular case of induction developed by Wittgenstein concerning the impossibility of determining what rule an actor is following and 'knowing positively in what sense others understand the rule that seems to us to govern his behaviour'. Only if there is *transgression* can we 'show that he is not following the rule in the sense we are giving the term' (Livet 1988). Yet while an idiot may be incapable of calculating, nothing prevents him from responding to violence with violence. Thus passivity in the face of violence is what allows an external observer to grasp the meaning of behaviour in a state of agape. We can see here one reason why hagiographies – whose authors, unlike the saints themselves, must produce a demonstration of holiness – grant such importance to the theme of temptation or *provocation* to which the saint does not respond.

22 The historical school of parable interpretation developed in opposition to the previously dominant allegorical tradition, which was challenged by Adolf Jülicher in the late nineteenth century. The allegorical interpretation, in use since the earliest centuries CE, treated parables 'as allegories, in which each term stood as a cryptogram for an idea' (Dodd 1961, 1). Thus St Augustine (cited by Dodd) interprets the parable of the Good Samaritan by substituting 'Adam' for 'a man', the 'heavenly city' for 'Jerusalem', the 'devil and his angels' for 'thieves', and so on. In contrast, the historical school, which benefits from Rudolf Bultmann's 'critical radicalism' (Bultmann 1963), stresses the realism of parables by showing how they fit into a specific historical context: thus, for example, Joachim Jeremias prefaces his interpretation of the parable of the Sower with ethnographic details on the customary technique for sowing seeds in first-century Palestine (Jeremias 1963, 11–12). Similarly, he treats the parable of the Prodigal Son as a 'story taken from life' in which the father is thus not God, but an earthly father, and he stresses the historical realism of the details concerning the feast (ibid., 128–32). This is how a parable can be distinguished from the biblical *mashal* to which it has often been compared. In fact, the mashal – a *sentence*, proverb or saying – is 'especially an enigma, a sort of allegory that has become obscure, which dissimulates and hides its true meaning in order to make the listener search' (Léon-Dufour 1965, 314). In addition, narratives more or less analogous to the parables in the gospels are found only in small numbers scattered throughout the Old Testament, where they appear chiefly in the wisdom literature and the prophetic writings (Perrot 1989, 390). The systematic use of parables is thus specific to the gospels, even if it was borrowed from rabbinical teaching. The gospels report forty parables to which some thirty brief analogies must be added (Marguerat 1989, 60–1).

But the historical tradition does not make room for metaphorical interpretation, either. Thus Jülicher, the founder of modern parable exegesis, explicitly rejects the notion of metaphor, because this notion is for him only the rhetorical tool of allegory (Ricoeur 1975, 89). Only with the development of the modern theory of metaphor (Ricoeur 1977b) could stress be placed not only on the realism of a plot's premises but also on the 'extravagance' of its dénouement, and thus on the tension between premise and dénouement that constitutes the force driving the interpretation towards the intended meaning.

23 The concept of 'redescription', applied to metaphor, comes from the theory of models proposed by Max Black and Mary B. Hesse, a theory itself built on a juxtaposition between model and metaphor. The theoretical models 'introduce a new language, like a dialect or idiom, in which the original is described without being constructed' (Ricoeur 1977b, 241). The theoretical explanation is then conceived as 'the metaphoric redescription of the domain of the *explanandum*' ... Indeed, 'if the model, like metaphor, introduces a new language, its description equals explanation ... To have recourse to models is to interpret rules of correspondence in terms of extension of the language of observation through metaphorical usage' (ibid., 242; here Ricoeur exploits the 'deployability' of the model, to use Stephen Toulmin's term). Ricoeur is interested in the way 'the theory of models reflect[s] back on the theory of metaphor' (ibid., 243); this leads him to look beyond isolated metaphorical statements for the equivalent of the model in the 'expanded

metaphor' or 'the metaphoric network' (ibid., 244). Stressing the creative function of metaphor that is associated with its power of redescription, he develops 'the thesis of the "tensional" character of metaphorical truth' (ibid., 255).

24 'Two claims will be made: a) that metaphor is more than a figure of style, but contains *semantic innovation*; b) that metaphor includes a denotative or referential dimension, i.e., the power of *redefining reality*' (Ricoeur 1975, 75).

25 'The signs of metaphoricity given by a single narrative, if there are any, have not to be found elsewhere than in the *plot*, . . . in the challenge which this plot displays for the main characters, and in the answer of these characters to the *crisis* situation' (ibid., 97).

26 Could we not say a poetic language, such as that of the parables, proverbs and proclamatory sayings, redescribes human reality according to the 'qualification' conveyed by the symbol Kingdom of God? This would indicate that the ultimate referent of parabolic (proverbial, proclamatory) language is human experience centred around the *limit-experiences* which would correspond to the *limit-expressions* of religious discourse. The task of hermeneutics, defined as the task of displaying the kind of 'world' projected by a certain type of text, would find its fulfillment at this stage: in the deciphering of the *limit-experiences* of human life. (Ibid., 34)

27 The term agape, which appears frequently in Paul's writings, is rare in the synoptic gospels (Léon-Dufour 1975, 111–12). In these gospels, the parables that rely on justice are the ones that bring to light the notion that the term covers.

28 To clarify what he means by a parable in action, Crossan gives examples from current events (his book was published in the United States in 1975), such as the gesture of a black preacher who takes a seat at a segregationist banquet, or that of a priest who burns the national flag. These actions, according to Crossan, 'forced the viewer to face [a] structural dilemma as the minister of God's word was led to jail.' One expects criminals, not priests, to be taken to jail, so that this type of action 'begets a series of very disturbing questions, and such is, of course, the very precise purpose of the action.' Crossan includes in this type of gestural parable, for example, the fact that Jesus appeared in the company of tax collectors (1975, 89–90).

29 When the constraint that weighs on the comparisons is ignored, the tension that inhabits the parabolic metaphor loses its point of application. One can then see in it the source of 'polysemy', understood as 'uncontrollable proliferation' or even, as for Beardslee (1978), as a technique that can lead – as can the koans of Zen Buddhist masters – to thinking of nothing, since 'meaning everything is equivalent to meaning nothing' (Fusco 1989, 37).

CHAPTER 12 AGAPE AND THE SOCIAL SCIENCES

1 After St Francis's death, the Franciscans twisted the article of the rule that forbade the order to own property, invoking a legal artifice that gave them the use of goods legally owned by the papacy (Lambert 1977, 184). Their hypocrisy is denounced in a passage of *The Romance of the Rose*, which

involves a Franciscan monk named 'False Seeming': 'If one of us has done something very good, we consider that we have all done it. . . . In order to win people's praise we tell lies to rich men and get them to give us letters bearing witness to our goodness, so that throughout the world people will think that every virtue abounds in us. We always pretend to be poor but no matter how we complain, we are the ones, let me tell you, who have everything without having anything' (Lorris and Meun 1995, 204 [lines 11661–78]).

2 The literature is too abundant to be surveyed even summarily here. Classic studies include Norman Cohn's *Pursuit of the Millennium* (1961), which is especially informative on the practitioners of the voluntary poverty that inspired all the great heretical movements of the second half of the Middle Ages (Vaudois, Spirituals, Beghards, Brethren of the Free Spirit, Beguins, and so on), and the acts of the Royaumont colloquium, *Hérésies et sociétés dans l'Europe pré-industrielle, XIe–XVIIIe siècles* (Le Goff 1968). The more recent work of M. D. Lambert, *Medieval Heresy: Popular Movements from Bogomil to Hus* (1977), is particularly useful on the heresies that derived from the Franciscans, Spirituals and Brethren of the Free Spirit. In the modern period, other forms of revolt have proclaimed the ideal of giving to the poor. See, among many other studies, those of Eric J. Hobsbawm, especially *Primitive Rebels: Studies in Archaic Forms of Social Movement in the 19th and 20th Centuries* (1963).

3 Rudolf Schnackenburg devotes a chapter of his book *The Moral Teaching of the New Testament* to the problem of putting the moral demands of Jesus into practice, and he surveys the modern debate on the question. For example, he enumerates the Jewish critiques that oppose the 'realism' of the Old Testament to the 'impracticability' of the gospels (1965, 81), while the Protestant tradition for its part stresses the primacy that must be granted to intention. Schnackenburg ridicules Tolstoy's attempt to construct a viable economic and social order on the basis of the Sermon on the Mount (ibid., 83) and offers a compromise solution: 'Most of Jesus' commandments are binding in their literal meaning; the principal commandment, of love, however, lays down an end which can only be attained by approximation, for love can and should perpetually increase' (ibid., 82).

4 It has been in the nature of our political thought (and for reasons we cannot explore here) to be highly selective and to exclude from articulate conceptualization a great variety of authentic political experiences, among which we need not be surprised to find some of an even elementary nature. Certain aspects of the teaching of Jesus of Nazareth which are not primarily related to the Christian religious message but sprang from experiences in the small and closely knit community of his followers, bent on challenging the public authorities in Israel, certainly belong among them, even though they have been neglected because of their allegedly exclusively religious nature. (Arendt 1958, 238–9)

5 This critique, in Nietzsche's writings and in those they have inspired, is often ambiguous, since denunciation – which includes a moral intention, at least implicitly – logically presupposes the possibility that the thing whose absence is denounced exists. Even in its most radical and most radically disenchanted forms, the unveiling of the always interested character of all practices, whatever those who carry them out may say or even think about

them, includes nostalgia for something whose absence is brought to light and thus whose existence is at least implicitly recognized. It is this fundamental ambiguity that is revealed by the paradoxical union between positivist forms of persuasion and the rhetoric of indignation (see *OJ* 340–6).

6   We shall say nothing about the morality that takes individual interest as its basis, for one can view it as abandoned. Nothing comes from nothing; it would be a logical miracle if we could deduce altruism from selfishness, love of society from love of self, the whole from the part. The best proof of this is moreover the form of this doctrine recently given by M. Spencer. He was able to remain consistent with his principle only by putting the most generally accepted morality on trial, treating as superstitious practices the duties that imply true disinterestedness, a more or less complete forgetting of the self. Thus he was able to say about his own conclusions that they probably would not find many adherents, for 'they are not in sufficient agreement either with prevailing ideas or with the most widespread sentiments.' What would one say about a biologist who instead of explaining biological phenomena challenged their right to exist? (Durkheim 1975, 263)

7   'Having given the name of *egoism* to the state of the ego living its own life and obeying itself alone, that of *altruism* adequately expresses the opposite state, where the ego is not its own property, where it is blended with something not itself, where the goal of conduct is exterior to itself, that is, in one of the groups in which it participates' (Durkheim 1951, 221).

8   We know that Marx devoted himself fully to the critique of capitalist society without making an effort to construct the model of a just society along the lines of classical political philosophies. This choice, which maintains the future in uncertainty, is related to the Marxist concept of the self-production of humanity in history. We do not even find in Marx a theory of the organization of the working class in its struggle for emancipation; this was developed later by Lenin and by Rosa Luxembourg. All Marx says on the subject is that the emancipation of the proletariat has to be won by the proletariat itself.

9   The relation between labour and utility is ambiguous in Marx's work, and this ambiguity, which underlies the many debates that have hinged on the definition of productive work, is at the root of the difficulties presented by the validation of the theory of capital gain.

10   This is why one cannot follow Hannah Arendt (1958, esp. 130–1) when she situates Marx entirely on the side of labour, defined by biological reproduction, as opposed to created works. To be sure, Marx's formulations, restrained by his effort not to shatter the compromise with the industrial world, are often ambiguous.

11   'I never recall without the most tender emotions the memory of the virtuous citizen to whom I owe my birth and who often spoke to me in childhood of the respect that is due you. I see him living still by the work of his hands and nourishing his soul with the most sublime truths. I see Tacitus, Plutarch, and Grotius intermixed with the tools of his trade in front of him' (Rousseau 1994a, 9).

12   On the opposition between the sociology of social phenomena and the

sociology of action and on the reinterpretation of Durkheim's sociology of social phenomena in the framework of a sociology of action, especially in the work of Parsons and Habermas, see Némedi 1989.

13 This point may be compared to Geoffrey MacCormack's critique challenging the uses of the concept of reciprocity in anthropology, particularly the application of the concept to the problem of gift exchange. According to MacCormack, it is not always clear whether the concept targets actual behaviours, rules, ideals or expectations, given that it functions sometimes as an instrument for describing practices, sometimes as a tool for constructing models (MacCormack 1976).

Chapter 13 Towards a Sociology of Agape

1 In using the term 'need', I may invite the objection that I am surreptitiously, and in a way fraudulently, reintroducing the reference to desire. Indeed, as has often been remarked in connection with, for example, the gap between desire and need in Marx (the two are opposed in Marx's work by differing degrees of necessity or objectivity), it is not obvious how the criterion for distinguishing desire from need can be defined except by an arbitrary decision based on the observer's preferences and applied on a case-by-case basis. In the construct sketched out here, the argument may be the following, or so it seems to me. I shall follow the intuition that informs all of René Girard's work – first developed in *Deceit, Desire, and the Novel* (1976) – on the opacity of desire; following Girard, I shall call *desire* what is experienced by persons who espouse the aim they believe they discern in another. To be sure, in agape, too, desire is opaque – all the more so in that it cannot attain on its own the manifestation that – whatever its form, is the condition for recognition. In agape, persons are unaware of what they require in order to live; that knowledge, as in mimetic desire, can be revealed to them only by another. But in agape it is the gift that bears the charge of revelation. It is in the presence of what is offered him or her that each one seizes what is needed. I shall thus propose, through a linguistic convention, to call *need* what is necessary when it is grasped in the immediacy of the gift, as opposed to desire, which is characterized by a specular necessity to be fulfilled in the future.

2 Self-reference thus constitutes one of the criteria making it possible to distinguish compassion from pity, according to Lawrence Blum: it is self-reference (and not reference to duty in the Kantian sense) in the dynamics of compassion that connects the capacity to conceive of distress with commitment to actions intended to relieve it. Conversely, in pity, distress is considered from the outside; self-reference is not actively engaged in order to grasp the distress and address it. This is probably why, where animals are concerned, for instance, people speak more readily of pity than of compassion (Blum 1980, 510–13).

3 Why are we interested in someone being the same person, and not merely the same human being or physical object? One reason is primarily retrospective: we need to know whom to reward and whom to punish for actions performed when 'they' were acknowledgedly different in some respects from the present population. But we have more forward-looking

reasons as well: we want to know what traits remain constant so that we can know what we can expect from the persons around us. We assign crucial responsibilities to individuals, assume important continuing relations to them in the belief that certain of their traits are relatively constant or predictable. And for ourselves, we are interested in our own identity because we make choices that will affect our futures: we set in motion a train of actions whose consequences involve 'our' well-being, without knowing whether we shall have, in the future, the desires and beliefs that now direct our planning. (Rorty 1976, 4–5)

4 Let us note nevertheless that this problem is not entirely foreign to classical economics, since, in the model of the invisible hand, the well-being of society as a whole is achieved by the aggregation of individual actions, which aim solely at selfish interest; the fact that these actions are aroused by passions, even if only 'calm passions' (Hirschman 1977, 65), means that they have much in common with violence. Here again, for an observer detached from the action, an 'impartial spectator', in Adam Smith's terms (2002), detached from self-interested memberships and positioned so as to observe from above, the equilibrium of the whole can appear as such. Nevertheless, there is a fundamental difference: the rebound effect of theory on practice helps reinforce the stability of exchanges in the case of classical economics, while it dismantles this stability in the hypothetical case of an economics of agape.

5 I am not referring here to something unsaid that would be, as in psychoanalysis, the product of a taboo or of censorship, or, as in constructs that extend notions originating in psychoanalysis to the objects of sociology, the product of a tension, impossible to assume other than in bad faith, between a covert selfish interest and overtly displayed altruistic beliefs. The constraints that keep agape from turning back on itself in a report are technical in nature, in a way, because they have to do, as we have seen, with the absence in this regime of instruments that could give a stable form to self-referential loops by relating them to a general equivalence through which they could be detached from persons.

6 This is to say, too, that in the state of agape one cannot conceive of Mary's ruse, when she wants Peter to fix her hairdryer but does not want to ask him directly, primarily so she won't owe him anything and, secondarily, for fear that he might refuse. Mary sets the stage as follows: she takes the hairdryer apart and spreads the pieces around her, as if she were in the process of fixing it herself. But she works things out so that Peter becomes aware that it is precisely a staged setting. Mary's intention is to inform Peter that she would like his help, and she transmits this information to Peter by making it obvious to him that she has the intention to inform him. However, this second-level intention – the intention to make it obvious that one has the intention of informing – has to remain concealed from Peter. Persons in the state of agape lack the competence to accede to these 'second-level intentions' (Dupuy 1988; Sperber and Wilson 1989, 52).

7 The idea according to which good deeds can be paid back by unspecified individuals who have not benefited from these deeds is at the heart of the liberal construction of society (I thank Professor Allan Silver for drawing my attention to this connection; see Silver 1989). This *generalized reciprocity* is supported, in Adam Smith, by the construction of *sympathy*, which makes it possible to pass without interruption in continuity from affection for those

near to us (a) to good will towards those who have obliged us, (b) to interest in society, (c) to attention to the public good and, finally, (d) to 'universal good will'. It is the possibility of adopting the viewpoint of an 'impartial spectator' that allows us to conceive of an exchange without stopping to take into account the singularity of those who accomplish it: 'Though . . . gratitude does not always correspond to . . . [a beneficent man's] beneficence, the sympathetic gratitude of the impartial spectator, will always correspond to it. . . . No benevolent man ever lost altogether the fruits of his beneficence. If he does not always gather them from the persons from whom he ought to have gathered them, he seldom fails to gather them, and with a tenfold increase, from other people' (Smith 2002, 265).

8 My research, pursued through the analysis of affairs that have given rise to lengthy disputes in justice and, in a number of cases, to public demonstrations and position-takings, is also extended by various studies (a summary of which is found in the booklet presenting the projects and accomplishments of the Groupe de sociologie politique et morale; GSPM 1988). A more complete presentation of a subset of cases is found in Boltanski and Thévenot, 1989, and especially in Francis Chateauraynaud's work on complaints focused on professional wrongdoing (Chateauraynaud 1989a, 1991).

9 Of course it is not certain that things such as love perfectly at peace, or a truly 'cold', absolutely emotionless violence have been attested. But this may be because persons never enter deeply enough and for a long enough time into these states to lose every vestige of the states that they exclude. Here again, relations between regimes must be conceptualized as continuous variations rather than as discrete oppositions. And, similarly, justice encounters emotion as soon as it takes into account the person of the actor to whom it applies; it then tends towards agape and, recognizing thereby its own limits, defines itself as *equity*.

10 This establishment is a secondary school in the suburbs of Paris, one with a reputation as a tough place in which to teach. The students, differing in age (from ten to eighteen) and in physical strength, represent thirty different nationalities or ethnic groups. The parents, most of whom are moderately or extremely poor, are blue-collar workers, low-ranking employees or unemployed. When there is violence (it has been decreasing), it is often associated with inter-ethnic conflicts. The likelihood of succeeding in school is very limited for all these children. The teachers suffer from the gap between the formal requirements of their task and what they can really accomplish. The proportion of union members is high. A significant number of the teachers belong to the Communist Party (the majority party in the municipality). Union or party membership offers a resource in situations in which cohesiveness has to be made manifest, especially in confrontations with the administration. (On the context in which this establishment is situated and on the sociology of public schools in France, see Derouet 1989.)

11 'There are things that have been misunderstood, things the others experienced as troublesome, as unjust. And one day, who knows why, there's one last incident that isn't any more serious than the others, but this one is the trigger, and then we have a crisis'; 'usually, it starts with people who aren't happy, it's not necessarily widespread; there's some arguing and then things explode, during recess or in the teachers' lounge.' For Mme A., the way the unification of local disputes comes about is incomprehensible: 'I don't

understand. Is it the build-up of things that people haven't settled, what the professors call "contentious issues"? Is it the whole set of these issues that leads to the explosion? I don't know. I don't see the connection between the affair that produces the general explosion and the rest.'

12 'When I say crisis, it's extremely violent. It's really a paralysis of the machine, it's the administration against the faculty. Everybody feels it very strongly in the school, even the students. Always, when there are these crises, there's always an aggravating effect on school life. The students are more troublesome, sad, tense. There's more absenteeism, there's always a backlash in the life of the school.' (During one of these crises, students waiting for the teachers to arrive in the courtyard lined the path on both sides and booed them.) 'Everything happens at once. Everything explodes. In general, I feel a sort of hardening, there's a kind of uneasiness and then there's the explosion in the teachers' lounge.' 'So things escalate slowly, there's an explosion, everybody is paralysed, it can last quite a few days. The record was ten days.'

13 'I told them, "That's enough, I'm not a doormat. Now, I'll see you, but we're going to decide together on a time and place for me to see you, which means that I'm a partner, you're a partner, so we're going to be on an equal basis. Now you take your students out of here." It was a brawl. The word came back to the teachers' lounge: "The administration doesn't want to see us." Result: a notice posted by me: "I'll receive the unions at the times and places we agree on together."'

14 'I'm obliged to put in hours, because I was challenged on everything. Someone who was coming to see me in the office, a union representative. I fell into the trap until I understood the rules of the game. They made decisions, and then I became aware that people were doing the opposite. They would say to me: "Wait, I came to see you, but I was not an appointed representative."'

15 'In this case, I pull in the sails, if I can put it that way. I don't go into the teachers' lounge, where I usually get a cordial welcome. But this time, I know it's better for me not to go there. Perhaps for me, because I would explode, because once or twice I did explode, and I regretted it. That's why I don't go there any more; I hole up. The teachers holed up too.'

16 'They made their case, I made mine, and the atmosphere was already clearing up at the level of the representatives. Things hadn't changed, but we had explained our positions. Then there was a general assembly. I remember very well. People talk. I ask somebody to lead the session . . . I designate a leader. The person leading the session is someone whose spirit of good will and impartiality people trust. There, people talk. "So-and-so has the floor", and talks, makes statements, more or less accurate, more or less false. There are reactions, and I intervened at the end.'

CHAPTER 14 THE AFFAIR AS A SOCIAL FORM

1 'It is very easy to know why the sovereign Power ought to leave every one at liberty to write against Authors, who are mistaken, but not to publish Satires. It is because Satires divest a Man of his Reputation, which is a kind of civil Homicide, and consequently a Punishment, which ought only to be inflicted by the Sovereign' (Bayle 1734–41, 2: 389 [Catius 812a, b]). To establish the autonomy of the 'Republic of Letters' and to delimit an apolitical space

where reappropriation of the political will can occur, it is necessary to establish the boundary between 'critique', which is legitimate, and 'diffamation', which usurps the 'majesty of the State'.

2 As a whole series of studies have shown, the existence of a mother population with clear-cut borders is most often the product of a legal or quasi-legal act of definition and delimitation. In all other cases, one cannot speak of a corpus without taking a position on the properties, dimensions and borders of the mother population; this always amounts to defining groups, and it also means intervening in a quasi-legal fashion in the social world by establishing criteria for determining belonging and non-belonging in a discrete fashion (see especially Desrosières and Thévenot 1979; Desrosières et al. 1983; Boltanski 1987a, 156–62 and 227–9).

Chapter 15 The Actantial System of Denunciation

1 The actantial system studied here differs in this respect from the system of roles in Bakhtin's sense (relations between author, hero, interlocutor, and so on). These roles, although dissociated from the 'real' author or reader, retain properties attached to an individual (or, rather, to an 'actor'), and this precludes analysing the relations between individual persons and collective persons and the procedures for shifting from one to the other (Todorov 1984, 46–8).

2 The terms in parentheses are labels for the various modalities of the code that I used in my analyses of the correspondence.

3 As soon as Dreyfus's defence ceased to be pursued in high places, as soon as it was construed and conducted as a private defence, as soon as the physical personality of the individual who until then had embodied an immaterial principle became the essential preoccupation for his friends (I was tempted to say for his partisans), the Dreyfus affair ceased to be a universal human affair. The events in Rennes and the acceptance of the pardon were terribly decisive. By accepting the pardon, Alfred Dreyfus did not in any way recognize his guilt. For reasons that it is not for me to judge, he preferred immediate freedom to the heroic, uninterrupted continuation of the quest for his legal rehabilitation. But he conducted himself in this as an independent and isolated being, not as a man passionate about humanity and conscious of the beauty of the duty to society: he acted as a pure individual, not as a member of the human collectivity in solidarity with all his fellow men. By the same token, and whatever the greatness of the role he was able to play, he no longer represents anything. (Cited in Vidal-Naquet 1982, 22)

4 Appendix 2 presents excerpts from typical letters corresponding to the various zones of the first factorial level.

Chapter 16 The Requirement of Desingularization

1 Conversely, the work of singularization that consists in declassifying a 'classificatory' relation, to use the language of anthropology, is best practised

309

with bodies, in part no doubt because bodily properties – odours, for example – are not used in our societies to define criteria of collective identities (with the obvious exception of sex, which poses a special problem).

CHAPTER 17 THE DIFFICULT DENUNCIATION OF KITH AND KIN

1 Psychoanalysis has contributed significantly to the formation of the feminist movement, helping it to achieve a higher power of generalization; this power makes it possible to constitute conflicts that previously would have been singular and manage them within a political logic.

CHAPTER 18 MANOEUVRING TO INCREASE ONE'S OWN STATURE

1 In other words, internal analysis does not suffice to account for rhetorical behaviour that is oriented by reference to expectations that the writer recognizes in others because they are familiar to the writer him- or herself. As studies of the language of schizophrenics show (see, for example, Hoffman et al. 1982), objective analyses of syntactic irregularities, categorial properties and modes of logical association do not suffice to characterize this particular use of language, either because internal analysis identifies features such as 'loose associations', without which ordinary conversation itself would be impossible or at least quite impoverished, or, conversely, because objectively grammatical sentences 'sound perfectly crazy', and this compels us to return to the experience of listeners and their sense of normality. Hoffman and his colleagues thus suggest completing the analysis of schizophrenic speech with an analysis of the linguistic and, as it were, psychiatric competence of the person who identifies the signs by means of which the discourse is recognized as deviant. These remarks are all the more applicable to the cases studied here, where the letters deemed most 'bizarre' on the continuum we are considering do not necessarily include 'objective' indices that would allow us to identify them as such if we were not reinserting the text in a context that we reconstruct by using our ordinary sense of social reality (for example, one reader deems 'nutty' the letter of a man lacking in importance who says he is being persecuted by famous people); most of us no doubt keep that sense of reality ready for use in the form of a repertory of typical anecdotes.

2 Simonnot faces a double task: he has to give an acceptable form to the public denunciation of the group (the 'work community', to use his own terms) of which he was a loyal member for several years, and at the same time he has to justify himself for not having spoken out earlier to denounce the 'errors' in which he can be accused of complicity. Thus he writes, in the introduction to the book in which he recounts his affair:

> I must also add this. Being the victim of dismissal, I imagine I shall be suspected of writing this book to get revenge. I reply: one does not avenge oneself for injustice. Moreover, why should this exemplary firing, carried out to serve as an example by a newspaper that is itself exemplary, not be cited as an example? I wrote this book with as much serenity as possible, but also with passion, sometimes with tenderness, the affection I still

310

have for a work community to which I belonged for eight years. The only critique that can honestly be addressed to me is that I did not write these pages earlier, when I was still on the rue des Italiens [site of *Le Monde*'s headquarters]. I shall answer: I had not understood. And that is why this book is also a self-critique. (Simonnot 1977, 13)

3 This holds true for all works of denunciation recounting an affair that has taken on the proportions of a 'political scandal'. The effect of abnormality exercised by the gossip form diminishes when the gossip has to do with important people and when the denouncers themselves are in a position to accredit the representation they offer of their relations with those people. The many books that exposed French political 'scandals' in the 1960s, 1970s and 1980s are all built on this principle; most of them were written by one of the actors, usually a politician involved in the affair as accused or as victim (depending on the position the interpreter occupied in the dispute that arose around the affair). No matter what position their author occupies in the political universe, these books possess common stylistic features – alternation between long sentences and concise formulas, irony, biting remarks, incisive portraits, and so on – whose function is to recall the corresponding legitimate genre, that of court gossip constituted by the seventeenth-century memorialists and moralists. This genre has the particularity of authorizing the publication of isolated incidents that might seem trivial or indecent if the importance of the actors in these incidents, their size and their representative power, their membership in the universe of collective action, politics or public affairs, did not confer on them an exemplary general dimension. Only state gossip can thus, in normality, be objectivized in a written text and integrated into a public denunciation.

4 Irregularities in the original spellings and syntax have been maintained and are reflected insofar as possible in the translation.

CHAPTER 20 GENERALIZATION AND SINGULARITY

1 In one incident, some teachers at the high-school level refused to be visited by inspectors. The gesture consisted in remaining silent while the inspector was present in the classroom. (See the document published in 1973 by a teachers' collective entitled *Non à l'inspection, dossier des profs sanctionnés* (No to Inspection: Dossier of the Sanctioned Teachers; Anonymous 1973). One of the pieces of evidence collected is called 'Éclaircissements sur les raisons et la signification de mon geste' [Clarifications of the reasons for and meaning of my gesture]).

2 There are associations in the United States today that bring together individuals known as whistle-blowers, following the model of Ralph Nader's movement. These denouncers demand legal recognition of their right to denounce, in public, the companies they work for or persons employed in these companies, in the name of the interests of the companies themselves, without being sanctioned (Westin 1981).

3 The most institutionalized protest technologies, such as strikes, were in the past unprecedented gestures that required interpretation by a group and that in turn helped mobilize such a group by the very act of provoking an

interpretation (see Tilly and Tilly 1981, especially 19ff.; see Tilly 1982 on the shift from the forms of protest used in the eighteenth century to the new forms that appeared in the nineteenth). To my knowledge, a systematic history of protest techniques (analogous to the history of technologies) does not exist. Let us take the hunger strike, for example, which in France today is a relatively common form of protest. When was it introduced? By what group? How did it spread? Why has it not been integrated into the arsenal of protest techniques in the workers' movement? And so on. One could raise the same questions, for example, about self-mutilation, whose introduction into France, especially in prison environments, is quite recent.

4 The intent to achieve the greatest possible originality through the fullest possible expression of the subject's singularity is related to the appearance of a new definition of the 'man of letters' (Starobinski 1979).

CHAPTER 21 DIGNITY OFFENDED

1 Acts of denunciation are often related by the denouncers themselves to life events, as attested by an abundance of biographical details or even in many cases life stories that accompany them. The twenty or so biographical interviews conducted in connection with my study made it possible to spell out this dimension, which is particularly relevant for analysing the relation between age and the denunciatory activity.

2 I used the periodic survey published by the Centre d'étude des supports de publicité [Centre for the study of the support structure for advertising]. The figures presented here were calculated on the basis of the 1970 survey, a year for which we have an additional survey, carried out by the same body, bearing exclusively on two categories: 'affairs' and 'upper-level cadres'. The table prepared by means of these two surveys is intended to shed light on trends.

3 These remarks were suggested by Yvette Delsaut.

4 This theme was particularly well developed by Alessandro Pizzorno during lectures given at the École de hautes études en sciences sociales.

5 The information used comes from four interviews with P., the hero of this affair, from press clippings (especially articles published in *Le Monde*) and from the work Maryvonne David-Jougneau devoted to this case, although her interpretation of the affair differs from mine.

CHAPTER 22 CONFIDENCE BETRAYED

1 A large number of affairs seem to hinge on the personal relationship between an individual endowed with legally guaranteed statutory authority and a trusted person who advises, supports and assists that individual without occupying a position that is officially recognized and consolidated by a title. Affairs involving such couples are particularly apt to link political and individual passions with dramatic ruptures and denials (denunciations on one side, betrayals on the other). These effects stand out in the 'Aranda affair', which arose around the association and subsequent disassociation between a bank director who had risen to a ministerial position and a personal advisor,

a self-educated former journalist from a 'modest background' (see especially *L'État piégé* [Aranda 1972] and Jean-Paul Sartre's interview with Gabriel Aranda [Sartre 1972]). A scandal has the paradoxical property of being an institution of political life that contributes to its ordinary functioning even while it is considered, in each of its manifestations, as the exceptional and monstrous product of a perverse mechanism.

2 For a better understanding of the relation that was established between P.'s protest and the teachers' organized movements, and also the gradual breakdown of that relation, one would have to analyse the evolution of the teaching profession in France between 1968 and about 1978, as has been done for higher education in the period 1960–1970 (Bourdieu, Boltanski and Maldidier 1971). It would also be necessary to resituate P.'s story in the long series of affairs that arose within French educational institutions during that period: this series has been studied by Jean-Louis Derouet.

3 The same thing seems to be true of politeness, which is also to a large extent a matter of size. Offences against 'face', to borrow the Goffmanian term used by Brown and Levinson (1978), consist very generally in not considering the interlocutor according to the dimensions that the latter attributes to himself (in 'diminishing', 'belittling' him), and especially in not accepting his discourse on the level of singularity or generality at which it is presented. One of the most common strategies thus consists in using interpretive capacities to belittle a discourse pronounced 'in general' about singular cases and interests.

313

REFERENCES

Angenot, Marc (1983) *La Parole pamphlétaire: typologie des discours modernes.* Paris: Payot.

Anonymous (1965) *Little Flowers of St Francis*, trans., rev. and emended by Dom Roger Hudleston. New York: Heritage Press; www.ewtn.com/library/mary/flowers.htm#Intro (accessed 10 December 2010).

Anonymous (1973) *Non à l'inspection: dossier de profs sanctionnés.* Paris: Cerf.

Ansart, Pierre (1969) *Marx et l'anarchisme.* Paris: Presses Universitaires de France.

Anspach, Mark Rogin (1987) 'La Raison du gratuit', *Bulletin du MAUSS* 22: 249–92.

Aquinas, Thomas ([1265–74] 1947) *Summa Theologica*, trans. Fathers of the English Dominican Province, 3 vols. New York: Benziger Brothers.

Aranda, Gabriel (1972) *L'État piégé.* Paris: Stock.

Arendt, Hannah (1958) *The Human Condition.* 2nd edn, Chicago: University of Chicago Press.

Aristotle (1926a) *Art of Rhetoric*, ed. J. H. Freese. Cambridge, MA: Harvard University Press [Loeb Classical Library].

—(1926b) *Nicomachean Ethics*, ed. H. Rackham. Cambridge, MA: Harvard University Press [Loeb Classical Library].

—(1933, 1935) *Metaphysics.* Vol. I, ed. Hugh Tredennick, Vol. II, ed. Hugh Tredennick and G. Cyril Armstrong. Cambridge, MA: Harvard University Press [Loeb Classical Library].

Aron, Raymond ([1976] 1985) *Clausewitz: Philosopher of War*, trans. Christine Booker and Norman Stone. Englewood Cliffs, NJ: Prentice-Hall.

—([1967] 1998) *Main Currents in Sociological Thought*, 2 vols. New Brunswick, NJ: Transaction.

Austin, J. L. ([1962] 1975) *How to Do Things with Words*, ed. J. O. Urmson and Marina Sbisà. Oxford: Clarendon Press.

Baker, Keith Michael (1987) 'Politique et opinion publique sous l'Ancien Régime', *Annales ESC* 1: 41–71.

Bakhtin, Mikail Mikaïlovich (Valentin N. Vološinov) ([1929] 1973) *Marxism and the Philosophy of Language*, trans. Ladislav Matejka and I. R. Titunik. Cambridge, MA: Harvard University Press.

Bally, Charles (1951) *Traité de stylistique française*, Vol. 1. Paris: Klincksieck.

Balthasar, Hans Urs von (1980) *Nouveaux points de repère*. Paris: Communio/ Fayard.

Bantman, P. S. (1979) 'Les Paranoïaques et la loi: contribution à l'étude historique des réactions médico-légales des sujets paranoïaques', MD dissertation, Paris, Université Pierre et Marie Curie.

Barthes, Roland ([1977] 1978) *A Lover's Discourse: Fragments*, trans. Richard Howard. New York: Hill & Wang.

Bastide, Roger (1947) 'Sociologie et psychanalyse', *Cahiers internationaux de sociologie* 2: 108–22.

Bayle, Pierre (1734–41) *A General Dictionary, Historical and Critical*, trans. John Peter Bernard, Thomas Birch, John Lockman and George Sale. London: J. Bettenham.

Beardslee, W. A. (1978) 'Parable, proverb and koan', *Semeia* 12: 151–77.

Benveniste, Èmile ([1966] 1971) *Problems in General Linguistics*, trans. Mary Elizabeth Meek. Coral Gables, FL: University of Miami Press.

—([1969] 1973) *Indo-European Language and Society*, trans. Elizabeth Palmer. Coral Gables, FL: University of Miami Press.

Berrendonner, Alain (1981) *Éléments de pragmatique linguistique*. Paris: Minuit.

Blum, Lawrence (1980) 'Compassion', in Amélie Oksenberg Rorty, ed., *Explaining Emotions*. Berkeley: University of California Press, pp. 507–17.

Blum, Léon (1935) *Souvenirs sur l'affaire*. Paris: Gallimard.

Boltanski, Luc (1969) *Prime éducation et morale de classe*. Paris: Mouton.

—(1971) 'Les Usages sociaux du corps', *Annales ESC* 26(1): 205–33.

—(1973) 'Erving Goffmann et le temps du soupçon', *Information sur les sciences sociales* 12(3): 127–47.

—(1975) 'Pouvoir et impuissance: projet intellectuel et sexualité dans le *Journal* d'Amiel', *Actes de la recherche en sciences sociales*, nos. 5–6: 80–108.

—([1982] 1987a) *The Making of a Class: Cadres in French Society*, trans. Arthur Goldhammer. Cambridge and New York: Cambridge University Press.

—(1987b) *Les Économies de la grandeur*. Cahiers du CEE, Protée series. Paris: Presses Universitaires de France.

Boltanski, Luc, and Pascal Maldidier (1977) 'La Vulgarisation scientifique et son public', Paris: mimeo, CSE/CORDES.

Boltanski, Luc, and Laurent Thévenot (1983) 'Finding one's way in social space: a study based on games', *Social Science Information* 22(4–5): 631–80.

—(eds) (1989) *Justesse et justice dans le travail*. Cahiers du Centre d'études de l'emploi. Paris: Presses Universitaires de France.

—([1991] 2006) *On Justification: Economies of Worth*, trans. Catherine Porter. Princeton, NJ: Princeton University Press [*OJ*].

Boltanski, Luc, Marie-Ange Schiltz and Yann Darre (1984) 'La Dénonciation', *Actes de la recherche en sciences sociales* 51 (March): 340.

Bourdieu, Pierre ([1972] 1977) *Outline of a Theory of Practice*, trans. Richard Nice. Cambridge and New York: Cambridge University Press.

—([1979] 1984) *Distinction: A Social Critique of the Judgment of Taste*, trans. Richard Nice. Cambridge, MA: Harvard University Press.

—([1982] 1990a) 'Lecture on the lecture', in Pierre Bourdieu, *In Other Words: Essays Toward a Reflexive Sociology*, trans Matthew Adamson. Cambridge: Polity, pp. 177–98.

—([1980] 1990b) *The Logic of Practice*, trans. Richard Nice. Stanford, CA: Stanford University Press.

Bourdieu, Pierre, and Luc Boltanski (1975) 'Le Titre et la poste', *Actes de la recherche en sciences sociales* no. 2: 95–107.

Bourdieu, Pierre, Luc Boltanski and Pascal Maldidier (1971) 'La Défense du corps', *Social Science Information* 10(4): 45–86.

Bourdieu, Pierre, Jean-Claude Chamboredon and Jean-Claude Passeron ([1968] 1991) *The Craft of Sociology*, ed. Beate Krais, trans. Richard Nice. Berlin and New York: Walter de Gruyter.

Braudel, Fernand ([1969] 1980) *On History*, trans. Sarah Matthews. Chicago: University of Chicago Press.

Brown, Penelope, and Stephen Levinson (1978) 'Universals in language usage: politeness phenomena', in E. N. Goody, ed., *Questions and Politeness*. Cambridge: Cambridge University Press.

Brun, Jean (1980) Introduction to Søren Kierkegaard, *Les Oeuvres de l'amour*. Oeuvres complètes, vol. 14. Paris: Orante, pp. xi–xxii.

Bultmann, Rudolf ([1930] 1947) 'To love your neighbor', trans. Ronald Gregor Smith. *Scottish Periodical* 1(1): 42–56.

—([1921] 1963) *The History of the Synoptic Tradition*, trans. John Marsh. New York: Harper & Row.

—([1933] 1987) *Faith and Understanding*. Philadelphia: Fortress Press.

Callon, Michel, and Bruno Latour (1981) 'Unscrewing the big leviathan', in Karin Knorr-Cetina and Aaron Victor Cicourel, eds, *Advances in Social Theory and Methodology: Toward an Integration of Micro- and Macro-Sociologies*. Boston: Routledge & Kegan Paul, pp. 277–303.

Cam, Pierre (1981) *Les prud'hommes, juges ou arbitres*. Paris: Presses de la Fondation nationale des sciences politiques.

Cameron, Norman (1943) 'The paranoid pseudo-community', *American Journal of Sociology* 46(1): 33–8.

—(1959) 'The paranoid pseudo-community revisited', *American Journal of Sociology* 65(1): 52–8.

Chamboredon, Jean-Claude (1984) 'Émile Durkheim: le social, objet de science: du moral au politique?', *Critique* 40: 460–531.

Chateauraynaud, Francis (1989a) 'La Construction des défaillances sur les lieux de travail: le cas des fautes professionnelles', in Luc Boltanski and Laurent Thévenot, eds, *Justesse et justice dans le travail*. Paris: Presses Universitaires de France, pp. 247–80.

—(1991) *La Faute professionnelle: une sociologie des conflits de responsabilité*. Paris: Métailié,

Chomsky, Noam (1975) *Reflections on Language*. New York: Pantheon Books.

Cicourel, Aaron Victor (1968) *The Social Organization of Juvenile Justice*. New York: Wiley.

—(1973) *Cognitive Sociology: Language and Meaning in Social Interaction*. Harmondsworth: Penguin.

—(1981) 'Notes on the integration of micro and macro-levels of analysis', in Karin Knorr-Cetina and Aaron Victor Cicourel, eds, *Advances in Social Theory and Methodology*. Boston: Routledge & Kegan Paul, pp. 51–80.

Clausewitz, Carl von ([1832] 1976) *On War*, ed. and trans. Michael Howard and Peter Paret. Princeton, NJ: Princeton University Press.

Claverie, Élisabeth (1984) 'De la difficulté de faire un citoyen: les "acquittements

scandaleux" du jury dans la France provinciale du début du XIXe siècle',
Études rurales, nos. 95–6: 143–66.

—(1987) 'Voltaire et la notion de cause judiciaire', *Journées de la Société
française de sociologie, Actes du colloque 'Normes sociales et règles jurid-
iques'*. Bordeaux; repr. as 'La Naissance d'une forme politique: l'affaire du
Chevalier de la Barre', in Philippe Roussin, ed., *Critique et affaires de blas-
phème à l'Époque des Lumières*. Paris: Honoré Champion, 1998.

—(2003) *Les Guerres de la Vierge: une anthropologie des apparitions*. Paris:
Gallimard.

Coates, Dan, and Steven Penrod (1980) 'Social psychology and the emergence of
disputes', *Law and Society Review* 15(3–4): 655–80.

Cohn, Norman (1961) *Pursuit of the Millennium: Revolutionary Messianism in
Medieval and Reformation Europe and its Bearing on Modern Totalitarianism*.
New York: Harper & Row.

Collange, Jean-François (1980) *De Jésus à Paul: l'éthique du Nouveau Testament*.
Geneva: Labor et Fides.

Coppet, Daniel de (1970) 'Cycles de meurtres et cycles funéraires: esquisse
de deux structures d'échange', in Jean Pouillon and Pierre Maranda, eds,
*Échanges et communications: mélanges offerts à Claude Lévi-Strauss pour son
60e anniversaire*, Vol. 2. Paris-La Haye: Mouton, pp. 759–81.

Corcuff, Philippe (1989) 'Sécurité et expertise psychologique dans les chemins
de fer', in Luc Boltanski and Laurent Thévenot, eds, *Justesse et justice dans le
travail*. Paris: Presses Universitaires de France, pp. 307–21.

Corcuff, Philippe, and Claudette Lafaye (1989) 'Une relecture critique du
Pouvoir périphérique – du fonctionnalisme au constructivisme', *Politix*, no.
7: 35–45.

Cothenet, Édouard (1988) *Exégèse et liturgie*. Paris: Cerf.

Crossan, John Dominic (1975) *The Dark Interval: Towards a Theology of Story*.
Niles, IL: Argus Communication.

David-Jougneau, Maryvonne (1988) 'La Dissidence institutionnelle: une
approche sociologique', *Revue française de sociologie* 29(3): 471–501.

Delamourd, Vinoli (1988) '"Monsieur le Président . . .": les formes de justification de l'état de chômeur', DEA thesis, Paris, École des hautes études en
sciences sociales.

Derathé, Robert ([1950] 1970) *Jean-Jacques Rousseau et la science politique de
son temps*. Paris: Vrin.

Derouet, Jean-Louis (1989) 'L'Établissement scolaire comme entreprise com-
posite: programme pour une sociologie des établissements scolaires', in Luc
Boltanski and Laurent Thévenot, eds, *Justesse et justice dans le travail*. Paris:
Presses Universitaires de France, pp. 11–42.

Desrosières, Alain (1988) 'Masses, individus, moyennes: la statistique sociale au
XIXe siècle', *Hermes* 2: 41–66.

—(2008) 'Historiciser l'action publique: l'état, le marché et les statistiques',
in Alain Desrosières, *Pour une sociologie historique de la quantification:
l'argument statistique*, Vol. 1. Paris: Presses de l'École des mines, pp. 39–56.

Desrosières, Alain, and Laurent Thévenot (1979) 'Les Mots et les chiffres:
les nomenclatures socioprofessionnelles', *Économie et statistique*, no. 110:
49–65.

Desrosières, Alain, Alain Goy, and Laurent Thévenot (1983) 'L'Identité sociale
dans le travail statistique', *Économie et statistique*, no. 152: 55–81.

Di Sante, Carmine ([1985] 1991) *Jewish Prayer: The Origins of the Christian Liturgy*, trans. Matthew J. O'Connell. New York: Paulist Press.

Dobry, Michel (1986) *Sociologie des crises politiques*. Paris: Presses de la Fondation nationale des sciences politiques.

—(1989) 'Février 1934 et la découverte de l'allergie de la société française à la "Révolution fasciste"', *Revue française de sociologie* 30: 511–33.

Dodd, Charles Harold (1961) *The Parables of the Kingdom*. London: Fontana.

Dodier, Nicolas (1988) 'Les Actes de l'inspection du travail en matière de sécurité: la place du droit dans les justifications des relevés d'infraction', *Sciences sociales et santé* 6: 7–28.

—(1989) 'Les ressources collectives de traduction de l'action', paper presented at the Journées annuelles de la Société française de sociologie, 'Action collective et mouvements sociaux', Paris, 29–30 September.

Dumézil, Georges (1949) *L'Héritage indo-européen à Rome*. Paris: Gallimard.

—([1948] 1988) *Mitra-Varuna: An Essay on Two Indo-European Representations of Sovereignty*, trans. Derek Coleman. New York: Zone Books.

Dumont, Louis (1977) *From Mandeville to Marx: The Genesis and Triumph of Economic Ideology*. Chicago: University of Chicago Press.

—([1966] 1980) *Homo hierarchicus: The Caste System and its Implications*, trans. Mark Sainsbury, Louis Dumont and Basia Gulati. Chicago: University of Chicago Press.

—(1983) Preface to Karl Polanyi, *La Grande Transformation: aux origines politiques et économiques de notre temps*, trans. Charles Malamoud. Paris: Gallimard, pp. i–xx.

—([1983] 1986) *Essays on Individualism: Modern Ideology in Anthropological Perspective*. Chicago: University of Chicago Press.

Dupuy, Jean-Pierre (1988) 'Common knowledge et sens commun', *Cahiers du CREA*, no. 11 (April): 11–51.

Durkheim, Émile ([1928] 1958) *Socialism and Saint-Simon*, ed. Alan Gouldner, trans. Charlotte Sattler. Yellow Springs, OH: Antioch Press.

—([1897] 1951) *Suicide: A Study in Sociology*, ed. George Simpson, trans. John A. Spaulding and George Simpson. Glencoe, IL: Free Press.

—(1970) *La Science sociale et l'action*. Paris: Presses Universitaires de France.

—([1934] 1973) *Moral Education: A Study in the Theory and Application of the Sociology of Education*, trans. Everett K. Wilson and Herman Schnurer. New York: Free Press.

—(1975) *Textes 2: religion, morale, anomie*, ed. V. Karady. Paris: Minuit.

—([1912] 1995) *The Elementary Forms of Religious Life*, trans. Karen E. Fields. New York: Free Press.

Elster, Jon (1981) 'States that are essentially by-products', *Social Science Information* 20(3): 431–73.

—(1985) *Making Sense of Marx*. Cambridge: Cambridge University Press.

Farge, Arlette, and Michel Foucault (1982) *Le Désordre des familles: lettres de cachet des archives de la Bastille*. Paris: Gallimard-Julliard.

Favret-Saada, Jeanne ([1977] 1980) *Deadly Words: Witchcraft in the Bocage*. Cambridge and New York: Cambridge University Press.

Felstiner, William L., Richard L. Abel and Austin Sarat (1980–81) 'The emergence and transformation of disputes: naming, blaming, claiming', *Law and Society Review* 15(3–4): 631–54.

318

Feuillet, André (1972) *Le Mystère de l'amour divin dans la théologie johannique.* Paris: Gabalda.

Filloux, Jean-Claude (1977) *Durkheim et le socialisme.* Geneva: Droz.

Fraisse, Jean-Claude (1976) *Aristote, anthropologie.* Paris: Presses Universitaires de France.

Francis of Assisi, St (1982) *Francis and Clare: The Complete Works*, trans. Regis J. Armstrong and Ignatius C. Brady. New York: Paulist Press.

Freidson, Eliot (1970) *The Profession of Medicine: A Study in the Sociology of Applied Knowledge.* New York: Harper & Row.

Freud, Sigmund ([1911] 1993) 'Psychoanalytic notes upon an autobiographical account of a case of paranoia (dementia paranoides)', in *Three Case Histories*, ed. Philip Rieff. New York: Touchstone, pp. 83–160.

—([1912] 2000) *Totem and Taboo: Resemblances between the Psychic Lives of Savages and Neurotics*, trans. A. A. Brill. Amherst, NY: Prometheus Books.

Furet, François ([1978] 1981) *Interpreting the French Revolution*, trans. Elborg Forster. Cambridge: Cambridge University Press.

—(1984) 'The conceptual system of *Democracy in America*', in François Furet, *In the Workshop of History*, trans. Jonathan Mandelbaum. Chicago: University of Chicago Press, pp. 167–96.

Fusco, Vittorio (1989) 'Tendances récentes dans l'interprétation des paraboles', in Association Catholique pour l'étude de la Bible, *Les paraboles évangéliques: perspectives nouvelles.* Paris: Cerf, pp. 19–50.

Gadamer, Hans Georg ([1960] 1982) *Truth and Method.* New York: Crossroad.

Gamson, William A. (1975) *The Strategy of Social Protest.* Homewood, IL: Dorsey Press.

Garfinkel, Harold (1967) *Studies in Ethnomethodology.* Englewood Cliffs, NJ: Prentice-Hall.

Ginzburg, Carlo (1980) 'Signes, traces, pistes: racines d'un paradigme de l'indice', *Le Débat* 7: 3–44.

Girard, René ([1961] 1976) *Deceit, Desire, and the Novel: Self and Other in Literary Structure*, trans. Yvonne Freccero. Baltimore: Johns Hopkins University Press.

—([1978] 1987) *Things Hidden since the Foundation of the World*, trans. Michael Metteer (Book I) and Stephen Bann (Books II and III). London: Athlone Press.

Gluckman, Max (1963) 'Gossip and scandal', *Current Anthropology* 4(3): 307–16.

Gobry, Ivan (1962) Introduction to *Fioretti de Saint-François*, trans. Alexandre Masseron. Paris: Seuil, pp. 7–16.

Goffman, Erving (1959) *The Presentation of Self in Everyday Life.* Garden City, NY: Doubleday.

—(1961) *Encounters.* New York: Bobbs-Merrill.

—(1967) *Interaction Ritual: Essays in Face-to-Face Behavior.* Chicago: Aldine Press.

—(1969) 'The insanity of place', *Psychiatry: Journal of Interpersonal Relations* 32(4): 357–87; repr. in Erving Goffman (1971) *Relations in Public: Microstudies of the Public Order.* New York: Basic Books.

Goody, Esther N. (ed.) (1975) *Questions and Politeness.* Cambridge: Cambridge University Press.

Gouldner, Alvin W. (1960) 'The norm of reciprocity: a preliminary statement', *American Sociological Review* 25(2): 161–78.

Greimas, A. J. ([1979] 1982) *Semiotics and Language: An Analytical Dictionary*, trans. Larry Crist. Bloomington: Indiana University Press.

Grenet, Paul Bernard (1962) *Les 24 thèses thomistes: de l'évolution à l'existence*. Paris: Téqui.

GSPM (Groupe de sociologie politique et morale) (1988) *Bilan et programme de recherches du Groupe de sociologie politique et morale, 1984–1992*. Paris: EHESS–CNRS.

Guitton, Jean (1971) *Le Temps et l'éternité chez Plotin et Saint Augustin*. Paris: Vrin.

Haarscher, Guy (1980) *L'Ontologie de Marx*. Brussels: Université libre de Bruxelles.

—(1984) 'Rawls, Marx et la théorie de la justice', in Jean Ladrière and Philippe Van Parijs, eds, *Fondements d'une théorie de la justice: essais critiques sur la philosophie politique de John Rawls*. Louvain-la-Neuve: Éditions de l'Institut supérieur de philosophie, pp. 104–28.

Habermas, Jürgen ([1981] 1984) *The Theory of Communicative Action*, trans. Thomas McCarthy. Cambridge: Polity.

—([1962] 1989) *The Structural Transformation of the Public Sphere: An Inquiry into a Category of Bourgeois Society*, trans. Thomas Burger and Frederick Lawrence. Cambridge, MA: MIT Press.

Heider, Fritz (1958) *The Psychology of Interpersonal Relations*. New York: Wiley.

Heller, Ágnes (1976) *A Theory of Need in Marx*. London: Allison & Busby.

Henry, Michel (1976) *Marx*, Vol. 1: *Une philosophie de la réalité*; Vol. 2: *Une philosophie de l'économie*. Paris: Gallimard.

Héran, François (1987) 'La Seconde Nature de l'habitus: tradition philosophique et sens commun dans le langage sociologique', *Revnue française de sociologie* 28: 382–416.

Hirschman, Albert O. (1970) *Exit, Voice, and Loyalty*. Cambridge, MA: Harvard University Press.

—(1977) *The Passions and the Interests*. Princeton, NJ: Princeton University Press.

—([1982] 2002) *Shifting Involvements: Private Interest and Public Action*. Princeton, NJ: Princeton University Press.

Hobbes, Thomas ([1651] 1996) *Léviathan*, ed. J. C. A. Gaskin. New York: Oxford University Press.

Hobsbawm, Eric J. (1963) *Primitive Rebels: Studies in Archaic Forms of Social Movement in the 19th and 20th Centuries*. 2nd edn, New York: Praeger.

Hoffman, Ralph E., Larry Kirstein, Susan Stopek and Domenic V. Cicchetti (1982) 'Apprehending schizophrenic discourse: a structural analysis of the listener's task', *Brain and Language* 15: 207–33.

Hollier, Denis (ed.) ([1979] 1988) *The College of Sociology*, trans. Betsy Wing. Minneapolis: University of Minnesota Press.

Isambert, François-André (1989) 'Alfred Schütz entre Weber et Husserl', *Revue française de sociologie* 30: 299–319.

Jeremias, Joachim ([1947] 1963) *The Parables of Jesus*, trans. S. H. Hooke. New York: C. Scribner's Sons.

Kierkegaard, Søren ([1847] 1995) *Works of Love*, ed. and trans. Howard V. Hong and Edna H. Hong. Princeton, NJ: Princeton University Press.

—(2009) 'Philosophical crumbs', in *Repetition* and *Philosophical Crumbs*, trans. M. G. Piety, ed. Edward F. Mooney. Oxford: Oxford University Press, pp. 83–173.

Kleist, Heinrich von (1967) *Michael Kohlhaas*, trans. James Kirkup. London and Glasgow: Blackie.

Kolakowski, Leszek (1978) *Main Currents of Marxism*, trans. P. S. Falla, 3 vols. Oxford: Clarendon Press.

Koselleck, Reinhart ([1959] 1979) *Critique and Crisis: Enlightenment and the Pathogenesis of Modern Society*. Cambridge, MA: MIT Press.

Labov, William (1972a) *Language in the Inner City: Studies in the Black English Vernacular*. Philadelphia: University of Pennsylvania Press.

—(1972b) *Sociolinguistic Patterns*. Philadelphia: University of Pennsylvania Press.

Lacan, Jacques ([1932] 1980) *De la psychose paranoïaque dans ses rapports avec la personnalité*. Paris: Seuil.

—([1975] 1988) *Freud's Papers on Technique, 1953–1954*, trans. with notes by John Forrester. New York: W. W. Norton.

—([1981] 1993) *The Seminar of Jacques Lacan, Book III: The Psychoses, 1955–56*, trans. Russell Grigg. New York: W. W. Norton.

Ladrière, Paul (1986) 'L'Herméneutique: le débat Gadamer–Habermas', *Sens et compréhension, éthique et pratiques symboliques*, no. 3: 112–24.

—(1991) 'La Notion de personne, héritière d'une longue tradition', in Simone Novaes, ed., *Biomédecine et devenir de la personne*. Paris: Seuil, pp. 27–85; repr. in Paul Ladrière (2001) *Pour une sociologie de l'éthique*. Paris: Presses Universitaires de France, pp. 319–68).

Lafaye, Claudette (1989) 'Réorganisation industrielle d'une municipalité de gauche', in Luc Boltanski and Laurent Thévenot, eds, *Justesse et justice dans le travail*. Cahiers du Centre d'etudes de l'emploi. Paris: Presses Universitaires de France, pp. 43–66.

—(1990) 'Situations tendues et sens ordinaire de la justice au sein d'une administration municipale', *Revue française de sociologie* 31–2 (April–June): 199–223.

Lagroye, Jean (1987) 'La Légitimation', in Madeleine Grawitz and Jean Leca, eds, *Traité de science politique*, Vol. 1. Paris: Presses Universitaires de France.

Lambert, Malcolm D. (1977) *Medieval Heresy: Popular Movements from Bogomil to Hus*. London: Edward Arnold.

Latour, Bruno (ed.) (1982) *La Science telle qu'elle se fait: anthologie de la sociologie des sciences de langue anglaise*. Paris: Pandore.

—(1984) *Les Microbes, guerre et paix,* suivi de *Irréduction*. Paris: Métailié.

—(1987) *Science in Action: How to Follow Scientists and Engineers through Society*. Cambridge, MA: Harvard University Press.

—(1988a) *Enquête sur les régimes d'énonciation*. Mimeo. Paris: École des Mines.

—([1984] 1988b) *The Pasteurization of France*, followed by *Irreductions*, trans. Alan Sheridan and John Law. Cambridge, MA: Harvard University Press.

—(1990) 'Post-modern? No, simply amodern! Steps towards an anthropology of science', *Studies in History and Philosophy of Science* 21(1): 145–71.

Latour, Bruno, and Steve Woolgar (1979) *Laboratory Life: The Social Construction of Scientific Facts*. Beverly Hills, CA: Sage.

Lefort, Claude (1978) *Les Formes de l'histoire: essais d'anthropologie politique*. Paris: Gallimard.

Légasse, Simon (1989) *Et qui est mon prochain? Étude sur l'objet de l'agapè dans le Nouveau Testament*. Paris: Cerf.

Le Goff, Jacques (ed.) (1968) *Hérésies et sociétés dans l'Europe pré-industrielle, XIe–XVIIIe siècles*. Paris-La Haye: Mouton.

—(1973) 'Le Vocabulaire des catégories sociales chez saint François d'Assise et ses biographies du XIIIe siècle', in Daniel Roche and Ernest Labrousse, eds, *Ordres et classes: colloque d'histoire sociale*. Paris-La Haye: Mouton, pp. 93–123.

Lemert, Edwin M. (1967) 'Paranoia and the dynamics of exclusion', in Edwin M. Lemert, *Human Deviance, Social Problems, and Social Control*. Englewood Cliffs, NJ: Prentice-Hall, pp. 197–211 [first pubd in *Sociometry* 25 (March 1962): 2–25].

Léon-Dufour, Xavier (1965) *Études d'évangile*. Paris: Seuil.

—(1975) *Dictionnaire du Nouveau Testament*. Paris: Seuil.

Lévi-Strauss, Claude ([1958] 1963) *Structural Anthropology*, 2 vols, trans. Claire Jacobson and Brooke Grundfest Schoepf. New York: Basic Books.

—([1950] 1987) *Introduction to the Work of Marcel Mauss*, trans. Felicity Baker. London: Routledge & Kegan Paul.

Levy-Bruhl, Henri (1964) *La Preuve judiciaire*. Paris: Marcel Rivière.

Lewis, David K. (1969) *Convention: A Philosophical Study*. Cambridge, MA: Harvard University Press.

Lidz, Charles W. (1978) 'Conspiracy, paranoia and the problem of knowledge', *Qualitative Sociology* 1(2): 3–20.

Livet, Pierre (1988) 'Conventions et limitations de la communication', *Hermès: Cognition, Communication, Politique* 1: 121–42.

Lorris, Guillaume de, and Jean de Meun (1995) *The Romance of the Rose*, trans. Charles Dahlberg. 3rd edn, Princeton, NJ: Princeton University Press.

Löwith, Karl ([1986] 1994) *My Life in Germany before and after 1933*, trans. Elizabeth King. Urbana: University of Illinois Press.

Luhmann, Niklas ([1982] 1986) *Love as Passion: The Codification of Intimacy*, trans. Jeremy Gaines and Doris L. Jones. Cambridge: Polity.

MacCormack, Geoffrey (1976) 'Reciprocity', *Man* 11: 89–103.

Marguerat, Daniel (1989) 'La Parabole, de Jésus aux évangiles: une histoire de réception', in Association Catholique pour l'étude de la Bible, *Les paraboles évangéliques: perspectives nouvelles*. Paris: Cerf, pp. 61–88.

Marion, Jean-Luc (1982) *Dieu sans l'être*. Paris: Communio/Fayard.

Marx, Karl (1922) *The Gotha Program*, by Karl Marx, and *Did Marx Err?* by Daniel de Leon. New York: National Executive Committee, Socialist Labor Party.

—(1964) *Economic and Philosophic Manuscripts of 1844*, trans. Martin Milligan. New York: International.

—([1843] 1970) *Critique of Hegel's 'Philosophy of Right'*, ed. Joseph O'Malley, trans. Annette Jolin and Joseph O'Malley. Cambridge: Cambridge University Press.

Marx, Karl, and Friedrich Engels ([1845] 1964) *The German Ideology*. Moscow: Progress.

Mauss, Marcel ([1938] 1979) 'A category of the human mind: the notion of person, the notion of "self"', in *Sociology and Psychology: Essays*, trans. Ben Brewster. London: Routledge & Kegan Paul, pp. 57–94.

—([1923] 1990) *The Gift: The Form and Reason for Exchange in Archaic Societies*, trans. W. D. Halls. New York: W. W. Norton.

Merton, Robert K. (1936) 'The unanticipated consequences of purposive social action', *American Sociological Review* 65 (March): 894–904.

Mesure, Sylvie ([1910] 1988) Introduction to Wilhelm Dilthey, *L'Édification du monde historique dans les sciences de l'esprit*. Paris: Cerf, pp. 5–26.

Miller, Richard E., and Austin Sarat (1980–81) 'Grievances, claims, and disputes: assessing the adversary culture', *Law and Society Review* 15(3–4): 525–66.

Mirowsky, John, and Catherine E. Ross (1983) 'Paranoia and the structure of powerlessness', *American Sociological Review* 48: 228–39.

Moore, Barrington, Jr. (1978) *Injustice: The Social Bases of Obedience and Revolt*. New York: Sharpe.

Moscovici, Serge (1988) *La Machine à faire des dieux*. Paris: Fayard.

Némedi, Dénes (1989) 'Durkheim and the modern sociological action theory', *Social Science Information* 19 (June): 211–48.

—(1990) 'Durkheim and the "strong programme" in the philosophy of science', *Revue européenne des sciences sociales*, 28(88): 55–75.

Nicolet, Claude (1982) *L'Idée républicaine en France*. Paris: Gallimard.

Nietzsche, Friedrich ([1901] 1967) *The Will to Power*, trans. Walter Kaufmann and R. J. Hollingdale, 2 vols. New York: Vintage Books.

—(1968) *The Antichrist*, in *Twilight of the Gods* and *The Antichrist*, trans. R. J. Hollingdale. Harmondworth: Penguin.

—([1901] 1990) *The Genealogy of Morals*, in *The Birth of Tragedy* and *the Genealogy of Morals*, trans. Francis Golffing. New York: Anchor Books.

Nisbet, Robert A. (1966) *The Sociological Tradition*. London: Heinemann.

Nygren, Anders ([1930–36] 1953) *Agapè and Eros*, trans. Philip S. Watson. London: SPCK.

Perelman, Chaim (1972) *Justice et raison*. Brussels: Éditions de l'Université libre de Bruxelles.

Perelman, Chaim, and Paul Foriers (1981) *La Preuve en droit*. Brussels: Émile Bruylant.

Perrot, Charles (1989) 'Images et paraboles dans la littérature juive ancienne', in Association Catholique pour l'étude de la Bible, *Les paraboles évangéliques: perspectives nouvelles*. Paris: Cerf, pp. 389–402.

Petit, Paul (1967) Introduction to Søren Kierkegaard, *Les Miettes philosophiques*. Paris: Seuil, pp. 11–25.

Pharo, Patrick (1985) *Le Civisme ordinaire*. Paris: Librairie des Méridiens.

Plato (1914) *Phaedrus*, in *Euthyphro; Apology; Crito; Phaedo; Phaedrus*, trans. Harold North Fowler. Cambridge, MA: Harvard University Press [Loeb Classical Library], pp. 405–579.

—(1924) *Meno*, in *Laches; Protagoras; Meno; Euthydemus*, trans. W. R. M. Lamb. Cambridge, MA: Harvard University Press [Loeb Classical Library], pp. 259–371.

—(1930–35) *The Republic*, ed. Paul Shorey, 2 vols. Cambridge, MA: Harvard University Press [Loeb Classical Library].

Polanyi, Karl ([1944] 2001) *The Great Transformation: The Political and Economic Origins of our Time*. 2nd edn, Boston: Beacon Press.

Pollak, Michael (1976) 'La Planification des sciences sociales', *Actes de la recherche en sciences sociales*, nos. 2–3: 105–21.

—(1986) 'La Gestion de l'indicible', *Actes de la recherche en sciences sociales*, no. 63: 30–53.

Puech, Henri-Charles (1978) *En quête de la gnose*, Vol. 1: *La Gnose et le temps*. Paris: Gallimard.

Racine, Luc (1986) 'Les Formes élémentaires de la réciprocité', *L'homme* 26(3): 97–118.

Rawls, John ([1971] 2005) *A Theory of Justice*. Cambridge, MA: Belknap Press.

Recanati, François ([1981] 1987) *Meaning and Force: The Pragmatics of Performative Utterances*. Cambridge: Cambridge University Press.

Ricoeur, Paul ([1950] 1966) *Freedom and Nature: The Voluntary and the Involuntary*, trans. Erazim V. Kohák. Evanston, IL: Northwestern University Press.

—(1975) 'Biblical hermeneutics', *Semeia* 4: 27–148.

—(ed.) (1976) *Cultures and Time*. Paris: Unesco Press.

—(1977a) 'Le Discours de l'action', in Paul Ricoeur and Dorian Tiffeneau, eds, *La Sémantique de l'action*. Paris: Éditions du Centre National de la Recherche Scientifique, pp. 3–137.

—([1975] 1977b) *The Rule of Metaphor: Multi-Disciplinary Studies of the Creation of Meaning in Language*, trans. Robert Czerny, with Kathleen McLaughlin and John Costello. Toronto: University of Toronto Press.

—([1983] 1984) *Time and Narrative*, Vol. 1, trans. Kathleen McLaughlin and David Pellauer. Chicago: University of Chicago Press.

—([1960] 1986) *Fallible Man*, trans. Charles A. Kelbley. New York: Fordham University Press.

—([1986] 1991) *From Text to Action*, trans. Kathleen Blamey and John B. Thompson. Evanston, IL: Northwestern University Press.

Rorty, Amélie Oksenberg (ed.) (1976) *The Identities of Persons*. Berkeley: University of California Press.

Rougemont, Denis de ([1938] 1974) *Love in the Western World*, trans. Montgomery Belgion. New York: Harper Colophon.

Rouiller, Grégoire (1981) 'Parabole et mise en abyme', in Pierre Casetti, Othmar Keel and Adrian Schenker, eds, *Mélanges Dominique Barthélemy*. Fribourg: Éditions universitaires, pp. 317–33.

Rousseau, Jean-Jacques ([1754] 1994a) *Discourse on the Origin of Inequality*, trans. Franklin Philip, ed. Patrick Coleman. Oxford: Oxford University Press.

—([1862] 1994b) *The Social Contract*, in *Discourse on Political Economy* and *The Social Contract*, trans. Christopher Betts. Oxford: Oxford University Press.

Sabel, Charles F. (1982) *Work and Politics: The Division of Labour in Industry*. Cambridge, Cambridge University Press.

Sahlins, Marshall (1972) *Stone Age Economics*. Chicago: Aldine.

Saint-Simon, Claude-Henri, comte de (1869) *Oeuvres*. Paris: E. Dentu.

Sartre, Jean-Paul (1972) Interview with Gabriel Aranda, *La Cause du peuple – J'accuse* 36 (22 December).

Saussure, Ferdinand de ([1916] 1966) *Course in General Linguistics*, ed. Charles Bally and Albert Sechehaye, with Albert Riedlinger, trans. Wade Baskin. New York: McGraw-Hill.

Scheler, Max ([1919] 1998) *Ressentiment*, trans. Lewis B. Coser and William W. Holdheim. Milwaukee: Marquette University Press.

Schelling, Thomas C. (1960) *The Strategy of Conflict*,Cambridge, MA: Harvard University Press.

Schiltz, Marie-Ange (1983) 'L'élimination des modalités non pertinentes dans un dépouillement d'enquête par analyse factorielle', *Bulletin de méthodologie sociologique* 1 (October): 19–40.

Schnackenburg, Rudolf ([1919] 1965) *The Moral Teaching of the New Testament*. New York: Herder & Herder.

Schreber, Daniel Paul ([1903] 1955) *Memoirs of my Nervous Illness*, ed. and trans. Ida Macalpine and Richard A. Hunter. London: W. M. Dawson & Sons.

Schumpeter, Joseph Alois (1954) *History of Economic Analysis*, ed. Elizabeth Boody Schumpeter. New York: Oxford University Press.

Schutz, Alfred (1970) 'Acting in the life-world', in Helmut Wagner, ed., *On Phenomenology and Social Relations*. University of Chicago Press, pp. 123–59.

Sérieux, Paul, and Joseph Capgras ([1909] 1982) 'Délire d'interprétation, délire de revendication', in *Classiques de la paranoïa*, Analytica, vol. 30. Paris: Navarin/Seuil, pp. 98–149.

Sider, John W. (1985) 'Proportional analogy in the gospel parables', *New Testament Studies* 31: 1–23.

Silver, Allan (1989) 'Friendship and trust as moral ideal: an historical approach', *Journal européen de sociologie* 30: 274–97.

Simmel, Georg ([1921–2] 1984) 'On love (a fragment)', in *Georg Simmel, On Women, Sexuality, and Love*, trans. Guy Oakes. New Haven, CT: Yale University Press, pp. 153–92.

—(1988) *Philosophie de l'amour*, trans. Sabine Cornille and Philippe Ivernel. Paris: Rivages.

Simonnot, Philippe (1977) *Le Monde et le pouvoir*. Paris: Presses d'Aujourd'hui.

Smith, Adam ([1759] 2002) *The Theory of Moral Sentiments*, ed. Knud Haakonssen. Cambridge: Cambridge University Press.

Sorokin, Pitirim A. ([1954] 1982) *The Ways and Power of Love*. Philadelphia and London: Templeton Foundation Press.

Sperber, Dan, and Deirdre Wilson (1989) *Relevance: Communication and Cognition*. Cambridge, MA: Harvard University Press.

Spicq, Ceslas (1955) *Prolégomène à une étude de théologie néo-testamentaire*. Louvain: Publications universitaires de Louvain.

—(1958) *Agapè dans le Nouveau Testament: analyse de textes*, 3 vols. Paris: Gabalda.

Starobinski, Jean ([1971] 1979) *Words upon Words: The Anagrams of Ferdinand de Saussure*, trans. Olivia Emmet. New Haven, CT: Yale University Press.

—([1971] 1988) *Jean-Jacques Rousseau: Transparency and Obstruction*, trans. Arthur Goldhammer. Chicago: University of Chicago Press.

Strawson, P. F. (1959) *Individuals: An Essay in Descriptive Metaphysics*. London: Methuen.

—(1962) 'Analyse, science et métaphysique', in Cahiers de Royaumont, *La Philosophie analytique*. Paris: Minuit, pp. 105–18.

Sulloway, Frank J. (1979) *Freud, Biologist of the Mind: Beyond the Psychoanalytic Legend*. New York: Basic Books.

Taieb, Paulette (1984) 'L'Oreille du sourd (à propos du *hau*)', *Bulletin du MAUSS*, no. 11: 39–67.

Tajan, Alfred, and Guy Delage (1981) *Écriture et structure*. Paris: Payot.

Teresa of Avila, St (1997) *The Autobiography of St. Teresa of Avila: The Life of St. Teresa of Jesus*, ed. Benedict Zimmerman, trans. David Lewis. Rockford, IL: Tan Books.

Thévenot, Laurent (1983) 'L'Économie du codage social', *Critique de l'économie politique*, nos. 23–4: 188–221.
—(1984) 'Rules and implements: investments in forms', *Social Science Information* 23(1): 1–45.
—(1989) 'Équilibre et rationalité dans un univers complexe', *Revue économique* 40(2): 147–98.
Thibaud, Paul (1988) 'Devant la crise de l'université: l'esprit libéral et l'esprit radical'. *Esprit*, nos. 7–8 [special issue on Paul Ricoeur]: 9–20.
Thompson, Edward Palmer (1963) *The Making of the English Working Class*. London: Victor Gollancz.
—(1975) 'The crime of anonymity', in Douglas Hay et al., eds, *Albion's Fatal Tree: Crime and Society in Eighteenth-Century England*. New York: Pantheon Books, pp. 255–308.
Tilly, Charles (1982) 'European violence and collective action since 1700', paper presented at the Conference on Political Violence and Terrorism, Bologna, Instituto Carlo Cattanea.
Tilly, Louise A., and Charles Tilly (1981) *Class and Collective Action*. Beverly Hills, CA: Sage.
Todorov, Tzvetan ([1981] 1984) *Mikhaïl Bakhtin: The Dialogical Principle*, trans. Wlad Godzich. Minneapolis: University of Minnesota Press.
Trepos, Jean-Yves (1988) 'La Construction sociale des conflits de consommation', PhD dissertation, Université de Lille.
Urlacher, Bernard (1984) 'La Protestation dans l'usine et ses modes d'objectivation: des graffiti aux tracts', DEA thesis, Paris, École des hautes études en sciences sociales.
Vidal-Naquet, Pierre (1982) 'Dreyfus dans l'Affaire et dans l'histoire', introduction to Alfred Dreyfus, *Cinq années de ma vie*. Paris: Maspero.
Villey, Michel (1975) *La Formation de la pensée juridique moderne*. Paris: Montchrestien.
—(1983) *Le Droit et les droits de l'homme*. Paris: Presses Universitaires de France.
Weber, Max ([1904] 1949) '"Objectivity" in social science and social policy', in *The Methodology of the Social Sciences*, trans. and ed. Edward A. Shils and Henry A. Finch. New York: Free Press, pp. 49–112.
—([1922] 1978) *Economy and Society: An Outline of Interpretive Sociology*, Vol. 1, ed. Guenther Roth and Claus Wittich, trans. Ephraim Fischoff et al. Berkeley: University of California Press.
Weil, Eric (1968) *Logique de la philosophie*. Paris: Vrin.
Weil, Simone (1957a) *Écrits de Londres*. Paris: Gallimard.
—(1957b) *Intimations of Christianity among the Ancient Greeks*. London and New York: Routledge.
—([1966] 1973) *Waiting for God*, trans. Emma Craufurd. New York: Harper & Row.
Westin, Alan F. (1981) *Whistle Blowing*. New York: McGraw-Hill.
Wittgenstein, Ludwig (1966) *Lectures & Conversations on Aesthetics, Psychology, and Religious Belief*, ed. Cyril Barrett. Berkeley: University of California Press.
Zumstein, Jean (1989) 'Jésus et les paraboles', in Association Catholique pour l'étude de la Bible, *Les paraboles évangéliques: perspectives nouvelles*. Paris: Cerf, pp. 89–108.

INDEX

Note: page numbers in italics denote figures or tables

Abel, Richard L. 6, 273n2
abnormality
  cognitive capacity 192
  denunciation 11, 58, 193–4
  disqualifying effect 246
  identification 40
  signs of 173–4
  singular/general dimension 11
  see also normality, judging of
abundance
  communist polity 134, 135, 137–8
  St Francis 122–3
accusation of injustice 7, 56, 162
actantial system of denunciation 9,
    178–90, 309n1
actants
  paranoia 160
  proximity 181–2, 188, 195, 196–7,
    202–4
  relations/aggrandizement *211*
  singular/collective acts 221
  size factors 178, 190, 192
  stylistic manoeuvres *218*
  worths 191
*Actes de la recherche en sciences
    sociales* vii
action
  civic 193–4
  individual/collective 42, 169,
    234–5
  power 65, 137

social 85–6, 304–5n12
  as test 65–6
  and theory 29–30, 37, 103
actors
  emplotment 84
  intentionality 113–14
  justice regime 81
  justification 38
  reports 30–2, 34, 80, 84–5
  researchers 31
  social sciences 141
  tradition 96–7
advertisers/target groups 280n11
affairs
  anecdotes 85–6
  duration of 203–4
  individual/collective 7, 8–9
  justice 6
  properties of 4–5, 7
  reports 16
  size 9, 10, 58
  study of 307n8, 312–13n1
  time 10
agape
  Aristotle 112–13
  in Christianity 70, 111
  constraints 306n5
  desire lacking 146, 151
  emotion 159–65, 292n9
  equivalence 110–14
  and eros 154, 298–9n13

agape (*cont.*)
  Aristotle 112–13
  gift 111
  insouciance of 114–16
  justice 79–80, 149–50
  Kierkegaard on 116–17
  language 125–6
  law 104, 113–14
  love 69
  model for 145–50
  neighbourliness 112
  opposition/complementarity
    152
  parables 128
  particular/general 289n8
  passivity 123–4
  political science 129–30
  in present 115–16, 123, 148
  reciprocity 112
  recognition 292n7
  relations in 102–3
  reports 293n1
  return to 75
  revelation 101–2, 116
  St Francis 121–2
  St Paul 302n27
  self-organization 148–9
  self-reference 146–7
  social sciences 129–31
  Spicq 299n15
  states of 78, 79, 103, 121, 149,
    150–3, 306n6
  time 116, 119–20
  utopia 145–6
  violence 300n21
aggrandizement 207, 208–9, *210*,
    211, 216, 218–19
agon/eros 297n8
alienation 132–3
allegory 301n22
altruism
  Durkheim 110, 130, 298n12,
    304n6, 304n7
  and egoism 110, 304n7
  Elster 136
  encouraged 163
  particular to general 109, 111
  public/private sector 243–4
  and selfishness 83–4, 298n12,
    304n6, 304n7

American Civil Litigation Research
    Project 273n2
anecdotes 85–6, 120–1, 171, 310n1
Angenot, Marc 15, 213
Annales school 25
Ansart, Pierre 277–8n4
Anspach, Mark Rogin 138–9, 142
anthropology
  critical capacity 29
  Durkheim 109
  evil 83–4
  exoticism 98, 100
  love 104
  and tradition 94–100
appetites, control of 109–10
Aquinas, St Thomas 111–12, 289n7
Aranda, Gabriel 217, 312–13n1
arbitration board 201
Arendt, Hannah 64, 115, 288n4,
    290n1, 303n4, 304n10
  The Human Condition 130
argument 38–9, 150, 204
Aristotle
  agape 112–13
  architect example 65, 288n5
  clarification 282n3
  disputes 65, 195
  friendship 297n2–n7
  justice 14, 47
  labour divisions 137
  philia 94–5, 105–6
  vengeance 297n7
Aron, Raymond 291–2n4
association 216, 248–9
attachment 145, 297n1
Augustine, St 60, 285n4, 301n22
Austin, J. L. 293n1
autobiography 56, 81–2

bad faith 83, 144
Bakhtin, Mikhail 206
Bally, Charles 228
Balthasar, Hans Urs von 111
Bantman, P. S. 257
Barthes, Roland 295n3
Bayle, Pierre 171, 308–9n1
Beauvoir, Simone de 250
belittling actions 313n3
belonging 199, 248
Benveniste, Émile 146, 293n1, 294n2

Benzecri, Jean-Paul 259
Bernard, Brother 124
Berrendonner, Alain 206
Best, Elsdon 138
betrayal 233
biography 56, 82
Black, Max 301–2n23
black box concept (Latour) 75
Blum, Lawrence 305n2
Blum, Léon 196
body politic 13–14
Boltanski, Luc 3–4, 9, 14–15, 33, 40,
    49–50, 65, 81, 91, 102, 148,
    172, 197, 202, 225, 246, 248,
    252, 272–3n1, 277n2, 279n9,
    307n8, 313n2
  Les Économies de la grandeur vii
  see also On Justification
Bossuet, Jacques-Benigne 16, 285n4
Boulin, Robert 217–18
Bourdieu, Pierre vii, 65, 82–3, 102–3,
    141–4, 149, 197, 213, 248,
    280n12, 313n2
  Distinction 83
  Outline of a Theory of Practice
    140–1, 149
Braudel, Fernand 280n12
Brown, Penelope 313n3
Brun, Jean 112
Bultmann, Rudolf 101–2, 296n6,
    296–7n7, 298n13, 301n22

cadres 3–4, 9, 40, 243, 246,
    279–80n10
calculability 82–3, 114–16, 141
Callon, Michel 178
Cam, Pierre 201
Cameron, Norman 256
Capgras, Joseph 203
capitalism 132, 134, 304n8
causes
  collective 8, 12
  groups 172
  as social form 274n4
  victims 173, 213–14
CGT (Confédération générale du
    travail) 214
Chamboredon, Jean-Claude 109,
    280n12
charity 111

Chateauraynaud, Francis 30, 67, 70,
    73, 282n4, 307n8
Chomsky, Noam 33
Christianity
  agape 70, 111
  love 296n6
  mysticism 72
  salvation 289n8
  tradition 285n3
Cicourel, Aaron Victor 24, 81, 207
civic action 193–4
civic polity 14–15, 16, 17, 276n3
clarification 44, 98, 102, 282n3
class struggle 214–15
Clausewitz, Carl von 75–6, 291–2n4
Claverie, Élisabeth 13, 294n4
cognitive capacity 96, 97–8, 192
Cohn, Norman 303n2
Collange, Jean-François 101, 129
collective resources 199, 202, 245
collective/individual *see* individual/
    collective dimension
collective/singular *see* singular/
    collective dimension
Collège de sociologie 145
Comment on James Mill (Marx) 134
common good
  defined 14–15
  denouncer/victim 195
  desire 110
  generality 232, 274n3
  legitimacy 45
  private interest 42, 194
  Rousseau 13, 285n4
  and scandal 13
  utilitarianism 282n1
communist polity 133, 134–5,
    137–8
competence
  for argument 33–4
  cognitive 96, 97–8, 192
  institutional certification 207–8
  for justice model 35, 38, 43, 66–7
complaints 163, 202, 274–5n6
compromise 34, 57–8
Confédération générale du travail
    (CGT) 214
Confessions (Rousseau) 276n2
confessions, in letters 230, 234
conspiracy 13, 219, 256

cooperation 157–9
Corcuff, Philippe 31, 274–5n6, 287n2
correspondence *see* factorial analysis of correspondence; letters
Cothenet, Édouard 110, 111
counter-gifts 138–44
creative work 133, 134, 136
critical capacity 29, 52–3, 60
critiques 29, 36, 37–8, 69–70
    see also sociologists of critique
Crossan, John Dominic 127, 302n28

David-Jougneau, Maryvonne 161
Delage, Guy 235
Delamourd, Vinoli 274n3
denouncers
    as actants 9, 178–9
    age 244, 245–6
    aggrandizement 208–9
    desingularization 215–16
    on factorial schema 221, 222–3, 224
    isolated 220–1
    mobilization of support 224
    normality 207
    political approach 229–30
    professions 242, 243–5
    public opinion 58
    singular/general 179–80
    social class 246–7
    and victim 181–2, 194–5, 200, 201, 210, 240, 243
denunciation
    abnormality 11, 58, 193–4
    actantial system of 9, 178–90, 309n1
    acts of 312n1
    as civic action 193–4
    as collective action 234–5
    collective resources 199
    desingularization 15
    duration of affair 203–4
    injustice 12, 15, 18, 26, 28, 41, 172–3, 191–2
    modes of 185–90
    normality 234, 240, 243
    public 167, 170, 171, 194, 239, 248
    of reality 75

reducing effects of 195
    scandals 16–17, 311n3
    social situation 57
    study of 28–9
    time 204–5
    worth 56
department heads study 288n6
dependency, personal 276n2
Derathé, Robert 13, 14
Derouet, Jean-Louis 66, 289n9, 313n2
descriptive metaphysics (Strawson) 32
desingularization
    aggrandizement 209
    complaints 202
    denouncers 215–16
    denunciation 15
    equivalence principle 197
    family/work context 197–8
    individuals 11, 207, 253
    power of 201
desire
    agape 146, 151
    common good 110
    deprivation 107
    Durkheim 109, 110
    Freud 133
    justice 155
    libido 108–9
    need 305n1
    particular/general 106–7, 108
    reciprocity 108–9
    Ricoeur 115
    social order 109–10
    social theory 297n9
    violence 123, 155
    see also eros
Desrosières, Alain 26, 81, 175, 276–7n2
detachment 112–13, 114
Di Sante, Carmine 114, 159, 299n17
Dilthey, Wilhelm 55
Discourse on the Origin of Inequality (Rousseau) 93
disproportionality 206
disputes 3
    abandonment 67
    in agape regime 160–1
    Aristotle 65, 195

closure 67
educational establishments 162–5
equivalence principle 68, 161
forgiveness 115
justice 18, 46, 70–1, 77, 90, 91–2,
  102, 159–62, 291n3
language 70–1
long-lasting 159–60, 161–2
trade unions 200–1
violence 68–9, 72–3, 77, 90, 291n3
Distinction (Bourdieu) 83
Dobry, Michel 294n3
Dodd, Charles Harold 125, 301n22
Dodier, Nicolas 29–30, 34, 67, 81, 85
domestic polity 16, 17, 285n2, 285n3
domestic relations 52, 194, 198,
  272–3n1
Dominic, St 123
dossiers 160, 227, 246
Dreyfus affair 7, 180–1, 196,
  216–17, 309n3
Dumézil, Georges 97, 152
Dumont, Louis 12, 15, 100–1, 132,
  138, 278n4
Durkheim, Émile
  altruism/selfishness 110, 130,
    298n12, 304n6, 304n7
  anthropology 109
  collective consciousness 93
  desire 109, 110
  holism 44
  ideals 282–3n1
  illusion 20
  individual action 42
  knowledge theory 283n2
  and liberal economics 48–9
  and Marx 277–8n4
  philosophy 284n2
  on religion 22, 101
  secular morality 21
  social justice 27
  social order 298n11
  society 14

Eckhart, Johannes 72
*Economic and Philosophic
  Manuscripts of 1844* (Marx)
  131
Les Économies de la grandeur
  (Boltanski & Thévenot) vii

Economy and Society (Weber)
  283–4n3
educational establishments
  disputes 162–5
  inspectors 249–52, 311n1
  sociology of 307–8n10–n16
  studies of 313n2
  tests 63–4, 66
egoism 110, 244, 304n7
elderly people 199, 245–6
electoral code of France 276n3
Elster, Jon 83, 115, 133, 134, 135,
  136, 156, 248
  Making Sense of Marx 132
emotion 159–65, 292n9
emphasis, devices for 222–3
emplotment 15, 30, 71, 79, 84,
  125
Engels, Friedrich, *The German
  Ideology* 137
equality 14, 47, 127, 213
equivalence
  agape 110–14
  eros 106–10
  establishing 80–1
  justice regime 75, 77–8
  love 94
  objectivized 92–3
  renounced 117–18
  tacit 69–70
  violence 291n3
equivalence principle 44, 284n1
  dependency 16
  desingularization 197
  disputes 68, 161
  justice 16
  polity 50–1
  setting aside 67
  universality 90
  worth 47, 48
eros 104
  and agape 154, 298–9n13
  and agon 297n8
  equivalence 106–10
  justice 110
  Plato 111
  renunciation 107–8
  Ricoeur 107
evil 83–4
exemplarity 215–16

factorial analysis of correspondence
    9, 10, 175–7, 182–3, 184–90,
    259–61
fairness 38–9, 60, 68, 69–70, 71, 75
Farge, Arlette 194
Favret-Saada, Jeanne 153, 252
Felstiner, William L. 6, 247, 273n2
feminist movement 200, 212
Feuerbach, Ludwig 112
Feuillet, André 110
Filloux, Jean-Claude 244
firings 199
Flechsig, Paul 226
forgiveness 115, 130, 299–300n19
Foriers, Paul 221
Foucault, Michel 194
Fraisse, Jean-Claude 105
Francis, St 72, 120–5, 300n20,
    302–3n1
Franciscans 302–3n1
Frappat, Bruno 5
Freidson, Eliot 81
French Revolution 12, 16, 276n3,
    278n5, 279n8
Freud, Sigmund 108, 109, 133, 258,
    276n1, 298n10
    Totem and Taboo 108
friendship 105–6, 297n2–n7
    see also philia
Furet, François 12, 279n8
Fusco, Vittorio 125, 126, 127,
    302n29

Gadamer, Hans-Georg 99, 295n4
Gamson, William A. 172
Garfinkel, Harold 81
Gary, Romain 287–8n3
generality 155, 244–5
    see also singular/general dimension
generalization 220, 235
generative grammar 33
The German Ideology (Marx &
    Engels) 137
gestures 229, 232–4
The Gift (Mauss) 138
gift exchange 79–80
    agape 111
    Bourdieu 142–4, 149
    cooperation 157–9
    counter-gifts 138–44

Lévi-Strauss 139–40
    memory 154–5
    mutual 147
    reciprocity 80, 112, 123, 138–9
    refusal 153–4, 158–9
    time lapse 142–3
    unconditional 164–5
Giles, Brother 124–5
Ginzburg, Carlo 235
Girard, René 101, 305n1
Gluckman, Max 193
Gobry, Ivan 120–1
Goffman, Erving 151, 161, 248, 255,
    278–9n7, 313n3
Good Samaritan parable 301n22
Goody, Esther N. 141, 151
gossip 192–3
The Gotha Program (Marx) 132,
    133, 137
Gouldner, Alvin 299n16
graphology 236
Greimas, Algirdas Julien 178
Grenet, Paul Bernard 64
grievance 6–7, 169
GSPM (Groupe de sociologie politique
    et morale) vii–viii, 307n8
Guattari, Félix 275n6

Haarscher, Guy 131–8, 132, 133, 137
Habermas, Jürgen 34, 45, 102,
    274n4, 279n7, 281n1
handwriting 231, 235, 236
Hegel, G. W. F. 134
Heider, Fritz 257
Heller, Agnes 135
Henry, Michel 134
Héran, François 284n2
Hesse, Mary B. 301–2n23
Hirschman, Albert O. 175, 282n1,
    297n9, 306n4
Hobbes, Thomas 76, 285n4,
    290–1n3, 292n5
Hoffman, Ralph E. 310n1
Hollier, Denis 145
homosexuality 298n10
The Human Condition (Arendt) 130
hunger strikes 233–4, 249

ideals 282–832n1
identification 14, 40

identity 48, 81, 253, 255, 258
  see also social identity
illness, exogenous/endogenous 202
illusion 19–20, 22, 23, 35
incorporation 299n18
indignation 76, 247
individual-becoming-cause 181
individual/collective dimension 7,
  8–9, 10, 44, 169
individuals
  action 42
  collective resources 245
  desingularization 11, 207, 253
industrial society 56–7, 122, 133
inequality 20–1, 25–6
injustice
  accusation of 7, 56, 162
  calculated 77
  denunciation 12, 18, 26, 28, 41,
    172–3, 191–2
INSEE 279n9
inspectors 249–52, 311n1
insults 45
interviews 272–3n1
invective 224
irony 206
Irreductions (Latour) 25
Isambert, François-André 294n2

Jaspers, Karl 126
jealousy 117
Jeremias, Joachim 125, 127, 301n22
Jouvenel, Bertrand de 82
judgement 55–6, 81–2
judges 9, 10, 12, 15, 30, 178–9
justice
  affairs 6
  agape 79–80, 149–50
  argument 150
  Aristotle 14, 47
  clarifications 44
  desire 155
  disputes 18, 46, 70–1, 77, 90,
    91–2, 102, 159–62, 291n3
  equality 14, 47, 127
  equivalence principle 16
  eros 110
  fairness 69–70, 75
  generality 151, 155
  as ideal 37–8, 59–60

labour/capital 132
language for 155
limits of 89–94
love 58, 74, 93–4, 100, 116–17
Marx 131–8
model of 11–12, 34, 37, 59, 67
normality 6, 9
passion 76
peace 75, 91–2
philia 95, 110
power 24–5, 41
reports 80
social 21, 59
sociology of 26
testing for 60–1
utilitarianism 133–4
violence 42–3, 89–90
worth 14, 46
justice regime 34, 75, 77–8, 81
justice theories 49, 94, 131–8
justification
  actors 38
  clarifications 98
  critiques 69–70
  as deceit 283–4n3
  imperative of 36, 37–8, 42–3, 44,
    56
  worths 49–50

Kierkegaard, Søren 112, 116–17,
  150, 153
  Philosophical Crumbs 296n5
  Works of Love 116–20, 146,
    156–7
kinship bonds 197
Kleist, Heinrich von, *Michael
  Kohlhaas* 167
Knobelspiess, Roger 181
Kolakowski, Leszek 21

Labori, Fernand 181
labour 81, 132–3, 304n9
labour divisions, abolished 135, 137
Labov, William 204, 247
Lacan, Jacques 76, 224, 228, 255
Ladrière, Paul 286n6, 288–9n7
Lafaye, Claudette 24, 286–7n1
Lagrove, Jean 284n3
Lambert, Malcolm D. 120–5,
  302–3n1

language
  agape 125–6
  disputes 70–1
  for emphasis 224
  for justice 155
  legalese 228
  love 102
  unconscious 281n12
Latour, Bruno 10, 20, 71, 73, 75, 81,
    92–3, 101, 115–16, 125, 178,
    277n3
  Irreductions 25
Law and Society Review 6, 273n2
Le Goff, Jacques 122
Lefort, Claude 140, 154
legal type manoeuvres 226–7
legalese 228
Légasse, Simon 299n17
legitimacy 45, 51, 53, 81, 283–4n3
Lemert, Edwin M. 6, 255, 256,
    273n2
Lenin, Vladimir Ilyich 304n8
Leo, Brother 124–5
Léon-Dufour, Xavier 125
letterhead, use of 209–11
letters
  abnormality signs 173–4
  analysis of 185, 204–5
  codified 175–7
  confessions 230, 234
  graphic properties 86, 176, 231,
    235, 236–7
  to *Le Monde* 171–5
  responses to 177
  samples of 262–71
  stylistic properties 176
  supporting documents 176
  see also factorial analysis of
    correspondence
letter-writers
  association 216
  biographic details 239–40
  changes to third person 208
  gestures 233–4
  identity 258
  legalese 228
  professions *241, 242, 244, 247*
  public opinion 205
  as representatives 212–13
  singularity 237–8

  social class 239–40, 247
  stylistic manoeuvres 228
  and victim 172–3
  as victims 160, 205–6
lettres de cachet 194
Leviathan and the Air-Pump (Shapin
    & Schaffer) 277n3
Levinson, Stephen 313n3
Lévi-Strauss, Claude 139–40, 141–2,
    277n4, 280n12
Levy-Bruhl, Henri 91, 224, 228
Lewis, David K. 90, 151
lex talionis 90–1
libel 199
libido 108–9
Lidz, Charles W. 256
linguistic turn 29, 35, 85
Little Flowers of St Francis of Assisi
    (Anon) 120–5, 146
Liver, Pierre 300n21
losing face 161
Louis, St 124–5
love
  agape 69
  anthropology 104
  as barter 116
  Christianity 296n6
  as edification 156–7
  equivalence 94
  exit from 153–5
  justice 58, 74, 93–4, 100, 116–17
  language 102
  law of 114
  mediation 103
  passion 294–5n3
  reciprocity 105–6
  St Francis 120–1
  social order 108
  states of 104
  violence 78
love in agape 69, 79, 82
Luhmann, Niklas 294–5n3
Luxembourg, Rosa 304n8

MacCormack, Geoffrey 305n13
Macquart, Gilbert 282n4
*The Making of the English Working
    Class* (Thompson) 274n5
Making Sense of Marx (Elster) 132
Maldidier, Pascal 225, 313n2

Maori society 138, 139
Marguerat, Daniel 125, 127
Marion, Jean-Luc 116
Marshall Plan 277n2
martyrdom 149–50
Marx, Karl
  capitalism 134, 304n8
  communism/abundance 135
  desire/need 305n1
  and Durkheim 277–8n4
  eschatological thrust 41
  on Hegel 42
  illusion 20
  justice theory 131–8
  labour divisions, abolished 137
  labour/utility 304n9
  on money 136–7
  ontology 132
  power relations 36
  reality 278n4
  works of
    Comment on James Mill 134
    Economic and Philosophic
      Manuscripts of 1844 131
    The German Ideology 137
    The Gotha Program 132, 133,
      137
Marxism 36
Masseo, Brother 123
Maurice, Philippe 181
Mauss, Marcel 138, 139, 288–9n7
  The Gift 138
Mead, George Herbert 177
medical diagnosis 81
membership of institutions 243
memory 61, 62–3, 64–5, 154–5,
  162
mentalities, history of 25
Merton, Robert K. 157
Mesure, Sylvie 148
metaphor
  parables 126–7, 302n28–n29
  redescription 301–2n23
  Ricoeur 125–6, 301–2n23,
    302n24–6
Michael Kohlhaas (Kleist) 167
Mirowski, John 257
Le Monde 5, 10, 171–5, 177, 213,
  216, 231–2, 239–40, 246
Moore, Barrington, Jr. 172

municipal services study 24
mysticism, Christian 72

Nader, Ralph 311n2
narrative 71, 85, 125, 204–5, 206
  see also parables
National Education Department 252
National Education Federation 250
natural laws 278n4
neighbourliness 112
Némedi, Dénes 37, 283n2
neologisms 224, 225
New Testament 299n17
nicknames 224, 225, 252, 275–6n1
Nicolet, Claude 244
Nietzsche, Friedrich 303–4n5
  agape 300n21
  Christianity inverted 130
  justification as deceit 283–4n3
  nihilism 278n6
  power 41
  religion objectified 21–2
  ressentiment 299n14
nihilism 278n6
Nisbet, Robert A. 109
normality
  common sense 258
  constraints of 214
  denouncers 207
  denunciation 234, 240, 243
  Hirschman 175
  judging of 177, 191, 207, 229,
    260
  justice 6, 9
  protests 169
  ratings for 191
  rules for 174–5
  supra-individual 93
notarized acts 237
Nygren, Anders 106, 107, 110, 114,
  298n13, 299n14

observation 85–6, 98, 160
Old Testament 299n17
On Justification (Boltanski &
  Thévenot)
  analysis of critiques 36
  constraints 39–40
  critical capacity 29
  equivalence principles 91

On Justification (Boltanski &
   Thévenot) (*cont.*)
  interviews 272–3n1
  justice model 11–12, 17, 34, 37,
    59, 67
  political philosophy 102
  polities 14–15, 49, 285–6n4,
    290n10
order, principles of 46–7
Outline of a Theory of Practice
  (Bourdieu) 140–1, 149

pamphlets 15, 213, 229
parables 79, 125–8, 171, 301n22,
  302n28–n29
paranoia
  actants 160
  affair 4
  cases on 76
  delirium 76–7
  file documents 5–6
  Freud 109
  interpretation 203
  as label 78
  Lemert 273n2
Pareto, Vilfredo 20
particular/general dimension 11, 12,
  106–7, 108, 109, 111, 133,
  289n8
Passeron, Jean-Claude 280n12
passion 76, 294–5n3
passivity 123–4, 157
Paul, St 111, 114, 299n18, 302n27
peace
  in agape 71–2
  in fairness 70
  in justice 75, 91–2
  re-established 164–5
  regimes 68, 69
  violence 92
Perelman, Chaim 221, 228
perpetrators 183
persecutions 185, *189*, 256, 257
persecutors
  as actant 9, 178–9
  aggrandizement 218–19
  individual/general 181
  and victims 202–3, 208, 219,
    234–5, 253
  violence 202–3

persona 288–9n7
persons
  construction of 55–6
  love in agape 79
  and things 69, 71, 72–3
Petit, Paul 296n5
petitions 231–2
Phaedrus (Plato) 107
Pharo, Patrick 81
philia 94, 95, 104, 105–6, 110, 116,
  153
Philosophical Crumbs (Kierkegaard)
  296n5
photocopies 227
plagiarism 203
Plato 111, 296n5
  Phaedrus 107
  The Republic 108
Polanyi, Karl 138
politeness 313n3
political action 8, 192
political parties 229
political philosophy 50, 98–9, 102,
  109, 132
polity
  civic 14–15, 16, 17, 276n3
  communist 133, 134–5, 137–8
  constraints 53
  domestic 16, 17, 285n2, 285n3
  equivalence principle 50–1
  just 132
  justice principle 78
  memory 61
  models 16, 289n8
  On Justice 14–15, 49, 285–6n4,
    290n10
  political philosophy 50
  utopian 41, 99
Pollak, Michael 78, 277n2
popular culture 50
potlatch 154
poverty, as choice 122, 303n2
power
  action 65, 137
  desingularization 201
  force 41
  justice 24–5, 41
  social sciences 41–2
power relations 24–5, 34, 36, 40–1,
  91

practice (Bourdieu) 102
prejudice 295n4
Prodigal Son parable 127, 301n22
protest
    documents 275–6n1
    gestures 229
    grammar of 10, 169
    grievance 6–7
    individual/collective action 169
    institutionalized 311–12n3
    normality 169
    objectivity 254–5
Prothèse software 282n4
psychiatrist's dismissal case 214–15
psychoanalysis 24, 55, 83, 169, 197,
    276n1, 310n1
public opinion
    appeal to 255–6
    defined 12
    denouncer 58
    denunciation 179
    and judges 10
    letter-writers 205
    mobilization 244–5
Puech, Henri-Charles 289n8

Racine, Luc 138
racism 190
ranking 60, 62
rape 212
rational choice theory 130
Rawls, John 61, 133, 135
reality
    denunciation of 75
    illusion 20, 35
    Marx 278n4
    objective 131
    social 19–20
reality test 54, 63, 94
Recanati, François 206
reciprocity
    agape 112
    desire 108–9
    generalized 306–7n7
    gift exchange 80, 112, 123, 138–9
    love 105–6
    philia 116, 153
    recognition 292n7
    universal 299n16
    violence 90–1, 294n1

recognition 148, 292n7
redescription 301–2n23
reidentification 148
religion 20, 21, 22, 101, 226
reports
    actors 30–1, 80, 84–5
    affairs 16
    agape regime 293n1
    emplotment 79
    judge 30
    justice 80
    researchers/actors 19, 23–4, 29
    retrospective constructions 102
    social action 85–6
    translation 82–3
representation 12–13, 24, 42
The Republic (Plato) 108
ressentiment 299n14
Revelation 114, 116
revelation 101–2, 116
Ricoeur, Paul
    allegory 301n22
    clarification 32
    desire 115
    on emotion 162, 164
    emplotment 15, 30, 125
    language/unconscious 281n12
    May 1968 events 292n8
    metaphor 125–6, 301–2n23,
        302n24–6
    power 64
    settlement of debt 76
    soul/eros 107
The Romance of the Rose 302–3n1
romantic sociology 145
Rorty, Richard 305–6n3
Ross, Catherine E. 257
Rougemont, Denis de 295n3
Rouiller, Grégoire 127
Rousseau, Jean-Jacques 47, 107,
    304n11
    Confessions 276n2
    Discourse on the Origin of
        Inequality 93
    The Social Contract 13–14, 276n2,
        285n4

Sabel, Charles F. 250
sacrifice 20, 34, 35, 80, 109, 134–6,
    234

Sahlins, Marshall 138
Saint-Simon, Claude-Henri, comte de 284n2, 285–6n4
salvation 289n8
Sarat, Austin 6, 273n2
sarcasm 224
Sartre, Jean-Paul 249, 250, 255, 313n1
Saussure, Ferdinand de 224, 225, 280n12
scandals 13, 15, 16–17, 191, 311n3
Schaffer, Simon, *Leviathan and the Air-Pump* 277n3
Scheler, Max 297n8
Schelling, Thomas C. 157
schizophrenia 310n1
Schnackenburg, Rudolf 129, 303n3
school teacher *vs.* inspector case 249–52
school tests 63–4, 66
Schreber, Daniel Paul 226, 258
Schumpeter, Joseph 130
Schutz, Alfred 293–4n2
science
controversies 81
culture 50
truth 255
universality claim 226
scientific psychology 257
self-actualization 137
self-aggrandizement 247
self-deception 143–4
selfishness 83–4, 298n12, 304n6, 304n7
self-love 130
self-organization 148–9
self-realization 133, 134, 135–6
self-reference 118–19, 125, 146–7, 150, 305n2
Sérieux, Paul 203
Service des informations générales 171–2, 173
sexism 190
Shapin, Steven, *Leviathan and the Air-Pump* 277n3
Sider, John W. 127
signatures, multiple 209–10, 212
Silver, Allan 306n7
Simonnot, Philippe 213, 310–11n2

singular/collective dimension 7, 8, 221
singular/general dimension 9–10, 11, 179–80, 237–8
singularization 309–10n1
Smith, Adam 132, 306–7n7, 306n4
The Wealth of Nations 285n4
SNCF 274–5n6, 287n2
social action 85–6, 304–5n12
social class 239–40, 246–7
The Social Contract (Rousseau) 13–14, 276n2, 285n4
social identity 248, 250–1, 252
social movements 169
social order 19–21, 31, 43–4, 108–10, 298n11
social sciences
actors 141
agape 129–31
natural laws 278n4
power 41–2
religion 101
representation of world 24
and social philosophy 27
sociologists
classical 18–20, 22–4, 29, 31, 49, 276–7n2
critical 23, 25–6, 34, 35
of critique 23, 25–6, 27, 30–1, 32–3
sociology
classical 19, 20, 29, 34, 49, 59, 276n2
critical 26, 27, 28, 29
of critique 29, 35
of justice 26
observation 85–6
philosophy and 284n2
of religion 294n4
tradition 284–5n3
solidarity 71, 77, 108, 110, 130, 232
Sorokin, Pitirim A. 295n3
Spicq, Ceslas 104, 105, 106, 112, 297n1, 299n15
spokespersons 229
spying 199
Starobinski, Jean 225
Stoics 110
Strawson, Peter F. 32

strikes 311–12n3
structuralist anthropology 52
stylistic manoeuvres *218*, 220, 228
suffering 247
suicide 203
Sulloway, Frank J. 108
support committees 230–1

Taieb, Paulette 146
Tajan, Alfred 235
Teresa, St 298n13
testing
  action 65–6
  factitious 63
  for justice 60–1
  memory 61, 62–3
  predictability 64, 66
  pre-selection 63–4
  retesting 286–7n1
  schools 63–4, 66
  for worths 61–2
Thévenot, Laurent 11–12, 30–1, 33,
  44, 49–50, 72, 81, 91, 102,
  148, 175, 196, 235, 252,
  276–7n2, 279n9, 307n8
  Les Économies de la grandeur vii
  see also *On Justification*
Thibaud, Paul 292n8
Thompson, Edward Palmer, *The
  Making of the English Working
  Class* 274n5
Thucydides 89–90
time dimension 10, 64–5, 74–5, 116,
  119–20, 122, 204–5
title-holders 207, 210, 211–12, 243,
  248
Tocqueville, Alexis de 12
totalization 148, 281n1
Totem and Taboo (Freud) 108
Toulmin, Stephen 301–2n23
Tournier, Michel 25
trade unions 200–1, 229, 275n6
tradition
  actors 96–7
  anthropology 94–100
  Christianity 285n3
  human sciences 97
  sociology 284–5n3
  theological 100–3
transgression 232–3, 300n21

uncertainty principle 60, 63
unconscious 25, 143–4, 280–1n12
universality claim 90, 170, 226,
  299n16
Urlacher, Bernard 207, 276n1
utilitarianism 133–4, 145, 282n1
utopia 41, 99, 129, 135, 145–6, 152

vehemence 185, 221, 236, 247
vengeance 297n7
victims 4, 178–9
  aggrandizement 216
  causes 173, 213–14
  collective resources 199
  compromise refused 160
  defenders 194–5
  as denouncers 181–2, 194–5, 200,
    201, 210, 240, 243
  individual/collective 180–1
  as letter-writers 160, 205–6
  and perpetrators 183
  and persecutors 202–3, 208, 219,
    234–5, 253
  rehabilitation of 170–1
  sacrifice 234
  singularity 235
  size 10
  spokespersons 229
  of state 188–9
Vidal-Naquet, Pierre 181
Villey, Michel 14, 47, 113, 195,
  300n20
'The Vineyard Workers' 127
violence
  acts of 153
  agape 300n21
  of crisis 253
  desire 123, 155
  disputes 68–9, 72–3, 77, 90,
    291n3
  equivalence 291n3
  force 41, 72, 73
  institutional 257
  justice 42–3, 89–90
  love 78
  passivity 124
  peace 92
  persecutors 202–3
  person–thing relationship 72–3
  power relations 91

violence (*cont.*)
  reciprocity 90–1, 294n1
  time 74–5
voting 13

The Wealth of Nations (Smith)
  285n4
Weber, Max 20, 21–2, 26, 41, 68,
  102, 123
  Economy and Society 283–4n3
Weil, Eric 35, 93
Weil, Simone 89–90, 148, 281n2,
  299n19
whistle-blowers 311n2
Wittgenstein, Ludwig 276n1,
  300n21
women
  as denouncers 245
  roles of 279n9
  as victims 199
  see also feminist movement
Woolgar, Steve 81, 92–3
workers' movement 214
workers' rights 57–8

Works of Love (Kierkegaard)
  116–20, 146, 156–7
worths
  actants 191
  agreement 48
  assessment of 56
  civic 15, 57
  constraints 53
  denunciation 56
  domestic 47
  embodiment 12–13
  equivalence principle 47, 48
  justice 14, 46
  justification 49–50
  legitimacy 51, 53
  order of 79
  principles of 54–5
  relative 9–10, 12, 90–1
  testing for 61–2
  values 47–8, 48–9
  written documents 162, 163–4
  see also handwriting

Zumstein, Jean 125, 126, 127